The Religionization of Israeli Society

During Israel's military operation in Gaza in the summer of 2014 the command-ing officer of the Givati infantry brigade, Colonel Ofer Vinter, called upon his troops to fight "the terrorists who defame the God of Israel." This unprecedented call for religious war by a senior IDF commander caused an uproar, but it was just one symptom of a profound process of religionization, or de-secularization, that Israeli society has been going through since the turn of the twenty-first century.

This book analyzes and explains, for the first time, the reasons for the reli-gionization of Israeli society, a process known in Hebrew as *hadata*. Jewish reli-gion, inseparable from Jewish nationality, was embedded in Zionism from its inception in the nineteenth century, but was subdued to a certain extent in favor of the national aspect in the interest of building a modern nation-state. *Hadata* has its origins in the 1967 war, has been accelerating since 2000, and is mani-fested in a number of key social fields: the military, the educational system, the media of mass communications, the *teshuvah* movement, the movement for Jewish renewal, and religious feminism. A major chapter of the book is devoted to the religionization of the visual fine arts field, a topic that has been largely neglected by previous researchers.

Through careful examination of religionization, this book sheds light on a major development in Israeli society, which will additionally inform our under-standing of the Israeli-Palestinian conflict. As such, it is a key resource for stu-dents and scholars of Israel Studies, and those interested in the relations between religion, culture, politics and nationalism, secularization and new social movements.

Yoav Peled is Professor Emeritus of Political Science at Tel Aviv University, Israel. His research interests include Israeli politics, religion and politics, citizen-ship, ethnic relations, and democratic theory.

Horit Herman Peled is a media artist and fine arts and media culture researcher. Her work deals with religion, art, and life under a "state of exception."

Routledge Studies in Middle Eastern Politics

80 **Israel's Military Operations in Gaza**
    Marouf Hasian, Jr.

81 **The Turkish AK Party and its Leader**
    Edited by Ümit Cizre

82 **Democratic Consolidation in Turkey**
    Edited by Cengiz Erisen and Paul Kubicek

83 **Saudi Arabian Foreign Relations**
    Rene Rieger

84 **Kurdish Politics in Turkey**
    Seevan Saeed

85 **Minority Rights in Turkey**
    Gözde Yilmaz

86 **Municipal Politics in Turkey**
    Charlotte Joppien

87 **Politics and Gender Identity in Turkey**
    Umut Korkut and Hande Eslen-Ziya

88 **Israel's Foreign Policy Beyond the Arab World**
    Jean-Loup Samaan

89 **Party Politics in Turkey**
    Edited by Sabri Sayari, Pelin Ayan Musil and Özhan Demirkol

90 **The Religionization of Israeli Society**
    Yoav Peled, Horit Herman Peled

For a full list of titles in the series: www.routledge.com/middleeaststudies/series/SE0823

The Religionization of
Israeli Society

Yoav Peled, Horit Herman Peled

LONDON AND NEW YORK

First published 2019
by Routledge
2 Park Square, Milton Park, Abingdon, Oxon OX14 4RN

and by Routledge
52 Vanderbilt Avenue, New York, NY 10017

First issued in paperback 2020

Routledge is an imprint of the Taylor & Francis Group, an informa business

British Library Cataloguing-in-Publication Data
A catalogue record for this book is available from the British Library

Library of Congress Cataloging-in-Publication Data
A catalog record has been requested for this book

ISBN 13: 978-0-367-58817-5 (pbk)
ISBN 13: 978-1-138-95479-3 (hbk)

Typeset in Times New Roman
by Wearset Ltd, Boldon, Tyne and Wear

To the memory of Zipora Lurie, a pioneer of art education in the national-religious sector

To the memory of E. Victor Wolfenstein, teacher and friend

Contents

List of figures   viii
List of tables   x
Acknowledgments   xi

1 Introduction: religion, secularization, nationalism, Zionism   1

2 The rise and fall of Labor Zionist hegemony   31

3 The Religious Zionist challenge   53

4 Return, renewal, and in-between   81

5 Education   100

6 The IDF: from religionization to theocratization   123

7 Nationalism and religion in the visual fine arts field   137

8 Orthodox feminism   187

9 Film, TV, media   201

10 Conclusion   214

Appendix   225
Glossary   227
Index   229

Figures

Paintings are oil on canvas unless indicated otherwise.

7.1 Ephraim Moshe Lilien. Illustration for *Der Jüdische Mai* (*Jewish May*) in Rosenfeld, Morris, *Lieder des Ghetto*, Berlin: Benjamin Harz Verlag (1902). 146

7.2 Meir Ben Uri, *Jacob's Ladder* (1957). Dry etching, 94 × 146 cm. Collection of Ben Uri Museum. Reproduced with permission of Ben Uri Museum. 162

7.3 Ziona Tager, *The Train Passing Through Neve Tzedek* (1920). 46 × 55 cm. Private collection. Reproduced with permission of Avraham Katz Oz. 164

7.4 Naftali Bezem, *In the Courtyard of the Third Temple* (1957). Gouache on cardboard, 70 × 100 cm. Collection of Tel Aviv Museum of Art. Reproduced with permission of Shlomo Bezem and Tel Aviv Museum of Art, photograph by Avraham Hai. 165

7.5 Igael Tumarkin, *He Walked in the Fields* (1967). Bronze, partly painted, 175 × 46 × 48 cm. Collection of Tel Aviv Museum of Art. Reproduced with permission of the artist and Tel Aviv Museum of Art, photograph by Ran Erde. 166

7.6 Andi Arnovitz, *Vest of Prayers* (2009). Found prayerbook pages, threads, and Japanese paper. Collection of the artist. Reproduced with permission of the artist. 169

7.7 Ruth Kestenbaum Ben-Dov, *Prayer Rug No. 2.* (2003) 125 × 80 cm. Collection of the artist. Reproduced with permission of the artist. 170

7.8 Debbie Kampel, *Reality Check* (2003). 100 × 110 cm. Collection of the artist. Reproduced with permission of the artist. 171

7.9 Horit Herman Peled, *Violinist at Beit Iba Checkpoint* (2004). Still from a videograph. Collection of the artist. Reproduced with permission of the artist. 172

7.10 Porat Salomon, *Shabbat* (2009). Photograph, 70 × 50 cm. Collection of the artist. Reproduced with permission of the artist. 173

7.11 Sigal Maor, *Tzuk Eithan* [solid rock], *Me?* (2014).
Embroidered IDF shirt. Collection of the artist. Reproduced
with permission of the artist.   174

7.12 Avner Bar Hama, *Hasam Gvulech Shalom* (2005). Digital
work, dibond print, 110 × 170 cm. Collection of the artist.
Reproduced with permission of the artist.   177

7.13 Fatma Shanan Dery, *Razan 2012* (2012). 80 × 100 cm. Private
collection. Reproduced with permission of the artist.   178

7.14 Shai Azulai, *Nimrod's Circumcision 2* (2008). 42 × 50 cm.
Collection of the artist. Reproduced with permission of the
artist.   181

8.1 Chana Goldberg, *Shulchan Aruch* (2003). Photocopies of
illustrations from books for children, and framed terylene
tablecloth, 20 × 30 × 40 cm. Ein Harod Museum of Art.
Reproduced with permission of the artist and Ein Harod
Museum of Art.   194

Tables

2.1 Percentage of total social expenditure on healthcare   44
2.2 Household healthcare expenditures (percent)   45
2.3 Income inequality   45
3.1 Religiosity of Israeli Jews by self-definition (percent)   54
3.2 Religiosity of Israeli Jews by observance of religious tradition
     (percent)   55
3.3 Students in all Jewish school systems, 2014–2015   55
3.4 Students in the different Jewish school systems (percentage of
     the total number of students)   55
3.5 Students in the different Jewish elementary school systems
     (percentage of the total number of Jewish students)   56
10.1 Political attitudes of Israeli Jews by level of religiosity,
     2014–2015 (percent)   217

Acknowledgments

While working on this book we were fortunate to be hosted by three great institutions of learning: the Jewish Studies program at the University of Virginia, the Centre for Conflict and Security Research at the University of Sussex (through a Leverhulme Visiting Professorship), and the Middle East Centre at the London School of Economics and Political Science. We are grateful to these institutions and to their respective directors: Gabriel Finder, Jeffrey Grossman, Jan Selby, and Robert Lowe for their generous hospitality and for the intellectual stimulation we experienced while resident in their institutions. Various sections of this book were presented at seminars in the following universities: Tel Aviv University, The University of Virginia, George Washington University, The New School for Social Research, University of Sussex, Oxford University, University of Bristol, London School of Economics and Political Science, University of Edinburgh, and Durham University. We thank the organizers and participants of these seminars for inviting us and for their very useful critical comments.

For permission to use their artworks or those of their parents special thanks are due to: Avraham Katz Oz (for the painting by his mother, the artist Ziona Tager), Yair Ben Uri (for the dry etching by his father, the artist Meir Ben Uri), Shlomo Bezem (for the painting by his father, the artist Naftali Bezem), Igael Tumarkin, Andi Arnovitz, Ruth Kestenbaum Ben-Dov, Debbie Kampel, Porat Salomon, Sigal Maor, Avner Bar-Hama, Fatma Shanan-Dery, Shai Azoulay, and Chana Goldberg.

Many friends and colleagues have helped us in various ways in writing this book. They are, in alphabetical order: Revital Amiran, Bat-Zion and Alex Eraqi Klorman, Shlomo Fischer, Jack Jacobs, Ilana and Ehud Kaufman, Natalie Kosoi, Nissim Leon, Gal Levy, Yagil Levy, Doron Navot, Vanessa and Peter Ochs, Fabio Petito, Noga Porat, Avshalom Schwartz, Osnat Sivron, Karnit Tumarkin, and Dana Yasur-Landau. We are grateful to all of them and to numerous other colleagues and friends who supported us during this project whose names we may have forgotten.

At Routledge we would like to thank Joe Whiting, Holly Jones, and Emma Tyce for their belief in this book and for bearing with us through a series of missed deadlines. Rene Bailey has done a wonderfully thorough and efficient job copy editing the manuscript and we thank her for that.

We dedicate this book to the memory of two extraordinary individuals who have affected each of our lives is a special way: Zipora (Zipi) Lurie, a West Bank settler whom Horit met while teaching digital art at the national-religious teachers' college, Talpiyot, and who appreciated very early on the artistic significance of the digital media; and E. Victor Wolfenstein, Yoav's dissertation adviser at UCLA, who remained a friend and critical supporter for many years afterwards.

1   Introduction

Religion, secularization, nationalism, Zionism

The anthropological student of particular religions should ... begin ... [by] unpacking the comprehensive concept which he or she translates as "religion" into heterogeneous elements according to its historical character.

(Talal Asad 1993:54)

There is no consensus, perhaps there will never be, as to what counts as religion.

(José Casanova 1994:26)

During Israel's military operation in Gaza in the summer of 2014 the commanding officer of the Givati infantry brigade, Colonel Ofer Vinter, called on his troops to fight "the terrorists who defame the God of Israel" (see Appendix). This unprecedented call for religious war by a senior commander of the Israel Defense Forces (IDF) caused an uproar among Israel's "enlightened public" (Peled 2012) but it was just one symptom of a profound process of religionization, or de-secularization, that Israeli society, including the Israeli military, has been going through since the turn of the twenty-first century. As noted by literary scholar Yaron Peleg,

> The tribalism that awakens in Israel during times of emergency bore clear religious signs for the first time during [the 2014 Gaza] war ... from the public's religious expressions of support – mass prayers and the wearing of phylacteries in public – to the religious expressions of soldiers and officers who took part in the fighting.

Thus the liberal *Haaretz* columnist Uri Misgav concluded that Colonel Vinter (who has been promoted in the meantime) should be asked for forgiveness by those who criticized his call for religious war (Peleg 2016:136).

In this book we describe, analyze and explain the reasons for the religionization of Israeli society, a process known in Hebrew as *hadata* and widely recognized and discussed in academia and in the public sphere (see, e.g., *Israel Studies Review* 2012). This process, we argue, had its origins in the 1967 war, has been accelerating since 2000, and is manifested in a number of key social fields. We further argue that Jewish religion, inseparable from Jewish nationality, was embedded in Zionism from its very inception at the end of the nineteenth century but was subdued to a certain extent in favor of the national aspect in the interest of building a modern nation-state. This building process proceeded under the hegemony of the Labor Zionist Movement (LZM) but was fraught with social, economic, political, and ideological contradictions. Paradoxically, these contradictions all came to a head in the 1960s due to the economic, political, and military success of the Zionist project. Of the various political tendencies that exist in Israeli society, for reasons we explore in this book it was Religious Zionism that was in a position to exploit those contradictions and claim the mantle of hegemony dropped by the LZM.[1] In the following chapters we will assess the success of this claim up to the time of writing and its future prospects.

A commonly held belief holds that Zionism was originally a modernizing, secular national movement, a "revolution" against traditional Jewish life in the Diaspora, which had been characterized, first and foremost, by strict adherence to *Halacha* (Jewish religious law). In the words of Eliezer Ben-Yehudah, "reviver" of the Hebrew language, in 1905, "All of us, all of us, have turned our backs on the past, that is our glory and splendor" (cited in Mirsky 2014:54). However, like all national movements, Zionism had to rely on primordial cultural elements, genuine or invented, in order to mobilize its target population for essentially modernizing aims. (Tom Nairn has therefore termed nationalism a "Janus Faced" ideology [Nairn 1977; Avineri 1998]).

For Zionism, moreover, the need to rely on primordial factors for mobilization and legitimation was particularly acute. Of all the political movements spawned by the crisis of Eastern European Jewry in the second half of the nineteenth century, Zionism alone claimed to speak on behalf of a world-wide Jewish *nation*, and there was no modern cultural marker common to all members of this purported nation. The only cultural attribute common to all Jews was Jewish religion, to which the vast majority of Jews still held (Almog et al. 1998:xi; Ben-Rafael 2008:91–2). The ultra-Orthodox *Agudat Yisrael*, established in 1912, was, until the Second World War, one of the largest political parties in the Jewish world.

Theodor Herzl himself wrote in his diary in 1895, "Our nation is not a nation except in its faith" (cited in M. Inbari 2008:43). This dictated, first, the choice of the movement's target territory (in dispute until Herzl's death in 1904 [Vital 1982, Chapters 9 and 10]) and then the use of a whole array of religious Jewish symbols and other cultural constructs. From the dubbing of immigration to Palestine *aliyah* (pilgrimage) and the use of the sacred Jewish language, Hebrew, as the *lingua franca* of the *yishuv* (pre-statehood Jewish community in Palestine), through the choice of the star of David and the seven-branch candelabrum (*menorah*) as the official emblems of the state, to the celebration of Jewish religious holidays as national holidays, traditional Jewish themes abound in Zionist lore (An. Shapira 2014:149–51; cf. Ben-Porat 2013:29–32; Charbit 2014:160–3).

While different tendencies in Zionism have tried, in varying degrees, to endow the traditional religious themes with secular national meanings, if Zionism was to maintain its ideological coherence, they could never be purged of their original religious content (Liebman and Don-Yehiya 1983; Liebman 1998:9; An. Shapira 1998:262–71).[2] This was brilliantly diagnosed already in 1926 by the philosopher and historian of Jewish mysticism, Gershom Scholem. In a letter to Franz Rosenzweig Scholem famously wrote of

[a] danger which follows of necessity from the Zionist enterprise. What will be the result of updating the Hebrew language? Is not the holy language, which we have planted among our children, an abyss that must open up? People here do not know the meaning of what they have done. They think they have turned Hebrew into a secular language and that they have removed its apocalyptic sting, but it is not so. The secularization of the language is mere empty words, a rhetorical turn of phrase … This Hebrew language is pregnant with catastrophe; it cannot remain in its present state – nor will it remain there. Our children will no longer have any other language; truth be told, they, and they alone, will pay the price for this encounter which we have imposed on them unasked, or without even asking ourselves. One day the language will turn against its own speakers … Will we then have a youth who will be able to hold fast against the rebellion of a holy tongue? … God cannot remain silent in a language in which He has been evoked thousands of times…

(Scholem 1997:27–9)

As explained by Daniel J. Levine,

[t]he promulgators of the "new" Hebrew, Scholem argues, lack reverence for the powers of the "old" one from which it had been extracted. Hebrew, he asserts, will not submit to being a passive, secular vernacular for late-modern political and social administration. Its "source code" – Biblical and medieval Hebrew – was entirely devoted to the transmission, interpretation, and application of revelation. The power and resilience of those foundational elements remained latent within the modern language – they were a staple of authentic Jewish self-understanding and they would, he feared, crowd their way back into Hebrew politics and discourse.

(Levine 2014:644)

Viewing the same potentiality with excitement rather than alarm, the eminent rabbi, Abraham Isaac Ha-Cohen Kook, future Chief Ashkenazi Rabbi of Palestine, wrote in 1906 that "Once the [pioneering Zionist] youth recognize that their own deepest ideals are those of the Torah, they will choose to serve God…" (Mirsky 2014:60–1).

Nor was the development feared by Scholem and hopefully anticipated by Kook a matter for the future only. Boris Schatz, a renowned sculptor and founder of Israel's leading art school, *Bezalel*, was a secular Zionist who had turned his back on his own religious background and on traditional Jewish society and sought to contribute to the founding of a modern, European Jewish society in Palestine. However, realizing the need of a modernizing national movement for a semiotic language drawing on the nation's glorious past, real or imagined, in the period from 1890 to 1900, he produced artworks depicting mythical Biblical and post-Biblical figures such as Moses, his mother, Jochebed, Matthias the Maccabee, and the heroine Judith. Moreover, in a utopian book written in 1918, *Jerusalem Rebuilt: A Daydream*, he imagined a secular temple devoted to Jewish culture to be erected on the Temple Mount in place of the existing Moslem shrines, which would be safely removed to another Jerusalem location, in recognition of the Moslems having taken care of the sacred Jewish site for so many centuries (Schatz 1924:9; Zalmona 1985; Chapter 7).

Claiming to speak in the name of world Jewry, both internally and externally, Zionism also needed at least the tacit approval of those universally recognized as the Jewish spokesmen – the Orthodox rabbis. Thus, already at the First Zionist Congress in 1897 Herzl declared: "Zionism is the return to Judaism even before the return to the land of the Jews."[3] In 1898 the Second Zionist Congress resolved that "Zionism will not act in any way to infringe upon the Jewish religion." The educational autonomy of *Mizrachi* (the small religious Zionist faction established in 1902) inside the formal bounds of the *yishuv* (unlike that of *Agudat Yisrael* which was outside of it) dates back to 1920 and survives today as the state-religious educational system. Not even the Labor Zionist Movement (LZM) really sought to completely secularize the traditional system of meaning.

At the Nineteenth Zionist Congress in 1935 an agreement was reached between the main Labor Zionist party, Mapai, and the *Mizrachi* movement, according to which "no public desecration of the Sabbath was to occur, and dietary laws were to be maintained in public institutions." This was the foundation of an "historic partnership" between the two movements, which lasted until 1977 (Liebman and Don-Yehiya 1984:33; Kolatt 1998:281; Chapter 3). As Norman Zucker has put it: "Mapai and the Mapai-led Israel Labor Party have surrendered to some of the demands of the religious parties because they do not totally reject religious values, nor do they desire a totally secular state" (Zucker 1973:3, 58; see also Kolatt 1998:290–1). The reasons for that were summarized succinctly by Zionist historian Anita Shapira:

> The founders of the Palestine labor movement attached great importance to instilling in the young generation clear, unquestionable *national* convictions. The components of this nationalism were rooted in the Jewish religion: the age-old ties of Jews to the Holy Land; the historical right to the land; the attempts of Jews all through the centuries to resettle in Palestine as manifested by the messianic movements.
>
> (An. Shapira 1998:259, emphasis added; see also An. Shapira 1991;
> Sorek and Ceobanu 2009)

Religion–secularity

Our understanding of religion, following Talal Asad, William Cavanaugh, and many others, is a non-essentialist one: the term "religion" for us does not connote a trans-historical, trans-cultural, universal phenomenon. It is, rather, a phenomenon that takes a particular shape, and performs particular functions, in the specific social-historical context in which it appears in different societies. In William Cavanaugh's words, "What counts as religion and what does not in any given context is contestable and depends on who has the power and authority to define religion at any given time and place" (Cavanaugh 2009:59). Moreover,

> the attempt to say that there *is* a transhistorical and transcultural concept of religion that is separable from secular phenomena *is itself* part of a particular configuration of power, that of the modern, liberal nation-state as it developed in the [Christian] West. In this context, religion is constructed as transhistorical, transcultural, essentially interior, and essentially distinct from public, secular rationality.
>
> (Cavanaugh 2009:59, emphasis in the original; cf. Asad 1993:29–30, 43)

Thus, a crucial element of what can be described as the "invention" of religion in the modern era is the identification of religion with personal, subjective, private "faith" or "belief," clearly distinguished from such public, *rational* spheres of activity as science, the market economy, and the state. Historically, this conceptualization of "religion" was significant because it helped "to separate [private] loyalty to God from one's public loyalty to the [sovereign] nation-state." Therefore, as Sarah Bracke has put it, "modernity and religion cannot be positioned as if they were mutually exclusive" (Cavanaugh 2009:59; Bracke 2008:57; cf. Asad 1993:39, 45–6; Batnitzky 2011:1).

Just like "religion," its twin concept, "secularity," is also a product of modernity and the liberal nation-state. Charles Taylor has famously discredited the "subtraction" notion of "the secular" as simply comprising all that has emancipated itself from religion. Secularity for him has a positive content, "the possibility of living within a purely immanent order … one that could be accounted for on its own terms, which thus leaves belief in the transcendent as a kind of 'optional extra'" (Taylor 2011:50–1; cf. Asad 1999:185; Bruce 2010:130). As elaborated by Ezra Kopelowitz:

> "Religion" is born from within the synthesis of private and public, at the moment when an individual *chooses to believe*. That the individual can choose a particularistic identity, is an option that is only possible within the framework of the secular public sphere. Religious authority does not exist in an either/or relationship to secular society, but is in itself part of the secular experience.
>
> (Kopelowitz 2003:94, emphasis added; cf. Davie 2010:172)

Historically, as Cavanaugh has pointed out, "the religious-secular distinction accompanies the invention of private-public, religion-politics, and church-state dichotomies. The religious-secular distinction also accompanies the state's monopoly over internal violence and its colonial expansion" (Cavanaugh 2009:59, 120; Bracke 2008:57; cf. Kopelowitz 2003:86; H. Lahav 2015).

Broadly following Taylor's and Asad's conceptualizations of the secular, Cavanaugh has argued that "Secularism need not be antireligion. It is rather against the undue influence of religion on public life," while Ingrid Creppell has defined secularity as "the relationship *between* religion and the worldly realm, the continual adjustment of the political and religious foundations of collective meaning and identity" (Cavanaugh 2009:121; Creppell 2010:29, emphasis in the original). As we saw, Kopelowitz has maintained that the secular is a necessary condition for the very existence of religion: "Religion as a form of association appears when there are people who maintain a sense of the sacred through belief in doctrine and ritual practice and at the same time interact with secular actors" (Kopelowitz 2003:86, see also 89, 92; Asad 1999:192; Casanova 2006:21, 24).

Nationalism

According to Rogers Brubaker:

> This process of differentiation – and in particular the emergence of under-standings of economy, society and polity as autonomous realms – was argu-ably a precondition for the emergence and widespread naturalisation of the social ontology, social imaginary and ascending understanding of political legitimacy that are characteristic of modern nationalism.
>
> (Brubaker 2012:16)

The close connection between the emergence of religion (and secularity) as a distinct category and the development of nationalism and the nation-state had a dual effect on the Jews of Europe. Medieval Judaism, like Medieval Christianity, was an all-encompassing communal way of life, wherein the idea of religion as a distinct sphere of activity, or consciousness, was inconceivable. Jewish com-munal life, inseparable from the lives of individual Jews, was regulated, accord-ing to Moses Mendelssohn, by

> divine *legislation* – laws, commandments, ordinances, rules of life, instruc-tion in the will of God as to how they should conduct themselves in order to attain temporal and eternal felicity. Propositions and prescriptions of this kind were revealed to them by Moses in a miraculous and supernatural manner, but no doctrinal opinions, no saving truths, no universal proposi-tions of reason. These the Eternal reveals to us and to all other men, at all times, through *nature* and *thing*, but never through *word* and *script*.
>
> (Mendelssohn 1983 [1783]:89–90, emphasis in the original)[4]

According to Mendelssohn, the "inventor" of Judaism as a religion (Batnitzky 2011:4), this character of Judaism as a religion of law, not of faith, that regulates its adherents' actions, not their thoughts, made Judaism more suitable for life in the modern liberal nation-state than Christianity.

In Western Europe, modernity, since the French Revolution, brought about "the dissolution of the corporate Jewish community and the concurrent shift of political agency to the individual Jew who became [a loyal] citizen of the modern nation-state" (Batnitzky 2011:4). Going well beyond Mendelssohn:

> Classical reform theology [in Germany] taught that the essence of Judaism lay in the teachings of the prophets rather than in *halakha* [Jewish religious law] ... Jews were obliged to conduct themselves according to standards of ethics and morality prevailing in the Western world and ... were free of ritual obligations...
>
> (Liebman and Cohen 1990:160; cf. discussion of Hermann Cohen in Chapter 7)

In Eastern Europe, meanwhile, where modernity lagged behind and where the multi-national empire was the prevailing political formation until 1918, another kind of relation between Jews and the nation-state emerged – Zionism, which sought to establish a nation-state for the Jews themselves (Abramov 1976; Vital 1982; Kopelowitz and Diamond 1998:672–3).[5]

Zionism, no less than the acculturated Jews of the West, had a clear interest in viewing Judaism as a religion, confined to its own sphere, and itself, as well as its future nation-state, as "secular." In Herzl's famous words:

> We shall keep our priests within the confines of their temples, in the same way as we shall keep our professional army within the confines of their barracks. Army and priesthood shall receive honours as high as their valuable functions deserve, but they must not interfere in the administration of the state which confers distinction upon them, lest they conjure up difficulties without and within.
>
> (Herzl 1934 [1896]:71, cited in Abramov 1976:63)

As Talal Asad has noted:

> Nationalism, with its vision of a universe of national *societies* (the state being thought of as necessary to their full articulation) in which individual humans live their worldly existence, requires the concept of the secular to make sense. The loyalty that the individual nationalist owes is directly and exclusively to the nation.
>
> (Asad 2003:193, emphasis in the original)

Moreover, as Mark Juergensmeyer has argued:

> Because religion ... and secular nationalism are [both] ideologies of order, they are potential rivals. Either can claim to be the guarantor of orderliness within a society; either can claim to be the ultimate authority for social order ... [C]ontained within these claims is the right to give moral sanction to life-and-death decisions, including the right to kill. When either secular nationalism or religion assumes that role by itself, it reduces the other to a peripheral social role.
>
> (Juergensmeyer 2008:21, see also 23–4)[6]

But secular nationalism and religion do not necessarily assume that role each by itself. Just as "the secular" in reality connotes a particular kind of entanglement with religion, so secular nationalism, in many cases at least, is engaged in various ways with religion. Asad, for example, has argued that

> [t]he established church, which was an integral part of the state, made the coherence and continuity of the English national community possible. We should not say that the English nation was shaped *or* influenced by religion: we should see the established church (called "Anglican" only in the nineteenth century) as its *necessary condition*.
>
> (Asad 2003:190, emphasis in the original; see also Asad 1999:178; Zubrzycki 2010; Abulof 2014)

These dialectical relations between secular nationalism and religion have certainly been at play in Zionism from the start.

Orthodox reactions to Zionism

The emergence of Zionism as a secular political movement actively seeking to "return" the Holy Land to Jewish sovereignty constituted a formidable theological dilemma for Orthodox Jews, a dilemma which has been aggravated by the Holocaust and by every Zionist success. While the return to Zion had been at the core of Jewish hopes for redemption for two millennia, it was never expected to materialize through the this-worldly efforts of heretics who had strayed from the fold. Initially, therefore, the vast majority of rabbis, whether Orthodox or Reform, and whether in Western or Eastern Europe, were vehemently opposed to Zionism, on both religious and political grounds.

The religious objections of the Orthodox rabbis focused on the traditional notion that redemption of the Jews – that is, their return to the Land of Israel – had to await the coming of the Messiah, and that the hand of the Almighty must not be forced in this matter by this-worldly action. Jewish tradition since the Talmud, although not necessarily the *Halacha*, held that God had made the people of Israel swear not to scale the wall (of Exile), not to hasten Redemption, and not to rebel against the (other) nations. (In another version God also made the nations swear not to subjugate the Jews excessively [Ravitzki 1993:277–305]).[7] In addition, these rabbis realized that the modern nation-state sought by Zionism was not going to be a theocracy governed by *Halacha*.[8] For Reform rabbis, the Jews' messianic mission was their very existence in the Diaspora, which enabled them to spread their universalist moral values among the nations. On that view, a return to the Land of Israel would constitute a betrayal, rather than fulfillment, of the Jews' religious calling (Abramov 1976:62–7; Charbit 2014:161).

Over time, the different ways in which various Orthodox groups and rabbinical authorities have responded to this dilemma can be classified, with some simplification, under four headings:

1 Pragmatic accommodationism

This response characterized the *Mizrachi* movement (established in 1902 as an Orthodox faction within Zionism) in its early period. The ideological position of this group, formulated originally by Rav I. J. Reines (1835–1915), viewed the Zionist enterprise as a project of physical survival, essentially indifferent in terms of religious values. Setting up a secular Jewish society in *Eretz Yisrael* (or anywhere else for that matter), where Jews could be safe and prosperous, was a worthwhile undertaking, although it had no bearing on the hoped-for messianic redemption.[9] Orthodox Jews, according to this view, should actively participate in this undertaking both because of its intrinsic value and because their participation could mitigate its secular character. This position has been associated with "modern orthodoxy," the tendency which in general has sought limited accommodation to modern secular society (Don-Yehiya 1983).

2 Principled accommodationism

This position was formulated by the eminent ultra-Orthodox rabbi, Rav Abraham Isaac Ha-Cohen Kook (1865–1935), Chief Ashkenazi Rabbi of Palestine from 1921 until his death. According to Kook's famous "synthesis," Zionist settlement in Palestine was the "advent of redemption" (*atchalta degeula*), a preliminary but essential stage in the holy process of redemption. Secular Zionists, while indeed sinners, were unknowingly carrying out God's will in setting up the physical prerequisites for the final spiritual redemption. Although final redemption required that all Jews repent and return to religion, the preparatory work done by secular Zionists was potentially and partially sacred, and so were its perpetrators (Hellinger 2008).[10] Moreover, within this school of thought the fact that the pioneers were Jews who had abandoned their religion was yet another indication of the divine guidance of their project. According to Rav Ben-Zion Uziel (1880–1953), an important Religious Zionist thinker and Chief Sephardic Rabbi of Palestine/Israel from 1939 to his death,

> ... the solution to this wondrous and unfathomable riddle, whereby the national awakening of ... Zionism, began only in the ranks of the people who had forsaken Judaism ... is no other than providing divine

enlightenment for those who are in need of repentance [*teshuvah*], and they return [*shavim*] to Zion, and through this repentance, they return to their people and escape assimilation and intermingling, in which they had almost drowned.

(Cited in D. Schwartz 2002:179)

A version of Kook's mystical messianic view was adopted by the *Mizrachi* movement after the First World War and the Balfour Declaration, precisely because it endowed the Zionist project with religious significance. However, since the forging of the "historic partnership" between the *Mizrachi* movement and Mapai in 1935, and partially because of it, the political leadership of the *Mizrachi*, where members of the labor-oriented *Ha-Poel Ha-Mizrachi* (see Chapter 3) played a prominent role, held a very moderate position with regard to the *yishuv*'s and Israel's use of force and policies toward the Palestinians and the Arab world in general. Thus, according to Dror Greenblum, two ideological streams had existed in the national-religious movement: A universalist-redemptive stream, which was wary of the use of military force and viewed war as foreign to Judaism, and a Kook-inspired activist-messianic stream, which viewed the use of military force as essential for the reconstruction of the Jewish homeland in the Land of Israel and considered Jewish military force as an arm of God hastening the forthcoming messianic redemption. Whereas the political leadership, by and large, adhered to the universalist-redemptive view, much of the party rank and file, including its then daily paper *Ha-Tzofe*, followed the activist-messianic one (Greenblum 2016:40–1, 58–208; cf. S. Fischer 2013; Don-Yehiya 2014).

After the 1967 war most religious Zionists adopted a radical version of the Kookist activist-messianic ideology developed by Rav Zvi Yehuda Kook (1891–1982), Rav A. I. Kook's son. Kook senior had attributed sanctity to an abstract, post-redemption, ideal Jewish society in *Eretz Yisrael*. From that he derived the potential and partial sanctity of the secular Zionist efforts that were preparing the groundwork for that society. In his son's version sanctity was attributed to the existing state, that "embodies the very fulfillment of the messianic ideal," and especially to its efforts to liberate the Holy Land by force (Aran 1991:268; Hellinger 2008:542; S. Fischer 2014:133–6; Sagi and Schwartz 2017). As the younger Rav Kook stated already in 1953:

Since the giving of the Torah in Sinai we have been commanded to conquer the land, and this is a commandment. Knowing that this is a commandment is knowing the sanctity of the IDF ... and that the Israel Defense Forces must be given a form of holiness ... The IDF is absolute holiness, symbolizing the rule of God's people over its land.

(Cited in Greenblum 2016:110; see also Luz 1999:368)

At the center of attention of the younger Kook's "messianic Zionism" was "political control of the territories of *Eretz Yisrael*, while the spiritual and universal dimensions of redemption, that played a central role in his father's messianic worldview, were pushed to the margin" (Atkes 2016:371–2; Hellinger 2008:534–5). Underlying this difference between father and son was a more profound difference, relating to the role of human agency in the process of messianic redemption. The father believed that the timing of redemption was up to God alone, and human beings could not affect it in any way; the son held that human initiative and struggle could trigger and expedite the process of redemption. Relatedly, the father believed that because of the universalist nature of Judaism, "the unique Jewish identity was not to be realized at the expense of other nations" (cited in Hellinger 2008:535). The son, on the other hand, did not have any such inhibition when it came to Jewish rule over the Greater Land of Israel (Hellinger 2008:542). After 1967 the younger Kook's formulation became the ideological cornerstone of a militant, messianic, territorially expansionist brand of religious Zionism epitomized by Gush Emunim (D. Schwartz 2003:132; Hellinger 2008; Don-Yehiya 2014:246–7, 250; Chapter 3).

3 Pragmatic rejectionism

This is the most common *Charedi* (non-Zionist ultra-Orthodox) position, distinguished by its rejection of ideological, though not necessarily practical Zionism. Most groups that adhere to this position seceded from the religious Zionist movement over the issue of Zionism's "cultural work" in the Diaspora. They came together under the title *Agudat Yisrael* in 1912 and have been grudgingly willing to take part in the Zionist enterprise on a limited basis and without endowing it with any theological legitimacy. Their cooperation with Zionism has been motivated by two sets of considerations. One had to do with defense of their own material interests in a society where all material resources were controlled by Zionist organs. In that sense cooperating with the Israeli state (or the pre-state Zionist institutions) was similar to cooperating with non-Jewish governments in the *galut* (exile), although the former is viewed by some *Charedim* as a greater abomination than the latter. The other consideration was similar to that of the religious Zionists, namely, an effort to minimize as much as possible the violation of Jewish religious codes in the society as presently constituted. In the words of the Lubavitcher Rebbe, head of the *Chabad* Chassidic sect:

> Our opposition to Zionism and to the state is not based on any objection to Jewish settlement in the Land of Israel, which is a *mitzvah* [commandment] ... Quite the contrary. It comes out of a desire to purify and sanctify these values which Zionism reduces and empties of significance, giving them meanings which are foreign.
>
> (Cited in Aran 1986:123)

4 Principled rejectionism

This position was held by the majority of Orthodox Jews when Zionism was first founded, but due to time and historical developments the number of people adhering to it has dwindled. Today it is held by the extreme, most religiously orthodox fringes of the *Charedi* community, who view Zionism and the State of Israel as demonic enterprises and refuse to have anything to do with them. According to Rav Mordechai Mintzberg, a prominent member of this group,

> I object to the very thing called the State of Israel, I object to this concept of the army, I don't agree to their wars and I don't agree to their operations, they are fighting against me ... Zionism is exile among Jews and this is the worst exile.
>
> (Hasson 2017)

Mintzberg's group counts for less than 1 percent of *Charedim* in Israel, but in spite of its small numbers it functions as an "ideological compass" for the entire *Charedi* leadership (Leon 2016:36).

In recent times, under the influence of the younger Rav Kook, the two tendencies described here as "principled accommodationism" and "pragmatic rejectionism" have increasingly been showing signs of convergence, with some Religious Zionists becoming more orthodox in their religious behavior and *Charedim* (with the exception of the "principled rejectionists") becoming more nationalist in their political outlook.[11] This phenomenon was very obvious in the election campaign of 1996, for example, when the officially non-Zionist *Charedi*, Chassidic Chabad Lubavitch movement campaigned aggressively for Benjamin Netanyahu under the slogan "Bibi is good for the Jews" (Liebman and Don-Yehiya 1984:122–33; Liebman 1993:138–9; 1994:139–40; S. Cohen 1997:102–4; Yefet 2016:276–9; Sagi and Schwartz 2017:107–11, 158–9).

A fifth type of response – "counter-nationalism" (Leon 2016) – which accepts Zionism but seeks to redefine it in an exclusively ethno-religious way, has been developed since the mid-1980s by the Mizrachi *Charedi* political party, Shas, that seceded from *Agudat Yisrael* because of the anti-Mizrachi discrimination that prevails in that party,[12] especially in admissions to its educational institutions (Peled 1998; 2001a; 2001b; Leon 2006; 2007; 2011; 2016; Lehman and Siebzehner 2006; Siebzehner and Lehman 2012:219). Since Shas has played a major role in the religionization of a sector of the Mizrachi community, turning it from mainly "traditionalist" in religious terms to increasingly *Charedi*, it will be discussed in Chapter 4, which deals with the "return" to religion of Israeli Jews.[13]

Israeli Judaism

Writing many years after the crystallization of Zionism and of what may be termed Western Judaism, and referring to a much later period, Charles Liebman and Steven Cohen pointed to the differences between Israeli and American Judaism in a way that reflected European Jews' dual encounter with the nation-state:

... the significance of the land of Israel and the concept of galut [exile] have been central to the Judaism of most Israelis but are virtually ignored by American Jews. To most Israelis (secular and religious alike), the land has a sacredness that few American Jews appreciate ... Jewish obligations and responsibility toward non-Jews have been interpreted and expanded by American Jews and virtually ignored by Israelis.

(Liebman and Cohen 1990:157–8, see also 171)

Thus, whereas American Jews' religious life is characterized by

personalism, voluntarism, moralism, and universalism ... Religion in Israel is very much a public affair ... Israelis in general and the Orthodox especially have chosen to emphasize the separateness and distinctiveness of Jews, and the special obligation that Jews have toward one another rather than toward gentiles.

(Liebman and Cohen 1990:158–9)

The modern era, then, brought about the development of (at least) two distinct types of Jewish religion: Zionist/Israeli Judaism has evolved into a publicly affirmed, national-state religion, while American Judaism (and, by extension, that of Jews in all Western liberal states, with the possible exception of the ultra-Orthodox) has adapted itself to the Protestant Christian conception of religion prevailing in American society (cf. Don-Yehiya 2005; G. Levy 2011; Pew 2016:46–65; Waxman 2016).

The emergence of Israeli Judaism as a national-state religion, which is what interests us in this book, came about necessarily as a result of Zionism's complex relations with Jewish religion. As we saw, Zionism originally presented itself as a modernizing, secular national movement, a "revolution" against traditional Jewish life in the Diaspora, which had been characterized, first and foremost, by strict adherence to *Halacha* (Abulof 2014:523–4). However, as we pointed out above and as we will show in some detail in Chapter 3, "secular" Zionism could not separate itself from Jewish religion, which defines its target population and legitimizes its claim to the Land of Israel (for an overview see Sharot 2007).

Israeli secularism

Just like "religion," "the concept of secularism cannot be imported easily from one culture to another, but requires special sensitivity to the particularistic features of the secularism examined" (H. Lahav 2015:357). Thus Jewish Israeli secularism

is not sustained by a comprehensive, consistent, and coherent philosophy ... [it] is not part of a long-range and systematic liberal *Weltanschauung*, but is, instead, a defensive and pragmatic attempt to reach and to protect something that is more a secular way of life than a secular way of thinking.

> [It is] pragmatic, incremental, empirical, spontaneous, and instinctive; ...
> it appears more as a reactive force than as a focus of proposal; ... it has no
> stable political representation, but knows outbursts of political expression...
>
> (Charbit 2014:159; see also G. Levy 2011)

The reason, according to Charles Liebman, a (late) political science professor at
the national-religious university, Bar-Ilan (who would not have necessarily
agreed with Charbit's characterization), is that

> [t]o be a Jewish secularist does not mean to be a Jew who is uninfluenced by
> Jewish values, untouched by matters of the spiritual or metaphysical con-
> siderations, and unconcerned with the Jewish heritage. Furthermore, secular
> Jewishness formulates its basic conceptions in religious language.
>
> (Liebman 1997:179)

For "There can be no secular Judaism which is not anchored in the Jewish tradition and there is no Jewish tradition that denies its religious roots." Thus "a
secular Jew is [merely] one who, at least in some aspects of his life and most
likely in the area of public policy choices, makes decisions independently of
halakha or of rabbinic decisors." Furthermore, in Liebman's view

> it is legitimate to term a culture or a public as secular even if it partially
> adheres to religious patterns of thought and defers to the religious tradition
> and is influenced by traditional Jewish values, consciously as well as uncon-
> sciously, in policy formation.
>
> (Liebman 1998:43; 1997:179, 182)

In Israel close to 50 percent of the Jews consider themselves to be secular,
but in 2009 only 16 percent of the Jews reported that they did not observe any
religious tradition (down from 23 percent in 1999), 72 percent reported that
they never eat pork, the hallmark prohibition of Jewish dietary law (*kashrut*),[14]
61 percent believed that public life should be conducted according to the
Jewish religious tradition, and fully 80 percent reported that they believed in
the existence of God (Guttman Center 2012:30, 33, 41, 50, 60, 62; Pew
2016:67, 97; see also H. Lahav 2015:357). The secularity of Israeli Jews thus
accords with Liebman's understanding of this concept. Most of the self-
defined seculars

> do not belong to religious institutions, but define themselves as belonging to
> the Jewish collective; most observe at least some of the Jewish religious
> precepts, especially those connected with the cycle of time and life (holi-
> days, marriage, circumcision, mourning and the like), although these are
> accorded more of a cultural–ethnic significance than a religious one.
>
> (H. Lahav 2015:357; see also H. Lahav 2016:19;
> Guttman Center 2012:48; Pew 2016:22)

An estimated half of those who define themselves as secular are "secular believers," i.e., they "believe in God or some kind of higher power(s)." About one third of them keep kosher at home, and 20 percent say religion is important in their lives. According to Hagar Lahav, these secular believers' "position is based on three principles: having faith, rejecting traditional religion, and practising secular (but not atheistic) Judaism" (H. Lahav 2016:29; 2015:355, 358; Pew 2016:24, 92, 97, 106). In view of these characteristics, to avoid misunderstanding we will henceforward refer to "secular" Israeli Jews not as secular but as non-observant.

According to Liebman, whose conclusion is affirmed by the survey data, self-defined secular Israeli Jews who perform religious rituals "are motivated by a conscious commitment to the continuity of the Jewish people" (Liebman 1997:184; Pew 2016:72; H. Lahav 2016:29). He contends that this commitment requires an alliance with the religious because "secular Jews alone do not have the will or the self-discipline that affirming a culture of responsibility and loyalty [to the Jewish people] requires" (Liebman 1998:45). This statement, we will argue, illuminates a crucially important aspect of the religionization process of Israeli society (see also Y. Fischer 2015:26–7).

The liberalization of Israeli society since the mid-1980s (see Chapter 2), motivated by economic considerations but extended to many other areas of social life as well, coupled with the arrival in the 1990s of about one million secular immigrants from the former USSR, many of them non-Jewish by *Halachic* criteria, resulted in a limited and temporary process of secularization (Shafir and Peled 2002, esp. 152–4; Ben-Porat 2013:27–59).[15]

Guy Ben-Porat has defined secularization in Israel as "a process in which religion loses its hold over public life … specifically … the erosion of the status quo as an institutional arrangement … and the erosion of the authority of the Orthodox rabbinical establishment over daily life" (Ben-Porat 2013:27). He examined this process with respect to four issue-areas, three of them specified in the Status Quo Letter (see Chapter 3) and one additional one: marriage and divorce, *kashrut* (Jewish dietary law), the Sabbath, and the availability of civil rather than religious burial arrangements.

In all of these areas, Ben-Porat argued, the status quo had eroded during the 1990s through the sub-political activities of secular entrepreneurs offering ways of circumventing the religious restrictions, not in the interest of an overarching secular ideology, but in the interest of the convenience of everyday life of non-observant Israeli Jews. As a result,

> neither the [formal] status quo arrangements … nor the status of religion in political life changed. Rules pertaining to religious monopoly largely remained in place, the privileges and rights of Orthodox Jews were protected, and religious parties' power did not diminish.
> (Ben-Porat 2013:59; see also Ben-Porat and Feniger 2009)

In other words, secularization in the 1990s was a superficial process, and the ground was ready for the religious upsurge beginning in the following decade, which saw a retreat of liberalism in all areas of social life, except the economy (Ram 2008).

Religionization

In their seminal book, *Civil Religion in Israel*, published in 1983, political scientists Charles Liebman and Eliezer Don-Yehiya identified a paradigm shift in Israel's "civil religion," from an essentially secular, statist (*mamlachtit*) civil religion to a new civil religion with much closer affinity to traditional Judaism. Civil religion, a civic republican concept, is

> the ceremonials, myths, and creeds which legitimate the social order, unite the population, and mobilize the society's members in pursuit of its dominant political goals. Civil religion is that which is most holy and sacred in the political culture. It forges its adherents into a moral community.
>
> (Liebman and Don-Yehia 1983:ix)

> The civil religion is thus of fundamental importance to a society because it integrates an entire people, drawing them into a common circle of identity, giving them a shared language about a common heritage, and defining certain absolutes about which they all agree.
>
> (Wuthnow 1994:131)[16]

According to Liebman and Don-Yehiya, the history of Zionist settlement in Palestine has known two major shifts of civil religion: from a socialist-Zionist one to a statist one in 1948, and from the statist to the "new" civil religion in 1967. The war of 1967 was a crucial turning point in that it generated a "legitimacy crisis" among Israeli Jews. The crisis was due to two ethical-political dilemmas that had confronted Zionism in Palestine/Israel all along but were heightened by the results of the war: the Jews' right to the Land of Israel, when exercising that right meant displacing or oppressing the Palestinians; and the justification for the sacrifices demanded of Israeli Jews themselves in order to preserve and defend the Zionist project. Paradoxically, both Israel's success in 1967 and the trauma it experienced in the 1973 Yom Kippur war made statist answers to these dilemmas, based as they were on survivalist arguments, unpersuasive, especially for the younger generation (Liebman and Don-Yehia 1983:128–31).

In very broad outline, the new civil religion can be described as a movement from socialist to religious Zionism, or from the universalist to the particularist pole within Jewish Israeli political culture. The tension between universalism and particularism was manifest already in the statist civil religion, as expressed in Israel's declaration of Independence: "The State of Israel [...] will be based on freedom, justice and peace as envisaged by the prophets of Israel." Namely, the new state will conduct itself as a modern, democratic liberal state, yet embedded within the spirit of the Jewish Biblical prophets, who extolled the worship of a monotheistic God as against the temptations of polytheism. For the prophets, subjugating the subjective personal, as well as social, body to faith in one God conditioned the possibility of social justice. Furthermore, the new state was going to be a "nationalizing state," in that it "will be open to *Jewish* immigration and the ingathering of the Exiles"[17] (see Brubaker 1996; Shafir and Peled 2002:1).

The value system espoused by the new civil religion was derived more clearly than the previous civil religions from traditional Judaism, adjusted to the requirements of a modern industrial society and a democratic nation-state. Thus, it sought to enhance the presence of religious Jewish symbols and values in the public sphere, both physically and culturally, but did not aspire to turning Israel into a theocracy; while affirming the primacy of Zionism for Jewish existence, it had a more positive attitude than the statist civil religion toward the preservation of Jewish identity in the Diaspora; and it was more tolerant than the statist civil religion of cultural pluralism within Jewish Israeli society. Whereas the dominant citizenship discourse of statism, as well as of socialist Zionism, was a republican discourse of pioneering civic virtue, the main citizenship discourse of the new civil religion was an ethno-national discourse of primordial belonging (Shafir and Peled 2002). Interestingly for a book published in 1983, Liebman and Don-Yehiya did not discuss the territorial aspects of the new civil religion in relation to those of statism (Liebman and Don-Yehiya 1983:131–7; Ravitzky 2004).

Fifteen years after the publication of *Civil Religion in Israel*, in 1998, Liebman lamented the decline of Israeli civil religion and national commitment in favor of post-modernism, post-Zionism, greater individualism and concern for personal fulfillment and the pursuit of personal interests. He warned that this process, that had affected primarily the secular intellectual elite, could lead, and has led, to the decline of what he called "Jewish secularism" and the rise of traditional religiosity as a substitute collective consciousness needed to fill the vacuum: "The passivity of secular Jews with regard to public issues renders them helpless in the face of the active religious public on the one hand and the assimilatory pressures of a global postmodern culture on the other." Therefore, "[s]trengthening secular Jewishness is necessary to secure a Jewish state and to make Israel a better place in which to live. It is a *sine qua non* for the flowering of Judaism" (Liebman 1998:44; 1997:187).

Liebman phrased his argument in very tentative language, but now, twenty years later, in this book we argue that, for reasons we are going to explore, traditional Jewish religion, in its Zionist variety, is well on its way to establishing itself firmly as the society's predominant integrative, legitimational and mobilizational ideology. Put in political terms, Religious Zionism is fast becoming the hegemonic sector in Israeli society.

The process of the replacement of Liebman and Don-Yehiya's new civil religion with traditional religion is known in Hebrew as *hadata* (religionization) (*Israel Studies Review* 2012; Abulof 2014). The trajectory of *hadata* – the consolidation of Religious Zionist hegemony – has manifested itself in various ways in many areas of social life. Among the most salient are:

- The growing prominence of religious individuals and/or religious themes in key institutions of the society such as the government, the military, the media, the arts, and various social movements. Nearly one third of the members of the Twentieth Knesset elected in 2015, including its Speaker, are Orthodox Jews, compared to one quarter in the Eighteenth Knesset elected in 2009 and similar to the Nineteenth Knesset elected in 2013. One sixth of the members the Nineteenth Knesset said they were subject to the authority of rabbis. Significantly, eleven of the religious Members of Knesset (MKs) in the Twentieth Knesset were elected on slates of non-religious political parties. After a 14-year hiatus, the former and current Education Ministers (from 2013 to the present) have again been Religious Zionists, the former a rabbi elected by a non-religious political party, Yesh Atid. Both ministers, but particularly the current one, Naftali Bennett of the Jewish Home party, have worked diligently to introduce religious themes and rituals in the *secular* state education system (Pery 2012; Levy 2015; Yefet 2016; Hermann et al. 2014:39n57).

- National-religious officers comprise about 40 percent of the junior officer ranks (up to company commander) in infantry units of the Israel Defense Forces (IDF) and about 50 percent of the cadets graduating from the combat branches of the IDF officers' school. Their presence in the upper echelon is no less impressive: in 2010 six out of the eight most senior commanders in the crack infantry brigade, Golani, were national-religious officers, as were half of the senior commanders in the Kfir brigade, stationed permanently in the West Bank, and three in the Givati brigade (Chapter 6).
- In the 1990s, with the encouragement of the Ministry of Education, impressively wide-ranging and thoroughgoing religious art production, art education and art discourse began to emerge, with the opening of art courses and art majors in state-religious high schools and in religious colleges. In 2012 the important art museum at kibbutz Ein Harod hosted an exhibition, *Matronita*, that presented for the first time in any major museum the work of feminist religious artists committed to observing the *Halacha* (Chapter 7).
- A movement "back" to Jewish religion (*teshuvah*) in many sectors of the society, most significantly, for its symbolic value, in kibbutzim. Thus Chassidic Chabad Lubavitch houses exist now in several kibbutzim of *Ha-Shomer Ha-Tzair*, historically the most left-wing and secular kibbutz movement. According to the Central Bureau of Statistics, in 2010 5.4 percent of the Jewish population aged 20 and over defined themselves as *chozrim biteshuvah* ("repentants," i.e., "returning" to religion) (Goodman 2002; CBS 2011:8–9; Mor-Chaim and Greenberg 2013; Spiegel 2016; Chapter 4).
- Increased Jewish religious content in the secular state school system, and the evolution of a joint secular-religious school system (Shikli 2004; Azulay 2006:3; Darom and Kashti 2013; Kashti and Skop 2014; Chapter 5).
- The growth of the movement for "Jewish renewal," in the form of "secular" religious institutions such as *midrashiyot*, prayer houses, *minyanim*, rabbis, and "learning communities" engaged in studying the traditional Jewish sources (Azulay 2006; Katz 2008; Hochman 2009; Ettinger 2013; Chapter 4).

• Resulting from all of the above, the growing prevalence of the national-religious Jewish worldview in Jewish Israeli culture and public life. To illustrate, in 2013 one third of Israeli Jews said they considered rabbinical decisions in the sphere of security and foreign affairs to be very important (Hermann et al. 2014:39n57).

The Jewish public in Israel is cognizant of these processes. In a survey conducted by the Israel Democracy Institute in June 2017, 50 percent of the respondents expressed the view that in recent years public life in Israel has tended to become more religious. One quarter of the respondents thought there was no change in this respect and 20 percent believed public life has tended to become more secular. Among those who define themselves as secular, fully 70 percent believed public life has tended to become more religious[18] (cf. Hermann et al. 2014:106; CBS 2011:94).

The resurgence of religion in the public sphere (dubbed de- or post-secularization or resacralization) is not limited to Israel, of course; it is a well-known and widely commented upon phenomenon in much of the world (Gorski et al. 2012). According to José Casanova, in the 1980s "religion, leaving its assigned place in the private sphere, had thrust itself into the public arena of moral and political contestation" (Casanova 1994:3). Bryan Turner has averred that "The idea that secularization is an inevitable outcome of modernization has been widely challenged by contemporary research and historical analysis" (Turner 2010:5).

Students of this phenomenon, such as Casanova (1994; 2006), Turner (2001; 2010; 2011), David Martin (1969; 1991), Peter Berger (1999), Jürgen Habermas (2006; 2010), Judith Butler (Butler et al. 2011), Craig Calhoun (Calhoun et al. 2011), and many others have explained the resurgence of public religion largely in terms of the failure of secular ideologies (such as nationalism, liberalism, and socialism) to provide normative and emotive foundations for collective identity and action, and the failure of scientific approaches (such as rationalism, positivism, and methodological individualism) to provide a meaningful understanding of reality (Mautner 2016).

Many have questioned the validity of the secularization thesis itself and the presumed close ties between secularization, modernity, and the Enlightenment. Thus, Grace Davie has argued that in the secularization thesis "The empirical connections present in Europe gradually – but inexorably – turned into theoretical assumptions, with the strong implication that secularization would necessarily accompany modernization whenever and wherever the latter occurred." In actual fact, however, "It is hardly an exaggeration to say that religion now dominates the agenda in many parts of the world" (Davie 2010:162, 167). Graeme Smith has gone farthest, it seems, arguing that secularism itself is "Christian ethics shorn of its doctrine" (Smith 2008:2).

Casanova has famously disaggregated the "secularization thesis" – viewing secularization as inherent in modernization and the Enlightenment – into three separate propositions: (1) differentiation of the secular spheres (science, market economy, the state) from religious institutions and norms, as part and parcel of the general process of social differentiation which constitutes modernization; (2) decline of religious beliefs and practices; (3) marginalization of religion to the private sphere. He further argued that propositions (2) and (3) are not "inherently concomitant with modernity," but proposition (1) is, and is therefore the defensible core of the secularization thesis (Casanova 2006:12–13). As we show in this book, in Israel the process described in proposition (3) did not happen; the process described in (2) happened partially and is now being reversed; and, most importantly, the process described in (1) happened only in part and is now being reversed with respect to the state. Israeli society, then, is undergoing religionization without having ever been fully secularized.

Our working hypothesis in this book is that, alongside the general explanations for the post-secularization of Western societies in general, stemming from heightened alienation caused by rapid technological change, neo-liberal economics, and the decline of the welfare state, there are specific reasons that account for the religionization of Israeli society. These are:

- Demographic growth of the Jewish religious sector due to its higher birth rates.
- Existential insecurity caused by a protracted conflict, which has increased significantly since 2000 due to the failure of the Oslo peace process and the onset of the second *intifada*. This existential insecurity is manifested, *inter alia*, in the number of Israeli Jews acquiring foreign citizenship – 60,000 (about 1 percent of the Jewish population of Israel at the time) in 2000–2010 (Harpaz 2012; on Zionist existential insecurity in general see Abulof 2015; 2016).
- The failure of the Oslo peace process signified the end of the two-state solution to the Israeli-Palestinian conflict, hence to the possibility of maintaining a Jewish demographic majority in Israel/Palestine (Herman Peled and Peled 2011; Ehrenberg and Peled 2016). Coupled with the halting and uneven, but still real, integration of Israel's Palestinian citizen into the mainstream of Israeli society, this intensified the siege mentality of many Israeli Jews and their need to erect higher cultural (as well as physical) walls around themselves in order to preserve their identity and security.
- The neo-liberalization of the Israeli economy since the mid-1980s (Shafir and Peled 2000; 2002; Chapter 2).
- The influence of the movement for Jewish renewal in the United States, as well as of the more established Conservative and Reform movements. These more liberal versions of Judaism have functioned to smooth the way for self-styled secular Israeli Jews, mainly middle-class Ashkenazim, back to religion.
- In certain circles, the idea that peace could be achieved through religious dialogue between Moslems and Jews has replaced the belief in peace through political negotiations.

Hegemony

The analytical framework within which we will examine our hypothesis is adapted from Antonio Gramsci's theory of cultural hegemony as sustained by a social historic bloc. Hegemony, for Gramsci, meant "an order in which a common social-moral language is spoken, in which one concept of reality is dominant, informing with its spirit all modes of thought and behavior" (Femia 1981:24; Anderson 1976). The concept of "social historic bloc" conveys the idea that a social group (for Gramsci, a class),

> as it develops itself historically, becomes more or less politically powerful not only because of its position within the economic structure but also because it is the carrier of certain values which, though certainly expressions of its experience in … everyday life, become detached as images or projections of its political outlook. Depending on the attractiveness of such images, the class will be able to attach itself to other political groups as joint power-seekers, potential power-shapers, and the social forces behind new cultural expressions.
>
> (Adamson 1980:177)

We will argue that the "social historic bloc" that sustained the hegemony of the Labor Zionist Movement during the pre-statehood and early statehood period began to disintegrate as a result of the 1967 and 1973 wars and the 1985 turn to neo-liberal economics, and that a new social historic bloc began to be formed around a reinvigorated national-religious camp. This social historic bloc was led by the younger members of the National Religious Party (NRP), disciples of Rav Zvi Yehuda Kook, who formed themselves as Gush Emunim in 1974 and took over the party in the mid-1980s (Don-Yehiya 1980; Raanan 1980; Liebman and Don-Yehiya 1983:194–206; Lustick 1988:42–71; Liebman 1990:82–4; Shafir and Peled 2002:165–72; M. Inbari 2012; Aran 2013:178–265; Chapter 3).

In addition to the young guard of the NRP, the new bloc included supporters of the Revisionist Zionist political party – Likud; major segments of the Labor Zionist Movement, especially from the *Ha-Kibbutz Ha-Meuchad* kibbutz movement and the former Rafi political party, led by such figures as Yitzhak Tabenkin, Yisrael Galili and Moshe Dayan and including intellectuals such as the poets Nathan Alterman and Haim Gouri, the songwriter Naomi Shemer, and the writers Chaim Hazaz and Moshe Shamir and organizations such as the Society for the Protection of Nature; and lower-class Mizrachim, ranging in religiosity from traditionalists to *Charedim* and organized in a political party – Shas – for the first time in 1984 (Peled 1998; 2001a; Barak 2013; Goodman and Yonah 2015:209; for a different view of the new social-historic bloc see Avigur-Eshel and Filc 2017). The myth around which this new social historic bloc was formed was the myth of Greater Israel: "the Land of Israel came to symbolize loyalty to both the State of Israel and to Judaism" (Liebman 1994:136).

A necessary corollary of the success of this new historic bloc was the transformation of the civil religion analyzed by Liebman and Don-Yehiya (1983). An important component of Israel's civil religion has always been what Grace Davie has termed "vicarious religion" – the religious establishment and religious people believing in doctrines, performing rituals, and embodying moral codes which many non-religious people put a high value on, even though they do not practice them themselves, primarily for reasons of convenience (Davie 2007). Thus, as stated by Liebman, and as we have pointed out in this Introduction, "the Jewish state, by its very definition, is a state where religion performs a public role and enjoys a public standing" (Liebman 1994:143), although formally religious people have never constituted more than 20 percent of the Jewish population. Vicarious religion was classically expressed by Ariel Sharon, the iconic right-wing political (and previously military) leader, when he said, "I am proud to be Jewish, but I'm sorry I am not a religious man" (cited in Liebman 1994:136).

Since 1967, and particularly since the failure of the Oslo peace process in 2000 and the second *intifada* that ensued, "the implicit has become explicit" in Davie's terms (Davie 2007:28–9), and the Religious Zionist social historic bloc, we will argue, has been joined by growing numbers of middle-class Ashkenazim, and is well on its way to establishing its worldview as the hegemonic worldview of Jewish Israeli society. As a result, in the words of sociologist Nissim Leon, a prominent student of religious-secular relations in Jewish Israeli society, "Israeli secular culture and politics [have shifted] from a position of dominance to one of defensiveness" (Leon 2012:24).

Summary

Our purpose in this book is to account for the religionization of Jewish Israeli society. We began by problematizing the concepts of "religion" and "secularity" and explaining what we understand them to mean in the Jewish Israeli context. We proceeded to do the same with the relations between religion and nationalism and argued that in the Jewish case the two cannot be separated from each other and that therefore a powerful religious element has always been embedded in Zionism. Because Zionism needs Judaism in order to legitimize both its claim to represent the Jewish *nation* and its claim on the Land of Israel, it has always made overtures toward religious Jews, whether Zionist or not, disproportionately to their electoral weight in its constituencies. This point will be more fully developed in Chapter 3.

This being said, in the following chapters we will show how the religious aspect of Zionism was subdued during the time when Labor Zionism enjoyed hegemony over the Zionist movement. As we show in Chapter 2, only when the hegemonic status of Labor began to erode, following the 1967 war and the liberalization of the Israeli economy, could Religious Zionism make a bid to replace it as the hegemonic group in society. We will show how, with a carefully thought-out strategy, Religious Zionism – led by its activist-messianic core epitomized by Gush Emunim – made inroads into several key social fields such as the IDF (Chapter 6), the educational system (Chapter 5), fine arts (Chapter 7),[19] film and television (Chapter 9), and most crucially, settlement in the occupied Palestinian territories (OPT). Aided by a broad hinterland of *Charedim* who wish to integrate into the larger society, at least to a certain extent, and of self-defined seculars who wish to (re)connect to Jewish tradition either with or without becoming fully observant Jews, Religious Zionism is now poised to achieve hegemony over the society.

Notes

1　We distinguish between *Religious* Zionism – a political movement possessing a well-established set of institutions: a political party; an autonomous educational system ranging from kindergartens to a university, with every intermediary level in between; a settlement movement; and major forays into the military establishment – and *religious* Zionism – a social, cultural, and political outlook that combines the basic tenets of Zionism with a whole range of levels of religious observance – from close to ultra-Orthodoxy to the "cultural Judaism" of the movement for Jewish renewal (see Chapters 3 and 4).

2　Talal Asad: "if we accept that religious ideas can be 'secularized,' that secularized concepts retain *a religious essence*, we might be induced to accept that nationalism has a religious origin" (Asad 2003:189, emphasis in the original). Asad himself does not accept this argument in a general way, but we believe it certainly holds true with respect to Zionism.

3　Available at: http://zionism-israel.com/hdoc/Theodor_Herzl_Zionist_Congress_Speech_1897.htm. Accessed December 21, 2016.

4　The Hebrew word for "religion" – *dat* – means "law."

5　While some of the more articulate formulators of Zionist ideology were Western European Jews, Theodor Herzl chief among them, the movement's constituency was clearly in Eastern Europe.

6　As phrased by Menachem Mautner, "religion and the project of the nation-state are the two chief systems of big meaning we have" (Mautner 2016:114).

7　According to Rav Zvi Yehudah Kook (see below) the Balfour Declaration, in which the British government committed itself to supporting the establishment of a Jewish national home in Palestine, annulled the three oaths undertaken by the Jews: not to scale the wall, not to hasten Redemption, and not to rebel against the nations (M. Inbari 2008:44).

8　For a literary depiction of this attitude see Potok 1967, Chapter 12 *passim*.

9　But see S. Fischer 2013:350 and D. Schwartz 2003:21–30 for a complication of Reines's position.

10　We realize that this is a highly simplified rendering of Kook's very complicated and sophisticated body of thought on this issue. For recent in-depth treatments of his thought see Sagi and Schwartz 2017:103n40.

11　For the history of the relations between these two religious-political streams see Mahla 2015.

12　In this book, Mizrachi (plural Mizrachim) refers to Jews originating in the Moslem world; *Mizrachi* refers to the Religious Zionist movement by that name.

13　On the religiously "traditionalist" sector of Jewish Israeli society see Yadgar 2011.

14　The Pew Research Center study, conducted five years after the Guttman Center study, found that 67 percent of self-defined *secular* Jews say they never eat pork (Pew 2016:108).

15　Children of immigrants from the former USSR are markedly more religious than their parents (Pew 2016:105).

16 On civil religion see also Cavanaugh 2009:113–18; Abulof 2014, esp. 519–20.
17 Emphasis added. Available at: www.knesset.gov.il/docs/eng/megilat_eng.htm. Accessed November 1, 2017.
18 Available at: www.idi.org.il/articles/16165?ct=t. Accessed August 8, 2017.
19 We devote a relatively long chapter to the field of fine arts because religionization in that field has been largely neglected by previous researchers.

References

Abramov, Z. S. (1976) *Perpetual Dilemma: Jewish Religion in the Jewish State*, Rutherford, NJ: Fairleigh Dickinson University Press.

Abulof, U. (2014) "The Roles of Religion in National Legitimation: Judaism and Zionism's Elusive Quest for Legitimacy," *Journal for the Scientific Study of Religion*, 53 (3): 515–33.

Abulof, U. (2015) *The Mortality and Morality of Nations*, Cambridge: Cambridge University Press.

Abulof, U. (2016) *Living on the Edge: The Existential Uncertainty of Zionism*, Haifa: Haifa University Press (in Hebrew).

Adamson, W. L. (1980) *Hegemony and Revolution: A Study of Antonio Gramsci's Political and Cultural Theory*, Berkeley, CA: University of California Press.

Almog, S., Reinharz, J., and Shapira An. (eds.) (1998) *Zionism and Religion*, Hanover, NH: University Press of New England.

Anderson, P. (1976) "The Antinomies of Antonio Gramsci," *New Left Review*, 100: 5–78.

Aran, G. (1986) "From Religious Zionism to Zionist Religion: The Roots of Gush Emunim," *Studies in Contemporary Jewry*, 2: 116–43.

Aran, G. (1991) "Jewish Zionist Fundamentalism: The Bloc of the Faithful in Israel (Gush Emunim)," in Marty, M. E. and Appleby, R. S. (eds.) *Fundamentalism Observed*, Chicago, IL: The University of Chicago Press, pp. 265–344.

Aran, G. (2013) *Kookism: The Roots of Gush Emunim, Settlers' Culture, Zionist Theology, Messianism in Our Time*, Jerusalem: Carmel (in Hebrew).

Asad, T. (1993) *Geneologies of Religion: Discipline and Reasons of Power in Christianity and Islam*, Baltimore, MD: Johns Hopkins University Press.

Asad, T. (1999) "Religion, Nation-State, Secularism," in Van der Veer, P. and Lehmann, H. (eds.) *Nation and Religion: Perspectives on Europe and Asia*, Princeton, NJ: Princeton University Press, pp. 178–95.

Asad, T. (2003) *Formations of the Secular: Christianity, Islam, Modernity*, Stanford, CA: Stanford University Press.

Atkes, E. (2016) "Contours of the Image of Religious Zionism," in Atkes, E., Assaf, D., and Kaplan, J. (eds.) *Milestones: Essays and Studies in the History of the People of Israel*, Jerusalem: Zalman Shazar Center, pp. 363–77 (in Hebrew).

Avigur-Eshel, A. and Filc, D. (2017) "Military Conflict and Neo-Liberalization in Israel (2001–2006): A Neo-Gramscian Approach," *Political Studies*, https://doi.org/10.1177/0032321717722356 (accessed December 12, 2017)

Avineri, S. (1998) "Zionism and the Jewish Religious Tradition: The Dialectics of Redemption and Secularization," in Almog, S., Reinharz, J., and Shapira, An. (eds.) *Zionism and Religion*, Hanover, NH: University Press of New England, pp. 1–12.

Azulay, N. (2006) "Jewish Renewal in the Secular Space in Israel – 2006 – Lecture Summary," *Panim for Jewish Renaissance*, www.panim.org.il/p-120/ (in Hebrew; accessed November 7, 2014).

Barak, Y. (2013) "The Society for the Protection of Nature and the Occupation of the Land," *Haaretz*, October 10 (in Hebrew).

Batnitzky, L. (2011) *How Judaism Became A Religion: An Introduction to Modern Jewish Thought*, Princeton, NJ: Princeton University Press.

Ben-Porat, G. (2013) *Between State and Synagogue: The Secularization of Contemporary Israel*, Cambridge: Cambridge University Press.

Ben-Porat, G. and Feniger, Y. (2009) "Live and Let Buy? Consumerism, Secularization, and Liberalism," *Comparative Politics*, 41 (3): 293–313.

Ben-Rafael, E. (2008) "The Faces of Religiosity in Israel: Cleavages or Continuum?," *Israel Studies*, 13 (3): 89–113.

Berger, P. (ed.) (1999) *Desecularization of the World: Resurgent Religion and World Politics*, Grand Rapids, MI: Erdmans Publishing Co.

Bracke, S. (2008) "Conjugating the Modern/Religious, Conceptualizing Female Religious Agency: Contours of a 'Post-secular' Conjuncture," *Theory, Culture & Society*, 25 (6): 51–67.

Brubaker, R. (1996) *Nationalism Reframed: Nationhood and the National Question in the New Europe*, Cambridge: Cambridge University Press.

Brubaker, R. (2012) "Religion and Nationalism: Four Approaches," *Nations and Nationalism*, 18 (1): 2–20.

Bruce, S. (2010) "Secularization," in Turner, B. S. (ed.) *The New Blackwell Companion to the Sociology of Religion*, Hoboken, NJ: Wiley-Blackwell, pp. 123–40.

Butler, J., Habermas, J., Taylor, C., and West, C. (2011) *The Power of Religion in the Public Sphere*, Mendieta, E. and Van Antwerpen, J. (eds.), New York: Columbia University Press.

Calhoun, C., Juergensmeyer, M., and Van Antwerpen, J. (eds.) (2011) *Rethinking Secularism*, New York: Oxford University Press.

Casanova, J. (1994) *Public Religion in the Modern World*, Chicago, IL: University of Chicago Press.

Casanova, J. (2006) "Rethinking Secularization: A Global Comparative Perspective," *The Hedgehog Review*, 8: 7–22.

Cavanaugh, W. T. (2009) *The Myth of Religious Violence: Secular Ideology and the Roots of Modern Conflict*, Oxford: Oxford University Press.

CBS (2011) "Selected Data from the Israel Statistical Annual No. 62, 2011," www.cbs.gov.il/reader/newhodaot/hodaa_template.html?hodaa=201111240 (accessed November 7, 2014).

Charbit, D. (2014) "Israel's Self-Restrained Secularism from the 1947 Status Quo Letter to the Present," in Berlinerblau, J., Fainberg, S., and Nou, A. (eds.) *Secularism on the Edge: Rethinking Church–State Relations in the United States, France, and Israel*, Basingstoke: Palgrave Macmillan, pp. 157–71.

Cohen, Stuart. (1997) *The Scroll or the Sword?: Dilemmas of Religion and Military Service in Israel*, Amsterdam: Harwood Academic Publishers.

Creppell, I. (2010) "Secularisation, Religion and the Roots of Innovation in the Political Sphere," in Katznelson, I. and Stedman Jones, G. (eds.) *Religion and the Political Imagination*, Cambridge: Cambridge University Press, pp. 23–45.

Darom, N. and Kashti, O. (2013) "How Are the Secular State Schools Making *Tshuvah*," *Haaretz Weekend Magazine*, December 27, www.haaretz.co.il/magazine/.premium-1.2200680 (in Hebrew; accessed November 7, 2014).

Davie, G. (2007) "Vicarious Religion: A Methodological Challenge," in Ammerman, N. T. (ed.) *Everyday Religion: Observing Modern Religious Lives*, Oxford: Oxford University Press, pp. 21–35.

Davie, G. (2010) "Resacralization," in Turner, B. S. (ed.) *The New Blackwell Companion to the Sociology of Religion*, Chichester: Wiley-Blackwell, pp. 160–77.

Don-Yehiya, E. (1980) "Stability and Transformations in a Camp Party: The NRP and the Young Revolution," *State, Government and International Relations*, 14: 25–52 (in Hebrew).

Don-Yehiya, E. (1983) "Ideology and Policy in religious Zionism: Rabbi Yitzhak Yaakov Reines' Conception of Zionism and the Policy of the Mizrahi under His Leadership," *Zionism*, VIII: 103–46 (in Hebrew).

Don-Yehiya, E. (2005) "Orthodox Jewry in Israel and in North America," *Israel Studies*, 10 (1): 157–87.

Don-Yehiya, E. (2014) "Messianism and Politics: The Ideological Transformation of Religious Zionism," *Israel Studies*, 19 (2): 239–63.

Ehrenberg, J. and Peled, Y. (2016) *Israel and Palestine: Alternative Perspectives on Statehood*, Lanham: Rowman & Littlefield.

Ettinger, Y. (2013) "Who's Afraid of Ruth Calderon?" *Haaretz*, March 2 (in Hebrew).

Femia, Joseph, V. (1981) *Gramsci's Political Thought: Hegemony, Consciousness, and the Revolutionary Process*, Oxford: Clarendon.

Fischer, S. (2013) "Change or Continuity? Torah Regime, Citizenship and the Origins of Radical Religious Zionism," in Shavit, Z., Sasson-Levy, O., and Ben-Porat, G. (eds.) *Points of Reference: Changing Identities and Social Positioning in Israel*, Jerusalem: Van Leer Jerusalem Institute, pp. 347–82 (in Hebrew).

Fischer, S. (2014) "The Crises of Liberal Citizenship: Religion and Education in Israel," in Seligman, A. (ed.) *Religious Education and the Challenge of Pluralism*, Oxford: Oxford University Press, pp. 119–49.

Fischer, Y. (ed.) (2015) *Secularization and Secularism: Interdisciplinary Perspectives*, Jerusalem and Tel Aviv: Van Leer Institute and Hakibbutz Hameuchad (in Hebrew).

Goodman, J. (2002) *Teshuvah and New Religious Identities in Israel in the 2000s*, Tel Aviv: Tel Aviv University, Pinhas Sapir Center for Development (in Hebrew).

Goodman, J. and Yonah, Y. (2015) "The Gordian Knot Between Religiosity and Secularism in Israel: Inclusion, Exclusion and Change," in Fischer, Y. (ed.) *Secularization and Secularism: Interdisciplinary Perspectives*, Jerusalem and Tel Aviv: Van Leer Institute and Hakibbutz Hameuchad, pp. 197–221 (in Hebrew).

Gorski, P. S., Kim, D. K., Torpey, J., and VanAntwerpen, J. (eds.) (2012) *The Post-Secular in Question: Religion in Contemporary Society*, New York: New York University Press.

Greenblum, D. (2016) *From the Bravery of the Spirit to the Sanctification of Power: Power and Bravery in Religious Zionism 1948–1967*, Ra'anana: Open University Press (in Hebrew).

Guttman Center (2012) *A Portrait of Israeli Jews: Beliefs, Observance, and Values of Israeli Jews, 2009*, Jerusalem: Israel Democracy Institute and Avi Chai–Israel.

Habermas, J. (2006) "Religion in the Public Sphere," *European Journal of Philosophy*, 14 (1): 1–25.

Habermas, J. (2010) *An Awareness of What is Missing: Faith and Reason in a Post-secular Age*, Cambridge: Polity Press.

Harpaz, Y. (2012) "'Israelis With an Option': The Demand for a European Passport in Israel – Dual Citizenship as a Family Legacy and Status Symbol," *Megamot*, 48: 626–55 (in Hebrew).

Hasson, N. (2017) "Their Resistance Is Their Vocation," *Haaretz*, August 20, www.haaretz.co.il/news/education/1.4364573 (in Hebrew; accessed August 20, 2017).

Hellinger, M. (2008) "Political Theology in the Thought of 'Merkaz HaRav' Yeshiva and its Profound Influence on Israeli Politics and Society since 1967," *Totalitarian Movements and Political Religions*, 9: 533–50.

Herman Peled, H. and Peled, Y. (2011) "Post-Post Zionism: Confronting the Death of the Two-State Solution," *New Left Review*, 67: 97–118.

Hermann, T., Be'eri, G., Heller, E., Cohen, C., Lebel, Y., Mozes, H., and Neuman, K. (2014) *The National-Religious Sector in Israel 2014*, Jerusalem: Israel Democracy Institute (in Hebrew).

Herzl, T. (1934 [1896]) *The Jewish State*, n.p., Library of Alexandria.

Hochman, R. (2009) "Rabbis Who Do Not Believe in God? Description of a Secular Humanist Rabbi in Israel – An Exploratory Study," MA thesis, Department of Sociology and Anthropology, Haifa University (in Hebrew).

Inbari, M. (2008) "Rav Zvi Yehudah Kook's Conception of Zionism and the Roots of 'Gush Emunim'," *Iyunim Betkumat Yisrael*, 18: 29–53 (in Hebrew).

Inbari, M. (2012) *Messianic Religious Zionism Confronts Israeli Territorial Compromises*, Cambridge: Cambridge University Press.

Israel Studies Review (2012) "The 'Religionization' of Israeli Society," 27 (1): v–208.

Juergensmeyer, M. (2008) *Global Rebellion: Religious Challenges to the Secular State, from Christian Militias to al Qaeda*, Berkeley, CA: University of California Press.

Kashti, O. and Skop, Y. (2014) "Education Ministry's New Baby: 'Jewish-Israeli Culture'," *Haaretz*, November 12, www.haaretz.com/misc/search-results (in Hebrew; accessed November 12, 2014).

Katz, G. (2008) "Secularism and the Imaginary Polemic of Israeli Intellectuals," *Israel Studies*, 13 (3): 43–63.

Kolatt, I. (1998) "Religion, Society and State in the Period of the National Home," in Almog, S., Reinharz, J., and Shapira, An. (eds.) *Zionism and Religion*, Hanover, NH: University Press of New England, pp. 273–301.

Kopelowitz, E. (2003) "Negotiating with the Secular: Forms of Religious Authority and their Political Consequences," in Greil, A. L. and Bromley, D. G. (eds.) *Defining Religion: Investigating the Boundaries between the Sacred and Secular* (*Religion and Social Order*, Vol. 10), Amsterdam: Elsevier Science, pp. 85–107.

Kopelowitz, E. and Diamond, M. (1998) "Religion That Strengthens Democracy: An Analysis of Religious Political Strategies in Israel," *Theory and Society*, 27: 671–708.

Lahav, H. (2015) "Post-Secular Jewish Feminist Theology?" *Journal of Modern Jewish Studies*, 14: 355–72.

Lahav, H. (2016) "What do Secular-Believer Women in Israel Believe in?" *Journal of Contemporary Religion*, 31: 17–34.

Lehman, D. and Siebzehner, B. (2006) *Remaking Israeli Judaism: The Challenge of Shas*, New York: Oxford University Press.

Leon, N. (2006) "Religion and Secularity," *Iyunim Betkumat Yisrael*, 16: 85–107 (in Hebrew).

Leon, N. (2007) "'Zikui Harabim': Ovadia Yosef's Approach Toward Religious Activism and His Place in the Haredi Movement Within Mizrahi Jewry," *Studies in Contemporary Jewry*, 22: 150–68.

Leon, N. (2011) "The Political Use of the Teshuva Cassette Culture in Israel," *Contemporary Jewry*, 31: 91–106.

Leon, N. (2012) "Secular Jews: From Proactive Agents to Defensive Players," *Israel Studies Review*, 27 (1): 21–6.

Leon, N. (2016) *Mizrachi Ultra-Orthodoxy and Nationalism in Israel*, Jerusalem: Van Leer Institute and Hakibbutz Hameuchad (in Hebrew).

Levine, D. J. (2014) "The Apocalyptic Sting and the Rise of Israeli Unrealism: Toward a Negative-Dialectical Critique," *Globalizations*, 11: 643–59.

Levy, G. (2011) "Secularism, Religion and The Status Quo," in Barbalet, J., Possamai, A., and Turner, B. S. (eds.) *Religion and the State: A Comparative Sociology*, London: Anthem Press, pp. 93–119.

Levy, Y. (2015) *The Divine Commander: The Theocratization of the Israeli Military*, Tel Aviv: Am Oved (in Hebrew).

Liebman, C. S. (ed.) (1990) *Religious and Secular: Conflict and Accommodation Between Jews in Israel*, Jerusalem: Keter (in Hebrew).

Liebman, C. S. (1993) "Attitudes Toward Democracy Among Israeli Religious Leaders," in Kaufman, E., Abed, S. B., and Rothstein, R. L. (eds.) *Democracy, Peace, and the Israeli-Palestinian Conflict*, Boulder, CO: Lynne Rienner, pp. 135–61.

Liebman, C. S. (1994) "Religion and Democracy in Israel," *Zmanim: A Historical Quarterly*, 50/51: 132–44 (in Hebrew).

Liebman, C. S. (1997) "Reconceptualizing the Culture Conflict among Israeli Jews," *Israel Studies*, 2: 172–89.

Liebman, C. S. (1998) "Secular Judaism and its Prospects," *Israel Affairs*, 4: 29–48.

Liebman, C. S. and Don-Yehiya, E. (1983) *Civil Religion in Israel: Traditional Judaism and Political Culture in the Jewish State*, Berkeley, CA: University of California Press.

Liebman, C. S. and Don-Yehiya, E. (1984) *Religion and Politics in Israel*, Bloomington, IN: Indiana University Press.

Liebman, C. S. and Cohen, S. M. (1990) *Two Worlds of Judaism: The Israeli and American Experiences*, New Haven, CT: Yale University Press.

Lustick, I. (1988) *For the Land and the Lord: Jewish Fundamentalism in Israel*, New York: Council on Foreign Relations.

Luz, E. (1999) *Wrestling in River Yabok: Power, Morality, and Jewish Identity*, Jerusalem: Magnes (in Hebrew). Available in English as *Wrestling with an Angel: Power, Morality, and Jewish Identity*, trans. Swirsky, M., New Haven, CT: Yale University Press, 2003.

Mahla, D. (2015) "No Trinity: The Tripartite Relations between Agudat Yisrael, the Mizrahi Movement, and the Zionist Organization," *The Journal of Israeli History: Politics, Society, Culture*, 34: 117–40.

Martin, D. (1969) *The Religious and the Secular*, London: Routledge.

Martin, D. (1991) "The Secularization Issue: Prospect and Retrospect," *The British Journal of Sociology*, 42: 465–74.

Mautner, M. (2016) "Meaning, Religion, and the State: On the Future of Liberal Human Rights," *Law & Ethics of Human Rights*, 10: 109–33.

Mendelssohn, M. (1983 [1783]) *Jerusalem, or On Religious Power and Judaism*, trans. Arkush, A., Hanover, NH and London: Brandeis University Press.

Mirsky, Y. (2014) *Rav Kook: Mystic in a Time of Revolution*, New Haven, CT: Yale University Press.

Mor-Chaim, N. and Greenberg, N. (2013) *The Holy Kibbutz*, Jerusalem: Israel Broadcasting Authority, Channel 1, Documentary Department [documentary film].

Nairn, T. (1977) *The Break-up of Britain*, London: New Left Books.

Peled, Y. (1998) "Towards a Redefinition of Jewish Nationalism in Israel? The Enigma of Shas," *Ethnic and Racial Studies*, 21 (4): 703–27.

Peled, Y. (ed.) (2001a) *Shas: The Challenge of Israeliness*, Tel Aviv: Yediot Aharonot (in Hebrew).

Peled, Y. (2001b) "Roar of the Lion: Shas and the Challenge to Israeli Identity," *Israel Studies Bulletin*, 16: 8–13.

Peled, Y. (2012) "From Oslo to Gaza: Israel's 'Enlightened Public' and the Remilitarization of the Israeli-Palestinian Conflict," in Stavrianakis, A., Selby, J., and Oikonomou, I. (eds.) *Militarism and International Relations: Political Economy, Security, Theory*, London: Routledge.

Peleg, Y. (2016) *Directed by God: Jewishness in Contemporary Israeli Film and Television*, Austin, TX: University of Texas Press.

Pery, Y. (2012) "Introduction," *Israel Studies Review* ("The 'Religionization' of Israeli Society"), 27 (1): 1–3.

Pew (2016) *Israel's Religiously Divided Society*, Washington, DC: Pew Research Center.

Potok, Ch. (1967) *The Chosen*, New York: Ballantine Books.

Raanan, T. (1980) *Gush Emunim*, Tel Aviv: Sifriat Poalim (in Hebrew).

Ram, Uri. (2008) "Why Secularism Fails? Secular Nationalism and Religious Revivalism in Israel," *International Journal of Politics, Culture, and Society*, 21 (1): 57–73.

Ravitzky, A. (1993) *Messianism, Zionism and Jewish Religious Radicalism*, Tel Aviv: Am Oved (in Hebrew).

Ravitzky, A. (2004) *Is a Halacha State Possible: The Paradox of Jewish Theocracy*, Jerusalem: Israel Democracy Institute (in Hebrew).

Sagi, A. and Schwartz, D. (2017) *From Realism to Messianism: Religious Zionism and the Six-Day War*, Jerusalem: Carmel (in Hebrew).

Schatz, B. (1924) *Jerusalem Rebuilt: A Daydream*, n.p., Jerusalem.

Scholem, G. (1997) *On the Possibility of Jewish Mysticism in Our Time, and Other Essays*. Philadelphia, PA: Jewish Publication Society.

Schwartz, D. (2002) *Faith at the Crossroads: A Theological Profile of Religious Zionism*, trans. Stein, B., Leiden: Brill.

Schwartz, D. (2003) *Religious Zionism: History and Chapters of Ideology*, Tel Aviv: Ministry of Defense (in Hebrew).

Shafir, G. and Peled, Y. (2000) *The New Israel: Peacemaking and Liberalization*, Boulder, CO: Westview Press.

Shafir, G. and Peled, Y. (2002) *Being Israeli: The Dynamics of Multiple Citizenship*, Cambridge: Cambridge University Press.

Shapira, An. (1991) "The Religious Motifs of the Labor Movement," in Shapira, R. and Kasher, A. (eds.) *Reshafim – Historical, Philosophical and Social Aspects of Education*, Tel Aviv: Tel Aviv University (in Hebrew).

Shapira, An. (1998) "Religious Motifs of the Labor Movement," in Almog, S., Reinharz, J. and Shapira, A. (eds.) *Zionism and Religion*, Hanover, NH: University Press of New England.

Shapira, An. (2014) "Israel's 'Religious Secularism'," in Berlinerblau, J., Fainberg, S., and Nou, A. (eds.) *Secularism on the Edge: Rethinking Church–State Relations in the United States, France, and Israel*, Basingstoke: Palgrave Macmillan, pp. 145–55.

Sharot, S. (2007) "Judaism in Israel: Public Religion, Neo-Traditionalism, Messianism, and Ethno-Religious Conflict," in Beckford, J. A. and Demerath, N. J. III (eds.) *The SAGE Handbook of the Sociology of Religion*, Los Angeles, CA: Sage Publications, pp. 670–96.

Shikli, E. (2004) "TALI Education: The Development and Realization of an Educational Idea under Conditions of a Changing Reality," PhD dissertation, Jewish Theological Seminary (in Hebrew).

Siebzehner, B. and Lehman, D. (2012) "Recruitment and Conversion in *Haredi* Society in Israel: Shas's *Teshuva* Enterprise," in Kaplan, K. and Stadler, N. (eds.) *From Survival to Consolidation: Changes in Israeli Haredi Society and its Scholarly Study*, Jerusalem: The Van Leer Jerusalem Institute (in Hebrew).

Smith, G. (2008) *A Short History of Secularism*, London: I.B. Tauris.

Sorek, T. and Ceobanu, A. M. (2009) "Religiosity, Identity and Legitimacy: Israel as an Extreme Case," *Sociology*, 43: 477–81.

Spiegel, N. (2016) "Kibbutzim Compromise Their Secular Character in Order to Survive and Fight for Their Complexion," *Haaretz*, April 28 (in Hebrew).

Taylor, C. (2011) "Western Secularity," in Calhoun, C., Juergensmeyer, M., and Van Antwerpen, M. (eds.) *Rethinking Secularism*, Oxford: Oxford University Press, pp. 31–53.

Turner, B. S. (2001) "Cosmopolitan Virtue: On Religion in a Global Age," *European Journal of Social Theory*, 4 (2): 131–52.

Turner, B. S. (ed.) (2010) *The New Blackwell Companion to the Sociology of Religion*, Chichester: Wiley-Blackwell.

Turner, B. S. (2011) *Religion and Modern Society: Citizenship, Secularisation, and the State*, Cambridge: Cambridge University Press.

Vital, D. (1982) *Zionism: The Formative Years*, Oxford: Clarendon Press.

Waxman, D. (2016) "A Tale of Two Jewries: The Pew Surveys of American and Israeli Jews," www.matzavblog.com/author/dwaxman/ (accessed September 29, 2017).

Wuthnow, R. (1994) *Producing the Sacred: An Essay on Public Religion*, Champaign, IL: University of Illinois Press.

Yadgar, Y. (2011) *Secularism and Religion in Jewish-Israeli Politics: Traditionists and Modernity*, London: Routledge.

Yefet, K. C. (2016) "Synagogue and State in the Israeli Military: A Story of 'Inappropriate Integration'," *Law and Ethics of Human Rights*, 10 (1): 223–94.

Zalmona, Y. (1985) *Boris Schatz*, Jerusalem: Keter (in Hebrew).

Zubrzycki, G. (2010) "Religion and Nationalism," in Turner, B. S. (ed.) *The New Blackwell Companion to the Sociology of Religion*, Hoboken, NJ: Wiley-Blackwell, pp. 606–25.

Zucker, N. L. (1973) *The Coming Crisis in Israel: Private Faith and Public Policy*, Cambridge, MA: The MIT Press.

2   The rise and fall of Labor Zionist hegemony[1]

The formation of Labor Zionist hegemony

The leadership achieved by the Labor Zionist Movement (LZM) over the *yishuv*, over the World Zionist Organization (WZO), and over the State of Israel, between 1933 and 1977, as well as the decline of that leadership and its potential replacement by the Religious Zionist "civil religion," can be most usefully analyzed in terms of Antonio Gramsci's concept of hegemony.

According to Gramsci, hegemony can be understood as:

> [T]he "spontaneous" consent given by the great masses of the population to the general direction imposed on social life by the dominant fundamental group; this consent is "historically" caused by the prestige (and consequent confidence) which the dominant group enjoys because of its position and function in the world of production.
>
> (Gramsci 1971 [1929–1935]:12, cited in Jackson Lears 1985:568)

By the same token, however:

> The fact of hegemony presupposes that account is taken of the interests and tendencies of the groups over which hegemony is to be exercised, and that a certain compromise equilibrium should be formed – in other words that the leading group should make sacrifices of an economic-corporative kind. But there is also no doubt that such sacrifices and such a compromise cannot touch the essential; for though hegemony is ethico-political, it must also be economic, must necessarily be based on the decisive function exercised by the leading group in the decisive nucleus of economic activity.
>
> (Gramsci 2000:211–12)

Hegemony may be attained when a social group, justifying its goals in universalistic terms, secures the leadership of a broad coalition of political parties and social strata. These parties and social strata are motivated to follow the hegemonic leader's broadly conceived moral and intellectual leadership by its promise to assimilate them into its own ranks. When successful, a hegemonic project results in the creation of a stable politico-economic "social-historic bloc," rather than merely a shifting political coalition (Anderson 1976:19; Shafir and Peled 2002:66). However, because the historic bloc is made up of a number of social groups, with divergent and shifting interests,

> hegemony is not a static concept but a process of continuous creation which, given its massive scale, is bound to be uneven in the degree of legitimacy it commands and to leave some room for antagonistic cultural expressions to develop.
>
> (Adamson 1980:174)

In Liebman and Don-Yehiya's terms (1983), a successful hegemonic project is able to constitute a new "civil religion."

The LZM's "prestige and confidence" stemmed from the fact that its goal – founding a Jewish nation-state in Palestine – was shared by the vast majority of Jews living in pre-statehood Palestine and by the world-wide Zionist movement as a whole (Liebman and Don-Yehiya 1983:28; Shalev 1992:81–99). The extra-market settlement strategy pursued by the LZM in order to achieve that goal – cooperative agricultural settlement on nationally-owned land financed by public funds and a corporatist economic system – was not as widely shared, but was grudgingly recognized even by the LZM's political rivals as the only feasible way to achieve the Zionist goal. As acknowledged by Ephraim Kleiman, a neo-classical Israeli economist:

> It would probably not be an exaggeration to say that it was in part because of this correspondence [between their "strong ideological proclivity toward interventionism and the planned economy … and the needs of the time"] that the founding fathers of [the] labor movement … became also the founding fathers of the country".
>
> (Kleiman 1997:159; Shapiro 1976:233)

Last but not least, between 1937 and 1973 it was widely believed that the LZM was the only political body capable of ensuring the physical security of the Zionist project.

Jewish colonization in Palestine began in 1882, even before the founding of the Zionist movement in 1897. Such settlement waves were known as *aliyah* [pilgrimage] and the First Aliyah (1882–1903) established plantation colonies (*moshavot*) consisting of privately owned farms that were meant to be economically self-sustaining. The owners of these farms therefore preferred to employ experienced and less costly Palestinian agricultural workers over their ideologically motivated but inexperienced and more expensive co-religionists of the Second Aliyah (1904–1914). By the same token, the financial resources available to the Zionist movement at the time did not afford the possibility of purchasing sufficient amounts of land in order to establish plantation colonies for the newly arriving settlers. Moreover, with land prices in Palestine skyrocketing due to Zionist demand, privately owned land could be re-sold to non-Jewish buyers.[2] Consequently, a strategy that would circumvent both the land and labor markets was required if the settlement project was to succeed (Shafir 1996; Kleiman 1997:155; Peled 2017).

The newly adopted "labor settlement" strategy – self-employing cooperative settlements on non-alienable, nationally owned land – was not devised originally by the LZM but by Franz Oppenheimer, a German Jewish physician-turned-sociologist who had been involved, as a physician, in the German settlement project in East Prussia. Oppenheimer's ideas were adopted by Otto Warburg and Arthur Ruppin, Chairman of the WZO's Palestinian Affairs Department and head of its Palestine Office, respectively, as a solution to the crisis of the Second Aliyah. The new strategy had to be sold to the leaders of the emergent LZM in Palestine, who saw themselves, ideologically, as revolutionary workers rather than settlers.

In 1907 the LZM agreed to adopt the new strategy, newly christened as "constructive socialism," only when they realized that the "conquest of labor" from the Palestinians could not be achieved without the "conquest of Land" (Vitkin 1908, cited in Shafir 1996:161–2; Gorny 1969:116–17; Horowitz and Lissak 1978:141–2; Peled 2017). All in all, the new settlement strategy "represented an attempt to deal with real or perceived failures of the market to create the conditions for the attainment of national or social goals," because "in no way could the aim of establishing a Jewish state have been attained by unaided market forces" (Kleiman, 1997:148, 158–9).

Following the adoption of the new settlement strategy, the economy of the *yishuv* was based on two pillars: the Jewish National Fund (JNF) that used funds raised by the WZO to purchase land from Palestinians and turn it into national Jewish land, and the LZM's *Histadrut* (Association), a top-down peak labor organization founded in 1920 by the workers' political parties. The *Histadrut* formally owned the cooperative enterprises and represented Jewish workers employed by private owners and by the British Mandatory administration (Shalev 1992; Shafir 1996; Grinberg 2017:31–2).[3]

The cooperative economy of the *Histadrut* gradually developed into a conglomerate encompassing, at its height in the 1970s, agricultural, manufacturing, construction, marketing, transportation and financial concerns, as well as a whole network of cultural and social service organizations, most importantly a health maintenance organization known as *Kupat Cholim* (Sick Fund), which provided healthcare to 70 percent of the population (Grinberg 2017:32, 41). Until the 1990s this conglomerate controlled about 25 percent of the Israeli economy and employed, through its holding company, *Chevrat Ha-Oovdim* (The Workers' Company), around a quarter of the labor force. (A roughly equal share of the economy, plus virtually all land, was owned directly by the state.) Through its labor union wing the *Histadrut* enjoyed a virtual monopoly on representing organized workers, even the workers in its own enterprises, where about one half of all economically active members of *Histadrut* were employed (Shalev 1992:101–2, 189–90).

"The *Histadrut*'s dual role as both union and boss has at times generated severe problems of internal co-ordination and external credibility" (Shalev 1992:105–6). However, its dominant position in the *yishuv* and, later on, the Israeli economy enabled the *Histadrut* (since 1948 jointly with the state) to distribute social rights, privileges and obligations differentially to different Jewish social sectors, thus playing a crucial role in allowing the LZM leadership to acquire and maintain "authority without sovereignty" – i.e., cultural hegemony – over the *yishuv* and the world-wide Zionist movement, that was to last for several decades after the achievement of sovereignty (Shapiro 1976; Horowitz and Lissak 1978; Shalev 1992; Shafir and Peled 2002).

The political culture of the *yishuv*, commensurate with the LZM's colonial strategy, combined three different discourses of citizenship: a Jewish ethno-national discourse of historical rights and primordial solidarity; a civic republican discourse of common moral purpose and "pioneering" civic virtue; and an individualist liberal discourse that reflected the voluntary, hence necessarily democratic character of the Zionist movement and the semi-voluntary character of the *yishuv* itself (Horowitz and Lissak 1978:106–7). The ethno-national and liberal discourses of citizenship were associated with Religious Zionism and with the *yishuv*'s middle class, respectively, while the LZM's own discourse was the civic republican one, which was able to mediate between the two other, contradictory, discourses and dominate over them (Shafir and Peled 2002). Moreover, the central role played by the LZM in the colonial project and in the creation of the nation-state and the rights associated with national citizenship, as well as its control of public resources, anchored its place at the heart of all three discourses of citizenship. As long as it could plausibly insist on the overlap between these three discourses, there was no platform from which it could be successfully assailed, and its hegemony was ensured (Shafir and Peled 2002:45; Peled 2014:96, 148–9). As we argue below, the loss of its hegemony would come about in the future, when the LZM's place at the center of all three discourses would be undermined.

The key concept of the LZM's hegemonic "ethico-political" ideational structure, and the foundation of its identification, in the mind of the Zionist movement, with the national-colonial state-building enterprise, was the ethos of "pioneering" (*chalutzyiyut*), the civic virtue of the Labor Zionist version of civic republicanism. The "first and foremost" element of pioneering, according to sociologist S. N. Eisenstadt, was "social and personal sacrifice" (Eisenstadt 1968:17; Neumann 2011; see also Herman Peled and Peled 2011:106–11). Self-imposed asceticism and deprivation for the sake of performing the common "redemptive" tasks of the community served as the basis of the LZM's cultural appeal for the Zionist movement. The "redemptive" activities – physical labor, agricultural settlement, and military defense – were undertaken voluntarily by the pioneers, as service to the collective they led by personal example. The pioneer exhibited "lack of interest in direct, immediate rewards of position, wages, material comforts, or even political power" (Eisenstadt 1968:18). Since these ideals were expressed in their fullness in the kibbutz, pioneering was most clearly bound up with that institution. The kibbutz was a close-knit, intimate, communitarian body: "Idealistic and deeply dedicated, the pioneers formed an elite group – they were the most esteemed members of the colonist society" (Weingrod 1965:8). By extension, the LZM leadership thought of itself, and was viewed by its following, as a "service elite," not interested in promoting its own interests but the common interests of the *yishuv* (Horowitz and Lissak 1978:105–10).

The pioneers were indeed an elite, the vanguard of the colonial-national effort. But the material benefits they gave up individually they regained collectively, and what they renounced directly was returned to them indirectly. The pioneers were placed at the head of the queue for national funds, public rewards, and access to institutions, and were thus the privileged recipients of these assets in comparison with other Jewish settlers in Palestine. "The organized workers' movement in Palestine [i.e., the LZM] is not the movement of the 'proletariat'," argued Haim Arlosoroff, one of its foremost leaders, in 1926. "The *Histadrut* is a *settlement aristocracy*. If a proletariat, which views itself as lacking public value, is to be found here, then it is among the Eastern [i.e., Mizrachi] groups and in [the *Charedi* Jerusalem neighborhood of] 'Mea Shearim'" (Arlosoroff 1934 [1926]:124, emphasis added; Horowitz and Lissak 1978:141–2).

Between 1927 and 1937 the LZM was able to successfully ward off two serious challenges to its hegemonic status – one internal, from within the WZO, and one external, from the Palestinian Arab population – and establish itself as the dominant political force of the WZO. The cooperation between the WZO and the worker's movement, which had begun in 1905 with the onset of the former's direct involvement in land purchase and colonization, focused on the facilitation of immigration, immigrant absorption, and settlement. It was transformed into a pragmatic alliance at the WZO's London Conference in 1920, where, to borrow Michael Shalev's telling formulation, a practical alliance was forged "between organized Zionism – a settlement movement without settlers, and the property-less pioneers – a worker's movement without work" (Shalev 1992:2; see also 1996; Shafir 1996). This alliance made possible the mobilization of the resources of the Zionist movement on the LZM's behalf. Thus the organized sectors of the Jewish agricultural laborers in Palestine were transformed from workers into settlers, while the WZO became a truly popular movement.

In 1927, however, against the background of a severe economic crisis in Palestine, the WZO Executive, headed by the British Zionist Harry Sacher, turned against fundamental aspects of the WZO-LZM alliance: unemployment benefits in Palestine were curtailed, public work projects were scaled back and, most significantly, subsidies to Jewish workers employed by the British Mandatory authorities at wages equal to those of their Arab employees were discontinued. In 1928 harsh criticism of the "alliance" policies was contained in the report of a committee of economic experts appointed by the Zionist Executive and headed by a number of wealthy Diaspora businessmen. The committee's report expressed the most hostile opinions heard until then toward the LZM's colonization strategy. The institutions and policies of the *Histadrut*, including the kibbutzim, came in for the severest rebuke: they were viewed as wasteful and the national-political considerations guiding their management were depicted as counter-productive. Instead of financing the cooperative settlement of penniless immigrants, the experts recommended, support should be redirected toward wealthier settlers who could establish profitable private enterprises (Shapiro 1976:150–1, 236–7).

The committee's conclusions were totally rejected, however, not only by the Labor movement itself but by middle-class circles in Palestine and abroad as well. This broad reaction clearly illustrated the support and moral authority already enjoyed by the LZM outside its own circles in the late 1920s. The middle-class elements of the *yishuv* especially stood shoulder to shoulder with the workers. Shlomo Kaplansky, an LZM leader who headed the WZO Executive's Settlement Department, and Meir Dizengoff, the General Zionist Mayor of Tel Aviv, submitted a joint proposal in which they demanded that investment in agriculture be enhanced and that investment and subsidies in Palestine be allocated on the basis of national, rather than market-based criteria. In view of this reaction the WZO Executive came around and reaffirmed its commitment to "Hebrew labor" and to nationally rather than privately owned land. The editor of *Haolam*, the official organ of the WZO, summed up the predominant sentiment in the organization:

> even the one who is not a socialist must support the wishes of the Jewish laborer even if it entails many concessions, since he is still our main support. He is the most loyal and the symbol of the devotion of our national ideal in the country.
>
> (Cited in Shapiro 1976:237–9)

In 1930 the badly scarred LZM underwent an internal consolidation. *Achdut Ha-Avoda* (Labor Unity), the workers' party founded in 1919, united with the other major workers' party, *Ha-Poel Ha-Tzair* (Young Worker), to form Mapai (Land of Israel Workers' Party), the key political party of the LZM and the nucleus of today's Labor party. Mapai built up a powerful party machine to receive, administer, control, and distribute to its members and supporters the resources placed at its disposal through the *Histadrut*. Some of these resources were deployed to co-opt other sectors of the *yishuv*, gaining for the LZM undertakings at least partial legitimacy from its religious and middle-class sectors. The religious *Mizrachi* movement split in 1922 with the formation of the labor-oriented *Ha-Poel Ha-Mizrachi* that joined some of the *Histadrut*'s institutions in 1927. After the formation of Mapai the petty-bourgeois General Zionists also split, between a faction that supported the LZM and joined some of its institutions and a faction that sought to preserve their party's autonomy (Horowitz and Lissak 1978:77–8; Yishai 1980:109–17).

The splits in these rival political parties reflected the central place of the LZM in the *yishuv*. Its appeal was now based not only on its pioneering role but also on the social services the comprehensive institutional framework of the LZM extended to its members and supporters. In 1934 David Ben-Gurion, leader of Mapai, reached a comprehensive economic and political agreement even with Vladimir Jabotinsky, founder and leader of the right-wing Revisionist Zionists, which would have allowed the latter to enjoy the services of the *Histadrut*'s labor exchanges in return for refraining from collaborating in breaking up the labor organization's strikes. This plan was scuttled by the *Histadrut* membership in 1935, in an atmosphere shaped by the assassination of Haim Arlosoroff in 1933 (Goldstein and Shavit 1979). The circumstances surrounding this murder are still unclear, but it was widely believed at the time that the crime was committed by Revisionist Zionists.

The electoral weight of the LZM in the WZO grew rapidly in the 1930s. Whereas before 1927 it was a pressure group with 22 percent of the vote, in 1933 Mapai attained 44 percent. As a result, by 1933 Mapai controlled not only the *Histadrut*, but also the Political Department of the Jewish Agency, and the *Vaad Leumi* (National Council) of the *yishuv*. It became the largest party in the WZO, and instead of having just a single member in the WZO Executive, Mapai now constituted it, with Ben-Gurion joining this body and, in 1935, becoming its Chairman (Horowitz and Lissak 1978:40).

It was not until the second challenge, however, this time not to the LZM alone, but to the whole Zionist enterprise, that the *yishuv*'s majority coalesced around the hard core of the LZM and confirmed its hegemonic position in leading the state-building effort. The Arab Revolt of 1936–1939, the most intense conflict prior to the 1947–1949 war, played the major role in placing the capstone on the institutional structure of the LZM's hegemony. The revolt began with a strike by Palestinian Arab producers and workers which paralyzed public services and sections of the Jewish private economy and led to a quick replacement of the strikers with Jewish hands, following the model established by the LZM. The monopoly of the *Histadrut* in supplying labor-power through its labor exchanges quickly convinced unorganized workers of its might. In historian Yoav Gelber's conclusion "the Arab Revolt transformed the character of the *yishuv*'s economic development by strengthening the standing of its central institutions." The import of private capital declined and construction, which had been financed largely by private capital, declined rapidly as well, and came to rely on "national capital." Private agriculture and industry also turned to national capital for support (Gelber 1994:377–80).

Under the new circumstances, the *Histadrut*'s military wing, the *Hagana* militia, evolved into a national body in charge of ensuring the safety of the entire Jewish population. In 1937 the first attempt to establish a standing Jewish military force took place, sponsored by the British Mandatory government. For the first time, security now came to be viewed as weightier than economic considerations (An. Shapira 1992). A popular song written in 1938 by Nathan Alterman, the LZM's poet laureate, included the line: "Your boys carried the peace of the plow for you, today they carry the peace of the guns." Most adept at handling and weathering the Jewish-Palestinian conflict through its separatist approach, the LZM proved the superiority of its nationalist strategy over opposing approaches when the national conflict reached its zenith for the first time (Shalev 1992:91). This success sealed the LZM's hegemony: it became identified in the public mind with the nation-state-building project, leading to a continuous and long-term domination of Israeli society, which lasted until 1977 (Shapiro 1991:151–3).

However, the LZM's reliance on the WZO – that is, on Diaspora middle-class Jews – for subsidies, and its primary devotion to its own members' welfare, had a decisive influence on the institutional structure and mode of operation of the *Histadrut*. This influence resulted in:

- the creation of a single and authoritative framework through which the labour movement could negotiate and channel Zionist aid;
- the formal distancing of party politics and purging of class-struggle ideology from this instrumentality;
- the placing of the Zionist tasks of immigration, absorption, and settlement at the head of the *Histadrut* agenda.

(Shalev 1992:152)

Coupled with the need to rely on non-socialist immigrants to achieve a Jewish majority in Palestine, this rendered the LZM incapable of installing the pioneering ethos in the community as a whole.

The criteria for membership in the *yishuv* thus remained fragmented. Among the Jewish non-pioneering groups were the middle-class, Mizrachim (Jews hailing from the Moslem world), and religious Zionists, groups whose Jewishness secured them a place in a common ethno-nationalist framework of membership, but who were perceived as lacking pioneering civic virtue and could therefore not be assimilated into the core ethno-republican community. These groups were co-opted into the LZM-based incorporation regime, where their relative ranking was determined by their perceived contribution to the state-building project (Peled 1992; Shafir and Peled 2002). In its effort to accommodate these groups and ensure their continuing support, the LZM, in the mode of any hegemonic group, had to take their interests and preferences into account to a certain extent. We will now turn to a discussion of the LZM's efforts to maintain its hegemony over the middle class – and the accommodations it had to make to the latter's interests. In the following chapter we will discuss the accommodation made by the LZM to the religious sector, both the Religious Zionists and the non-Zionist *Charedim*. The accommodations made to these groups, we will argue, were at the root of the decline of the LZM's hegemony beginning in 1967.

A corporatist economy

Like the elites of many newly independent and late developing countries that fashioned their societies into self-conscious "developmental states" (Öniş 1991), the LZM elite also identified state-building with economic development. But in contrast with many other new states, Israel was already at its inception a "strong state" in Joel Migdal's terms, with a long and successful practice of developmentalism since the 1920s (Migdal 1988). This developmental model continued to fulfill the expectations attached to it for about two-and-a-half decades after the establishment of Israel: "[T]he practical needs of building and the conditions of the country in the pre- and early statehood years seem to have been well-served by the leading ideological stances of the day" (Kleiman 1997:154).

After the achievement of statehood, Israeli Labor governments were supportive of private, public, and *Histadrut* investments, using the criterion of job creation as their main yardstick. In addition to encouraging state- and *Histadrut*-owned enterprises, "the government aggressively searched for private entrepreneurs and investors and heavily subsidized them. In this respect, the economic system was far from a socialist command economy. Indeed, Israel has always had a flourishing private sector..." (Razin and Sadka 1993:1–2; see also Sternhell 1998; Khenin 2000). As a ruling party, Mapai also encouraged the development of a " 'state-made middle class' – entrepreneurs and middlemen who made their fortunes through government concessions and subsidies, as well as the considerable salariat of managerial and professional workers in public employ" (Shalev 1992:110). In the context of a mixed economy, the latter adopted the profit orientation of the former and were instrumental, later on, in bringing the LZM's hegemony to an end (see below).

Many observers who associated the LZM with its declared socialist ideology were puzzled by its lukewarm and opportunistic commitment to socialism when it finally came to hold governmental power. However, as Shalev (1992), Sternhell (1998), and Shafir and Peled (2002), among others, have shown, socialism was no more than the handmaiden of the LZM's national-colonial aims. The LZM did not seek to nationalize the means of production, except for land – the main resource over which the struggle with the Palestinians was waged. Nor was the LZM opposed to private enterprise, provided that it was geared toward creating employment and willing to employ "Hebrew labor" only. Thus, even during the *yishuv* era,

> Mapai did its best to appease employers and their allies by reining in union militancy; ... [by] its handling of labour relations issues at enterprise level; [by maintaining] informal contacts with top employer representatives; and [by] its willingness to sanction joint business ventures with private capital.
> (Shalev 1992:91)

One of the main reasons for the LZM's willingness to pursue its aims within a plural economy was its ability to exert considerable control not only over the land and labor markets, but also over flows of capital into the Israeli economy. Whereas before 1948 "national capital" constituted only about 40 percent of capital imports (Kleiman 1997:149–50), after 1948 the state became the greatest importer of capital, in the form of untaxed US savings bonds, German reparations and personal compensations to Holocaust survivors, long-term loans, and private philanthropic donations. These unilateral transfers enabled the state to maintain the corporatist structure of the economy.

In no other area was the combination of state-centered economic development with the institutions of pioneering as evident as in the capital market or, actually, in its practical absence. According to Kleiman's calculation in 1967, approximately three-quarters of all capital imports were received by the public sector, which in turn financed nearly two-thirds of all capital formation (Kleiman 1967:239). The distribution of foreign funds and control over foreign currency served as key elements in buttressing the state's economic weight, but domestic capital formation was also tightly controlled by the state and the *Histadrut*, thus enhancing and reproducing their economic influence (Shafir and Peled 2002:56–8).

State control over capital formation and, to a large extent, over capital allocation as well, not only had the effect, until the mid-1980s, of preventing the formation of a free internal capital market, but also had a number of far-reaching consequences for the structure of the economy and the relationship between the spheres of "politics" and "economics." First, it was difficult to tell where the *Histadrut* ended and the state began, since they pooled their resources and both operated under the same sheltered conditions (Grinberg 2017:33). Second, this arrangement ensured sturdy ties between the political and economic elites of the LZM and reduced the possibility of conflict between them. While the economic wing of the LZM elite sought on occasion to invoke an economic rationale in order to gain a measure of autonomy, the political wing on the other hand was afraid of such autonomy and sought to curtail it. Hence until the mid-1960s the two wings remained tied to each other within the given set of institutional arrangements (Shafir and Peled 2002:58).

By importing foreign capital itself, the government was in a position to favor those sectors of the economy that provided maximum employment, a goal Israel shared with other developing countries (although in Israel's case the target population was exclusively Jewish). In the early 1950s priority was therefore assigned to labor-intensive industries, most prominently agriculture. Only with the exhaustion of agricultural assets (most of which were the expropriated lands of Palestinian refugees and "present absentees") was the first industrial policy adopted, aiming, as in many other newly industrializing countries, to substitute local production for imports in order to ease foreign currency shortages. The main tools of the new industrial policy were exchange-rate controls, direct administrative allocation of foreign currency, investment subsidies, and tariff barriers to protect infant industries. "Israel thus followed other newly industrializing countries in establishing a highly protective trade regime" (Kleiman 1997:153). This economic strategy turned out to be a great success: the period 1955–1965 witnessed an average of 12 percent per annum growth of industrial production, accompanied by a 5.5 percent growth in employment, 10 percent in capital reserves, and 20 percent in exports (Bar 1990:29).

Economic liberalization

As Emma Murphy has pointed out, in Israel "the high living standards required to attract immigrants were achieved through the subsidization of the economy by foreign aid, Diaspora revenues and international loans rather than through high productivity" (Murphy 1993:241). By the mid-1960s, however, a number of the conditions that enabled the state to maintain the corporatist arrangements summarized by the category of "attracting immigrants" – rapid economic growth, a relatively decent standard of living for workers in the primary labor market, sufficiently high profit for employers, and relative industrial peace – began to deteriorate. Immigration, unilateral transfers, long-term loans, and foreign investment declined, while the foreign trade deficit and workers' militancy, fueled by labor shortages, were on the increase. Significantly, "[t]he proportion of strikes lacking *Histadrut* authorization [i.e., "wild strikes"] rose from 25 percent in 1960 to an average of 60 percent during the remaining full employment years" (until 1965) (Shalev 1992:209–12; Grinberg 2017:33).

The state, with the *Histadrut*'s cooperation, responded with a two-pronged move: on the demand side, it sharply reduced its own expenditures, primarily in the construction of public housing; and, on the supply side, it opened the Jewish labor market to Palestinian citizens by ending the military regime which had been imposed on them in 1948 and which restricted their ability to move freely throughout the country. The spending cuts plunged the economy into the worst recession in its history – still known in Israel as "The Great Recession" (*mitun*) – and achieved the desired effect: "As the Bank of Israel concluded in its annual report for 1966 … the recession 'undoubtedly induced workers to adapt themselves to employers' demands and to tone down their own demands'" (Shalev 1992:218–19; 1984). The recession came to an abrupt halt due to the prosperity that followed the territorial acquisitions of 1967, but the stratum of managers of state and *Histadrut* enterprises concluded from the crisis that the state's developmental model had exhausted its usefulness and that economic policy needed to be "rationalized," that is, conducted solely on the basis of profit considerations.

The first severe political challenge to the corporatist regime and call for economic liberalization came from within the LZM itself as early as 1965, with the secession from Mapai of the Israel Workers' List (Rafi), headed by none other than David Ben-Gurion and including such luminaries as Moshe Dayan, Shimon Peres and Teddy Kollek. Rafi "denounced the existing structure of labour representation … called for depoliticization and internal democratization of the Histadrut, transfer of its non-union functions to the state, and statutory controls over labour disputes" (Shalev 1992:214). In spite of its star-studded candidate list Rafi did not do well in the 1965 general elections, gaining only ten seats in the Knesset (out of 120).

The boom period that followed the 1967 war caused the demands for liberalization to be suspended until after the 1973 war, the war that ended that period of prosperity. In the aftermath of that traumatic war a whole number of protest groups emerged, most of them demanding a change of government. One of those groups, and the only one to have survived for any length of time other than Gush Emunim (see Chapter 3), was Shinuy (Change), constituted by people "belonging to the successful, bourgeois class of Ashkenazi Israel" (Urieli and Barzilay 1982:88; Shapiro 1980). In Shapiro's overview, Shinuy's initial political goals were distinctly liberal, yet unfocused:

It concentrated on issues of social integrity and on honesty and rationality in government. It was satisfied with the demand for a rational approach in both domestic and foreign policy and for greater democracy in the state. It did not deal with the questions of Israel's integration into the region ... nor did it demand radical change in the pseudo-socialist structure of the economy....
Most of its practical proposals dealt with changing this or that law or with an amorphous demand for change in the general atmosphere.

(Shapiro 1980:102; see also A. Rubinstein 1982:45–6)

In 1976 Shinuy joined a number of other groups and prominent individuals, many of them members of the upper managerial strata of the *Histadrut* and state economic sectors, to form the Democratic Movement for Change (DMC). The new party was headed by Yigael Yadin, a Hebrew University archeologist and highly esteemed former Chief of the IDF General Staff (Torgovnik 1980; Urieli and Barzilay 1982; A. Rubinstein 1982). The DMC was truly a center party, in that its platform combined a liberal critique of the prevailing economic institutions of the LZM, in the spirit of Likud, with a "moderate" stance on the Arab-Israeli conflict akin to that of Labor. (Moderation in those days meant willingness to forego Israel's "historical right" to the occupied Palestinian territories and accept the need for territorial compromise with Jordan, and agreement to establish new settlements in the occupied territories for security reasons only.) But the party's main focus was clearly on the domestic front. Out of seven key points in its platform, only one dealt with foreign policy, while the other six were equally divided between issues of economic policy and demands for governmental and electoral reform (Urieli and Barzilay 1982:204; Torgovnik 1980:87; Arian 1998:133–7).

This formula appealed to many members of the second-generation Ashkenazi elite who supported Labor's way of managing the Arab-Israeli conflict but were increasingly disillusioned with the constraints put on the market by the institutions of the pioneering era. They concluded that radical economic reform required loosening the control of the *Histadrut* over the economy, and perhaps even the removal of Labor from political office, because the party had too many vested interests in the existing institutional and socio-economic system. In the general elections of 1977 the DMC won 11.6 percent of the vote and fifteen Knesset seats, an unprecedented showing for a first-time contender (Arian 1980; Torgovnik 1980; Shalev 1992:289; Arian and Shamir 1995). After arduous negotiations that lasted five months, the DMC joined the Likud coalition government headed by Menachem Begin, which until then had only a four-seat majority in the Knesset, with a coalition that included Likud, the National Religious Party, *Agudat Yisrael*, and two smaller factions. Since the DMC joined that government without having secured any of the political principles it had defined as its minimum requirements for joining, it lost all credibility and disintegrated even before the next general elections.

Labor's fall from political dominance was caused, then, not by a rebellion of the downtrodden in society, but by a defection of the social stratum that was the most privileged under its political-economic regime. But the loss of political dominance cannot be equated with an immediate loss of cultural hegemony. As we will argue in the next chapter, Labor's hegemony had already suffered a major blow due to its paralysis and inaction in 1967 and the blunders that led to the war of 1973, but the effects of that development were slow in materializing on the surface of political reality. It would take another two decades, and the renunciation by Labor itself of its political-economic system, to complete the process of its loss of hegemony.

As soon as Likud assumed control of the government in 1977, it launched an economic liberalization program designed to dismantle the corporatist political-economic structure that was the mainstay of Labor's power. However, since it did not control the *Histadrut*, which refused to cooperate with it in laying off workers and cutting wages, Likud's economic policy brought the economy to the brink of hyper-inflation – 466 percent annually in 1984 (Grinberg 2017:37). As an unintended consequence, perhaps, the high inflation rates contributed to the weakening of Labor's economic institutions, many of which were subsidized by the state or provided it with goods and services and were dependent on timely payments from the state to maintain their cash flows. By delaying such payments even for a short time, in a situation of very rapid monetary inflation, the state was able to erode their value, force its creditors to seek high-interest bank loans, and thus undermine their economic viability. This greatly hastened the downfall of the *Histadrut* (Grinberg 2017:37).

After the general elections of 1984, which resulted in a tie between Labor and Likud, Labor made a strategic decision to rid itself of the crisis-ridden *Histadrut* enterprises, which it came to see more as a burden than a benefit for the party. In 1985 a national unity government, in which Labor and Likud shared power, instituted the Emergency Economic Stabilization Plan that halted monetary inflation and laid the groundwork for the successful liberalization of the economy (Shafir and Peled 2002:231–59; Grinberg 2017:30, 37–9).

When Labor returned to power on its own, in 1992, a momentous struggle developed between its neo-liberal wing and its welfarist wing, based in the *Histadrut*. The aim of the neo-liberal Laborites was to dismantle the *Histadrut* and the public-sector economy in general, and to undermine the welfare state, in order to enable the economy to be thoroughly liberalized (Grinberg 2017:39, 43). Significantly, the major issue over which this clash between the two wings of the party took place was control over the *Histadrut*'s extensive healthcare system.

By the 1990s the *Histadrut* had already been stripped of much of its productive resources through privatization. Its pension funds, together with its healthcare system, which had always been its main vehicle for attracting membership, had by then become its only significant assets. *Kupat Cholim* pre-dated the First World War and the *Histadrut* itself, and was one of the primary manifestations of the LZM's republican commitment to Jewish social solidarity and mutual aid. At its peak, this system provided healthcare services to 70 percent of the Israeli population, on the basis of voluntary membership in the *Histadrut* (Grinberg

2017:41). Most of the rest of population was covered by similar, smaller, organizations, generally associated with various political parties. By many experts' accounts, this was one of the most efficient systems of healthcare provision in existence throughout the world.

In 1995, under a Labor-led government, a new State Health Insurance Law came into effect, authorizing the state to take over the healthcare system and shift its financial basis from voluntary subscription to a mandatory health tax. In a different social context, such as in the United States, this may have meant a major expansion of the welfare state. In Israel, however, in spite of the universalization of healthcare coverage entailed by this act, it signified a retreat of the welfare state and a major step toward the privatization of the healthcare system.

Historically, the healthcare system operated on a deficit financing basis, with the state covering its deficits at the end of each year. Since the reform, the sick funds – which continue to provide healthcare services – are required by law to operate within an authorized budget limit made up of the proceeds of the health tax plus an unspecified contribution by the state. Since the state, in the form of the Treasury bureaucracy, tries to contribute as little as possible, this means an inevitable deterioration of services, with the shortfall being picked up by private health providers for those who can afford to pay (Peled 2004:51–2; Filc 2009).

As can be seen in Tables 2.1 and 2.2, the burden of paying for healthcare expenditures has shifted, to a significant extent, from the state to the consumers of those services. As a result, in June 2012 the High Court of Justice (HCJ) determined that "the right to health of all of Israel's citizens … that was established by and anchored in the State Health Insurance Law, is being slowly emptied of content, in view of the systematic erosion of the sick funds' budgets…" (HCJ 8730/03, §37 of Justice Joubran's opinion).

In the interest of free competition, the new State Health Insurance Law also required the sick funds to accept all applicants, and forbade them to make their own membership conditional on membership in any other organization. This provision was introduced in order to sever the ties between the *Histadrut* and its *Kupat Cholim*, causing the *Histadrut* to lose two thirds of its membership and reconstitute itself as a fledgling labor organization. As a result, the unionization rate of Israeli workers (not including non-citizen Palestinian workers and labor migrants) declined from 80 percent in the 1970s to 49 percent in 1996, and continued to decline through the 2000s with the progression of the liberalization process. Nonetheless, the much-weakened *Histadrut* has been the only force

Table 2.1 Percentage of total social expenditure on healthcare

Paid by:	1995	2010
State	70.0	35.5
Households (beyond health tax)	26.0	43.0
NGOs	4.0	21.5

Sources: B. Swirski 2007; 2012; *The Marker*, June 13 and 18, 2012.

Table 2.2 Household healthcare expenditures (percent)

	1997	2005
Healthcare expenditures out of all household expenditures	3.8	5.1
Extra insurance expenditures (beyond the health tax) out of total household expenditures on healthcare	10.5	25.5

Sources: B. Swirski 2007; 2012; *The Marker*, June 13 and 18, 2012.

trying to stand up to the juggernaut of economic liberalization, to the chagrin of businessmen, Treasury officials, academic economists and economic journalists (Ram 2007; Grinberg 2017:41–4).[4]

In the first fifteen years of liberalization and globalization – from 1985 to 2000 – the Israeli economy experienced relatively high growth rates and a parallel increase in the inequality of income distribution. Per capita GDP rose from 5,612 US dollars in 1985 to 17,804 US dollars in 2000, as 83 state-owned (not including *Histadrut*-owned) corporations worth 8.7 billion US dollars were privatized. By the same token, between 1990 and 2002 the economic income share of the top decile of income earners rose from 25 to 30 percent, that of the second highest decile remained unchanged, while the share of all other income earners declined.

However, until Likud's return to power in 2001, following the outbreak of the second or *al-Aksa intifada*, the project of dismantling the Israeli welfare state was stymied by path dependency, lack of resolve on the part of political elites, and concern over the possibility of massive popular discontent. As can be seen in Table 2.3, while inequality of economic income rose rather sharply between 1993 and 2002, with a particularly sharp increase between 2001 and 2002 (the first full year of Ariel Sharon's tenure as Prime Minister), inequality of disposable income grew much more moderately but picked up steam after 2001 (Arian et al. 2003:83; Swirski and Konnor-Attias 2004:7, 13; Ram 2007; Shalev 2007; NII 2011:9; 2012:81).

Table 2.3 Income inequality

	1980	1993	2001	2002	2010
Gini coefficient (economic income)		0.498	0.528	0.509	0.50 (OECD 0.46)
Gini coefficient (disposable income)		0.339	0.350	0.357	0.38 (OECD 0.31)
% families below poverty line (economic income)	28	34	34	34	34
% families below poverty line (disposable income)					20

Sources: Arian et al. 2003:83; Swirski and Konnor-Attias 2004:7, 13; Shalev 2007; Ram 2007; NII 2011:9; 2012:81.

The new economic policy was greatly beneficial, however, to the upper layers of the business class. It has granted them lower labor costs, greater labor market "flexibility," and lower taxes. As a result, the profits of the top 25 companies traded on the Tel Aviv Stock Exchange *tripled* between 2002 and 2003, and those of the major banks increased by 350 percent. In 2002 the average salary of senior executives of all companies traded on the Tel Aviv Stock Exchange was 17 times higher than the average income in the economy, and 36 times higher than the minimum wage. In 2006 nineteen families controlled 54 percent of the business sector GDP, with five of those families controlling 61 percent of the total income of the group. In 2010 about one third of all families were below the poverty line in terms of their economic income, and one fifth remained poor after taxes and transfer payments. In 2011 the top two deciles of families earned 39.3 percent of all net family income, while the two bottom deciles earned only 6.7 percent (Ram 2007; NII 2012:68–81; CBS 2012).

This transformation of Israeli society was duly recognized by the international agencies monitoring the global economy. In early 2004 Moody's rating service declared the economic policy of the current Israeli government to be the best in Israel's history. In May of 2010 Israel was admitted to membership of the Organization for Economic Co-operation and Development (OECD), the organization of the economically most developed countries. In 2013 the United Nations (UN) ranked Israel among the twenty most highly developed countries in the world and in 2015 it was ranked by the World Economic Forum as the third most innovative economy and among the thirty most competitive ones (Campbell 2017:vii).

By the new millennium the socio-economic transformation of Israeli society had erased practically all traces of the period of Labor hegemony. Symbolically, perhaps, in July 2000 the Oslo peace process, launched by the second Rabin government in 1993, was brought to an end at Camp David, and with it the last Labor-headed government to be in power until the time of writing. In the next chapter we discuss the challenge posed by Religious Zionism to Labor's hegemony since 1967. In Chapter 4 we will discuss the other arm of the religionization process – the "return" of many non-observant and traditionalist Israeli Jews to Jewish religion – which is an essential component in Religious Zionism's quest for hegemony.

Summary

The Labor Zionist Movement's hegemony, which lasted 45 years, was based on the crucial role it played in carrying out a successful strategy for settling Jews in Palestine, culminating in the establishment of a Jewish state. That settlement strategy had three major components: (1) a territorial component; (2) a political-economic component based on circumventing the land and labor markets in order to separate the Jewish from the Palestinian economy and absorb Jewish immigrant-settlers, and on a corporatist mode of managing the economy once sovereignty had been achieved; and (3) especially since 1937, a national security component that enabled the *yishuv* and Israel to prevail in the wars of 1947–1949 and 1967.

The success of this settlement strategy established an identification between the LZM and the state-building project not only in the minds of its members and supporters, but also in the minds of most Jewish social groups in Palestine/Israel and the world-wide Zionist movement. That identification was augmented by skillful use of the *Histadrut*'s material resources to reward, in a measured and variegated way, the support and loyalty of these other groups. As formulated by Michael Shalev, there were "three conspicuous features of Mapai dominance":

> One is the all-important role played by Mapai's judicious use of *material incentives* to individuals and communities via the Histadrut, the urban party machine, and (after statehood) the electoral business cycle. A second is the fact that, following sovereignty, the party managed to mobilize a plurality of voters within *all* classes and exercised a determinate influence over *all* major organized economic interests. Third is Mapai's conscious identification with the interests of the (Jewish) nation as a whole, built upon its paramount role in the struggle for sovereignty and construction of the state.
>
> (Shalev 1992:116, emphasis in the original)

However, both the material and the ethico-political aspects of Mapai's, and the LZM's, hegemony were rife with contradictions. In order to achieve and maintain its hegemony, the LZM had to accommodate to some degree the interests of non-pioneering groups, particularly, for our purposes, Orthodox Jews and the owners of private capital, as well as the Diaspora Jewish middle class, who supplied the funds for the settlement project. The *Histadrut* itself was based on a contradiction that was rooted in the historical role it played in the settlement project – it was at one and the same time both the largest industrial employer in the county and the sole representative of organized labor. These contradictions all came to a head in the 1960s, as Israel overcame the crises of war and mass migration and emerged as a viable concern both economically and militarily. In other words, it was the very success of the LZM that exposed its vulnerabilities and brought its hegemony over Israeli society to an end.

Territorially, the LZM's strategy in the pre-statehood period was to acquire as much territory as possible, compatible with the maintenance of a Jewish majority. In 1947–1949 Israel extended its borders well beyond the area designated as the Jewish state in the 1947 UN Partition Resolution and proceeded to expel the majority of Palestinian Arabs from its territory (Morris 2004; Pappe 2006). In 1967, in a war that was the height of its military prowess, Israel occupied the West Bank and Gaza, among other areas, precisely the locations where most of the 1948 Palestinian refugees had found refuge. Mass expulsion of Palestinians from these areas was no longer possible (although some limited expulsions did take place; Pappe 2006:169, 173, 175, 192) so the territorial-demographic dilemma came to face the Labor government head on.

As we show in the next chapter, because it was unable to deal successfully with this dilemma, Labor lost the political initiative to a reinvigorated Religious Zionism armed with a mystical-messianic ideology that left no room for hesitation about incorporating the newly acquired territories into Israel. Labor's inability to decide on a clear course of action also led directly to the disastrous 1973 war (Maoz 2006:140–70) and to complete loss of confidence in its ability to safeguard Israel's security among a very large portion of the Jewish public. Thus Labor lost its hold on both the territorial and the security aspects of the Zionist project.

Economically, as soon as it reached its declared goal of full employment for Jews, in the mid-1960s, Labor had to face workers' militancy fueled by full employment just as the unilateral transfers that had sustained its corporatist economic policy up to that point were beginning to dry up. Committed as it was to the profitability of *Histadrut* enterprises, as well as to that of private capital (heavily subsidized in some cases), Labor responded by instigating an economic recession that most probably went out of hand and brought about the loss of its credibility as a manager of the economy. This loss of credibility was submerged by the spectacular military victory of 1967, but reappeared after the 1973 war that brought in its wake another economic recession (Grinberg 2017:33–5). Thus, by the mid-1970s all three components of the LZM's settlement strategy – the territorial, the security and the economic – seemed to be heading toward a dead end.

Ian Lustick has listed three conditions as being necessary in order "to overthrow an established ideologically hegemonic conception or explain its breakdown":

- a severe contradiction between the conception advanced as hegemonic and the stubborn realities it purports to describe;
- an appropriately fashioned alternative interpretation of political reality capable of reorganizing competition to the advantage of particular groups;
- dedicated political-ideological entrepreneurs who can operate successfully where fundamental assumptions of political life have been thrown open to question, and who see better opportunities in competition over basic "rules of the game" than in competition for marginal advantage according to existing rules.

(Lustick 1993:123–4)

By the mid-1970s all three conditions listed by Lustick were in place: the LZM's moderate social democratic economic worldview and its cautious territorial-security outlook both seemed to be incompatible with the post-1967 realities. On both fronts alternative conceptions were offered – the openly expansionist territorial vision of Religious Zionism and (somewhat more pragmatically) of the new governing party, Likud, and the free market orthodoxy espoused by Likud and shared by many members of the LZM's own salaried managerial class. And dedicated political-ideological entrepreneurs, committed to bringing about the end of Labor's political and cultural dominance, were also on the scene

– in addition to the old-timer Revisionist Zionists of Likud, they were the leaders and activists of Shinuy, dedicated to transforming Israel's political economy in a (neo-)liberal way, and the young guard of Religious Zionism, spearheaded by Gush Emunim, determined to ensure Israel's rule over the territories captured in 1967 and working to enhance the prominence of Jewish religion in the public sphere. It is to the latter challenge that we now turn.

Notes

1 For the period prior to 2000 this chapter draws in a general way on several sections of Shafir and Peled 2002.
2 Between 1922 and 1944 the price of rural land in Palestine rose from 34 to 1,050 US dollars per acre. In 1944 the price of rural land in the United States was 45 US dollars per acre (Warwick 2001:10).
3 The *Histadrut* is oftentimes mistakenly referred to as a trade union federation (e.g., Kleiman 1997:146). In reality the *Histadrut* was established as, and is still today, a federation of political parties that operates trade unions under its administrative authority (Shalev 1990:91n11; Grinberg 2017:31).
4 For the privatization of the Histadrut's pension funds, which resulted in significant weakening of pensioners' income security, see Grinberg 2017:42–3.

References

Adamson, W. L. (1980) *Hegemony and Revolution: A Study of Antonio Gramsci's Political and Cultural Theory*, Berkeley, CA: University of California Press.
Anderson, P. (1976) "The Antinomies of Antonio Gramsci," *New Left Review*, 100: 5–78.
Arian, A. (1980) "The Israeli Electorate, 1977," in Arian, A. (ed.) *The Elections in Israel – 1977*, Jerusalem: Jerusalem Academic Press, pp. 253–76.
Arian, A. (1998) *The Second Republic: Politics in Israel*, Chatham, NJ: Chatham House.
Arian, A. and Shamir, M. (1995) "Two Reversals: Why 1992 Was Not 1977," in Arian, A. and Shamir, M. (eds.), *The Elections in Israel – 1992*, Albany, NY: SUNY Press, pp. 17–53.
Arian, A., Nachmias, D., Navot, D., and Shani, D. (2003) *Democracy in Israel: 2003 Follow Up Report, "Democracy Index" Project*, Jerusalem: Israel Democracy Institute (in Hebrew).
Arlosoroff, H. (1934 [1926]). "Class Struggle in the Reality of Eretz Israel," in Steinberg, J. (ed.), *Haim Arlosoroff's Writings in Six Volumes, Vol. 3: New Life*, Tel Aviv: Shtibel, pp. 121–32 (in Hebrew).
Bar, A. (1990) "Industry and Industrial Policy in Israel: Landmarks," in Brodet, D., Justman, M., and Tuval, M. (eds.), *Industrial-Technological Policy for Israel*, Jerusalem: Jerusalem Institute for Israel Studies, pp. 22–46 (in Hebrew).
Campbell, John L. (2017) "Foreword: Israel, Neoliberalism, and Comparative Political Economy," in Maron, A. and Shalev, M. (eds.) *Neoliberalism as a State Project: Changing the Political Economy of Israel*, Oxford: Oxford University Press.
CBS (2012) *The Face of Israeli Society; Report No. 5*, Jerusalem: Central Bureau of Statistics (in Hebrew).
Eisenstadt, S. N. (1968) *Israeli Society*, London: Weidenfeld & Nicolson.
Filc, D. (2009) *Circles of Exclusion: The Politics of Health Care in Israel*, Ithaca, NY: Cornell University Press.

Gelber, Y. (1994) "The Consolidation of Jewish Society in Eretz-Israel, 1936–1947," in *The History of the Jewish Community in Eretz-Israel Since 1882, Part Two: The Period of the British Mandate*, Jerusalem: Israeli Academy for Sciences and Humanities, pp. 303–463 (in Hebrew).

Goldstein, Y. and Shavit, Y. (1979) *The Agreement Between D. Ben-Gurion and V. Jabotinski and its Failure (1934–1935)*, Tel Aviv: Yariv Publishing Co. (in Hebrew).

Gorny, J. (1969) "The Idea of Constructive Socialism in the Poale Zion Party (Eretz Israel) During the Years 1906–1914," *Proceedings of the World Congress of Jewish Studies*, 2: 114–18 (in Hebrew).

Gramsci, A. (1971 [1929–1935]) *Selections from the Prison Notebooks*, trans. Hoare, Q. and Nowell Smith, G. New York: International Publishers.

Gramsci, A. (2000) *The Gramsci Reader: Selected Writings 1916–1935*, Forgacs, D. (ed.), New York: New York University Press.

Grinberg, L. (2017) "Paving the Way to Neoliberalism: The Self-Destruction of the Zionist Labor Movement," in Maron, A. and Shalev, M. (eds.), *Neoliberalism as a State Project: Changing the Political Economy of Israel*, Oxford: Oxford University Press.

HCJ 8730/03 (Ruling of the Israeli High Court of Justice). *Clalit Health Services vs. Minister of Finance and Others.*

Herman Peled, H. and Peled, Y. (2011) "Post-Post Zionism: Confronting the Death of the Two-State Solution," *New Left Review*, 67: 97–118.

Horowitz, D. and Lissak, M. (1978) *Origins of the Israeli Polity: Palestine under the Mandate*, Chicago, IL: University of Chicago Press.

Jackson Lears, T. J. (1985) "The Concept of Cultural Hegemony: Problems and Possibilities," *The American Historical Review*, 90: 567–93.

Khenin, Dov. (2000) "Discourse and Hegemony in Mapai and the British Labour Party: Patterns of Change and Continuity," PhD dissertation, Department of Political Science, Tel Aviv University.

Kleiman, E. (1967) "The Place of Manufacturing in the Growth of the Israeli Economy," *Journal of Development Studies*, 3: 226–48.

Kleiman, E. (1997) "The Waning of Israeli *Etatisme*," *Israel Studies*, 2: 146–71.

Liebman, C. S. and Don-Yehiya, E. (1983) *Civil Religion in Israel: Traditional Judaism and Political Culture in the Jewish State*, Berkeley, CA: University of California Press.

Lustick, I. (1993) *Unsettled States, Disputed Lands: Britain and Ireland, France and Algeria, Israel and the West Bank-Gaza*, Ithaca, NY: Cornell University Press.

Maoz, Z. (2006) *Defending the Holy Land: A Critical Analysis of Israel's Security and Foreign Policy*, Ann Arbor, MI: University of Michigan Press.

Migdal, J. (1988) *Strong Societies and Weak States: State-Society Relations and State Capabilities in the Third World*, Princeton, NJ: Princeton University Press.

Morris, B. (2004) *The Birth of the Palestinian Refugee Problem Revisited*, Cambridge: Cambridge University Press.

Murphy, E. (1993) "Israel," in Niblock, T. and Murphy, E. (eds.), *Economic and Political Liberalisation in the Middle East*, London: British Academy Press, pp. 237–55.

Neumann, B. (2011) *Land and Desire in Early Zionism*, trans. Watzman, H., Waltham, MA: Brandeis University Press.

NII (2011) *Dimensions of Poverty and Social Gaps, 2010: Annual Report*, Jerusalem: National Insurance Institute (in Hebrew).

NII (2012) *Annual Report*, Jerusalem: National Insurance Institute (in Hebrew).

Öniş, Z. (1991) "The Logic of the Developmental State," *Comparative Politics*, 24: 109–26.

Pappe, I. (2006) *The Ethnic Cleansing of Palestine*, London: Oneworld Publications.

Peled, Y. (1992) "Ethnic Democracy and the Legal Construction of Citizenship: Arab Citizens of the Jewish State," *The American Political Science Review*, 86: 432–43.

Peled, Y. (2004) "Profits or Glory? The 28th Elul of Arik Sharon," *New Left Review*, 29: 47–70.

Peled, Y. (2014) *The Challenge of Ethnic Democracy: The State and Minority Groups in Israel, Poland and Northern Ireland*, London: Routledge.

Peled, Y. (2017) "Delegitimation of Israel or Social-Historical Analysis? The Debate Over Zionism as a Colonial Settler Movement," in Jacobs, J. (ed.), *Jews and Leftist Politics: Judaism, Israel, Antisemitism, and Gender*, Cambridge: Cambridge University Press, pp. 103–22.

Ram, U. (2007) *The Globalization of Israel: McWorld in Tel Aviv, Jihad in Jerusalem*, New York: Routledge.

Razin, A. and Sadka, E. (1993) *The Economy of Modern Israel: Malaise and Promise*, Chicago, IL: University of Chicago Press.

Rubinstein, A. (1982) *A Certain Political Experience*, Jerusalem: Idanim (in Hebrew).

Shafir, G. (1996) *Land, Labor and the Origins of the Israeli-Palestinian Conflict, 1882–1914*, updated edition, Berkeley, CA: University of California Press.

Shafir, G. and Peled, Y. (2002) *Being Israeli: The Dynamics of Multiple Citizenship*, Cambridge: Cambridge University Press.

Shalev, M. (1984) "Labor, State and Crisis: An Israeli Case Study," *Industrial Relations* 23: 362–86.

Shalev, M. (1990) "The Political Economy of Labor Party Dominance and Decline in Israel," in Pempel, T. J. (ed.), *Uncommon Democracies: The One-Party Dominant Regimes*, Ithaca, NY: Cornell University Press, pp. 83–127.

Shalev, M. (1992) *Labour and the Political Economy of Israel*, Oxford: Oxford University Press.

Shalev, M. (1996) "The Labor Movement in Israel: Ideology and Political Economy," in Goldberg, E. J. (ed.), *The Social History of Labor in the Middle East*, Boulder, CO: Westview Press, pp. 131–61.

Shalev, M. (2007) "The Welfare State Consensus in Israel: Placing Class Politics in Context," in Mau, S. and Veghte, B. (eds.), *Social Justice, Legitimacy and the Welfare State*, Farnham: Ashgate.

Shapira, An. (1992) *Land and Power: The Zionist Resort to Force, 1881–1948*, Oxford: Oxford University Press.

Shapiro, Y. (1976) *The Formative Years of the Israeli Labour Party: The Organization of Power, 1919–1930*, London: Sage.

Shapiro, Y. (1980) "Epilogue," in Shira, B. (ed.), *The Shinuy Movement: From Protest to Party*, Tel Aviv: Shira Public Relations, pp. 100–2 (in Hebrew).

Shapiro, Y. (1991) *The Road to Power: Herut Party in Israel*, Albany, NY: SUNY Press.

Sternhell, Z. (1998) *The Founding Myths of Israel: Nationalism, Socialism, and the Making of the Jewish State*, trans. Maisel, D., Princeton, NJ: Princeton University Press.

Swirski, B. (2007) *Privatization in the Public Healthcare System in Israel; Manifestations and Implications*, Tel Aviv: Adva Center (in Hebrew).

Swirski, B. (2012) *The State Does Not Look After Health: On Financing the Healthcare System in Israel*, Tel Aviv: Adva Center (in Hebrew).

Swirski, S. and Konnor-Attias, E. (2004) *Social Report – 2003*, Tel Aviv: Adva Center (in Hebrew).

Torgovnik, E. (1980) "A Movement for Change in a Stable System," in Arian, A. (ed.), *The Elections in Israel – 1977*, Jerusalem: Jerusalem Academic Press, pp. 75–98.

Urieli, N. and Barzilay, A. (1982) *The Rise and Fall of the Democratic Movement for Change*, Tel Aviv: Reshafim (in Hebrew).

Vitkin, Y. (1908) "The Conquest of Land and the Conquest of Labor" *Ben-Yhudah Project*, http://benyehuda.org/vitkin/articles_03.html (in Hebrew; accessed January 25, 2018).

Warwick, P. T. (2001) *State Lands and Rural Development in Mandatory Palestine, 1920–1948*, Brighton: Sussex Academic Press.

Weingrod, A. (1965) *Israel: Group Relations in a New Society*, New York: Praeger.

Yishai, Y. (1980) "Factionalism in Labour Zionism and Religious Zionism – A Comparative Perspective," *Cathedra: For the History of Eretz Israel and Its Settlement*, 16: 109–24 (in Hebrew).

3   The Religious Zionist challenge

Religious Zionism – demography

Identifying the national-religious (or Religious Zionist, the terms are synonymous) sector in Israeli society is not a straightforward matter. Conventionally researchers have identified this group with respondents who define themselves as "religious" (as opposed to "secular," "*Charedi*," or "traditionalist") in public opinion surveys. By that measure the size of the national-religious group has been quite stable since the turn of the millennium – about 11 percent of the Jewish population, a figure that corresponds, more or less, to the share of the national religious party(ies) in national elections (CBS 2011:8–9; Hermann et al. 2014:23, 44; Pew 2016:7, 43, 67).[1]

Sensing that in view of the growing social, political, and cultural weight of Religious Zionism in the society, the conventional method of identifying this sector was inadequate, in 2013 a research team of the Israel Democracy Institute (IDI) decided to take another approach. In their periodic survey of the state of democracy in Israel conducted in April 2013 they included the question: "Do you feel part of the Religious-Zionist public?" The result was that nearly 29 percent of the (Jewish) respondents answered that they did feel part of that public "in large measure" or in "very large measure."

Suspecting that this high level of identification with Religious Zionism may be an artifact of the phrasing of the question, in a test conducted in July of that year they asked a different question: "To what extent would you say you belong to the national-religious sector by your lifestyle and by your views?" In the test respondents were offered two types of answers to this question: (1) "both by my lifestyle and by my views, by my lifestyle only, by my views only, neither by my lifestyle nor by my views, don't know"; (2) "not at all, in small measure, in large measure, in very large measure, don't know." The answers to the first formulation indicated the same level of identification with Religious Zionism as in the previous survey – nearly 29 percent – and the answers to the second formulation indicated a lower level of identification – 22 percent who answered that they belonged to the national-religious sector "in large measure" or "in very large measure." To be methodologically cautious, the IDI researchers decided to take the lower finding as the valid one and included the second formulation in a survey they conducted between August and November 2013. The findings of that survey were identical to those of the test – 22 percent replied that they belonged to the national-religious sector "in large measure" or "in very large measure" (Hermann et al. 2014:24, 42).

Breaking down the respondents who identified with the national-religious sector by level of religiosity (see below), only 49 percent were found to hold the religious views conventionally identified with that sector. In addition, 33 percent belonged to the "traditionalist" religious category, 11 percent to the "*Charedi*" one and 3 percent, within the range of the statistical error, identified themselves as secular (4 percent did not know or refused to answer) (Hermann et al. 2014:43). In light of these findings, what might be viewed as the national-religious sphere of influence is at least as large as the core national-religious sector itself and includes people holding the whole range of levels of religiosity that exist in the society.

Based on the findings of this study the national-religious sector is significantly younger than the general Jewish population in Israel. Twenty percent of respondents in this study were between the ages of 18 and 24, compared with 13 percent in the general Jewish population, while 26 percent were aged 55 or older, compared to 33 percent in the general Jewish population (Hermann et al. 2014:45). This age distribution results from the much higher birth rate among the national-religious (and the *Charedim*) than among the rest of the Jewish population: in a survey conducted by the Pew Research Center in 2014–2015, 84 percent of the national-religious (defined in the survey as "dati" [religious]) had between three and six children and 5 percent had more than seven children, compared with 50 percent and 0 percent among secular ("hiloni") respondents, respectively. (Among *Charedi* respondents 63 percent had between three and six children and 28 percent had more than seven children.) (Pew 2016:44; Hermann et al. 2014:52).

In classifying Israeli Jews by level of religiosity there is a significant difference between the way people define themselves religiously and what they report that they actually observe in practice (Guttman Center 2012:30; CBS 2011:8). Comparing the top two categories in Tables 3.1 and 3.2, it is obvious that people under-report their level of religiosity – as opposed to their observance of

Table 3.1 Religiosity of Israeli Jews by self-definition (percent)

	2009	1999
Haredi	5	7
National religious	11	15
Traditional (from MENA*)	33	32
Secular not anti-religious	46	43
Secular anti-religious	6	3

Source: Guttman Center 2012.

Note
* MENA: Middle East and North Africa.

Table 3.2 Religiosity of Israeli Jews by observance of religious tradition (percent)

	1999	*2009*
Observe meticulously	14	14
Observe to a great extent	19	26
Observe to some extent	45	44
Do not observe at all	23	16

Source: Guttman Center 2012.

religious practices – if this self-reporting is taken at face value. The same conclusion is reached when comparing the third category in each table – "traditionalist" and "observe to some extent" (which is commonly understood to mean "traditionalist"). Most significantly, comparing the two "secular" categories in Table 3.1 to those who do not observe religious traditions at all, it is clear that people over-report themselves as secular by a very large factor.

The two types of self-reporting are much closer together when it comes to the trajectories of change in people's self-definition and reporting of their religious practices. By self-definition the top two categories of religiosity increased by 6 percent between 1999 and 2009 while the two secular categories decreased by exactly the same factor. In terms of actual religious practices, the top two categories increased by 7 percent, while the secular category decreased by the same factor (Guttman Center 2012:13).

A good indication of the demographic trends of the different groups is the number of students in the three Jewish school systems: state-secular, state-religious, and *Charedi* (Table 3.3). As can be seen in Table 3.4, according to the

Table 3.3 Students in all Jewish school systems, 2014-2015

	State-secular	*State-religious*	*Charedi*	*Total*
Number	1,017,066	354,751	289,108	1,660,925
%	61.2	21.4	17.4	100.0

Source: Knesset 2015:9.

Table 3.4 Students in the different Jewish school systems (percentage of the total number of students)

	2001	*2012*	*2019 (expected)*	*Expected % growth 2012–2019*
State-secular	52	43	41	5.8
State-religious	14	13	14	17.7
Charedi	12	17	19	23.8
Total Jewish	78	73	74	

Source: CBS 2013b.

Table 3.5 Students in the different Jewish elementary school systems (percentage of the total number of Jewish students)

	1989–1990	*2009–2010*	*2019 (expected)*
State-secular	71.0	53.2	Just below 50.0
State-religious	21.3	18.7	19.0
Charedi	7.6	28.0	31.5
Total %	100	100	100

Sources: Faitelson 2011; CBS 2013a; Zelba n.d. [2016]:11.

Central Bureau of Statistics (CBS) the share of the state-secular system in the total number of students is declining, that of the state-religious (Religious Zionist) remains stable, while the share of the *Charedi* system is growing. The share of Jewish students as a whole in the total population (including the Arab state system) declined since the turn of the millennium but is expected to remain stable at about 75 percent due to the decline in the birth rate among Palestinian citizens (CBS 2013b:139).

A similar but starker picture emerges when comparing the different *elementary* Jewish school systems: As can be seen in Table 3.5, while in the school year 1989–1990 71 percent of Jewish elementary school pupils were enrolled in the secular state system, 21.3 percent in the national-religious system and 7.6 percent in the *Charedi* systems, in the school year 2009–2010 53.2 percent were enrolled in the secular state system, 18.7 percent in the national-religious system and 28 percent in the *Charedi* systems (Faitelson 2011:71). The Central Bureau of Statistics has projected that by 2019 the number of pupils in the elementary secular state system will decline for the first time to just below 50 percent, while in the national-religious system it will grow to 19 percent and in the *Charedi* systems it will grow to nearly 32 percent (CBS 2013a:405; Zelba n.d. [2016]:11; see also Chapter 5).[2]

The "historic partnership"

The so-called "historic partnership" was forged between Mapai and the *Mizrachi* movement in 1935, when the Labor Zionist Movement became dominant in the World Zionist Organization and Ben-Gurion was elected Chairman of the Zionist Executive. Between 1933 and 1935 the *Mizrachi* had been in opposition to the Zionist Executive within the WZO, because of what it perceived as less than rigorous observance of *kashrut* and the Sabbath in Zionist institutions and activities (D. Schwartz 2003:70; Ha-Cohen 2005:265). However, the political and financial consequences of being outside the governing body of the WZO induced the *Mizrachi* to rejoin it. Ben-Gurion, on his part, was concerned that the *Mizrachi* would follow Vladimir Jabotinsky's Revisionist Zionists and secede from the WZO altogether, as voices within it were urging it to do. Another factor that facilitated the alliance between the two parties was the fact that the workers' faction that had split from the *Mizrachi* in 1922, *Ha-Poel Ha-Mizrachi* (The

Mizrachi Worker), had already signed an agreement with the *Histadrut* in 1927 which granted its members access to the *Histadrut*'s labor exchanges and health-care services. Hence a compromise formula was worked out about the observance of the Sabbath and of *kashrut*, and *Mizrachi* rejoined the Executive and formed a partnership with Mapai that was to last until 1977 (D. Schwartz 2003:57, 64, 70; Ha-Cohen 2005:266–8).

In the "historic partnership" between Mapai and the *Mizrachi* the Religious Zionist movement was clearly the junior partner. Its inferiority was not merely a matter of its small numbers. The *Mizrachi* was for the most part an urban middle-class movement, removed from the spirit and activities of pioneering (with the exception of the small but increasingly influential *Ha-Poel Ha-Mizrachi*, which had its own kibbutz movement) (D. Schwartz 2009:143; S. Fischer 2013:353–4; Greenblum 2016:159–60; Sagi and Schwartz 2017:127). Its petty-bourgeois character and overt religiosity did not comport well with the image of the "new Jew" that Zionism, and especially the LZM, sought to create: "He was to be secular and modern, love his people and homeland, draw close to nature, have clean hands and a courageous heart" (An. Shapira 1997:264; Triger 2005; D. Schwartz 2009:143–4; Conforti 2009; Recanati 2010:35).[3] "Negation of the Diaspora" was a constitutive element of Zionist ideology, and the negation included Jewish religious observance as practiced in the *galut* (exile): "Religion was to the pioneers one of numerous outdated conventions that was shed on becoming a pioneer in Palestine" (S. Almog 1998:239). In their eyes, "adherence to Halakhah retarded both individual and communal development and represented the negative aspect of *galut* society" (Kolatt 1998:277).

For Zionists, and especially for the Labor Zionist pioneers in Palestine, religious Jews, whether in the Diaspora or in Palestine, were "poor, uneducated, superstitious, cowardly, zealous, lacking in self-respect" and unproductive. Therefore, "the image of the new Jew as the direct descendant of the ancient Jew, and the antithesis of the diaspora Jew, was imparted to the youth of the Yishuv..." (An. Shapira 1997:261; 1998:252; Raz-Krakotzkin 1993/1994; Ufaz 1998:132; Zisenwine 1998:147; Guttwein 2009; Neumann 2011:116–23; Presner 2007). In textual terms, Zionism's foundational text was the Bible (Old Testament), while the text mainly studied in the Diaspora for centuries was the Talmud with its many interpretations (An. Shapira 1992:58–9; 1998:260–2; Sharot 2007:674; Sheleg 2010:37, Raz-Krakotzkin 2015:123–9). The great Zionist poet, Shaul Tchernichovsky, in his famous poem, "In Front of the Statue of Apollo," described Diaspora Jews as "rebels against life," who took "the God of the wonderous deserts, the God of the conquerors of Canaan in a storm, and bound Him up with the straps of the phylacteries" (Tchernichovsky 1899; cf. Kolatt 1998:275; Peleg 2016:151n4).

As a result of their marginalization, "Religious Zionists were ... self-conscious about their minimal contribution to the leadership and development of Zionism, and to the establishment and maintenance of the state. They felt obliged, therefore, to adopt defensive, segregationist policies to protect themselves from secularism" (Liebman and Don-Yehiya 1983:202; Aran

1991:312). By the same token, Religious Zionists felt religiously inferior to the ultra-Orthodox, non-Zionist *Charedim*, with their more exacting observance of Jewish religious strictures (Liebman and Don-Yehiya 1983:203; Luz 1999:379; M. Inbari 2008:38; Sagi and Schwartz 2017:128–9).[4]

Status Quo Letter

Mapai's greatest overture toward the religiously Orthodox was not aimed at the Religious Zionists, with whom it had an "historic partnership," however, but at the non-Zionist *Agudat Yisrael*, which had seceded from the *yishuv* when women were enfranchised in 1925.[5] The context was the expected arrival in Palestine in June 1947 of UNSCOP, the committee charged by the UN to investigate the situation in the country and propose a solution, in the wake of Great Britain surrendering its Mandate in February of that year. In order to forestall the possibility of *Agudat Yisrael* appearing before the Committee as representing a distinct community, separate from the *yishuv* (as it did before the British Peel Commission in 1936), the Jewish Agency Executive sent a letter to *Agudat Yisrael*, signed by its Chairman, David Ben-Gurion, Yitzhak Grünbaum of the General Zionists and Rav Judah Leib Fishman of *Mizrachi*, outlining the place of Jewish religion in the public life of the future State of Israel.

Commonly referred to as the "Status Quo Letter,"[6] it stipulated that the future state would continue to observe the religious arrangements that had prevailed in the *yishuv* in four specific areas: Saturday would become the national day of rest, *kashrut* would be observed in all government kitchens, rabbinical courts would retain exclusive jurisdiction over marriage and divorce of Jews, and the autonomy of the existing religious educational systems would be preserved. Aside from the immediate circumstances of the issuing of this letter, in a more general way, as put by Zionist historian Israel Kolatt, "no Jewish national body could allow itself to set conditions that would bar participation by the religious parties"[7] (Kolatt 1998:298; Marmorstein 1969:86–8; Liebman and Don-Yehiya 1984:32; Varhaftig 1988:35–6; Friedman 1988; Don-Yehiya 1997; Shafir and Peled 2002:140–6; Jamal 2009:1157–62; G. Levy 2011; Greilsammer 2014:136–8; Jobani and Perez 2017:36–8).

The conditions stipulated in the Status Quo Letter have, by and large, been maintained since the time of its writing. Moreover, Orthodox privileges have been augmented in two important areas not mentioned in the letter: all Orthodox women, and ultra-Orthodox (*Charedi*) *yeshiva* students, have been exempted, fully or in part, from mandatory military service, and the Orthodox conception of "who is a Jew" has become increasingly influential in defining the boundaries of the Jewish Israeli collectivity (Liebman 1993:154–5). Both of these extensions were effected while Labor was the political party in power. The issues concerning education and military service will be discussed in some detail in Chapters 5 and 6 below, respectively. Here we will present only a brief discussion of the issues concerning family law and "who is a Jew?," two issue areas that touch directly on the identity of the Jewish Israeli collectivity.

Family Law

During the Ottoman and Mandatory periods, jurisdiction over family law (primarily marriage and divorce) was the purview of the various officially recognized religious communities of Palestine (*millets*). This situation was written into the Israeli legal system in the Rabbinical Courts Jurisdiction (Marriage and Divorce) Law of 1953. This statute granted rabbinical courts exclusive jurisdiction over marriage and divorce of Jews in Israel. (Similar laws were enacted with respect to the religious courts of non-Jewish communities.) The most important practical consequence of this law has been that, officially, non-religious civil marriage and the possibility of inter-religious marriage are not available in Israel. Moreover, since both Jewish and Moslem law do not consider women to be equal to men, the status of Israeli women in marriage and divorce procedures is clearly inferior to that of men, a situation that reflects on many other aspects of civil law as well. Thus the 1951 Women's Equal Rights Law specifically excluded from its purview matters of marriage and divorce, and its amendment enacted in 2000 excluded religious institutions from the requirement to appoint women that is mandatory for all other kinds of public institutions (Zucker 1973:100–21; Abramov 1976:179–8; Liebman and Don-Yehiya 1984:25; Shifman 1995; Raday 1996; Halperin-Kaddari 2000; Triger 2005; Barak-Erez 2009; Chapter 8).[8]

The stated rationale underlying the surrender of jurisdiction in this crucially important area to parochial courts and religious laws was the need to preserve Jewish national unity. Had the choice of non-religious marriage and divorce been available to Jews in Israel, Orthodox Jews would have refrained from marrying non-Orthodox ones because of their concern that religiously illegitimate divorces, sanctioned by civil courts, may have occurred in the candidates' families in the past, so that a suspicion of *mamzerut* (bastardness) would hover over all non-Orthodox Israeli Jews.[9] Since *mamzerim* are not eligible to marry Jews (except for other *mamzerim* or religious converts), it was argued, two separate, endogamous Jewish communities would have developed in Israel (Zucker 1973:100–21; Shifman 1995; Halperin-Kaddari 2000:349; Triger 2005:198–204). In reality, however, marriages between Orthodox and non-Orthodox Jews rarely occur anyway, unless one of the partners adopts the religious convictions of the other (Pew 2016:29–30, 212, 216).

Legal scholar Zvi Triger has explained the granting of exclusive jurisdiction in matters of marriage and divorce to religious authorities in terms of Zionism's quest to create a "new Jew" by, *inter alia*, recovering the patriarchal authority of Jewish men:

> ... the aim of the Zionist project was to create a new Jewish man, while rejecting the image of the Diasporic "feminine" and "degenerate" Jew. Thus the adoption of religious law in the sphere of family law, in the way in which it serves to reconstitute the patriarchal social order, can be seen not only as a product of political compromise but also, perhaps mainly, as an almost natural consequence of the development of Zionist ideology.
>
> (Triger 2005:175, 213–20; cf. Shakdiel 2002:153)

Thus the "status quo," at least in the area of family law, was "a very convenient 'compromise' for the Zionist leadership, a 'compromise' that did not require it to retreat from principles it believed in," including the subjection of women's rights to the overriding need for national unity and resilience (Triger 2005:176, 182, 207–11).

Problematic cases from the perspective of Jewish law, such as when one of the partners is non-Jewish or doubtfully Jewish, or when a *Cohen* (priest) and a divorced woman wish to be married, as well as same-sex unions, have been settled in practice by the expansion, through judicial decisions, of legally recognized non-marriage forms of cohabitation, such as common law marriages, and by civil marriages conducted abroad. These options, as well as non-Orthodox Jewish marriage ceremonies, have also been used by couples who wish to have an egalitarian wedding ceremony.[10]

As a result, the increase in the number of Jews in Israel has not been reflected by a similar increase in the number of official, that is, religious marriages. Thus, while in 1975, with close to 3 million Jewish citizens, the number of officially sanctioned Jewish marriages was 28,583, in 2011, when the number of Jewish citizens had doubled, the number of officially sanctioned marriages had risen to only 38,936. Between 1995 and 2011 the number of (officially sanctioned) marriages per 1,000 people in the Jewish population of Israel had actually declined from 8.5 to 6.7 (Shifman 1995; Hemdat 1996:46; Etner-Levkovitch 1997:45–50; Sapir and Statman 2009; Ben-Porat 2013:60–101; CBS 2013c). In addition, since the mid-1990s the establishment of civil family courts has eroded the role played by rabbinical courts in family matters other than the performance of marriage and divorce.[11]

"Who is a Jew?"

This is a vitally important political question in Israel, in view of the role played by the ethno-national discourse in defining the Jewish Israeli collectivity and the privileged status of Jews in the society. Thus, a person's nationality is not defined by citizenship, but rather by his or her ascriptive religious affiliation. In 2013 the Supreme Court turned down an appeal by a group of Israeli citizens, prominent in various fields of culture and politics, who demanded to be registered in the population registry as belonging to the *Israeli* nation. Their appeal was turned down on the grounds that an Israeli nation, distinguishable from the Jewish nation, does not exist in Israeli law or political culture. In other words, the State of Israel distinguishes between a person's citizenship and her/his national identity and does not derive the latter from the former (CA 8573/08; J. Shapira 2014; see also CA 630/70). This legal understanding is expressed most clearly in the Law of Return of 1950, the Nationality Law of 1952, and the Law of Population Registry of 1965. Over the years, the official definition of "Jew" for the purposes of these laws has become progressively restricted and more closely aligned with Orthodox thinking.

In 1958, Yisrael Bar-Yehuda, the Minister of the Interior who belonged to *Achdut Ha-Avoda* (a left-leaning Labor Zionist party), issued a directive to the offices of the Population Registry that "any person declaring in good faith that he is a Jew, shall be registered as a Jew and no additional proof shall be required" (Zucker 1973:173). This directive expressed the civil, rather than ethnic conception of nationality, in that it made entry into the Jewish national collectivity in Israel a voluntary matter, distinct from belonging to Judaism as a religion. Precisely for this reason that directive was very short-lived. Through a series of government crises, coalition agreements, and judicial rulings too tedious to be related here, in 1970 a definition of a "Jew" was added to the Law of Return: "a person born of a Jewish mother, or who converted to Judaism, and is not a member of another religion" (Zucker 1973:206, slightly altered translation; see also 172–207; Abramov 1976:270–320; Schiff 1977:195–207; Eilam 2000a; 2000b).

This religious definition was too restrictive, however, in view of the demographic aim of Zionism, to maintain and increase the Jewish majority in Israel. As a result, in 1970, with the relaxation of emigration restrictions in the USSR, the same amendment to the Law of Return also stipulated that only one Jewish grandparent would be required in order to entitle a person and her/his spouse and minor children to the privileges provided by the law (the so-called "grandfather clause"). Thus, it is estimated that up to 400,000 of the immigrants from the former Soviet Union living in Israel today are non-Jews by the Orthodox definition, and that non-Jewish "Law of Return Eligibles" throughout the world currently number 15,000,000. As marriage, divorce, and burials in Israel are all under the exclusive jurisdiction of religious authorities (whether Jewish or non-Jewish), these non- and doubtful Jews run into problems when they come to need these services, unless they convert to Judaism. One paradoxical result of the amended Law of Return, reflecting a contradiction between the demographic and legitimational imperatives of Zionism, and between the republican and ethno-national discourses of citizenship, is thus the development of a diverse non-Jewish, non-Arab group of citizens in Israel (Lustick 1999).

The Orthodox political parties are still struggling to restrict the definition of a Jew in the Law of Return even further, by having the law read, following the word "converted," "in accordance with *Halacha*." This is because, as it now stands, the definition covers people who may have converted to Judaism according to non-Orthodox procedures. In 1989 an attempt to institute this change was narrowly defeated in the Knesset, after the Reform and Conservative Jewish establishments in the United States had threatened to cut their contributions to Israel. In this case, then, when a core Zionist interest was at stake, Orthodox demands were accommodated only to a limited degree (Landau 1996; cf. Hoffman 1989, 215–40).

In 1997–1998 another, more moderate attempt to deprive non-Orthodox conversions to Judaism of official recognition, if performed *in Israel*, has also been shelved. At the time of writing, non-Orthodox conversions performed in Israel are recognized for the purpose of the population registry, but not for the Law of Return, while such conversions performed abroad are recognized for all state purposes, but not for functions that are under the jurisdiction of the Rabbinate

(*Haaretz*, April 1, 1997; *New York Times*, April 17, 1997; T. L. Friedman 1997; Don-Yehiya 1997; Hirschl 2010:145–7; Reform Center for Religion and State[12]).

Return of the repressed

With time, members of the younger generation of the *Mizrachi*, educated in the network of institutions it had set up and controlled – the state-religious educational system, encompassing kindergartens to high schools; the *Bnei Akiva* youth movement; the high-school *yeshiva* network, where high-level religious studies are coupled with secular education; and the national-religious university, Bar-Ilan – came to resent the inferior role their movement was playing *vis-à-vis* both Labor and the *Charedim* (Aran 1991:275; M. Inbari 2008:38; Recanati 2010:36–7; S. Fischer 2013:367; Greenblum 2016:208; Sagi and Schwartz 2017). As explained by Dror Greenblum, graduates of this system, who became leaders of Religious Zionism in the 1970s (see below) and sought to assume leadership positions in the society as a whole, took Rav A. I. Kook's "activist-messianic worldview and turned it into the central stream in religious Zionism, and in our own days – to the only stream defining the national-religious public" (Greenblum 2016:287; Barzel 2017:245–86).

Of particular importance in this new generation of Religious Zionists, the generation born shortly before or after the establishment of the state, was a group within *Bnei Akiva* known as *Gachelet* (Ember): Pioneering Torah Scholars' Group, that was formed in 1952–1953 by 14–18-year-old students in two Religious Zionist schools belonging to the "romantic-expressive" stream of Religious Zionism inspired by Rav A. I. Kook. *Gachelet* was critical of the Religious Zionist establishment for not being orthodox enough in its religious observance and for lacking in nationalist fervor because of its subservience to the Labor Zionist Movement. In line with this critique they formed their own nationalist religious *yeshivot*, and helped establish the first *hesder yeshiva*, combining religious studies with military service, in 1958 (Aran 1986; 2013; Rodick 1989; Lustick 1988:34; D. Schwartz 2003:127; S. Fischer 2013:355–7; Sagi and Schwartz 2017:132; on *yeshivot hesder* see Chapter 6).

The vision motivating *Gachelet* was that the ideal of "Torah state" or "Torah regime," fusing Jewish nationalism and Jewish religion, should be implemented in practice. In addition to "full observance of the Torah of Israel" in everyday life, they were committed to "nationalism and patriotism, dedication to the nation and loyalty to the state, readiness to sacrifice for the sake of the nation" (Aran 1986:130). Already in 1961 they called for the establishment of a supreme *Halachic* institution that would prepare a program for the implementation of the Torah regime (Azrieli 1990:24–6). As explained by Shlomo Fischer:

> [The] concept of [Torah state] includes two separate, yet connected, ideas. The first is that religious value and fulfillment can be realized in the "secular" or mundane realms of politics, settlement, economic production, cultural production and the military, that is realms outside of the narrow

sacramental-religious arena of prayer, religious ritual and interpersonal ethics. The second idea is that these realms have to be ordered according to some religious vision, principle or regulations. In other words, the unification of the religious and the national frameworks of collective identity entailed the de-compartmentalization of the religious life. The various institutional arenas of life: political, economic, cultural, military etc. were to be brought within an overall religious meaning and regulative system.

(S. Fischer 2013:351; see also 2014:131–2; Aran 1991:295–6;
Sagi and Schwartz 2017:124)

By implication, initially, and after 1967 explicitly, the vision of "Torah state" included Jewish sovereignty over the entire Land of Israel (S. Fischer 2013:371–4; Barzel 2017:183–4).

Members of *Gachelet* realized that implementing their concept of "Torah state" in practice required that its adherents should break the "historic partnership" with Mapai and assume leadership positions themselves in all areas of social life, from the military to fine arts. And they were critical of the current Religious Zionist leadership, which adhered to this ideal in principle, for failing to work to achieve it in practice (S. Fischer 2013:352–4, 357–8, 365–6, 379; D. Schwartz 2003:138). The war of 1967 gave *Gachelet* the opportunity to launch their move to acquire leadership positions, both in their own movement and in the society as a whole (see below), but to take advantage of that opportunity they needed a much more solid ideological basis than they were capable of developing by themselves. This ideological basis was provided by Rav Zvi Yehuda Kook, son of the formidable Rav A. I. Kook. In 1959–1960 members of *Gachelet* met with the rabbi, came under his influence, and moved to his *yeshiva*, *Merkaz Ha-Rav*, founded by his father in 1924. Their arrival revitalized the *yeshiva* and elevated its status, and the status of Rav Kook himself, in the Religious Zionist world (Aran 1986:134–5; Rodick 1989:22; Hellinger 2008). According to sociologist Shlomo Fischer, that move was "the fateful moment … of religious Zionism in its entirety" (S. Fischer 2013:364).

Gachelet's influence was felt first in *Bnei Akiva*, the religious Zionist youth movement from which it had sprung. Under its influence the movement abandoned its ideal of life on a religious kibbutz and replaced it with a life devoted to Torah study in a *yeshiva* and, after 1967, to settling in the occupied Palestinian territories. *Gachelet*'s ideas then spread through the network of high school *yeshivot* established by the youth movement and the *hesder yeshivot* where many of their graduates spend their military service (Aran 1986:132–3; Sagi 2011; Don-Yehiya 2014; cf. Sagi and Schwartz 2017:94–6, 109; Barzel 2017:252–61).

1967–1973

The war of 1967 enabled the young guard of the National Religious Party, which had crystalized around the graduates of *Gachelet* and *Merkaz Ha-Rav*, to shift from a war of position to a war of maneuver, to use Gramscian terms (Anderson

1976:8–9; Sagi and Schwartz 2017:89–111). On Israel's Nineteenth Independence Day in 1967, three weeks before the outbreak of the war, Rav Kook gave a homily in which he lamented, *inter alia*, the separation from the State of Israel of "our Hebron … our Nablus … our Jericho … our lands on the other side of the Jordan" (cited in Peleg 2016:92). Three weeks later Israel was in control of all those places (except for the East bank of the Jordan), which elevated the rabbi to the status of a prophet in the eyes of his followers (Sagi and Schwartz 2017:61–9).

The 1967 war was preceded by a three-week "waiting period" during which the country was gripped by widespread, albeit unfounded, fear for the very existence of Israel. Against that background the stunning victory in the war itself and the occupation of the West Bank, encompassing the heart of the Biblical Land of Israel, were seen by many as a supernatural miracle (Liebman and Don-Yehiya 1983:203; Lustick 1988:29; Oren 2002; 2005; Segev 2005, esp. p. 15; Maoz 2006:80–112; Gluska 2007; S. Fischer 2013:369; Laron 2017; Barzel 2017: 385–401). The results of the war thus contributed to a process of "Judaization" of Israeli society, forcing "Israelis to re-confront their relationship with Jewish peoplehood and with Judaism itself":

> This meant rediscovering a positive relationship with both the past of the Jewish people and the present-day Jews of the Diaspora. Terms such as "eternal unity," "common fate," and "destiny" were revived in the process. Nationalism and statehood, permeated by the values of modernism and secularity, were suddenly placed in a new proximity and sympathy with the values of religion and tradition. This in turn led to a renewed identification between the two value systems but also to a heightened consciousness of their differences.
>
> (Aran 1991:273; cf. R. Shapira 1975; Sagi and Schwartz 2017;
> Barzel 2017:404–7)

Following the 1967 war the governing Labor party was internally split with respect to the future of the territories that had been captured – keep them under Israeli rule or return most of them for peace. The split was in large measure generational: the old, foreign-born leadership favored withdrawal from most of the territories under certain conditions, primarily out of concern for international public opinion. (However, "Jerusalem," which by the Israeli definition included a large portion of the West Bank as well, was immediately annexed to Israel.) The younger generation of leaders, consisting mostly of retired military technocrats, wanted to keep some or all of the territories, primarily for alleged security reasons (Lustick 1988:42; Shapiro 1991:153–9; Naor 1999).

More fundamentally, the two sides to this debate represented two conflicting imperatives whose synthesis had guided Labor's historical settlement strategy: the geographic and the demographic. The geographic imperative dictated trying to acquire through settlement as much territory as possible; the demographic imperative dictated maintaining a Jewish majority, and thus the possibility of

democracy, even at the price of limiting territorial expansion. The older generation, by and large (Golda Meir was a notable exception), continued to abide by
the demographic imperative, while their younger colleagues embraced the geographic one. This split resulted in indecision and policy paralysis and inconsist-
ency which created a political vacuum into which the young Religious Zionists
were only too happy to enter (Shafir and Peled 2002:40, 160–3).

Lacking a coherent policy on the future of the occupied territories, the Labor
party engaged, by default, in piecemeal settlement activity in response to political pressures from within and without:

> Labor ... did invest substantial resources in settling the Golan Heights, the
> Jordan Valley, the greater East Jerusalem area and the Gush Etzion area [half
> way between Jerusalem and Hebron] ... [but] continued to resist ... demands
> to create a large Jewish presence in the heavily populated highlands of the
> West Bank ... in anticipation of [their] eventual return to Arab rule.
>
> (Lustick 1988:45)

It was precisely this possibility of eventual return to Arab rule that the young
guard of Religious Zionism was determined to forestall:

> The Six Day War ... turned the conception of Jewish sovereignty over all
> the Land into an operational concept. The commitment of so many religious
> Zionists to this ideology, contrasting with the hesitation and misgiving in
> most secularist circles, ended their status as political satellites. For the first
> time in the history of political Zionism, they asserted leadership in political
> and social fields – in their own settlement of the newly captured territories
> and in their political defense of Israel's foreign policy.
>
> (Liebman and Don-Yehiya 1983:203)

For Rav Z. Y. Kook and his followers, who had now become hegemonic
within Religious Zionism (Lustick 1988:29; S. Fischer 2013:376; Greenblum
2016: 287; Sagi and Schwartz 2017), the victory of 1967 was an incontrovertible
sign of a divine plan to return the entire Land of Israel to the People of Israel, as
a major step in the process of messianic redemption:

> The State of Israel stopped being a "normal" state and became a state pos-
> sessed of metaphysical significance, embodying the processes of redemption
> awaiting the Jewish people. The real state is now judged in light of its meta-
> physical goals, since it is the embodiment of the divine presence in the
> world.
>
> (Sagi and Schwartz 2017:156)

The close connection, on this view, "between the notion of the Torah State
and the Greater Land of Israel [was] thus rooted in the fundamental expressivist
religious ideal of the higher synthesis of the mundane and sacred worlds"

(S. Fischer 2013:374; Barzel 2017:183–98). *Merkaz Ha-Rav* circles saw the Land of Israel as an indivisible organic whole and keeping the occupied Palestinian territories under Jewish sovereignty as a divine commandment not subject to utilitarian considerations of any kind. In the words of Rav Kook:

> These borders, these kilometers of ours, are sanctified with divine sanctity and we cannot give them up under any circumstances. Besides, we have to remember the simple fact that these kilometers … are not only ours; we are just small representatives of the People of Israel … This land belongs not only to the three million Jews who are here but no less than that – to all the millions of Jews in Russia and the United States and the whole world. We have no permission even to consider – we have not received a legal power of attorney from them – giving up these lands, under any circumstances! This is a positive commandment [*mitzvat aseh*] from the Torah – not to be transgressed even at the price of one's life and no political calculations and complications, no government arrangements and no ministerial pronouncements of ours will change that.
>
> (Rav Z. Y. Kook, 1974, cited in Atkes 2016:371; see also Luz 1999:367)

In sum, as Shmuel Sandler, among others, has pointed out:

> By turning the issue [of settling the West Bank] into both a national and a religious cause the *Mizrachi* camp emerged as a leading force in both areas, for in taking the lead on settlement in the territories, it could demonstrate its loyalty to the sacred ideals of settling the land and security, while at the same time criticizing the *Agudah* circles for their disloyalty to the Land of Israel. Thus, while the old leadership continued to play second fiddle to Labor, an issue had arisen in which the NRP camp could potentially provide leadership in both the national and the religious areas…
>
> (Sandler 1981:164; see also Don-Yehiya 1979:37–8;
> Sagi and Schwartz 2017; the classic depiction of this transformation
> from a personal standpoint is Michael 1984)

Gush Emunim

If the war of 1967 was a necessary condition for radical national-religious activism to take shape, its combination with the war of 1973 was a sufficient one (Aran 1991:275; D. Schwartz 2003:125). Until 1973 the young guard of Religious Zionism were involved in only two rather limited spontaneous settlement activities that received government approval *ex post facto* – in Gush Etzion and in Hebron, where Jewish communities had existed before 1948 (Sagi and Schwartz 2017:91). However, a new stage in the process of colonization opened up in February 1974, with the foundation of Gush Emunim (GE; Block of the Faithful), in the aftermath of the traumatic 1973 war, the loss of Labor's credibility as the guardian of Israel's security, and American pressure to withdraw

Israeli forces from Sinai and the Golan Heights in order to separate the hostile armies from each other (Lustick 1988:42–3, 44–5; Maoz 2006:140–70; M. Inbari 2008:38, 48, 52; Barzel 2017:310–17, 330–74).

Gush Emunim vehemently opposed any Israeli withdrawal as part of these disengagement agreements and demanded the removal of the restrictions imposed on the settlement process by the by now wholly discredited Labor government. These far-reaching goals were accompanied by new and militant methods. Yearly marches across the West Bank of 30,000–40,000 participants, frequent street demonstrations (in some of which Secretary of State Henry Kissinger was castigated as a "Jew boy"), and most significantly, repeated attempts to settle forcefully at chosen sites, in spite of evacuations by the military. Certain elements within GE and its offshoots even resorted to violent terrorist activities against Palestinians and Palestinian sites, including the Temple Mount (Lustick 1988:65–71; Rodick 1989:159–99; Aran 1991:293, 299; D. Schwartz 2003:129; Don-Yehiya 2014:251–2; Rubin 2014:57–8; Barzel 2017:271–4, 281–2, 422, 550–1). These methods placed GE on the margins of Israeli democracy but at the heart of Israeli politics. While its successes during the era of the first Rabin government (1974–1977) were scant (Gorenberg 2006), GE displayed a vitality and persistence that had not been encountered in Israeli society since the end of the 1948 war.

The vitality and persistence of GE, as well as its puritanism and "pioneering" spirit, drew a great deal of sympathy even from their supposed political opponents, especially against the background of the traumatic 1973 war. Thus Hanoch Bartov, a non-observant author with a left-wing Labor Zionist background, wrote in 1975 that in his heart,

> as in the hearts of many, there is sympathy, or better yet, yearning or jealousy, for the enthusiastic youth of Gush Emunim. When you see the other side of our life in this country ... the violence, the vulgarity ... the gossip columns about the provincial so-called high society, the dwarfs of all social classes, the heart goes out to these young people whose national path is fed by the fire of religious faith. The entire cruel reality of our day is turned into a heap of bones by one fiery speech of [GE leader] Rav Levinger.
>
> (Cited in Barzel 2017:430)

In terms of internal party politics, until 1967 the religiously and nationally moderate foreign-born leadership of the NRP successfully maintained its hold over the party by preventing intra-party elections and substituting for them power-sharing arrangements. Following the 1967 war, however, leaders of the party's young guard moved to assume the political representation of the Hebron and Gush Etzion settlers and urged the NRP to take the lead in forcing the settlement of the West Bank (Hornstein and Goldstein 2017; Sagi and Schwartz 2017:91).

This position served the NRP young guard well in their intra-party generational conflict, as it was a source of influence within the national-religious community, beyond the ranks of their age group. After the death of the party's long-time moderate leader, Moshe Chaim Shapira in 1970, the young guard succeeded in forcing democratic elections on the foreign-born leadership, from which they emerged greatly strengthened. In 1986, Zevulun Hammer, a founder and leader of the young guard and GE, replaced the veteran Dr. Joseph Burg as head of the NRP. The takeover was completed (Lustick 1988:162; Azrieli 1990; Don-Yehiya 2014; Barzel 2017; Sagi and Schwartz 2017:124).

The militant expansionist stance of the NRP young guard provided a key element in the crystallization of an independent nationalist-religious worldview that came to vie for primacy with Labor's security-mindedness as the central component of Israeli nationalism. As GE leader Chanan Porat wrote in March 1975:

> The struggle [between GE and the Labor government] results from different worldviews regarding the correct dimensions of Zionism. Does Zionism constitute a safe haven for Jews and [do] we have to exert efforts for providing the certain number of Jews who are found here with a life of security, so they can succeed in holding their own and exist? Or maybe the process of redemption in its concrete sense – the redemption of the people, and the redemption of the land – and in its divine sense – the redemption of the godhead, the redemption of the world – is taking place?
>
> (Porat 1975:8)

These two different worldviews came into sharp relief in the celebrated case of Elon Moreh, adjudicated before the High Court of Justice in 1979. Elon Moreh was a settlement established by GE on private Palestinian land in the Nablus area that had been expropriated for that purpose by the Israeli military, ostensibly for security reasons (Gorenberg 2006:180–95; Hornstein and Goldstein 2017:57). The Palestinian owners of the land appealed to the High Court of Justice against its expropriation. Lieutenant General Rafael Eitan, Chief of the IDF General Staff (and later on a prominent ultra-nationalist politician; Lustick 1988:64), defended the expropriation on the grounds of the strategic importance of the area for the security of Israel. GE, however, submitted a brief to the Court arguing that "the settlement itself does not stem from security reasons or physical requirements but from the force of destiny and by virtue of the return of Israel to its land" (HCJ 390/79 cited in Hornstein and Goldstein 2017:57).

Since the Minister of Defense, Ezer Weitzman, a retired air force general, did not support General Eitan's argument (but submitted to the Cabinet's decision to defend the expropriation in court), and since two retired generals, one of them a former Chief of the IDF General Staff himself, contradicted General Eitan's security arguments, the Court decided that the expropriation could not be justified on security grounds and the land had to be returned to its Palestinian owners. GE's honest intervention, revealing the true purpose of expropriating the land and settling on it, undoubtedly diminished the credibility of the security argument in the eyes of the Court (HCJ 390/79; Lustick 1988:48–51; Hornstein and

Goldstein 2017:58). This tactical setback, however, opened the way for a strategic triumph: the government proceeded to declare about 22 percent of the West Bank territory state lands, on which settlement did not have to be justified on security grounds, thus de facto, though not de jure, annexing the West Bank to Israel (Barzel 2017:354–60).

The republican discourse of citizenship, which had been diluted by the LZM due to the need to accommodate non-pioneering groups under its hegemony, was now available for religious redefinition. Its new champions, spearheaded by GE, were well placed to construct a new historic bloc and move to acquire hegemony over the society. GE took great pride in presenting itself, in the words of Rav Moshe Levinger, as "the direct and legitimate offspring of the pioneers of Zionism" (*Yediot Aharonot*, June 18, 1976; Avruch 1979).

Gush Emunim's "symbolic system owes much to the pioneer legacy identified with the left" (Aran 1991:289, 301). Its activists self-consciously adopted the language, demeanor, and even casual dress style and bearing of kibbutz members, and demanded the same recognition that in the past had been accorded the vanguard of Zionism in the colonial struggle to inherit the land. They grafted their own messianic religious discourse onto the old discourse of republican virtue, and claimed the mantle of the moral community attending to the common good by settling the Land of Israel (Aran 1991:302; Shafir and Peled 2002:167–72; D. Schwartz 2003:127; Barzel 2017:360–2, 374; S. Fischer 2013:359–60).

Aiming to replace the LZM as the core hegemonic group, GE pointed out – correctly – that the Labor movement was substituting for its own tradition of ethno-republican citizenship a new, liberal orientation. In this comparison the liberal discourse, with its emphasis on individual subjectivity and individual rights, was denigrated as hedonistic. In one of its early publications, GE ridiculed the "phenomena of decadence and retreat, indifference and ignorance ... pursuit of easy and comfortable life, luxuries, and an atmosphere which brings in its wake unwillingness for self-realization, aversion to physical labor, wild strikes and acts of corruption" (D. Rubinstein 1982:129). In 1996, Rav Elisha Aviner, a rabbi in a West Bank settlement *yeshiva* close to GE, published a textbook on "Jewish democracy" where he castigated liberalism, which he referred to as "democratic culture,"

> as a system of ultimate values that is designed to *replace* Judaism as a central component of Israeli identity. These values include an extreme individualism that talks exclusively in the language of "rights" and not of duties, and endorses atomizing economic competition and "self-realization." Secondly, they include an extreme universalism, or cosmopolitanism ... [and do] not recognize the essential importance of national groupings, nor of national history or culture.
>
> (S. Fischer 2014:137, emphasis in the original)

Chanan Porat rudely told the initiators of *Siach Lochamim* (see Chapter 4): "you finished your role, just don't interfere with our efforts to continue it" (cited in Barzel 2017:420). In short, to contend for cultural hegemony Religious Zionism adopted as its own the great legacy of colonization and reasserted, even as it reinterpreted it in a religious vein, the LZM's own ethno-republicanism as being against its endeavor to liberalize Israeli society in the 1990s (Shafir and Peled 2000; 2002).

As heir to the Zionist settlement project, GE certainly succeeded in forming an historic bloc that incorporated non-religious groups and individuals as well. The Movement for Greater Israel, established in 1967 by "well-known writers, intellectuals, poets, generals, kibbutz leaders, and other personalities prominent in the pre-1948 Zionist struggle" (Lustick 1988:43), and the *Ein-Vered* circle, established in 1976 on the initiative of Rav Z. Y. Kook, that included members of kibbutzim and moshavim, were both rooted in the Labor movement (M. Inbari 2008:45; S. Fischer 2013:369–70; Goodman and Yonah 2015:209; Barzel 2017:339–40, 416–21; Sagi and Schwartz 2017:96).

Efraim Ben-Chaim, a kibbutz member and Secretary General of a short-lived ultra-nationalist political party formed by GE in 1979, *Techiya* (Revival), saw the value of the *Ein-Vered* circle precisely in the symbolic act of conferring on GE the mantle of the old pioneering movement. The new movement replaced the old and, in the process, he argued, "synthesized" Rav Kook's theology "with the best values of the Second Aliyah" (Raanan 1980:213, 218–19).

These Labor veterans supported GE precisely because it followed the traditional course of settlement, which carried with it an inherent aura of legitimacy, in a society where pioneering had been a core element of nationalism and a major source of prestige and influence. Even Prime Minister Yitzhak Rabin who (in his first term as Prime Minister) ordered the dismantling of several early GE settlements, found it useful to express his admiration for their "pioneering zeal" (Sachar 1987:17). Moreover, without the help of key Labor leaders – Yigal Allon, Rabin, Yisrael Galili and Shimon Peres – the early settlements of Gush Etzion, Kiryat Arba (Hebron), Ofra, and Kedumim would not have been established (A. Rubinstein 1980:126; Zertal and Eldar 2007:32–6, 53; Hornstein and Goldstein 2017:50–2).

While GE claimed the mantle of pioneering, its settlements did not follow the LZM's collective agricultural model based on manual labor, such as the kibbutz and moshav, but replaced it with *yishuv kehilati* (community settlement), a bedroom community. The bare act of settlement in the occupied Palestinian territories now became co-terminous with pioneering, preempting its social attributes and discarding its socialist justification. Colonialism pure and simple became the civic virtue of this new vanguard of nationalism, now justified through religiously accented terms of republican virtue.

Likud's electoral victory in 1977 consolidated the historic bloc that sustained Religious Zionism's claim for hegemony over Jewish Israeli society and the world-wide Zionist movement. In spite of some tactical disputes, most importantly over Israel's withdrawal from the Sinai as part of the peace agreement with Egypt in 1979–1982 and the disengagement from Gaza in 2005, the two parties shared the strategic goal of maintaining the occupied territories under

Israeli sovereignty (Aran 1991:280; M. Inbari 2007; 2012; Goodman and Yonah 2015:209). The justification for that policy was no longer just the value of those territories as security assets, but, more importantly, the messianic nationalist-religious worldview espoused by Rav Z. Y. Kook and GE. Not surprisingly, the WZO recognized *yishuv kehilati* as a "pioneering settlement" in 1977, arguing that it may be

> a substitute for kibbutz and moshav, more suitable for the generation of Zionist realization, better prepared for coping with the limitations and possibilities of the mountain region and for integrating into the Israeli economy of the 1980s and 90s.
>
> (Cited in Barzel 2017:309)

This recognition made *yishuv kehilati* eligible for financial support from the world-wide Zionist movement (Benvenisti 1984:52–3; Shafir and Peled 2002:172–82; Barzel 2017:308–10).

Socio-economic orientation

The newly established ex-urban *yishuv kehilati* conformed not only to the Religious Zionist worldview but also to the emerging middle-class Israeli lifestyle, which valued "a detached home, fresh air, quiet streets" (Barzel 2017:308). Moreover, the compatibility between Religious Zionism and the newly emerging middle-class lifestyle was not limited to GE and to this new type of settlement. As mentioned already, through most of the years of LZM hegemony the leading body within Religious Zionism was *Ha-Poel Ha-Mizrachi*, a labor-oriented political and social movement which was formed out of the *Mizrachi* in 1922 and had its own kibbutz movement. In 1956 *Ha-Poel Ha-Mizrachi* reunited with *Mizrachi* to form the National Religious Party (NRP). In 1954 Chaim Druckman, then a member of *Bnei Akiva*'s board of directors and later on a rabbi and leader of GE and a Member of Knesset wrote:

> For *Ha-Poel Ha-Mizrachi* a Torah state does not mean only a state where everyone observes the Sabbath, but also a state where everyone lives by the product of their own hands, without exploiting others … The argument that "there are others who would worry about socialism, we worry about religious matters," is very superficial and very far from the thought of *Torah Va'avoda* [Torah and Labor, the title of *Ha-Poel Ha-Mizrachi*'s ideology]. For us there are no "religious matters." Our holy Torah encompasses our whole life and all our matters and socialist approach stem from it.
>
> (Cited in Hominer 2016–2017:1)

The constitution of the newly founded NRP indeed stated, in part, that the role of the party was "to stand by the working and laboring man, regardless of [inter-Jewish] ethnic origin; to defend his rightful interests and to fight for social legislation that would guarantee him decent living conditions" (cited in Hominer 2016–2017:1).

However, as "the natural tendency of Religious Zionism is to emulate trends in the Israeli mainstream with a slight delay and with ideological enthusiasm surpassing that of their original carriers" (Hominer 2016–2017:4), with the liberalization of the economy and society that began in 1985 the Religious Zionist elite, now under the spell of GE, took a leading part in promoting the ideology of neo-liberal economics, seeking to ground it in Jewish religion. The main civil society organization promoting neo-liberalism "in the spirit of Judaism" is the Tikvah Fund, founded by the late neo-conservative American investment fund owner Zalman Bernstein, who also established the Avi Chai Foundation (see Chapter 4).

The Tikvah Fund describes itself on its website as "politically Zionist, economically free-market oriented, culturally traditional, and theologically open-minded."[13] All of its programs in Israel are headed by Religious Zionists. These Religious Zionist promoters of neo-liberalism claim that Judaism supports conservative economics in that it defends personal freedom and encourages personal and communal responsibility, rather than coercion by the state. Even the religious limitations imposed on economic activity, such as the prohibition of charging interest on loans or the obligation to let the land lie fallow every seventh year, are to be enforced by the individual's own conscience rather than by the state (Hominer 2016–2017:3–4).

Regardless of the theological validity or otherwise of these claims, in 2013 leadership of the Jewish Home, successor party to the NRP, was captured by Naftali Bennett, a staunch neo-liberal hi-tech entrepreneur. The constitution of the remade party stated, in part, "the Party sees a free economy together with social sensitivity, and the strengthening of mutual responsibility, as principles which would provide all citizens of the state with a safety net for decent life" (cited in Hominer 2016–2017:2). Be that as it may, in its quest for cultural hegemony Religious Zionism clearly does not mean to challenge the neo-liberal socio-economic philosophy or institutional arrangements that have dominated Israeli society since the mid-1980s.

Summary

Writing in 1989, Gideon Aran already argued that GE "consistently, although indirectly, strives to impose religion on secular sectors, using power to dominate state and society and make them abide by the movement's particular norms" (Aran 1991:296). In 2014, Chaim Retig, a rabbi and important member of the Jewish Home party, who is Chairman of *Zehut* (Identity), an umbrella organization uniting forty-five state-funded non-governmental organizations (NGOs) that engage in teaching "Jewish identity" in *secular* state schools (see Chapter 5), stated:

> For many years we felt like second class. For many years we wanted to be on the front line with the general public in leading the country, but we never thought or dared imagine that there could be a religious Chief of [the IDF]

General Staff or a Prime Minister of our own. We always attached ourselves to others. But we need something else. We need to advance a stage and take a hold of the wheel and sail the ship of state in the right direction ... towards the great horizon of building the Kingdom of Israel in the Land of Israel ... The public has a duty to build the [Third] Temple ...

(Cited in Molad 2017:39, see also 42)

Twenty-seven years after Aran's observation, and taking GE as representing Religious Zionism as a whole, which it has long dominated, it would seem that the movement has made great progress toward achieving its goal.

On the face of it, the rise of Religious Zionism to the position of potential contender for hegemonic status in the society may seem surprising, given the secondary role it played in the Zionist movement and in the State of Israel prior to 1967. But a closer observation of the historical trajectory of Zionism reveals the underlying factors that helped Religious Zionism achieve the position that it now holds. With all its efforts to present itself as a "revolution" against traditional Jewish life in the Diaspora, including its religiosity, Zionism could never really divorce itself from Judaism, for two obvious reasons: the only cultural marker shared by all members of the Jewish nation that Zionism claimed to represent was Jewish religion, and the connection between that nation and its "homeland" was a religious connection. These realities secured for Judaism and the Orthodox political parties that represent it a privileged status in the Zionist movement and in the State of Israel far beyond the weight of Orthodox religious Jews in the relevant populations.

The educational autonomy granted the Religious Zionist movement (as well as the *Charedim*) in the *yishuv* and in Israel enabled it to nurture in its young generation its own conception of the "new Jew," in contradiction with the mainstream Zionist conception. According to Dov Schwartz, whereas the mainstream Zionist "new Jew" was meant to replace the traditional Orthodox Jew of the Diaspora, the national-religious "new Jew" was seen as its extension and completion. This "new Jew" (unlike the *Charedi* "old Jew") would combine modernity with religious Orthodoxy, would be enterprising, politically involved in order to attain political leadership, ready to do physical labor and military service, and in general ready to share in the burden of realizing the Zionist project. The idea of this "new Jew" drew its religious legitimacy from the belief that the current era is the era of messianic redemption (D. Schwartz 2009:163–4).

When the hegemony of the Labor Zionist Movement was eroded due to the reasons elaborated in Chapter 2, the "new Jews" produced by the national-religious educational system were ready and eager to fill the vacuum. Beginning in 1967 they have been playing a leading role in settling the occupied Palestinian territories and in subverting any and all attempts to make peace through the two-state solution. Although, electorally, the representation of Religious Zionist political parties has never exceeded 10 percent of Knesset membership, their occupation of key government ministries, such as Interior and Education, and currently the Ministry of Justice as well, has enabled them to wield great influence over the shaping of Israel's social and political life. As will be related in the following chapters, Religious Zionists have also made significant inroads into the military, the media, and the arts, which are all areas of great importance for achieving cultural hegemony.

Notes

1 The 2009 Guttman Center survey is an outlier in this sense, identifying 15 percent of the Jewish population as national-religious ("Orthodox") (Guttman Center 2012:30).
2 For a somewhat different interpretation of the data see Zelba n.d. [2016].
3 For the Religious Zionist conception of the "new Jew" see D. Schwartz 2009.
4 Despite the post-1967 developments to be related below, these feelings toward the secular and the *charedim* were still evident in films made by graduating students of the Religious Zionist film school *Ma'aleh* between 1994 and 2007 (see Chapter 9) (Recanati 2010:236–7).
5 The British Mandatory government allowed Jews in Palestine to exclude themselves from membership in the *yishuv*. This was done with the agreement of the Zionist authorities, in order to accommodate the non-Zionist Orthodox Jews (M. Friedman 1988:195–6).
6 The letter is oftentimes referred to as the "Status Quo Agreement" (e.g., Kolatt 1998:295–8; Hirschl 2010:139; An. Shapira 2014:145; Jobani and Perez 2017:36–8). However, it was not a two-sided agreement, but rather a strictly one-sided set of commitments undertaken by the Jewish Agency.
7 Although enfranchising women was precisely such a condition.
8 The conventional way of describing Israeli family law is to say that the option of civil marriage in not available in Israel. A more accurate description, however, would be that there is a legal identity between religious and civil marriage, so that neither one of them is available without the other (Shifman 1995).
9 A *mamzer* is someone born to a married woman by another man. In 2001 it was reported that there were 115 "definite *mamzerim*" in Israel (Triger 2005:224).
10 An important reason for the opposition of the Orthodox establishment to the recognition of the non-Orthodox streams of Judaism is the fact that the latter conduct egalitarian wedding ceremonies (Raday 1996:226–7).
11 At the time of writing a legislative move is on the way to expand the jurisdiction of rabbinical courts to civil matters, if both sides to the dispute agree to adjudication there. If realized, this would turn the rabbinical courts, which rule in accordance with *Halacha*, into arbitration courts in civil cases, in addition to their role in the performance of marriage and divorce of Jews (Kashti 2017).
12 Available at: www.irac.org.il/IssuePage.aspx?id=13#.VFtH2fmsWqA (accessed November 6, 2014).
13 Available at: https://tikvahfund.org/about/ (accessed December 26, 2017).

References

Abramov, Zalman S. (1976) *Perpetual Dilemma: Jewish Religion in the Jewish State*, Rutherford, NJ: Fairleigh Dickinson University Press.
Almog, S. (1998) "The Role of Religious Values in the Second Aliyah," in Almog, S., Reinharz, J., and Shapira An. (eds.), *Zionism and Religion*, Hanover, NH: University Press of New England.
Anderson, P. (1976) "The Antinomies of Antonio Gramsci," *New Left Review*, 100: 5–78.

Aran, G. (1986) "From Religious Zionism to Zionist Religion: The Roots of Gush Emunim," *Studies in Contemporary Jewry*, 2: 116–43.

Aran, G. (1991) "Jewish Zionist Fundamentalism: The Bloc of the Faithful in Israel (Gush Emunim)," in Marty, M. E. and Appleby, R. S. (eds.), *Fundamentalism Observed*, Chicago, IL: The University of Chicago Press, pp. 265–344.

Aran, G. (2013) *Kookism: The Roots of Gush Emunim, Settlers' Culture, Zionist Theology, Messianism in Our Time*, Jerusalem: Carmel (in Hebrew).

Atkes, E. (2016) "Contours of the Image of Religious Zionism," in Atkes, E., Assaf, D., and Kaplan, J. (eds.), *Milestones: Essays and Studies in the History of the People of Israel*, Jerusalem: Zalman Shazar Center: 363–77 (in Hebrew).

Avruch, K. A. (1979) "Gush Emunim: Politics, Religion, and Ideology in Israel," *Political Psychology*, 1: 47–57.

Azrieli, Y. (1990) *The Knitted Kipot Generation: The Political Revolution of the Young in the NRP*, n.p: Avivim (in Hebrew).

Barak-Erez, D. (2009) "Law and Religion under the Status Quo Model: Between Past Compromises and Constant Change," *Cardozo Law Review*, 30: 2495–507.

Barzel, N. (2017) *"Redemption Now": The Beliefs and Activities of the Jewish Settlers in the West Bank and Israeli Society*, Bnei Brak: Hakibbutz Hameuchad (in Hebrew).

Ben-Porat, G. (2013) *Between State and Synagogue: The Secularization of Contemporary Israel*, Cambridge: Cambridge University Press.

Benvenisti, M. (1984) *The West Bank Data Project: A Survey of Israel's Policies*, Washington, DC: American Enterprise Institute.

CA 630/70 (Ruling of the Israeli Supreme Court). George Tamarin vs. State of Israel (in Hebrew).

CA 8573/08 (Ruling of the Israeli Supreme Court). Uzi Ornan and Others vs. Ministry of the Interior and Others http://versa.cardozo.yu.edu/sites/default/files/upload/opinions/Ornan%20v.%20Ministry%20of%20the%20Interior.pdf (in Hebrew; accessed October 16, 2017).

CBS (2011) "Selected Data from the Israel Statistical Annual No. 62, 2011," www.cbs.gov.il/reader/newhodaot/hodaa_template.html?hodaa=201111240 (in Hebrew; accessed November 7, 2014).

CBS (2013a) *Israel Statistical Abstract 2013*, Jerusalem: Central Bureau of Statistics (in Hebrew).

CBS (2013b) *The Face of Israeli Society: Israel Where To?* Jerusalem: Central Bureau of Statistics, www.cbs.gov.il/publications13/rep_06/pdf/4box1_h.pdf (in Hebrew; accessed August 10, 2017).

CBS (2013c) *Israel in Numbers, 2013*, Jerusalem: Central Bureau of Statistics (in Hebrew).

Conforti, I. (2009) "The New Jew in Zionist Thought: Nationalism, Ideology and Historiography," *Israel*, 16: 63–96 (in Hebrew).

Don-Yehiya, E. (1979) "Stability and Change in a 'Camp-Party': The NRP and the Youth Revolution," *Medina, Mimshal Viahasim Beuleumyim*, 14: 26–39 (in Hebrew).

Don-Yehiya, E. (1997) *The Politics of Accommodation: Settling Conflicts of State and Religion in Israel*, Jerusalem: The Floersheimer Institute for Policy Studies (in Hebrew).

Don-Yehiya, E. (2014) "Messianism and Politics: The Ideological Transformation of Religious Zionism," *Israel Studies*, 19: 239–63.

Eilam, Y. (2000a) *The End of Judaism – The Religio-Nation and the State*, Tel Aviv: Yediot Aharonot (in Hebrew).

Eilam, Y. (2000b) *Judaism as Status-Quo: The 1958 Who Is A Jew Controversy as Illuminating Religious-Secular Relations in Israel*, Tel Aviv: Am Oved (in Hebrew).

Etner-Levkovitch, G. (1997) "The Politics of Marriage: Legitimation Crises and the Rabbinate in Israel," MA thesis, Department of Political Science, Tel Aviv University (in Hebrew).

Faitelson, J. (2011) *Demographic Trends and their Implications for the Educational System in Israel*, Jerusalem: The Institute for Zionist Strategy (in Hebrew).

Fischer, S. (2013) "Change or Continuity? Torah Regime, Citizenship and the Origins of Radical Religious Zionism," in Shavit, Z., Sasson-Levy, O., and Ben-Porat, G. (eds.), *Points of Reference: Changing Identities and Social Positioning in Israel*, Jerusalem: Van Leer Jerusalem Institute, pp. 347–82 (in Hebrew).

Fischer, S. (2014) "The Crises of Liberal Citizenship: Religion and Education in Israel," in Seligman, A. (ed.), *Religious Education and the Challenge of Pluralism*, Oxford: Oxford University Press, pp. 119–49.

Friedman, M. (1988) *Society and Religion: The Non-Zionist Orthodox in Eretz-Israel – 1918–1936*, 2nd edn., Jerusalem: Ben-Zvi Institute (in Hebrew).

Friedman, T. L. (1997) "Exodus," *New York Times*, April 21.

Gluska, Ami (2007) *The Israeli Military and the Origins of the 1967 War: Government, Armed Forces and Defense Policy 1963–1967*, New York: Routledge.

Goodman, J. and Yonah, Y. (2015) "The Gordian Knot Between Religiosity and Secularity in Israel: Inclusion, Exclusion and Change," in Fischer, Y. (ed.), *Secularization and Secularity: Interdisciplinary Studies*, Jerusalem: Van Leer Jerusalem Institute, pp. 197–221 (in Hebrew).

Gorenberg, G. (2006) *The Accidental Empire: Israel and the Birth of the Settlements, 1967–1977*, New York: Times Books.

Greenblum, D. (2016) *From the Bravery of the Spirit to the Sanctification of Power: Power and Bravery in Religious Zionism 1948–1967*, Ra'anana: Open University Press (in Hebrew).

Greilsammer, I. (2014) "Ben-Gurion's Status Quo and Moving the Frontlines Between Hilonim (Secularists) and Datiim (Religious)," in Berlinerblau, J., Fainberg, S., and Nou, A. (eds.), *Secularism on the Edge: Rethinking Church–State Relations in the United States, France, and Israel*, Basingstoke: Palgrave Macmillan, pp. 135–44.

Guttman Center (2012) *A Portrait of Israeli Jews: Beliefs, Observance, and Values of Israeli Jews, 2009*, Jerusalem: Israel Democracy Institute and Avi Chai–Israel.

Guttwein, D. (2009) "Critique of 'Negation of the Diaspora' and the Privatization of Israeli Consciousness," in Ben-Rafael, E., Bareli, A. Chazan, M., and Schiff, O. (eds.), *The Jews in the Present Time: Ingathering and Dispersion – For Yoseph Gorny*, Jerusalem: Yad Ben-Zvi, pp. 201–19 (in Hebrew).

Ha-Cohen, D. (2005) "'The Historic Partnership': Between Ideology and Politics," in Don-Yehiya, E. (ed.), *Between Tradition and Innovation*, Ramat Gan: Bar-Ilan University Press, pp. 259–95 (in Hebrew).

Halperin-Kaddari, R. (2000) "Women, Religion and Multiculturalism in Israel," *UCLA Journal of International Law and Foreign Affairs*, 5: 339–66.

HCJ 390/79 (Ruling of the Israeli High Court of Justice). *Muhammad Mustafa Duweikat and Other vs. Government of Israel and Others*.

Hellinger, M. (2008) "Political Theology in the Thought of 'Merkaz HaRav' Yeshiva and its Profound Influence on Israeli Politics and Society since 1967," *Totalitarian Movements and Political Religions*, 9: 533–50.

Hemdat (1996) *Free Choice in Marriage*, Jerusalem: Hemdat (Council for Freedom of Science, Religion and Culture in Israel) (in Hebrew).

Hermann, T., Be'eri, G., Heller, E., Cohen, C., Lebel, Y., Mozes, H., and Neuman, K. (2014) *The National-Religious Sector in Israel 2014*, Jerusalem: Israel Democracy Institute (in Hebrew).

Hirschl, R. (2010) *Constitutional Theocracy*, Cambridge, MA: Harvard University Press.

Hoffman, Ch (1989) *The Smoke Screen: Israel, Philanthropy and American Jews*, Silver Spring, MD: Eshel Books.

Hominer, A. (2016–2017) "Religious Zionism: From Equality and Social Justice to Ultra-Capitalism," *Deot*, 77: 1–4.

Hornstein, E. and Goldstein, Y. (2017) "Elon Moreh as a Symbol," *Israel Affairs*, 23 (1): 40–65.

Inbari, M. (2007) "Fundamentalism in Crisis – The Response of the Gush Emunim Rabbinical Authorities to the Theological Dilemmas Raised by Israel's Disengagement Plan," *Journal of Church and State*, 49: 697–717.

Inbari, M. (2008) "Rav Zvi Yehudah Kook's Conception of Zionism and the Roots of 'Gush Emunim'," *Iyunim Betkumat Yisrael*, 18: 29–53 (in Hebrew).

Inbari, M. (2012) *Messianic Religious Zionism Confronts Israeli Territorial Compromises*, Cambridge: Cambridge University Press.

Jamal, A. (2009) "Democratizing State-Religion Relations: A Comparative Study of Turkey, Egypt and Israel," *Democratization*, 16: 1143–61.

Jobani, Y. and Perez, N. (2017) *Women of the Wall Navigating Religion in Sacred Sites*, Oxford: Oxford University Press.

Kashti, O. (2017) "A Competing Court System: The State will Support Arbitration Courts that Rule in Accordance with *Halacha*," *Haaretz*, December 29.

Knesset (2015) *The Educational System in Israel – Selected Issues under the Purview of the Knesset Education, Culture and Sports Committee*, Jerusalem: The Knesset Research and Information Center (in Hebrew).

Kolatt, I. (1998) "Religion, Society and State in the Period of the National Home," in Almog, S., Reinharz, J., and Shapira, An. (eds.), *Zionism and Religion*, Hanover, NH: University Press of New England, pp. 273–301.

Landau, David (1996) *Who is a Jew? A Case Study of American Jewish Influence on Israeli Policy*, Jerusalem: The American Jewish Committee and Ramat Gan: Bar-Ilan University.

Laron, G. (2017) *The Six-Day War: The Breaking of the Middle East*, New Haven, CT: Yale University Press.

Levy, G. (2011) "Secularism, Religion and the Status Quo," in Barbalet, J., Possamai, A., and Turner, B. S. (eds.), *Religion and the State: A Comparative Sociology*, London: Anthem Press, pp. 93–119.

Liebman, C. S. (1993) "Attitudes Towards Democracy Among Israeli Religious Leaders," in Kaufman, E., Abed, S. B., and Rothstein, R. L. (eds.), *Democracy, Peace, and the Israeli-Palestinian Conflict*, Boulder, CO: Lynne Rienner, pp. 135–61.

Liebman, C. S. and Don-Yehiya, E. (1983) *Civil Religion in Israel: Traditional Judaism and Political Culture in the Jewish State*, Berkeley, CA: University of California Press.

Liebman, C. S. and Don-Yehiya, E. (1984) *Religion and Politics in Israel*, Bloomington, IN: Indiana University Press.

Lustick, I. (1988) *For the Land and the Lord: Jewish Fundamentalism in Israel*, New York: Council on Foreign Relations.

Lustick, I. (1999) "Israel as a Non-Arab State: The Political Implications of Mass Immigration of Non-Jews," *Middle East Journal*, 53: 417–33.

Luz, E. (1999) *Wrestling in River Yabok: Power, Morality, and Jewish Identity*, Jerusalem: Magnes (in Hebrew). Available in English as *Wrestling with an Angel: Power, Morality, and Jewish Identity*, trans. Swirsky, M., New Haven, CT: Yale University Press, 2003.

Maoz, Z. (2006) *Defending the Holy Land: A Critical Analysis of Israel's Security and Foreign Policy*, Ann Arbor, MI: University of Michigan Press.

Marmorstein, E. (1969) *Heaven at Bay: The Jewish Kulturkampf in the Holy Land*, Oxford: Oxford University Press.

Michael, B. (1984) "How and Why I Became a Settler?" *Haaretz Weekend Magazine*, March 2 (in Hebrew).

Molad (2017) *Propagating: How the Religious Right Took Control of Values Education in the [Secular] State System*, Jerusalem: Molad – The Center for Democratic Renewal (in Hebrew).

Naor, A. (1999) "The Security Argument in the Territorial Debate in Israel: Rhetoric and Policy," *Israel Studies*, 4: 150–77.

Neumann, B. (2011) *Land and Desire in Early Zionism*, trans. Watzman, H., Waltham, MA: Brandeis University Press.

Oren, M. (2002) *June 1967 and the Making of the Modern Middle East*, Oxford: Oxford University Press.

Oren, M. (2005) "The Revelations of 1967: New Research on the Six Day War and Its Lessons for the Contemporary Middle East," *Israel Studies*, 10 (2): 1–14.

Peleg, Y. (2016) *Directed by God: Jewishness in Contemporary Israeli Film and Television*, Austin, TX: University of Texas Press.

Pew (2016) *Israel's Religiously Divided Society*, Washington, DC: Pew Research Center.

Porat, C. (1975) "For They Shall See, Eye to Eye, the Lord Returning to Zion," *Ptachim*, 32: 3–12 (in Hebrew).

Presner, T. S. (2007) *Muscular Judaism: The Jewish Body and the Politics of Regeneration*, Abingdon: Routledge.

Raanan, T. (1980) *Gush Emunim*, Tel Aviv: Sifriat Poalim (in Hebrew).

Raday, F. (1996) "Religion, Multiculturalism and Equality: The Israeli Case," *Israel Yearbook on Human Rights*, 25: 193–241.

Raz-Krakotzkin, A. (1993/1994) "Exile within Sovereignty: Toward a Critique of the 'Negation of Exile' in Israeli Culture," *Theory and Criticism*, 4: 23–55, 5: 113–32 (in Hebrew).

Raz-Krakotzkin, A. (2015) "Secularization and the Christian Ambivalence towards Judaism," in Fischer, Y. (ed.), *Secularization and Secularism: Interdisciplinary Perspectives*, Jerusalem and Tel Aviv: Van Leer Jerusalem Institute and Hakibbutz Hameuchad, pp. 108–36 (in Hebrew).

Recanati, I. S. (2010) "Religious Zionism and the Screen Arts: 'Ma'aleh' School, Its Students and Their Films as a Test Case," PhD dissertation, Department of Contemporary Jewry, Bar-Ilan University (in Hebrew).

Rodick, Y. B. (1989) *Land of Redemption: Ideological Roots of Religious Zionism, Gush Emunim and the Jewish Underground and their Relations with the Secular World in the State of Israel*, Jerusalem: The Institute for Research in Rav Kook's Thought (in Hebrew).

Rubin, A. (2014) "Bifurcated Loyalty and Religious Actors' Behaviour in Democratic Politics: The Case of Post-1967 Religious Zionism in Israel," *Religion, State and Society*, 42: 46–65.

Rubinstein, A. (1980) *From Herzl to Gush Emunim and Back*, Jerusalem: Schocken (in Hebrew).

Rubinstein, D. (1982) *On the Lord's Side: Gush Emunim*, Tel Aviv: Hakibbutz Hameuchad (in Hebrew).

Sachar, H. M. (1987) *A History of Israel: Vol. 2: From the Aftermath of the Yom Kippur War*, New York: Oxford University Press.

Sagi, A. (2011) "Requiem to Religious Zionism – Testimony," in Sagi, A. and Stern, Y. Z., *Barefooted Homeland: Israeli Reflections*, Tel Aviv: Am Oved, pp. 137–44.

Sagi, A. and Schwartz, D. (2017) *From Realism to Messianism: Religious Zionism and the Six-Day War*, Jerusalem: Carmel (in Hebrew).

Sandler, S. (1981) "The National Religious Party: Towards a New Role in Israel's Political System," in Lehman-Wilzig, S. N. and Susser, B. (eds.), *Public Life in Israel and the Diaspora*, Jerusalem: Bar-Ilan University Press.

Sapir, G. and Statman, D. (2009) "Religious Marriage in a Liberal State," *Cardozo Law Review*, 30: 2855–80.

Schiff, G. (1977) *Tradition and Politics: The Religious Parties of Israel*, Detroit, MI: Wayne State University Press.

Schwartz, D. (2003) *Religious Zionism: History and Chapters of Ideology*, Tel Aviv: Ministry of Defense (in Hebrew).

Schwartz, D. (2009) "Religious Zionism and the Idea of the New Man," *Israel*, 16: 143–64 (in Hebrew).

Segev, T. (2005) *1967: Israel, the War, and the Year that Transformed the Middle East*, New York: Metropolitan Books.

Shafir, G. and Peled, Y. (2002) *Being Israeli: The Dynamics of Multiple Citizenship*, Cambridge: Cambridge University Press.

Shakdiel, L. (2002) "Women of the Wall: Radical Feminism as an Opportunity for a New Discourse in Israel," *Journal of Israeli History*, 21: 126–63.

Shapira, An (1992) *Land and Power: The Zionist Resort to Force, 1881–1948*, Oxford: Oxford University Press.

Shapira, An (1997) "The Origins of the Myth of the 'New Jew': The Zionist Variety," *The Fate of European Jewry, 1939–1945 – Continuity or Contingency? Studies in Contemporary Judaism*, 31: 253–68.

Shapira, An (1998) "Religious Motifs of the Labor Movement," in Almog, S., Reinharz, J., and Shapira, An. (eds.), *Zionism and Religion*, Hanover, NH: University Press of New England.

Shapira, J. (2014) "On National Identity," *Judicial Ruling Flashes*, 21: 5–21, Rishon Le-Zion: College of Administration School of Law, The Emile Zola Chair for Human Rights (in Hebrew).

Shapira, R. (1975) "Jewish Identification of Israeli Students: What Lies Ahead," *Jewish Social Studies* 37: 251–66.

Shapiro, Y. (1991) *The Road to Power: Herut Party in Israel*, Albany, NY: SUNY Press.

Sharot, S. (2007) "Judaism in Israel: Public Religion, Neo-Traditionalism, Messianism, and Ethno-Religious Conflict," in Beckford, J. A. and Demerath, N. J. III (eds.), *The SAGE Handbook of the Sociology of Religion*, Los Angeles, CA: Sage Publications, pp. 670–96.

Schwartz, D. (2009) "Religious Zionism and the Idea of the New Man," *Israel*, 16: 143–64 (in Hebrew).

Shafir, G. and Peled, Y. (2000) *The New Israel: Peacemaking and Liberalization*, Boulder, CO: Westview Press.

Sheleg, Y. (2010) *From Old Hebrew to New Jew: The Jewish Renaissance in Israeli Society*, Jerusalem: Israel Democracy Institute (in Hebrew).

Shifman, P. (1995) *Civil Marriage in Israel: The Case for Reform*, Jerusalem: The Jerusalem Institute for Israel Studies (Research Series No. 62) (in Hebrew).

Tchernichovsky, S. (1899) "Before the Statue of Apollo," *Ben-Yehuda Project* http://benyehuda.org/tchernichowsky/lenoxax_pesel_apollo.html (in Hebrew; accessed May 25, 2017).

Triger, Z. (2005) "There is a State for Love: Marriage and Divorce between Jews in the State of Israel," in Ben-Naftali, O. and Nave, H. (eds.), *Trials of Love*, Tel Aviv: Tel Aviv University, The Buchman Faculty of Law (in Hebrew).

Ufaz, G. (1998) "The Shdemot Circle Members in Search of Jewish Sources," *Israel Affairs*, 4: 132–45.

Varhaftig, Z. (1988) *Constitution for Israel – Religion and State*, Jerusalem: Messilot (in Hebrew).

Zelba, M. (n.d. [2016]) *Demography of Religiosity: Secularization Processes in the Religious and Traditional Public*, Jerusalem: Hotam–Judaism on the Agenda.

Zertal, I. and Eldar, A. (2007) *Lords of the Land: The War Over Israel's Settlements in the Occupied Territories, 1967–2007*, New York: Nation Books.

Zisenwine, D. (1998) "Jewish Education in the Jewish State," *Israel Affairs*, 4: 146–55.

Zucker, N. L. (1973) *The Coming Crisis in Israel: Private Faith and Public Policy*, Cambridge, MA: The MIT Press.

4   Return, renewal, and in-between

As Jewish-Israeli society progressively despairs of integrating in the region, and seeks to enclose itself between the walls of the "villa in the jungle"[1] it had built for itself, so it deepens its preoccupation with its distinct Jewish identity ... As the Jewish majority becomes less "Israeli" and more "Jewish," so the identity common to Jews and Arabs [in Israel] seems to weaken – that is, the common Israeli space weakens and the divisive elements are getting stronger ... [I]n the coming phases the focus on Jewish cultural identity could sharpen and intensify Jewish consciousness in the political sphere as well (in an anti-Arab direction).

(Sheleg 2010:167)

The legitimation crisis identified by Liebman and Don-Yehiya (1983) as originating in the era of the 1967–1973 wars gave rise to two seemingly contradictory but, we argue, essentially complementary movements: (1) a movement of "return" to Jewish religion by previously "secular" or traditionalist Jews, and (2) a movement of "Jewish cultural renewal" purporting to be a secular alternative or antidote to the former but, in reality, a major element in the constitution of the new civil religion and a vehicle for easing the tension between non-observant and religious Jews and a way for Israeli Jews who see themselves as secular to adopt a more religious outlook (cf. Tzaban 2007; Jobani 2008; Ben-Porat 2013:42–3). In between these two movements, *hadata* has taken various forms of blurring the distinction between religiosity and secularity in general, and in Israeli Judaism in particular (Yonah and Goodman 2002; Shenhav 2008; H. Lahav 2015; 2016). The overall effect of these phenomena has been a movement toward the establishment of the Jewish religious outlook as hegemonic in Israeli society.

The *teshuvah* movement

"Teshuvah" in Hebrew literally means both "a return" and "an answer," and in the religious context describes a process whereby an individual Jew becomes increasingly more observant of the strictures of Jewish religion. The people undergoing this process are referred to as *Ba'alei Teshuvah*, or *Chozrim*

Biteshuvah, which can be translated as either "converts" (Aviad 1983), "repentants" (Caplan 2001), or "penitents" (Sharabi 2012; 2014; Doron 2013).

While sporadic *teshuvah* by individual Jews, in Israel and abroad, has
always been present, as a significant social phenomenon the movement clearly
owes its origin to the 1967 and 1973 Arab-Israeli wars (Sheleg 2010:19). As
mentioned above, the three-week "waiting period," between the onset of the
Sinai crisis in May 1967 and the outbreak of war on June 5, were characterized in Israel by unfounded but widespread fear that the very existence of the
country was under threat. In view of this atmosphere of public panic, the
astounding victory achieved by the IDF was interpreted by many as a miracu-
lous delivery from mortal danger. Coupled with the conquest of the heartland
of Biblical *Eretz Yisrael* in the West Bank and East Jerusalem, which enabled
Israeli Jews, for the first time since 1948, to visit the sites considered most
sacred for Judaism, this naturally gave rise to heightened religious feelings
among many of them (Aviad 1983:133, 137–40; Maizlish 1984:73; Sagi and
Schwartz 2017: 164). More profoundly, as pointed out both by Liebman and
Don-Yehiya and by Aviad, among others, the wars gave rise to questions
about the justice of Zionism, about its promise of providing security to the
Jewish people, and about the sacrifices it demanded of Israelis; questions to
which the prevailing statist "civil religion" could not provide satisfactory
answers (Liebman and Don-Yehiya 1983:128–31; Aviad 1983:137–40). In the
words of sociologist Janet Aviad, who was the first to study the sociology of
teshuvah in Israel,

> ... the [1967] Six Day War, and the [1973] Yom Kippur War ... destroyed
> the sense that the future of Israel was guaranteed. Both demonstrated clearly
> that Israel's survival is threatened and that the struggle for that survival will
> continue to make great demands upon each individual and upon the col-
> lective. The questions arose among many tired of that struggle: Why? What
> for? Is it worthwhile?
>
> (Aviad 1983:10; cf. Ufaz 1986:282)

The dilemmas raised by the 1967 war for many young non-observant Israeli
Jews who had fought in it were brought into sharp relief in *Siach Lochamim,* a
book that recorded the (heavily censored, as it turned out)[2] soul-searching conversations of young non-observant kibbutz members immediately following the
war (Av. Shapira 1967). Moderated by the likes of Amos Oz, the famous Israeli
novelist who was a kibbutz member at the time, these conversations reflected in
a naïve and direct way the impact left by the war on the consciousness of the
younger generation of what was still considered at the time the elite of Israeli
society.[3]

The issues raised in the book are the most profound issues faced by a
colonial-settler society that, nevertheless, retains some commitment to universal
humanistic values. In the words of Nachman, one of the more articulate
participants:

It begins with the issue of Zionism in general. The existence of the Jewish people and its ability to come back to this land is connected to the eviction of those who were here. If you were not to evict anyone, you had to stay in the Diaspora, and there you would have been slaughtered. [But] ... this war [1967] is just ... because we never had any intention to destroy, or take over, or oppress others ... On the contrary, they had such intentions and we defended ourselves and this is why we were just ... We would like to see a world of valuing human life, of respect for the other, and toleration – and at the same time, towards the Arabs – aggressiveness ... We talk to them about a situation of equality, not of domination, and they don't want to accept that ... And this is the tragic thing here, this matter of Zionism. For them the penetration of our people into this area is seen as domination, while for us it is a matter of life. We say that we have something to give this Orient: culture, enlightenment. They say: Leave us alone, we are not interested in your culture. We have our own culture ... We don't want you here at all. This is tragic.

(Av. Shapira 1967:132, 139)

Still:

The big problem is educational. How – with all the justice of this war from our perspective – not to turn into militarists, not to devalue human life. And this is the contradiction, this is the paradox we have in this whole affair. Not to cheapen human life, and not to turn into conquerors, not to turn into expansionists at the expense of other peoples, and not to turn into haters of Arabs. And how not to ... [become] cynical and say "Justice – there is no such thing"; "the UN – nonsense" ...

(Av. Shapira 1967:134)[4]

The significance of the 1967 war for the *teshuvah* movement, and of *Siach Lochamim* as an expression of that significance, did not escape the notice of the promoters of *teshuvah*. Thus Rav Yoel Schwartz, who was teaching at a *yeshiva* for *ba'alei teshuvah* (see below), wrote in a book aimed at such penitents and published in 1979, that following

"the Six Day War," that period which was filled with light due to the many miracles seen in the great victories and the liberation of Jerusalem and the other territories of the Holy Land, the people began to think about the connection of the Jew to the Torah.

(Y. Schwartz 1979:13)

To illustrate, he cited Hagai, one of the participants in *Siach Lochamim*, who had said:

The Jewish nation exists thanks to [Jewish] religion, thanks to the religious faith. And it exists thanks to the religious people. And we are here thanks to the fact that these religious people saw in front of their eyes, in the Diaspora ... this thing of *Eretz Yisrael*. And not of Uganda and not of anywhere else, but of *Eretz Yisrael*.

(Y. Schwartz 1979:16, translated here from the original,
Av. Shapira 1967:124; see also Barzel 2017:152, 160–1)[5]

According to Schwartz, the Yom Kippur War provided an even greater impetus to the *teshuvah* process, for that traumatic war "exploded the many idols which ruled in the Jewish street, such as military strength and the worship of leaders. Secular society was undermined, and many doubts filled the hearts of Israelis" (Y. Schwartz 1979:13, cited in Aviad 1983:133–4; see also Maizlish 1984:172; Barzel 2017:412–15).

Schwartz emphasized the growing interest in Judaism among "public institutions," such as the IDF and kibbutzim, including kibbutzim of *Ha-Shomer Ha-Tzair*, the most left-wing and secular kibbutz movement (Y. Schwartz 1979:14; Aviad 1983:134). Indeed, Aviad has noted that in the late 1970s "[t]he journal of the kibbutzim, *Shdemot*, reflects in its many articles by young kibbutz members a new interest in Judaism and a driving pressure to work out a new relationship between Judaism and Zionism" (Aviad 1983:140; see also Maizlish 1984:171–2; Ufaz 1986; 1998; Azulay 2010:80–1; Cahaner and Leon 2013; Mor-Chaim and Greenberg 2013). Writing in *Shdemot* shortly after the 1967 war, the poet Eli Allon, a member of *Ha-Shomer Ha-Tzair* kibbutz, explained:

I hunger to probe the nature of the belief that, through the generations, Jews were willing to die for ... I am looking for a direct link to the world, to the truth, to God. I do not know if this has a particularly religious significance, and I cannot say what God is for me. This is something I cannot define or explain, and the ongoing search is part of its significance. I feel within myself the ability to live this ... My God may even be the reaction to everything [about] life, and thinking about Him may even lead to love for the earthly experience and small mortal creatures.

(Cited in Ufaz 1998:139)

Aviad has argued, correctly, we believe, that this growing interest in Judaism must be seen in light of the decline of socialist Zionism as the hegemonic ideology of Israeli society and the resurgence of Jewish religious elements that had always been there, hidden under the surface (Aviad 1983:137–8; Ufaz 1986; 1998; Barzel 2017:75–80, 108–16, 153–4).

In the words of Tsvi Raanan, a member of *Ha-Shomer Ha-Tzair* kibbutz and scholar of Jewish thought at Oranim College (see below), secular Zionism was inflicted with two debilitating shortcomings:

Over-optimism about the willingness of the majority of the Jewish people to make Aliyah to the Land of Israel, and the shallowness of its understanding of the problematic of the secular Jew, who needed not only a state and a well-ordered society, but also a new home of Jewish identity and integrated culture, Jewish and general, in the image of his own secularity.

(Raanan 1986:306–7)

With the post-1967 legitimation crisis, into the vacuum created by the latter shortcoming stepped the purveyors of religious legitimacy, of both the national-religious and the Ultra-Orthodox variety.

Shas and Mizrachi teshuvah

The *teshuvah* phenomenon is not limited to members of the veteran Ashkenazi elite represented, for our purposes, by members of kibbutzim.[6] A parallel process of even greater magnitude has been taking place among second-generation Mizrachim, children of the immigrants from the Moslem world who had come to Israel in the 1950s and 1960s. Unlike their Ashkenazi counterparts, many of whom came from a purportedly secular background, most Mizrachi penitents came from "traditionalist" homes, where religious strictures were observed selectively and where secular ideology (as well as ultra-Orthodoxy) had never taken root (Sharot 2007:681–2; Yadgar 2011).

According to the Central Bureau of Statistics, in 2009 11 percent of the *Charedim* had grown up in a traditionalist, meaning almost exclusively Mizrachi home, while only 8 percent grew up in a secular home. Of the "religious" (i.e., national-religious), 22 percent grew up in traditionalist homes and only 6 percent in secular ones (CBS 2010:4). In the IDI survey of the national-religious sector, a *majority* of Shas voters belonging to that sector, more than double the rate among voters of any other political party, indicated that they had come closer to religion in recent years (Hermann et al. 2014:106).

For these Mizrachi *ba'alei teshuvah*, another powerful incentive to embrace religion was added to the post-1967 legitimation crisis – the marginalization of their communities by the state (Aviad 1983:10; Goodman 2002:12; Shafir and Peled 2002:74–109; Sharabi 2010; 2012:278; 2015:229–30; cf. H. Lahav 2016:21). As noted by Shlomo Fischer and Zvi Beckerman, many Mizrachim were drawn to the ultra-Orthodox variety of *teshuvah* because the ultra-Orthodox critique and (at least formal) rejection of Zionism "is the most effective language available to [them] to express their rejection, disdain and alienation from the Zionist State of Israel, where they have experienced exclusion, discrimination, humiliation and lack of equal opportunity" (Fischer and Beckerman 2001:327; cf. Leon 2006).

Much of the Mizrachi *teshuvah* movement was inspired and facilitated by Shas, the Mizrachi ultra-Orthodox political party established as a national party in 1984. Shas, which seeks to replace secular Zionism with religious Judaism as the hegemonic ideology in Israeli society, and presents this as the remedy for both the socio-economic and the cultural grievances of its constituency, is the first specifically Mizrachi political party that succeeded in mobilizing large numbers of Mizrachi voters (Peled 1998; 2001a; 2001b; Leon 2006:99–100;

2016:29; cf. Lehmann and Siebzehner 2006:95–6). Its success stemmed from its ability to forge a credible political platform on the basis of politicized Jewish religiosity, an ideology that is seen by lower-class Mizrachim as integrative, rather than separatist, with respect to Jewish Israeli society. As Erik Cohen has argued, the Mizrachi claim against official Zionist ideology has always been that "mere Jewishness, rather than the internalization of any particular Zionist or 'Israeli' values, attitudes and patterns of behavior, [should be] sufficient for participation [in the center of Israeli society]" (E. Cohen 1983:121).

This assertion of the primacy of ethno-national identity over all other possible bases of solidarity is at the heart of Shas's ideology (and success). As a semi-peripheral group, located between the Ashkenazim on top and the Palestinians – both citizens and non-citizens – at the bottom, Mizrachim have been inclined to emphasize their religious affinity to the dominant Ashkenazi group, rather than their class and cultural affinity to the subordinate Palestinians, with whom they share many socio-economic and cultural attributes. This choice was consonant with Zionist ideology, which has always stressed the value of unity among Jews, and has militated against autonomous ethnic political organizations (Peled 1998; Leon 2016:94–101).

Unlike the Ashkenazi ultra-Orthodox, Shas, an open church and not a closed sect in Weberian terms (Fischer and Beckerman 2001; Leon 2007; 2011) does not demand of its penitents a complete transformation of their way of life:

> There are no secular persons amongst us [Mizrachim]. Even if some of our brothers have estranged themselves they are still believers. Shas does not conceive of the return to Judaism as isolation in secluded *yeshivas* while leaving behind community and family. It does not mean changing the dress code. This is the Ashkenazi return to Judaism. We would like people to keep on wearing blue jeans. For us to return to Judaism is to conduct a normal life and to maintain our traditions.
>
> ("It is the Time," *Shorashim*, 7 January 1992, p. 5, cited in Abutbul-Selinger 2016:11; see also Lehmann and Siebzehner 2006:87–8)

In this way

> a new form of haredi community [was created] with far more fluid boundaries, a community based on joint observance of the halakhah as a way of life. In such a community, the balance moves from the responsibility of the religiously observant public for what happens in the world of nonobservant individuals to the responsibility of observant individuals – be they rabbis or lay believers – for the nonobservant collectivity that nevertheless maintains some link with religious life.
>
> (Leon 2007:164)

Given its political project of mobilizing the Mizrachim, its character as an open church, and the traditionalist social milieu in which it operates, "[t']shuva is, and perhaps has to be, the central mission of Shas, an integral part of its institution-building project, and the recruiting ground for core activists and followers" (Lehmann and Siebzehner 2006:78, 80). And indeed, Shas cabinet ministers have funneled great sums of money from their ministries' budgets to organizations promoting *teshuvah* and to establishing educational institutions for Mizrachi *ba'alei teshuvah*, as well as to other Shas institutions.[7] The party has also promoted *ba'alei teshuvah* to senior political positions, including as cabinet ministers (Leon 2011:96–7).

Ideologically, an important motivation of *teshuvah* entrepreneurs, whether in Shas or elsewhere, is *zikui harabim*, a doctrine that stipulates that those who cause others to perform religiously virtuous deeds – observing the strictures of Jewish religion – will be remunerated handsomely in the afterlife (Leon 2007; 2016:56–9; Sharabi 2015:224). In the words of the late Rav Ovadia Yosef, spiritual leader of Shas:

> One who repairs only his own soul, attains only small merit, but one who repairs his own soul and many other souls with him attains double merit, as it is taught: "Whosoever enables the people to attain religious merit will not come to any sin, but whosoever leads the people astray will not be permitted to repent." One who teaches his friend's son Torah attains the merit of "sitting" in the yeshiva on high [that is, in the world-to come].
>
> (Cited in Leon 2007:164)

Under Rav Ovadia's guidance, *zikui harabim* was the ideological mainstay of Shas's national project of spreading religious knowledge and observance beyond the boundaries of Mizrachi ultra-Orthodoxy and into the Mizrachi community as a whole in order to "return the people to its legacy" (Leon 2016:60).

Institutionalization

As for Jewish Israeli society as a whole, it has been estimated that between 1967 and 1983 there were 8,200 *ba'alei teshuvah* in Israel. By 1997 their number had grown to 210,000, and in 2009 the Central Bureau of Statistics found that 5.4 percent of the Jewish population aged 20 and over, or 200,000 people, defined themselves as *chozrim biteshuvah*, while 790,000 people aged 20 and over, or over 20 percent of the Jewish population, reported that they were more religious than they used to be (CBS 2010:4; Yogev and El-Dor 1987:5; Sharabi 2014:443).

In a 1978 survey by the Israeli Institute of Applied Social Research (now the Guttman Center) 68 percent of (Jewish) respondents said that Israeli society needed a strengthening of religious values and 51 percent stated that *teshuvah* was the way to accomplish that. Accordingly, 46 percent opined that the *teshuvah* movement had a positive effect on Israeli society, while only 4 percent believed it had a negative effect. According to Janet Aviad, "so high a level of positive response is truly surprising" (Aviad 1983:141).

The organized nature of the post-1967 *teshuvah* movement was manifested by the establishment of *yeshivot* and other types of religious organizations designed specifically for *ba'alei Teshuvah*. The *yeshivot* were originally established by American rabbis of the Lithuanian (i.e., anti-Chassidic) stream of ultra-Orthodoxy, and were meant for young American Jews who had experienced, and been frustrated by, the "counterculture" of the 1960s, and were in search of spiritual sustenance (Rosenberg Farber 2017:57). The first such *yeshiva*, the Diaspora Yeshiva, located on Mount Zion in Jerusalem, was established in 1967 and was followed very closely by a number of additional *yeshivot*. Although they were meant for Americans, these institutions increasingly attracted young Israelis as well, so they soon established special wings to accommodate them.[8] Later on, other streams of Orthodoxy – Chassidism, especially the Chabad and Breslav movements, Religious Zionism, and Sephardic ultra-Orthodoxy, inspired primarily by Shas – established their own institutions for promoting *teshuvah* (Aviad 1983:68; Goodman 2002; Sharabi 2012). Already in the late 1970s, when Aviad's book *Return to Judaism* was being written, the IDF was encouraging its soldiers to visit *yeshivot* for *ba'alei teshuvah* in order to enrich their knowledge of (Orthodox) Judaism and, one would presume, allay the doubts expressed in *Siach Lochamim* and referred to by Aviad in the citation above (Aviad 1983:17, 24, 30).

Teshuvah is also a big business, handsomely paid for by the state and by private donors. The exact magnitude of state financial support for *teshuvah* organizations is hard to determine, because it appears under various budgetary items in the budgets of different government ministries, especially the Ministry of Education, the Ministry of Culture and the Ministry of Religious Services. Shahar Ilan, a journalist and blogger specializing in covering the ultra-Orthodox community (and, at the time of writing, deputy director of *Hiddush*, a secularist NGO), estimated that in 1999 state support for *teshuvah* organizations amounted to 100 million shekels (about 25 million US dollars) a year (Ilan 2000:330). In addition, *teshuvah* organizations enjoy generous support from private donors. Thus, the Wolfesohn Fund, established by Zeev Wolfesohn, founder of Ness Technologies, contributed in the four years ending in 2013 an average of 155 million shekels a year to such organizations, a decline from the roughly 200 million a year it was contributing before the financial crisis of 2008. Some of Wolfesohn's contributions are made on the basis of matching funds from the state (Hiddush 2012). In can be safely estimated, then, that *teshuvah* represents a business of at least 300 million shekels a year.

A prominent theme in the current scholarship on *teshuvah* is that the transformation undergone by *ba'alei teshuvah* does not lead necessarily from one clearly defined religious identity to another. *Ba'alei teshuvah* come from a variety of religious backgrounds, ranging from completely non-observant, such as in the kibbutzim of *Ha-Shomer Ha-Tzair*, to various degrees of partially observant. On the supply side, *teshuvah* is being offered by a whole range of organizations, from strictly rationalist Lithuanian ultra-Orthodox *yeshivot* to various "new age" groups (Goodman 2002; Sharabi 2012; Kaplan and

Werczberger 2015). Asaf Sharabi (2012) has therefore characterized this scene as a "*teshuvah* market" offering a whole array of "*teshuvah* baskets." In this variegated context, many *ba'alei teshuvah* do not commit themselves to one version of Jewish religiosity but move from one institutional setting to another and/or create their own hybrid amalgam of religious practices (cf. Goodman 2002).

Most students of *teshuvah* do not include the movement for Jewish renewal as part of their field of study, accepting this movement's own self-definition as an alternative or antidote to Jewish religiosity. In the next section of this chapter we will argue that, in reality, the movement for Jewish renewal should be understood as one more offering in the *teshuvah* market (cf. Ravid 2013b:13, 39).

"Inspiration, not authority": the Jewish renewal movement

The movement for "Jewish renewal" was launched right after the 1967 war by *Shdemot Circle*, a group of young kibbutz members, some of whom were also instrumental in publishing *Siach Lochamim* (Ufaz 1998:134; Werczberger and Azulay 2011:117; Ravid 2013b:27). The aim of the Jewish renewal movement was

> to bring Judaism back to the masses by creating a multifaceted Jewish identity for secular society that is based on Israeli culture as well as on traditional Jewish sources, and to do it in a positive and unapologetic manner. The hope is that this will help nonreligious Israeli Jews become more engaged with their Jewish heritage.
>
> (Azulay and Tabory 2012:5)

A different formulation mentioned a three-fold purpose: to renew the connection between Israelis and their Jewishness, to renew Jewish ceremonies and tradition, and to revitalize the community supportive of its members (Azulay 2010:113; Werczberger and Azulay 2011; Ravid 2013b). The motivation for launching the movement was stated, not surprisingly, in a collection of essays published by *Ha-Shomer Ha-Tzair* in 1986:

> It is about time to declare the complete emancipation of the [Jewish] legacy, its liberation from traditional religious approaches of learning, research, evaluation and drawing pleasure ... No more "the Heritage of Israel" [i.e., Jewish heritage], but Jewish culture through the generations, with its sublime and beautiful values, as well as its other components, which intellectual integrity permits or obliges [us] to question. Only men and women who acquire their Jewish education in secular academies, with rational and scientific methods and analytic tools, will be able to get to the truth of Jewish culture, rich in history, and convey it to the many, not as an imposition or an obligatory model, but as a spring of contemplative inspiration, ethical and aesthetic. This emancipation of Jewish spiritual treasures is already a fact, as witnessed by the secular Hebrew culture in

Israel, and it must be enhanced and glorified: it must not retreat in the face of religious coercion.

(Rabi 1986:164)

By the same token, however, as stated by the collection's editor, Yehoshua Rash:

We must beware of the bulliness of all sorts of "leagues against religious coercion"[9] which stand for disengagement from the tradition, view it as mere clericalism, and offer condescending emptiness – instead of communal warmth (free of Diasporic imitation and rabbinical ceremonialism).

We expect of the Israeli Left to oppose any renunciation … of the primacy of Zionism … *He who renounces the past, which leads "in spite of everything" to Zionism, to the resurgence of Israel, necessarily renounces the justice of our existence here* … [Therefore] a page of the Talmud cannot be strange to a man of the Left, on the argument that it was a liberal or socialist Torah that was allegedly given to him in the Sinai…

(Rash 1986:198, emphasis added)

Twenty years later, a policy document written by "the coordination unit for the promotion of Jewish secularism in Israel," funded by the Posen Foundation, which funds many projects of this nature, stated the rationale behind Jewish renewal in terms of the justice of Zionism and the cohesion of Jewish Israeli society:

In the last 20 years one can diagnose clear patterns of an identity … crisis among the secular public in the Jewish context … The issue of Jewish identity in the secular space has a direct bearing on the deterioration of the elements of *national resilience* of the society and state in Israel in two major areas:

a   *Doubts about the justice of the Zionist project and the State of Israel.*
b   Serious impairment of the cohesion of the Jewish collectivity – polarization to the point of tearing apart different groups in the [Jewish] people.

(Arad and Yaffe 2006:2, emphasis added)

Clearly, then, at least according to the authors of this document,[10] the aim of the Jewish renewal movement in Israel is not only to provide spiritual sustenance to individuals, but to reinforce the national resilience of the Jewish collectivity as well. This goal was shared by the Shenhar Committee, which was appointed in 1991 by the Minister of Education to investigate the state of Jewish studies in the secular state educational system and recommend improvements. The Committee submitted its report in 1994 and called for teaching Jewish studies in the secular state school system in a positive, pluralist, humanistic, and critical context, in tune with the values of the Jewish secular public. The Arad-Yaffe document called for implementing this approach (Shenhar 1994; Arad and Yaffe 2006:3; Chapter 5).

The concern with Jewish national identity and resilience, and with ways of enhancing them, is repeated in other writing of the promoters of Jewish renewal. Yaakov Malkin, a major theoretician of "Judaism as culture" and founder of a number of institutions promoting "secular Judaism," is worried primarily about the rift between secular and religious Jews in Israel, which weakens Jewish Israeli solidarity. Another concern is the alienation of educated Jews, in Israel and abroad, from their *national* identity as a result of their estrangement from Jewish religion. Educating such people in "humanistic Jewish culture," stripped of the overtly religious aspects of Judaism, would reconnect them to their national roots. And "humanistic Jewish culture," drawing on both Jewish and general humanistic values and sources, could help bridge the gap between secular and religious Jews in Israel by educating them to the value of pluralism in Judaism (Malkin 1997).

In the Epilogue of her book dealing with young kibbutz members who had immigrated to Los Angeles in the 1980s, Naama Sabar, a professor of education and prominent intellectual of the Jewish renewal movement, argues that

> [W]hen the secular public is fed up with the restrictions of extreme ortho-doxy … the danger that lies in the counter-reaction of purely universal-humanistic education is that the public will also disavow everything of a Jewish or Zionist hue … One of the main aims of our educational system, along with teaching universal humanistic values, must be to impart deeper knowledge about all facets of Jewish creation throughout the ages … The underlying idea is that one can be a secular Jew without cutting oneself off from the past … If the State of Israel has no roots in or orientation to the Jewish people, its greatness is diminished.
>
> (Sabar 2000:147–8)

A guide for American donors published by the Avi Chai Foundation, a major funder of Jewish renewal activities, states, among the issues addressed by that movement: "Young Israelis suffer from an under-developed or passive Jewish identity. One possible result is that they feel less connection to Israel as a Jewish State, which impacts their motivation *to serve in the army*" (Goldwater 2015a:14, emphasis added; cf. the Hebrew version in Goldwater 2015b:30).

The movement for Jewish renewal, which began as study circles, is clearly a movement of "the old elites of Israeli society: middle class, academic and of Ashkenazi origin [as well as] the new middle class" that includes middle-class Mizrachim (Werczberger and Azulay 2011:114–15; Sheleg 2010:47). From the very beginning it was in close contact with the Conservative and Reform move-ments in the United States and it is still supported financially primarily by American Jewish philanthropic organizations, including the Jewish Federations of various American cities (Arad and Yaffe 2006:10, 14; Calderon 2010; Azulay 2010:229; Werczberger and Azulay 2011:117, 122; Dardashti 2015:99n18).

Its first formal institution was the Institute for Zionist Education, established in 1977 as the kibbutz branch of the Jewish Agency's network of Zionist institutes and located at the kibbutz teachers' seminar (now Academic College of Education) Oranim (Azulay 2010:81). In 1989 the Zionist institute at Oranim was given the religious-sounding name, *Midrasha* (a post-secondary institution of religious Jewish learning). Two key initiators of this project were Ruth Calderon, who later served one term as Member of the Knesset (2013–2015), and Moti Bar-Or, a graduate of the *hesder yeshiva* in the West Bank settlement bloc of Gush Etzion, a relatively liberal Religious Zionist *yeshiva*. Later on the two of them together established Elul, a *beit midrash* for Jewish renewal, and then each one of them established her/his own institution, Alma and Kolot, respectively. All of these institutions still operate today as major centers of "Jewish renewal" (Arad and Yaffe 2006:4–5; Azulay 2006:2–3; 2010:61).

Since then the development of the movement, in the form of "secular" religious institutions such as synagogues, *yeshivot*, *midrashiyot*, prayer groups, *minyanim*, rabbis, and "learning communities" engaged in studying the traditional "Jewish bookshelf," as well as widespread publishing activity, has been quite remarkable (Sheleg 2010:13). The paradoxical choice of using religious terms to describe the movement's institutions and activities was explained by Motti Zeira, director of the *Midrasha* at Oranim College, in a way that is revealing of an important element of the movement's rationale:

> We don't want to forego Jewish terminology. Why give it up? Because one sector of Judaism took full control of it? "Our" Beit Midrash, "Our" synagogue, "Our" prayers," "Our" God. Everything is "ours" [i.e., theirs – the Orthodox]. I don't want to forego use of these terms. Just the opposite! Why do I have to try and define myself and invent a new dictionary? Because the basic vocabulary is already expropriated [by the Orthodox] or carries so much [Orthodox] meaning?
>
> (Cited in Werczberger and Azulay 2011:113)

Going beyond these learning activities:

> In recent years, the movement has taken part in legal struggles against the state for funding equivalent to that of the Orthodox institutions; for the recognition of secular conversion (*giyur*); and for the establishment and institutionalization of secular lifecycle ceremonies in general and secular marriages in particular.
>
> (Werczberger and Azulay 2011:113)

For that purpose the movement for Jewish renewal established a Forum to Promote Secular Pluralistic Judaism in the Knesset, a lobby advocating separation of religion and state, the establishment of civil marriage, recognition of secular conversions to Judaism, funding for secular Jewish education, and "in the long run, the establishment of a pluralistic Judaism movement" (Werczberger and Azulay 2011:121).

The movement received a major impetus following the assassination of Prime Minister Yitzhak Rabin by Yigal Amir, a *hesder* yeshiva graduate and law student at the national-religious university, Bar-Ilan, in 1995. The assassination caused intellectuals of both camps – non-observant and Religious Zionist – to try and bridge the gap between them. *Tzav Piyus* (reconciliation order), a program set up especially for this purpose by the US-based and funded Avi Chai Foundation, a major promoter of Jewish renewal in Israel, declares that its purpose is "to close the gaps that threaten national resilience and social solidarity in Israeli society ... by preserving and enhancing the Jewish-Israeli identity of every individual and group in Israeli society."[11] However, "bridging the gap" always entails moving from the secular pole toward the religious one, not vice versa, because Jewish religion is viewed as the unifying bond between all Jews while secularity is viewed as divisive (Artzieli 2003; Gavison and Medan n.d. [2003]; Yanay and Lifshitz-Oron 2003; A. Cohen and Rynold 2005; Dromi 2005:263–313, 365–438; Azulay 2006:3; Arad and Yaffe 2006:4; Sheleg 2010:105; Werczberger and Azulay 2011:116–17, 119; Ravid 2013b:13; Dardashti 2015; Molad 2017:4, 13).

As noted by culture critic Arianna Melamed, producers of TV series (a favorite medium of the Avi Chai Foundation)

> [c]an always count on the generous support of the Avi Chai Foundation provided that the script possesses some essential ingredients: a diverse assortment of the religious shown in a completely positive light while blurring the enormous social conflicts between them and secular viewers, or turning such conflict into a moving human story ... The possibility of seeing [*Charedim*] as belonging to an insular sect with offensive beliefs no longer exists now that the Avi Chai Foundation funds the script and the production.
> (Cited in Peleg 2016:137; see also Dardashti 2015)

Although accurate numbers are hard to come by (Ravid 2013a:11–13; Goldwater 2015a:48–50), estimates are that the movement for Jewish renewal currently encompasses between 250,000 and half a million Israeli Jews who participate in various activities offered by a loose network of at least 350 different organizations, having a combined annual budget (in 2011) of at least 700,000,000 shekels. Some of these organizations operate in state schools, in state-run community centers, and in the IDF, garnering at least 150,000,000 shekels of state funds (Werczberger and Azulay 2011:109; Ravid 2013a:14, 19; Goldwater 2015a:50). One indication of the widespread interest in Jewish renewal is the fact that Ruth Calderon's maiden speech as a Member of the Knesset in February 2013, which she opened by reading from the Talmud, was played 200,000 times on YouTube within three weeks of its delivery[12] (Azulay 2006; Katz 2008; Hochman 2009; Werczberger and Azulay 2011:108; Ettinger 2013; Persico 2013).

Summary

A "return" to Judaism, whether in one of its traditional forms or under a "renewed," supposedly secular appearance, has been a major component of the religionization of Israeli society. The main reason behind this phenomenon is the inseparability of Zionism from Jewish religion. The legitimacy crisis caused by the 1967 and 1973 wars that, coupled with the introduction of neo-liberal economics, brought about the decline of Labor Zionist hegemony, raised doubts among many Israeli Jews about both the justice and the success of Zionism. In response, both individuals and major social institutions, in Israel and abroad, turned to Jewish religion in search of an alternative worldview that could provide reassurance about Zionism and the future of Israel and enhance Jewish Israeli solidarity that seemed to be fraying as well. The need for reassurance and for enhancing Jewish solidarity was intensified due to the passionate internal conflicts caused by the 1993 Oslo Accords with the PLO, the assassination of Prime Minister Rabin in 1995, the failure of the Oslo peace process and the outbreak of the second *intifada* in 2000, and the disengagement from Gaza in 2005.

Whereas the need to "return" to Judaism was felt among all sectors of society, from bohemian artists (Wexler n.d.; Chapter 7) to lower-class Mizrachim, "Jewish renewal" was initiated by members of kibbutzim, who felt most acutely the decline of Labor Zionist hegemony, and was spread later on throughout the society. Both these movements, "return" and "renewal," have been supported by the state and by major Jewish American and international funding organizations, concerned about the resilience of Jewish Israeli society.

For American Jews the legitimacy crisis in Israel coincided with the "counterculture" crisis in the United States, which made many of them reassert their Jewish identity and bolstered their concern for Israel. Their influence has been felt in every aspect of the religionization process, from the first *yeshivot* for *ba'alei teshuvah*, through the TALI educational system (Chapter 5) and the Jewish renewal movement, to NGOs working to bring Orthodox and non-observant Israeli Jews together, and Women of the Wall (Chapter 8). The involvement of American and other Diaspora Jews in the "return" and "renewal" movements does not mean, however, that these are not authentic Israeli phenomena, or that they do not come to answer genuine concerns of Israeli Jews. As we have shown in this chapter, many Israeli Jews have turned and are turning to Judaism in order to find reassurance in a volatile situation to which previous forms of the civil religion have failed to provide adequate answers (Sheleg 2010:167).

Notes

1 "A villa in the jungle" was a phrase coined by former Prime Minister Ehud Barak to describe Israel's position in the Middle East.
2 *Censored Voices: War, Uncut*. 2015. Director: Mor Loushi. Producers: kNow Productions; One Man Show. *Siach Lochamim* was published in English as *The Seventh Day* (Av. Shapira 1970).

3 The initiators of *Siach Lochamim* held one discussion with a number of students at *Merkaz Ha-Rav yeshiva*, who would later become prominent in GE. That discussion was not included in the book, however, because of the ethno-centric, messianic sentiments and lack of moral sensitivity expressed by some of the participants from the *yeshiva*. The exchange was published in 1968 in *Shdemot*, literary organ of the group of kibbutz members who were behind the publication of *Siach Lochamim* (*Shdemot* 29:15–27; Barzilai 2002; Barzel 2017:141–3).

4 Reference is being made to Ben-Gurion's famous dismissive remark about the UN, "um-shmum."

5 The *Mizrachi* movement actually supported Herzl's Uganda proposal at the Sixth Zionist Congress.

6 "Even though … [chazarah bi-teshuvah in kibbutzim] is a relatively marginal phenomenon, both within the kibbutz and against the background of the Israeli chazarah bi-teshuvah movement as a whole, its symbolic significance is considerable" (Cahaner and Leon 2013:212).

7 Shas has participated in all government coalitions since 1984, with the exception of the 2003–2006 government.

8 The awakening of the *teshuvah* movement following the 1967 war caused Jewish women, initially American ones, to demand to be allowed to study the *Halacha* too, hence the establishment of special institutions for that purpose (Ross 2007:146–8; see Chapter 8).

9 "The League Against Religious Coercion" was established in 1951 and declined after the 1967 war. It called for the separation of state and religion, the establishment of civil marriage, and operating public transportation on Saturday.

10 The Arad and Yaffe document credits, in addition to the two authors, other key figures in the movement for Jewish renewal: Professor Hayim Adler (a well-known professor of education), Dr. Zvi Zameret (a noted historian and educator), Martin Ben Moreh, Dalia Goren, and Yair Tzaban, a former Meretz cabinet minister of *Hashomer Hatzair* background who initiated the writing of the encyclopedia, *New Jewish Time: Jewish Culture in a Secular Age*, another Posen Foundation project (Yovel 2007).

11 Available at: www.tzavpius.org.il/node/6001 (accessed April 1, 2017). Note the identification of Israeli society with *Jewish* Israeli society (cf. Dardashti 2015:96).

12 Available at: www.youtube.com/watch?v=ktDfdxLcUtk&feature=youtu.be (accessed April 1, 2017).

References

Abutbul-Selinger, G. (2016) "Shas and The Resignification of the Intersection between Ethnicity and Religion," *Journal of Ethnic and Migration Studies* (Online), http://dx.doi.org/10.1080/1369183X.2016.1245606 (accessed 10 January 2017).

Arad, U. and Yaffe, M. (2006) "The Place, Contribution and Role of NGOs in the Area of Education for Judaism as Culture in the General State Educational System and its Community Space," *Panim: Everyone Deserves Jewish Culture* www.panim.org.il/p-120 (in Hebrew; accessed October 25, 2013).

Artzieli, Y. (2003) *The Gavison-Medan Covenant: Key Points and Principles*, Jerusalem: Israel Democracy Institute (in Hebrew).

Aviad, Janet. (1983) *Return to Judaism: Religious Renewal in Israel*, Chicago, IL: The University of Chicago Press.

Azulay, N. (2006) "Jewish Renewal in the Secular Space in Israel – 2006 – Lecture Summary," *Panim for Jewish Renaissance*, www.panim.org.il/p-120/ (in Hebrew; accessed November 7, 2014).

Azulay, N. (2010) "Hebrews We Are and We Shall Worship Our Heart: The Jewish Renewal Movement in the Secular Space in Israel," PhD dissertation, Department of Sociology and Anthropology, Bar-Ilan University (in Hebrew).

Azulay, N. and Tabory, E. (2012) "The Formulation of Contemporary Tradition: Jewish Renewal in Israel's Secular Sector, *Contact*, 14: 5.

Barzel, N. (2017) *"Redemption Now": The Beliefs and Activities of the Jewish Settlers in the West Bank and Israeli Society*, Tel Aviv: Hakibbutz Hameuchad (in Hebrew).

Barzilai, A. (2002) "This is How Siach Lochamim of Merkaz Ha-Rav was Shelved," *Haaretz*, August 17 (in Hebrew).

Ben-Porat, G. (2013) *Between State and Synagogue: The Secularization of Contemporary Israel*, Cambridge: Cambridge University Press.

Cahaner, L. and Leon, N. (2013) "Returning to Religious Observance on Israel's Non-Religious Kibbutzim," *Journal of Israeli History*, 32: 197–218.

Calderon, R. (2010) "Tel Aviv and the Flowering of Jewish Renewal," *Journal of Jewish Communal Service*, 85: 77–80.

Caplan, K. (2001) "Israeli Haredi Society and the Repentance (Hazarah Biteshuvah) Phenomenon," *Jewish Studies Quarterly*, 8: 369–98.

CBS (2010) *Israel in Numbers 2010*, Jerusalem: Central Bureau of Statistics (in Hebrew).

Cohen, A. and Rynhold, J. (2005) "Social Covenants: The Solution to the Crisis of Religion and State in Israel?" *Journal of Church and State*, 47: 725–45.

Cohen, E. (1983) "Ethnicity and Legitimation in Contemporary Israel," *The Jerusalem Quarterly*, 28: 111–24.

Dardashti, G. (2015) "Televised Agendas: How Global Funders Make Israeli TV More 'Jewish'," *Jewish Film & New Media: An International Journal*, 3: 77–103.

Doron, S. (2013) *Shuttling Between Two Worlds: Coming To and Defecting From Ultra Orthodox Judaism in Israeli Society*, Tel Aviv: Hakibbutz Hameuchad (in Hebrew).

Dromi, U. (ed.) (2005) *Brothers Sitting Together – Religious-Secular Relations: Positions, Proposals, Covenants*, Jerusalem: Israel Democracy Institute (in Hebrew).

Ettinger, Y. (2013) "Who's Afraid of Ruth Calderon?" *Haaretz*, March 2 (in Hebrew).

Fischer, S. and Beckerman, Z. (2001) "'Church' or 'Caste'?" in Peled, Y. (ed.), *Shas: The Challenge of Israeliness*, Tel Aviv: Miskal–Yediot Ahronoth Books, pp. 321–42 (in Hebrew).

Gavison, R. and Medan, Y. (n.d. [2003]) *The Gavison-Medan Covenant*. Online: www.gavison-medan.org.il/english/ (accessed 17 October 2013).

Goldwater, C. (2015a) *Jewish Renewal in Israel*, Jerusalem: Avi Chai Foundation.

Goldwater, C. (2015b) *Jewish Renewal in Israel*, Jerusalem: Avi Chai Foundation (in Hebrew).

Goodman, Judah. (2002) *Teshuvah and New Religious Identities in Israel in the 2000s*, Tel Aviv: Tel Aviv University, Pinhas Sapir Center for Development (in Hebrew).

Hermann, T., Be'eri, G., Heller, E., Cohen, C., Lebel, Y., Mozes, H., and Neuman, K. (2014) *The National-Religious Sector in Israel 2014*, Jerusalem: Israel Democracy Institute (in Hebrew).

Hiddush: For Religious Freedom and Equality (2012) "All Time High in Yeshiva Student Numbers: About 114,000" http://hiddush.org/article-2344-0-All_time_high_in_yeshiva_student_numbers_about_114000.aspx (accessed April 10, 2018).

Hochman, R. (2009) "Rabbis Who Do Not Believe in God? Description of a Secular Humanist Rabbi in Israel – An Exploratory Study," MA thesis, Department of Sociology and Anthropology, Haifa University (in Hebrew).

Ilan, S. (2000) *Charedim Ltd.*, Jerusalem: Keter (in Hebrew).

Jobani, Y. (2008) "Three Basic Models of Secular Jewish Culture," *Israel Studies*, 13: 160–9.

Kaplan, D. and Werczberger, R. (2015) "Jewish New Age and the Middle Class: Jewish Identity Politics in Israel under Neoliberalism," *Sociology*, 51: 575–91.

Katz, G. (2008) "Secularism and the Imaginary Polemic of Israeli Intellectuals," *Israel Studies*, 13: 43–63.

Lahav, H. (2015) "Post-Secular Jewish Feminist Theology?" *Journal of Modern Jewish Studies*, 14: 355–72.

Lahav, H. (2016) "What do Secular-Believer Women in Israel Believe in?" *Journal of Contemporary Religion*, 31: 17–34.

Lehman, D. and Siebzehner, B. (2006) *Remaking Israeli Judaism: The Challenge of Shas*, New York: Oxford University Press.

Leon, N. (2006) "Religion and Secularity," *Iyunim Betkumat Yisrael*, 16: 85–107 (in Hebrew).

Leon, N. (2007) " 'Zikui Harabim': Ovadia Yosef's Approach toward Religious Activism and His Place in the Haredi Movement within Mizrahi Jewry," *Studies in Contemporary Jewry*, 22: 150–68.

Leon, N. (2011) "The Political Use of the Teshuva Cassette Culture in Israel," *Contemporary Jewry*, 31: 91–106.

Leon, N. (2016) *Mizrachi Ultra-Orthodoxy and Nationalism in Israel*, Jerusalem: Van Leer Institute and Tel Aviv: Hakibbutz Hameuchad (in Hebrew).

Liebman, C. S. and Don-Yehiya, E. (1983) *Civil Religion in Israel: Traditional Judaism and Political Culture in the Jewish State*, Berkeley, CA: University of California Press.

Maizlish, S. (1984) *Chazara Biteshuvah: Phenomenon and People*, Tel Aviv: Massada (in Hebrew).

Malkin, Y. (1997) "Teaching Judaism to Secular Jews," *Ravgoni: Framework for Contemporary Jewish Thought and Identity*, 1: 6–9.

Molad (2017) *Propagating: How the Religious Right Took Control of Values Education in the [Secular] State System*, Jerusalem: Molad – The Center for Democratic Renewal (in Hebrew).

Mor-Chaim, N. and Greenberg, N. (2013) *The Holy Kibbutz*, Jerusalem: Israel Broadcasting Authority, Channel 1, Documentary Department [documentary film].

Peled, Y. (1998) "Towards a Redefinition of Jewish Nationalism in Israel? The Enigma of Shas," *Ethnic and Racial Studies*, 21: 703–27.

Peled, Y. (ed.) (2001a) *Shas: The Challenge of Israeliness*, Tel Aviv: Miskal–Yediot Ahronoth Books.

Peled, Y. (2001b) "Roar of the Lion: Shas and the Challenge to Israeli Identity," *Israel Studies Bulletin*, 16: 8–13.

Peleg, Y. (2016) *Directed by God: Jewishness in Contemporary Israeli Film and Television*, Austin, TX: University of Texas Press.

Persico, T. (2013) "Who's Afraid of Ruth Calderon?," www.bac.org.il/society/article/my-mphd-mrvt-kldrvn (in Hebrew; accessed January 28, 2018).

Raanan, T. (1986) "The Struggle for the Legitimacy of Jewish Secularity," in Rash, Y. (ed.), *Thus See and Renew: The Free Jew and His Legacy*, Tel Aviv: Sifriat Poalim (in Hebrew).

Rabi, J. (1986) Man of Israel, People of Israel, Culture of Israel," in Rash, Y. (ed.), *Thus See and Renew: The Free Jew and His Legacy*, Tel Aviv: Sifriat Poalim (in Hebrew).

Rash, Y. (1986) "Left, Right, Religion: The Political Aspect," in Rash, Y. (ed.), *Thus See and Renew: The Free Jew and His Legacy*, Tel Aviv: Sifriat Poalim (in Hebrew).

Ravid, G. (2013a) *Analysis of the Field of Jewish Renewal in Israel – Summary*, n.p., Midot (in Hebrew).

Ravid, G. (2013b) *Jewish Renewal in Israel – Conceptualization and Theoretical Framework*, n.p., Midot (in Hebrew).

Rosenberg Farber, R. (2017) "The Role of Life Motifs in Commitment Journeys of *Ba'alei Teshuvah*," *Studies in Judaism, Humanities, and the Social Sciences*, 1: 57–72.

Ross, T. (2007) *Expanding the Palace of Torah: Orthodoxy and Feminism*, Tel Aviv: Am Oved (in Hebrew).

Sabar, N. (2000) *Kibbutzniks in the Diaspora*, trans. Naor, Ch., Albany, NY: SUNY press.

Sagi, A. and Schwartz, D. (2017) *From Realism to Messianism: Religious Zionism and the Six-Day War*, Jerusalem: Carmel (in Hebrew).

Schwartz, Y. (1979) *An Opening for Chozrim Biteshuvah*, Jerusalem: Dvar Yerushalayim (in Hebrew).

Shafir, G. and Peled, Y. (2002) *Being Israeli: The Dynamics of Multiple Citizenship*, Cambridge: Cambridge University Press.

Shapira, Av (ed.) (1967) *Siach Lochamim: Chapters of Listening and Observing*, Tel Aviv: A Group of Young Kibbutz Members (in Hebrew).

Shapira, Av (1970) *The Seventh Day: Soldiers' Talk about the Six Day War*, trans. Near, H., London: Deutsch.

Sharabi, A. (2010) "'Boundary Work' in the Teshuvah Movement in Israel," PhD dissertation, Department of Sociology and Anthropology, Bar-Ilan University (in Hebrew).

Sharabi, A. (2012) "'Teshuvah Baskets' in the Israeli Teshuvah Market," *Culture and Religion*, 13: 273–93.

Sharabi, A. (2014) "'Soft' Religion and 'Strict' Religion: The Teshuvah Movement in Israel," in Yadgar, Y., Katz, G., and Ratzabi, S. (eds.), *Beyond Halacha: Secularism, Traditionalism and "New Age" Culture in Israel*, Beer Sheva: Ben-Gurion University of the Negev (in Hebrew).

Sharabi, A. (2015) "Religion and Modernity: Religious Revival Movement in Israel," *Journal of Contemporary Ethnography*, 44: 223–48.

Sharot, S. (2007) "Judaism in Israel: Public Religion, Neo-Traditionalism, Messianism, and Ethno-Religious Conflict," in Beckford, J. A. and Demerath, N. J. III (eds.), *The SAGE Handbook of the Sociology of Religion*, Los Angeles, CA: Sage Publications, pp. 670–96.

Sheleg, Y. (2010) *From Old Hebrew to New Jew: The Jewish Renaissance in Israeli Society*, Jerusalem: Israel Democracy Institute (in Hebrew).

Shenhar, A. (1994) *People and the World: Jewish Culture in a Changing World*, Jerusalem: Ministry of Education – The Committee for Examining Judaic Studies in State Education (in Hebrew).

Shenhav, Y. (2008) "An Invitation to a 'Post-Secular' Sociology," *Israeli Sociology*, 10: 161–88 (in Hebrew).

Werczberger, R. and Azulay, N. (2011) "The Jewish Renewal Movement in Israeli Secular Society," *Contemporary Jewry*, 31: 107–28.

Yonah, Y. and Goodman, J. (eds.) (2002) *In the Vortex of Identities: A Critical Discussion of Secularity and Religiosity in Israel*, Bnei Brak: Hakibbutz Hameuchad (in Hebrew).

Tzaban, Y. (2007) "Foreword," in Yovel, Y. (ed.), *New Jewish Time: Jewish Culture in a Secular Age – Encyclopedic View*, Jerusalem: Keter, pp. xi-xii (in Hebrew).

Ufaz, G. (1986) "Affinity of the Kibbutz to the Jewish Sources in the Thought of 'Shdemot Circle'," PhD dissertation, Tel Aviv University (in Hebrew).

Ufaz, G. (1998) "The Shdemot Circle Members in Search of Jewish Sources," *Israel Affairs*, 4: 132–45.

Wexler, E. (n.d.) "Dahn Ben-Amotz, the Zionist Ethos and a Spiritual Crisis," n.p., copy on file with the authors (in Hebrew).

Yadgar, Y. (2011) *Secularism and Religion in Jewish-Israeli Politics: Traditionists and Modernity*, London: Routledge.

Yanay, N. and Lifshitz-Oron, R. (2003) "Mandatory Reconciliation (Tzav Piyus): The Violent Discourse of Moderation," *Israeli Sociology* 5: 161–91 (in Hebrew).

Yogev, A. and El-Dor, J. (1987) "Attitudes and Tendencies toward Return to Judaism Among Israeli Adolescents: Seekers or Drifters?" *Jewish Journal of Sociology*, 29: 5–17.

Yovel, Y. (ed.) (2007) *New Jewish Time: Jewish Culture in a Secular Age – Encyclopedic View*, Jerusalem: Keter (in Hebrew).

5 Education

A dialectical tension between secular and religious elements has characterized the Israeli educational system from its inception.[1] Under the British Mandate, the *yishuv* enjoyed complete autonomy in educational matters. Jewish public education (at the elementary level only) was organized in political-ideological streams: General Zionist, Labor Zionist and Religious Zionist (*Mizrachi*). In addition, *Agudat Yisrael*, which seceded from the *yishuv*'s Elected Assembly in 1925, after women had been granted the right to vote in elections to *yishuv* institutions (Kolatt 1998:285; Boaz 2002), had its own independent school system, partially subsidized by Zionist organizations.

In 1948 about 50 percent of the students enrolled in the official *yishuv* systems attended General Zionist schools, about 27 percent attended the Labor Zionist schools, and about 22 percent attended the Religious Zionist ones. The independent *Agudat Yisrael* schools were attended by roughly the same number of students as the Labor and Religious Zionist schools (Eliav 1988:218–19; Swirski 1990:41; Zameret 1997:21). As a result of being in power, the share of the Labor Zionist system had increased by 1953 to 43 percent of all Jewish students, while the General Zionist's had declined to only 27 percent, the Religious Zionist's to 19 percent and *Agudat Yisrael*'s to 11 percent (Swirski 1990:41–2; cf. Zameret 1997:191–4).

With massive immigration beginning in 1948, the three Zionist systems competed fiercely for the enrollment of immigrant children. Initially, education in the immigrants' camps was "unified education" provided by a special educational organization controlled by the ruling party, Mapai, and aiming to set off a "melting pot" process. The principles guiding education in the immigrant camps at that stage were "no *galutiyut* [Diasporism], no religious conservatism, no [inter-Jewish] ethnic culture" (Zameret 1997:142). "Unified education" was accused by the religious political parties of fostering anti-religious coercion, especially with regard to Mizrachi immigrant children, whose family background was much more traditional than that of most Ashkenazi immigrants (Zameret 1997:147–9, 172–80).

Political pressure exerted by *Mizrachi* and by Jews abroad resulted in the appointment of a commission of inquiry to examine these accusations, headed by a judge, Gad Frumkin. The Frumkin Commission affirmed the accusations of anti-religious coercion in the camps and recommended that education in the camps be transferred from the "unified education" system to the Ministry of Education and that all educational streams be allowed to operate there. The government accepted the commission's recommendations, and even prior to that agreed that all Yemenite immigrant children be assigned to religious education. Still, the bickering over the assignment of children, particularly Mizrachi children, to the different educational streams continued until the government fell following a no-confidence vote in the Knesset in February 1951 (Zameret 1997:152–9, 180–5).

In 1953 the State Education Law was enacted, ostensibly abolishing the independent school systems and establishing two state systems instead, one secular and one religious, the latter under the de facto control of the *Mizrachi*.[2] The independent system of *Agudat Yisrael* was brought under partial state financing, without real state supervision (Zucker 1973:134–8; Liebman and Don-Yehiya 1984:35; Zameret 1997; Biton 2014; S. Fischer 2014, 125–6; Ben David-Hadar 2016). Effectively, then, the only school system abolished by the Mapai-led government was the Labor Zionist system. The reason for this move was that, in the view of the Mapai leadership, the Labor educational system had become excessively influenced by Mapai's left-leaning, more thoroughly secular, Labor Zionist rival, Mapam (United Workers' Party). Thus the Labor movement deprived itself of the major institution that had been socializing its youth into its "secular" pioneering ethos, and gave state sanction to institutions propagating Jewish religion (Kafkafi 1991; Liebman and Don Yehiya 1983:84, 126; Shapiro 1984; see also Zucker 1973:123–43; Schiff 1977:170–94; Zameret 1997:190–210).

The nationalization of the school systems brought to an end the competition over immigrant children, with the majority of Mizrachi immigrant children now being assigned to the state-religious schools. As a result, between 1953 and 1968 the state-religious system's share of Jewish elementary school pupils grew from 19 percent to 29 percent. By 1970, 84 percent of the students in the state-religious system were of Mizrachi origin, compared to 51 percent in the secular state system. In 1965, 21 percent of the teachers in the secular state system, but fully 40.5 percent in the religious system, lacked proper teaching credentials (Swirski 1990:41–2, 53).

The religious educational sector

The education provided by the state-religious system is based on four integrated principles: "The Torah of Israel, the State of Israel, the People of Israel and the Land of Israel." Texts written by the elder Rav Kook began to appear in state-religious textbooks in the 1950s and their weight had increased during the 1960s. With time, especially after 1967, these texts were sanctified, and became central in shaping the state-religious system's national-mystical ideology, as well as its attitude toward the body and sexuality:

Sexual morality was expropriated from human mores and became an expression of the divinity and of the divine plan. Now the voice of the rabbis, especially those of the messianic orientation who motivated "Gush Emunim," became dramatic. They turned the body and sexuality into the main arena of redemption and messianism and in this way blocked the discourse of sexuality and the body that had prevailed [in Religious Zionist circles] in the first decades of the state.

(Sagi and Schwartz 2017:143, see also 41n78, 144–8, 153–61; Greenblum 2016:212–13)

As a result, the enhanced religiosity and militant nationalism of the state-religious school system since the 1970s has been manifested in gender segregation in elementary schools – beginning, in some cases, in the first grade (state-religious high schools have been gender segregated all along) – as well as in the nature of the material being taught and in the values imparted to the students. Between 2001 and 2010 the number of sixth-grade students enrolled in mixed gender classrooms in the state-religious system declined from 50 to 37 percent. In 2010 in 58 percent of the schools of that system sixth-grade classes were gender segregated, and in 50 percent of the schools *first-grade* classes were gender segregated. Beginning in the school year of 2014–2015 *all* fourth-grade classes and above in the state-religious system are supposed to be gender segregated, while the first to third grades are gender mixed, unless two-thirds of the parents prefer otherwise (Finkelstein 2014:19, 22–8; Shir 2014:3, 7, 8; Skop 2015; Kashti 2017e).

Interestingly, the level of gender segregation in elementary schools is positively related to both the size and the socio-economic status of the students' families. This means that better-off, more highly educated families in the national-religious sector tend to be more conservative, a quality that manifests itself in larger numbers of children per family and in the parents' preference that the children be educated in a gender segregated environment. Generally speaking, only 26 percent of the people belonging to the national-religious sector, broadly defined, oppose gender segregation in primary school, while 45 percent believe the genders should be segregated in primary school or even earlier (Shir 2014:9–10; Hermann et al. 2014, especially 203–6).

Gender segregated classes are smaller than mixed gender ones and, as indicated, students in gender segregated schools come from more affluent families. In spite of that, the educational attainments in the gender segregated schools are similar to those of the non-segregated or partially segregated schools. This may have to do with the fact that mixed gender schools are less prone to violence than segregated ones, even though the students in the mixed schools tend to come from a lower socio-economic background, which in the educational system as a whole would tend to raise the level of violence (Shir 2014:9–10; Finkelstein 2014:29–31, 41; Skop 2015).[3] Gender segregation applies not only to the students, but to the teachers as well, so there is a growing correspondence between the gender of the students and that of the teachers in the state-religious schools.

Thus, whereas in 2008 17 percent of the teachers in the state-religious system were men (compared to only 4 percent in the secular state system), in boys-only schools the figure was 55 percent (Shir 2014:10, 12).

All single gender schools and schools where the classes are gender segregated emphasize religious studies in their educational activity, while less than 80 percent of the mixed gender schools do so. The precise opposite is true with respect to the subjects of democracy, mathematics, science, and social studies, as well as sports. A corollary of the weaker emphasis on the study of democracy in the segregated schools is the fact that in 2010 students' councils existed in only 68 percent of the gender segregated schools, and in 85 percent of mixed gender schools where the classes were gender segregated, whereas such councils existed in 95 percent of the non-segregated schools (Shir 2014:25–6).

The *Charedi* independent educational sector is made up of a number of systems with differing degrees of state supervision and state financing, manifested in the extent to which the "core curriculum" – languages and literatures, mathematics, science and technology, humanities, and social science – are taught in the system's elementary schools, in addition to religious studies. In boys' schools the systems range from full state funding and complete adherence to the core curriculum in the state-*Charedi* system established in 2014, in Shas's *Bnei-Yosef: Maayan ha-chinuch ha-torani* (Sons of [Rav Ovadia] Yoseph: Spring of Torah Education) system established in 1984, and in the independent Lithuanian (non-Chassidic) system, to no state funding and no core curriculum in the schools of the most extreme *Charedi* sects. Most *Charedi* girls' schools do teach the core curriculum because, unlike men, women are not required to study the Torah and are destined to be the main income earners of their families (Malach and Kahaner 2016:23; Brown 2017; Rabinowitz 2017; on Shas see Chapter 4).

While in the school year 1989–1990 71.1 percent of Jewish elementary school students were enrolled in the secular state system, 21.3 percent in the national-religious system, and 7.6 percent in the *Charedi* systems, in the school year 2009–2010 53.2 percent were enrolled in the secular state system, 18.7 percent in the national-religious system and 28.1 percent in the *Charedi* systems (Faitelson 2011:71). In the school year 2017–2018 about 10 percent of *Charedi* students are in the state-*Charedi* system and about 12 percent are in *Bnei-Yosef: Maayan ha-chinuch ha-torani* (Rabinowitz 2017). The rest are in the Ashkenazi independent systems of *Agudat Yisrael* (Chassidic) and *Degel ha-torah* (Lithuanian). As mentioned in Chapter 3, Israel's Central Bureau of Statistics (CBS) has projected that by 2019 the number of students in the elementary secular state system will decline for the first time to just below 50 percent, while in the state-religious system it will grow to 19 percent and in the *Charedi* systems it will grow to almost 32 percent. By 2021 in elementary schools the number of students in the secular state system in projected to grow by 10.7 percent as compared to 2016, in the state-religious system by 14.8 percent and in the *Charedi* systems by 16.5 percent; the projection for high schools is 5.1 percent, 5 percent and 12.7 percent, respectively (CBS 2013:405; 2016: Tables 5 and 6).

Jewish education in the secular state system

The history of the thorny issue of Jewish education in the *secular* state school system has been marked by a series of committees set up in order to recommend ways of dealing with it. During most of the *yishuv* period the secular Zionist school systems in Palestine were concerned primarily with forming their students as "new Jews," which meant negating Jewish experience in the Diaspora, including, generally speaking, Diaspora Jews' religious practices (O. Almog 1997, especially 127–34). Ben-Zion Dinur, a prominent Zionist historian who was to serve as Israel's powerful Minister of Education at the time of the enactment of the State Education Law in 1953, stated in 1939:

> What is the ideological foundation of Zionism? First of all negation of the Diaspora – knowing the Diaspora, teaching the students what Diaspora is with all of its phenomena from Egypt until today, explaining to them the matter of adaptation, of the falsehood of Diaspora, of the instability, of its ups and downs ... Zionism is a rebellion against Diaspora, a war on it.
>
> (Cited in Shikli 2004:25; Conforti 2009:88–90)

Nonetheless, Dinur also warned against collapsing negation of the Diaspora as a state of being in the world into contempt for the "wonderful cultural and social values created [by Jews] in the Diaspora" (cited in Conforti 2009:89–90; see also Kafkafi 1991:16–20). It is doubtful, however, that this fine distinction could be appreciated by less sophisticated minds.

Negating the religious practices of the Diaspora did not mean abandoning Jewish religion. It meant, rather, *inter alia* shifting the focus of Jewish studies from the Talmud and its interpretations to the Bible (Old Testament), as part of establishing the Jews' historical connection to the Land of Israel and imparting Zionist values to the students. In the words of Ben-Zion Mosenson, a Bible teacher and future principal of the Hebrew Gymnasium Herzlia, in 1910, if the Bible

> is placed at the foundation of our children's education, our youth will not turn their backs on their people. And a new generation will rise, a strong and healthy generation, a generation that aspires to revival, a generation that loves its people and its land, a Hebrew generation.
>
> (Cited in Sagiv 2011:107)

In this spirit, in 1939 in the General [Zionist] Educational System, which was the largest one (enrolling 57 percent of the students in the *yishuv* educational systems), Jewish studies, both secular and religious, occupied on average nearly half of the instructional time, with one sixth of instructional time devoted to Bible study (Riger 1940:60–1, 107; Firer 1985:110; Kafkafi 1991:7–11; Zameret 2003:24; Dror 2007; Sagiv 2011).

Eliezer Riger, Inspector General of the General Educational System (between 1928 and 1939) and later Director General of the Ministry of Education

(1951–1954), wrote in the late 1930s that "our national culture was in its best manifestations throughout the generations a religious culture and therefore we cannot, nor do we want to abandon it." He further argued that the Hebrew school in Palestine should

> nurture a religious spirit that will be manifested in: a) love of the Sabbath and [Jewish] holidays and their observance, b) inspiring to mend the world (*tikkun olam*), c) interest in both the visible and hidden questions relating to the creation of the world.

Finally, "our national and human future demands the revival of religion amongst us" (Riger 1940:103, 105–7).

The educational attitude toward the Diaspora began to change in the mid-1940s, as news of the Holocaust began reaching the *yishuv*. In 1944 a committee headed by Moshe Talmi was charged with enhancing Jewish education in the Labor educational system. The committee recommended including two new major categories in the curriculum: "Jewish cultural creation through the ages" and "the Jewish calendar." This was one element in a broader process of shifting from "negation of the Diaspora" to "Jewish consciousness" in shaping the "new Jew" by the secular educational systems of the *yishuv* (Dror 2009:6–7; Chemo n.d.[2012]:3).

The educational approach that characterized the final years of the *yishuv* continued during the first decade of the State of Israel. But in 1957, in response to "widely felt ... anxiety about Israeli youth's possible estrangement from their Jewish heritage" (Herman 1970:35),[4] the Mapai-headed government launched an intensive program of "Jewish consciousness" instruction in the secular state school system. The rationale for adopting the program was articulated by none other than David Ben-Gurion himself. In a letter to Education Minister Zalman Aranne dated November 7, 1955, he stated:

> As far as I know [our] youth (and I mean the good youth!) – they are very very deficient in Jewish consciousness, in understanding our historical heritage and in moral affinity to world Jewry, and it must be seen to it that an educational program [be established] that will correct this deficiency without harming other vital educational values.
>
> (Cited in Zameret 2003:59)

In setting up the program, described by Aranne as "Jewish inoculation," he averred that knowledge of the Jewish tradition was essential "for the *national* education of the Hebrew nation" (Liebman and Don-Yehiya 1983:173; Zameret 2003:60; emphasis added). The program was criticized, however, by both religious and left-wing Zionist circles. The former viewed it as too shallow and the latter objected to the "cult of religion" allegedly promoted by the program. In general, Aranne's program was widely considered a failure for merely imparting passive knowledge of religious Jewish subjects rather than nurturing the personality and the Jewish national identity of the students (Zucker 1973:139–42; Liebman and Don-Yehiya 1983:172–4, 170–7; Shapiro 1996:48–50, 56–60; Shikli 2004:35–8; Dror 2009:8; Chemo n.d.[2012]:4–5).

Aranne's Jewish consciousness program was discontinued by the mid-1970s. Precisely at that time, in the wake of the 1973 Arab-Israeli war, a new "semi-state" Jewish-oriented educational system was initiated by a group of American Conservative rabbis and educators, most of them graduates of Jewish Theological Seminary, who had recently immigrated to Israel and found fault with both of the existing Jewish educational systems – secular and religious. In the words of the founders of the new initiative, that came to be known as TALI (Hebrew acronym for "reinforcing Jewish studies"):

> … secular schools, while often excelling in general studies, see little if any value in introducing the serious study of rabbinical texts or religious thought, and fail to foster any deep sense of identification with the Jewish people, its history, traditions, customs or values.
>
> The state-religious schools were dogmatic and imposed religious behavior on children and their families. They did not deal with Jewish tradition in its historical context and they could not cope with the pluralistic nature of a broad spectrum of interests in Jewish culture.
>
> (Cited in Shikli 2004:41)

The challenge the founders of TALI set themselves was to "try and develop an alternative system that would provide serious, liberal and pluralist Jewish education that would train [the students] for tolerance while nurturing feelings of identification and sympathy, openness together with commitment to the Jewish tradition,"[5] because

> we cannot expect the younger generation to *serve in the army*, remain in Israel, and contribute meaningfully to its society without supplying it with the knowledge and commitment to reinforce it in its tasks, without elucidating the meaning of the State of Israel and its significance in Jewish life.
>
> (Cited in Shikli 2004:41, 45; emphasis added)

The TALI initiative was adopted by Zevulun Hammer, erstwhile leader of the Young Guard of the NRP, who became Minister of Education after Likud's victory in the general elections of 1977 and was to serve in that capacity until his untimely death in 1998, with some interruptions. Under his guidance the Ministry of Education began to assume responsibility for the TALI program in 1981, diluting its liberal elements in the process (Azrieli 1990:136–60; Shikli 2004:63–4).

Hammer left his post as Minister of Education in 1984, and when he came back to that position in 1990 his enthusiasm for the TALI system, or at least that of his aides, had cooled off considerably, primarily because of the continued association of TALI with the Conservative movement and because of turf wars between the

Ministry and the initiators of the TALI program (Shikli 2004:81–2, 87–9). In spite of this cooling off, and continuing ideological and bureaucratic friction with the Ministry of Education under several ministers, by 2013 the TALI system had 94 schools and 34 kindergartens affiliated with it with a total enrollment of 46,000 students[6] (Kelman 2010:81). In 2008, under a liberal Minister of Education, Professor Yael Tamir (Labor), the State Education Law was amended and a new educational stream – the Integrative Stream, offering enhanced Jewish studies – was recognized as a stream occupying a middle position between the secular and the religious state school systems (Laws of the State of Israel 2008).

In 1991, following his failure to turn TALI into an instrument of religionization of the secular state school system, Hammer appointed a committee to investigate the state of Jewish studies in that system and to recommend improvements. This was done in the context of economic liberalization, the first *intifada*, massive immigration of secular Jews and a large number of non- or doubtfully Jews from the former Soviet Union and Ethiopia, and a prevailing feeling that interest in Jewish studies was declining in Israeli society. (Paradoxically, this was precisely the time when Jewish studies as an academic discipline was flourishing in the United States.) The underlying concern which led to the appointment of this committee was articulated by its Chair, Professor Aliza Shenhar, several years later: "The crisis of Jewish identity in the secular space raises doubts among Israeli youths about the *justice of Zionism and of the State of Israel* and seriously harms the unity of the Jewish-Israeli collective" (Shenhar 2007:78; emphasis added).

The Shenhar Committee attributed the decline of Jewish studies in Israel to a number of factors, both general and specific to Israel: the decline of ideology, the rise of consumer society and the global village, the information explosion, growing professional specialization, the politicization of religion in Israel – especially around issues related to the Israeli-Palestinian conflict and the peace process – and the growing class and ethnic gaps in Israeli society. It assumed the students in the Jewish secular state educational system to come from largely secular families, although it noted that the (Jewish) secular public in Israel does not like to refer to itself as "secular," preferring the terms "free" or "general" public. The Committee recommended that interest in Jewish studies in the secular state system be enhanced by presenting them in a positive, pluralist, humanistic, and critical context, in tune with the values of the Jewish secular public (Shenhar 1994:5, 8–9; Dror 2009:14; Knesset 2010).

The Shenhar Committee's recommendations to enhance Jewish studies in the secular state system were adopted by the government in 1994, and a special unit within the Ministry of Education was set up for the purpose of implementing them. Since then implementation has been uneven, subject to all kinds of political and budgetary calculations, and, in the words of Shenhar, "has raised many questions and discontent" (Shenhar 2007:80; Arad and Yaffe 2006:16–18; Chemo n.d. [2012]:6–7). One clear outcome of the committee's report, however, was that, in the context of wide-ranging budget cuts, privatization and outsourcing in the educational system, numerous Orthodox religious organizations have been entrusted with teaching Jewish subjects in the *secular* state system, and they have been doing so with taxpayers' money and with a national-religious or *Charedi* orientation (Sheleg 2010:56–62; Silver et al. 2012:6; Darom and Kashti 2013; Hod 2017; Kashti 2017a; Molad 2017).

In 2011, under a Likud Minister of Education, Gideon Sa'ar, the title of the Jewish studies program was officially changed from the universalist-sounding title recommended by the Shenhar Committee – "People and the World – Jewish Culture in a Changing World" – to the parochial "Heritage and Culture of Israel" (i.e., of Judaism) (Shenhar 2012:18). As for its content, the Secular Forum, an NGO established in 2011 to fight the religionization of Israeli society, examined textbooks used in the *secular* state system to teach the "Heritage and Culture of Israel" program and found "wide ranging use of religious language, and a religious bias, in all books offered on the market, whether they were written by orthodox bodies or published through pluralist bodies in the name of Jewish renewal" (Secular Forum 2017a:1). In general, the Forum found that the program contributed to the religionization of the secular state educational system through "enhancing ethnocentrism, belittling Israeliness as against Judaism, exacerbating the imbalance between teaching about the [Jewish] people and teaching about the world, and engaging in religious indoctrination of young children" (Secular Forum 2017b:1).[7]

The forum further examined 80 textbooks used in the secular state system to teach Hebrew, Bible, geography, social studies, civics, history, science, mathematics, values, road safety, and art in elementary schools. It found in the books "indoctrination into a national-Jewish worldview" through

> stories about miracles that happened to those who observed the Sabbath, the need to pray for grandpa to get well, phrases like "we are commanded" and "we have to behave," Memorial Day [commemorating fallen soldiers of the IDF] is meant to defend "the [Greater] Land of Israel," [claiming] that even the Pioneers "prayed for a Jewish State" ... The texts construct a reality where there is a close connection between Israeli nationalism and Jewish religion, presented in its Orthodox version only.
>
> (The Secular Forum website, accessed April 26, 2017; in Hebrew)

The educational program adopted under Sa'ar was criticized by Avi Sagi, a professor of philosophy in the national-religious University, Bar-Ilan, who had headed yet another committee dealing with these issues that had been appointed in 2008 by the previous Minister of Education, Professor Tamir. Sagi argued that

> [w]hen the Ministry of Education assigns canonical status to certain [Jewish religious] texts it enables indoctrination. It is hard to understand why the studies of secular youth should be shaped by the weekly Torah portion or *Pirkei Avot*,[8] which are of interest to religious students. Gideon Sa'ar and his people don't understand that the meaning of secular identity is not derived from the religious world. Being secular does not mean being a little less religious.
>
> (Cited in Chemo n.d. [2012]:9; cf. Taylor 2011)

Sagi's criticism notwithstanding, the underlying imperative in respect of both these approaches – i.e. Shenhar's Judaism as culture and Sa'ar's Judaism as religion – is identical: to enhance the unity of the Jewish Israeli collective and its belief in the justice of Zionism.

Since 2015 a Religious Zionist Minister of Education, Naftali Bennett, who heads the Jewish Home party, has greatly increased the budgetary allocation for "Jewish culture" organizations and activities: from 125,800,000 shekels in 2013 to 176,900,000 shekels in 2015 and 210,000,000 shekels in 2017, representing close to 20 percent of the entire budget of the Ministry of Education (Molad 2017:17; Dattel 2017; Kashti 2017f). A large portion of these funds goes to Orthodox NGOs that work to enhance the religious Jewish identity of students, teachers and parents in secular schools, focusing on primary schools and kindergartens. For example, in 2017 the Ministry of Education signed a 1,000,000 shekel contract with a national-religious NGO called *Binyan Shalem* (Whole Building) to conduct workshops for teachers and parents in secular primary and secondary schools about Jewish family values. *Binyan Shalem*'s idea of Jewish family values can be gleaned from one of the articles appearing on its website – "Happy Women." This article instructs newly married women that as wives and mothers God wants them to worship him through taking care of the practical details of life, such as "making sandwiches for the children in the morning," rather than through "prayer, [Torah] study, and charity," which are important, but secondary for married women. In sum:

> If we understand that taking care of the practical details of life is our task at this stage of our life; if we internalize that this is what God wants from a woman who is a wife and mother – it will be much clearer to us what we have to aspire for and in relation to what we should not be frustrated. When we worship God and not our fantasies and wishes, we will be blessed to feel liberation, relief and happiness in the stage where we are.[9]
>
> (Kashti 2017c)

The argument behind the entrusting of Jewish consciousness instruction in the secular school system to Orthodox organizations is that secular Jewish children's Jewish identity has been eroded and their commitment to (Jewish) values has weakened. While liberal, secular Israeli Jews are up in arms about this argument (Molad 2017), it is actually quite similar to the rationale that had motivated the secular Shenhar Committee.

Civic education

Between the enactment of the State Education Law in 1953 and 1985 civic education in Israel was focused on the formal and legal aspects of state institutions and on the citizens' duties, rather than their rights. In line with Ben-Gurion's doctrine of *mamlachtiyut* (Peled 1992; Kedar 2009), the notion of pioneering was expanded from physical labor, settlement, and defense to include science and industry as well. In 1985, as Israeli society was undergoing a process of liberalization, and in the wake of the election of the blatantly racist Rabbi Meir Kahane to the Knesset in 1984, "the Ministry of Education was alerted to the need to foster democratic education in the schools." Thus,

> [a] policy directive issued in 1985 ... assigns unprecedented importance to the universalistic aspects of citizenship while allotting national values a much more minor role. The document asserts that there exists an inevitable conflict between national and humanistic-universal values. Educators are instructed to teach students that when faced with dilemmas emanating from the clash between national and universalistic values "citizenship rights that are derived from fundamental democratic principles and procedures should gain precedence [over national values] and provide behavioural guidance."
>
> (Ichilov et al. 2005:308; see also Pedahzur and Perliger 2004:73)

In March 1995, as Israeli society was gripped by intense, sometimes violent conflict over the Oslo peace process (which was to lead to the assassination of Prime Minister Yitzhak Rabin in November of that year), the liberal Minister of Education, Amnon Rubenstein (Meretz), appointed a committee charged with developing a civics education program for the state school systems in order to foster a common civic identity for all (or at least most) groups in the society. The committee, headed by Hebrew University law professor Mordechai Kremnitzer, submitted its interim report in February 1996 (Kremnitzer 1996).[10] The report stated that:

> Whereas the conception of democracy as majority rule is prevalent among the [Israeli] public, the conception of democracy as a regime centered on a sovereign individual, free to form and develop its personality in a society whose purpose is to defend individual rights while safeguarding the rights of different groups in society, has not been sufficiently internalized. There is conspicuous weakness in the internalization of universal values ... manifested, for example, in attitudes toward Arabs and *Charedim* and toward freedom of expression and freedom of the press.
>
> (Kremnitzer 1996:8)

The Kremnitzer Committee also found that a significant number of Israelis hold a passive, rather than active, conception of citizenship. To correct these problems the Committee called for expansion and profound revision of the existing civics education program in the schools, in order to

> establish a *commitment to the democratic regime* and an internalization of a worldview that sees human rights as belonging to all human beings and citizenship rights as belonging to all citizens ... [as well as] *nurture civic responsibility, civic engagement and civic initiative of an active and responsible citizen*
>
> (Kremnitzer 1996:16, emphasis in the original; Ichilov et al. 2005:311)

The Kremnitzer Committee's report was adopted by the Ministry of Education and a special unit within it was established to implement both the Shenhar and Kremnitzer reports. A new high school civics textbook, written in the spirit of the Kremnitzer Report, *To be Citizens in Israel: A Jewish and Democratic State*, was published as well, in both Hebrew and Arabic, in 2000 and 2001, respectively (Ministry of Education 2000; Pinson n.d. [2013]:8). In the same year the State Education Law of 1953 was amended with the stated goals of state education expanded to include, *inter alia*, "equal opportunities for self-development, acceptance of and support for 'others,' inculcating intellectual curiosity and critical thinking, voluntary work and social involvement" (Ichilov et al. 2005:312). The law also designated gender equality and environmental concerns among the goals of civic education, as well as "knowing the unique language, culture, history, legacy and tradition of the Arab population and of other population groups in the State of Israel and recognizing the equal rights of all citizens of Israel" (Laws of the State of Israel 2000).

However, regardless of the amended law, the change of government to one dominated by Likud in 1996 and then again in 2001 have caused the Kremnitzer recommendations, just like the Shenhar ones, to be implemented only partially and haphazardly, if at all (Pedahzur and Perliger 2004; S. Fischer 2014:129).

The adoption of the Kremnitzer Report by the Ministry of Education came under fire in 2009 in a position paper written by a veteran Religious Zionist civics teacher, Isaac Geiger, for the right-wing, settler-oriented think tank, The Institute for Zionist Strategy (Geiger 2009; see also Geiger 2013). Geiger accused the Kremnitzer Committee, and the Ministry of Education as well, of promoting an exclusively liberal-individualist conception of democracy and ignoring alternative conceptions – "republican, communitarian, or 'thin' [procedural]" (Geiger 2009:52). As a result, he argued, in its current form civic education in Israel undermines "Zionist and patriotic education and students' commitment to the existence of the State of Israel as a Jewish nation-state."

Overall, Geiger further argued, under the influence of liberal academics, especially those in the social sciences and law, civic education in Israel has been characterized by a post-modern, post-Zionist, post-colonial, feminist and sometimes multicultural approach, rather than a Jewish, Zionist, republican, collectivist approach. Thus the Jewish component of Israel's definition as a Jewish and democratic state had been completely obfuscated in civic education by the emphasis on its democratic element, leading, potentially, to "the weakening of our existence as a Jewish and democratic state" (Geiger 2009:1). As far as the Israeli-Palestinian conflict was concerned, Geiger also argued, the civics textbook *To be Citizens in Israel* presented this topic from an exclusively Arab and left-wing Jewish perspective (Geiger 2009:36, 38–49).[11]

To correct these problems, Geiger proposed the following: discard the Kremnitzer Committee's report and the book, *To be Citizens in Israel*, altogether; prepare a new core curriculum for civic education that would incorporate "Zionist, national, republican and communitarian perspectives"; limit civic education to "individual–state relations" only (i.e., the formal structure of the state and formal citizenship), so as to prevent the ideological bias that is bound to creep in whenever the scope of civic education is expanded beyond that topic to include a discussion of social cleavages or of normative values; and prepare different curricula and instructional materials for the Arab, the Druze and the three Jewish state school systems (secular, religious, and vocational) (Geiger 2009:3, 34–5, 54–7).

Although the Ministry of Education rejected many of Geiger's claims as unfounded, it did concede one point, which is crucially important for our argument. In its response to the position paper, stated in a letter to the Institute for Zionist Strategy, the Ministry agreed that an imbalance existed in the civics education program in regard to the emphasis laid on the Jewish and on the democratic aspects of the state's definition. By way of explanation it stated that the value of democracy was emphasized since it was shared by all sectors of the society, while it agreed that the Jewish aspect should have been presented through "the world of Jewish values" (i.e., Jewish religion), not only through the symbols of the state and its national identity, as was currently being done. This would require, the Ministry further agreed, incorporating Jewish (religious) sources in the civics education program (Ministry of Education 2009:11).

Geiger's recommendations set the tone for the conversation about civic education in Israel and were largely adopted by the Likud Minister of Education, Gideon Sa'ar, in 2009 (S. Fischer 2014:139–40; Pinson n.d. [2013]:8; Liefschitz 2017). In 2011, under the supervision of another member of the Institute for Zionist Strategy, the textbook *To be Citizens in Israel* began to be revised in accordance with Geiger's recommendations, in a way that would also be compatible with the new program for Jewish education, "Heritage and Culture of Israel." The partially revised book was published in 2013, and a completely new book was published in 2016, when the Religious Zionist Naftali Bennett was already Minister of Education.

Liberal critics of the new book, including Kremnitzer himself, have argued that whereas the original book, and Kremintzer's recommendations that served as its basis, tried to strike a balance between Israel's definition as a Jewish and a democratic state, the new book subsumed the democratic aspect completely under the Jewish aspect and promoted an ethno-national rather than liberal conception of citizenship (Pinson n.d. [2013]). According to Kremnitzer, the new book is a product of "a new, nationalist-religious elite whose flag is an anti-liberal Jewish republic in the service of the [West Bank] settlement project, depriving the Palestinians of their lands, and denying their right to [national] self-determination." By turning the education provided by the secular state educational system into "nationalist-religious education," this new elite "presents Israeli democracy with a first-rate challenge" (Kremnitzer 2016a:6; 2016b:2).

Between Bennett's appointment as Minister of Education in 2015 and the publication of the new civics textbook in 2016 a policy directive titled "Essential Concepts for the Teacher" was issued by the Ministry. That directive promoted a majoritarian conception of democracy, downplaying the protection of individual and minority rights, and an ethno-national conception of citizenship presented as a republican one (cf. Shafir and Peled 2002:4–11). The result, according to Hebrew University political scientist Dan Avnon, is "legitimation of a nationalist civic consciousness that is turned against minorities" who live among the Jewish majority in Israel (Avnon 2016:7).

Charedim in higher education

In 2016 the Israel Democracy Institute (IDI) reported that

> The proportion of the haredi community living beneath the poverty line is much greater than that of the general population (52% as opposed to 19%), with poverty levels among haredim remaining constant since 2006. A majority of haredi families are living in poverty, and the share of haredi children defined as poor is extremely high (67%). A quarter of haredi families suffer from food insecurity and per capita income is 47% lower than that of the general public.
>
> (IDI 2016a:16)

The reasons for these high poverty rates are not hard to fathom: to avoid military service, *Charedi* men have to be registered as full-time students in a *yeshiva* and cannot work (at least not formally) or undertake any kind of vocational training until the age of forty-one (see Chapter 6).[12] Thus their very large families depend on their wives' earnings and on welfare payments of various kinds, primarily child support (Malach 2014:12, 27–8).

In 2015 only 50 percent of *Charedi* men aged 25–64 were gainfully employed, compared to 87 percent of non-*Charedi* Jewish men; among women the gap was much smaller: 73 percent of *Charedi* women were gainfully employed, compared to 81 percent of non-*Charedi* Jewish women. The trend in employment of both *Charedi* men and women is clearly upwards, however: in 2003 only 36 percent of the men and 51 percent of the women were gainfully employed. This trend results from the growing number of *Charedi* men who do serve in the military and can therefore work for a living afterwards and from periodical cuts in government subsidies due to the changing composition of government coalitions. However, in 2015 the average income from employment among *Charedim* was only 71 percent of the national average due to low hourly pay (primarily among the men) and part-time work (primarily among the women) (IDI 2016a:19–20).[13]

Efforts to ameliorate this problem, which costs the Israeli economy an estimated 9.4 billion shekels (about 2.5 billion US dollars) annually in lost production, and to integrate the *Charedi* men into the labor market, have taken primarily two forms: (1) state initiatives to induce *Charedi* young men to perform military service, which would free them from being shackled to the *yeshiva*; and (2) various programs, initiated originally by Shas, to provide *Charedi* men with access to higher education (Malach 2014; CHE 2016:3, 7, 12; Cohn 2016:4–5).

The main requirements for admission to institutions of higher education in Israel are possession of a "matriculation certificate," granted to high school students who pass successfully a set of state-administered examinations, and a certain score in a psychometric test.[14] Because most *Charedi* schools, especially boys' schools, do not teach the complete core curriculum, in 2014–2015 only 10 percent of *Charedi* 17-year olds gained the certificate, compared to 75.6 percent among the non-*Charedi* Jewish population (Steinmetz 2016). Moreover, not all matriculation certificates are alike. Only the better ones in terms of grades qualify their holders to admission to a university, as opposed to other institutions of higher education. Thus in 2011–2012 only 1 percent of *Charedi* boys and 9 percent of *Charedi* girls gained matriculation certificates that enabled them to enter a university (IDI 2016b:82–6; Malach et al. n.d. [2016]:51n1).

The Council on Higher Education (CHE), the body that regulates higher education in Israel, has developed two five-year plans catering to *Charedim* in order to increase their presence in the secular institutions of higher education, for 2011–2016 and for 2017–2022. These plans have three essential elements: lowering the bar of admission to specially designed academic programs for *Charedim;* separation between the male and female *Charedi* students as well as between the *Charedi* students and the general student population; and generous financial aid to the *Charedi* students, especially the men among them, and to the institutions they attend (Knesset 2014; Malach 2014:9, 49–51; CHE 2016; Malach et al. n.d. [2016]; Regev 2016; HCJ 6500/17:9, 37, 44).

The stated rationale of the CHE for the special treatment accorded potential *Charedi* students is their lack of academic preparation and unique, strictly Orthodox, cultural background. Thus, in 2014, 53 percent of *Charedi* students were accepted for academic studies without a matriculation certificate or psychometric test score, compared to only 26 percent in 2000, before the onset of the first five-year plan. But in spite of all these efforts, in 2014 there were fewer than 9,500 *Charedi* students in higher education, out of whom only slightly more than 3,000 were men, for whom the program was particularly designed in the first place. Percentage-wise, in the *Charedi* 25–35 age cohort only 8 percent of the men and 15 percent of the women were studying or had studied for a degree in an institution of higher education. Some, but not all, colleges and universities offer academic preparatory programs for students lacking a matriculation certificate, so in many cases *Charedi* students enroll in academic studies without any formal qualifications or academic preparation. As a result, dropout rates among these students are very high, up to 50 percent, especially among the men. Thus "[a]s of 2014, only 2.4 percent of Haredi men and 8.3 percent of Haredi women aged 25–35 held academic degrees – compared to 28 percent of non-Haredi men and 43 percent of non-Haredi women" (Malach 2014:9, 24; CHE 2016; Regev 2016:219–21, 226–9, 235; Malach et al. n.d. [2016]:9, 20, 29).

The normatively problematic concession to the *Charedim* in these programs is, of course, the segregation of men and women, which affects classrooms, corridors, sometimes entire campuses, and threatens to spread to other areas of social life (Kashti 2017d). Moreover, since the *Halacha* prohibits women from being in positions of authority over men (see Chapter 8), female professors are prohibited from teaching male students, unless they are defined officially as teaching assistants.[15] (Male professors are not prohibited from teaching female students, so the issue is not one of modesty.) Needless to say, gender segregation violates the principle of equality and is harmful to the human dignity of the gender that is being discriminated against – women.[16] It also diminishes the prospects of *Charedi* students to integrate into the labor market, which in most cases is not segregated by gender (yet?). According to the CHE the legal basis for its policy of gender segregation, as well as the preferential treatment accorded to *Charedim* in admissions, is Articles 4(b) and 9(b) of the Students' Rights Law, 2007 (obviously written for this very purpose), which exempt these practices from the prohibition of any kind of discrimination in admission to institutions of higher education (Malach 2014:32, 60; CHE 2016; Cohn 2016:5; HCJ 6500/17:8–9, 11, 17–18, 23–4, 31–7; Malach et al. n.d. [2016]:18; cf. Malach and Kahaner 2016).[17]

Critics of the program have argued, on the other hand, that the recruitment of academically unprepared *Charedim* to higher education is not an effective way of improving their economic status, as evidenced by the alleged failure of the CHE's first five-year plan (2011–2016); that there are more effective ways of achieving the same goal; and that therefore the harm inflicted by the violation of the principles of gender equality and equality between different student populations ("separate but equal is not equal"), as well as the infringement of the human dignity of female students and professors, are unjustified and the program as a whole is illegal (Cohn 2016:6; HCJ 6500/17; cf. Malach et al. n.d. [2016]).

Summary

Education is a key arena in which the religionization of Israeli society is taking place. Summarizing his survey of the development of "Jewish consciousness" in the secular state school system, Yuval Dror has concluded that

[in] spite of the deep cleavages and intensifying individualism in Israeli society – or perhaps because of them – it seems that [the goal of] "nurturing Jewish consciousness" in the [secular] educational system for the purpose of "Jewish unity" is strengthening and stabilizing in the last decades: history curricula present both the Zionist and the Jewish stories ... as do the arts and literature curricula; the presence of Mizrachi Jews in the curricula is increasing...; the scope of formal and informal programs for teaching the Holocaust is growing, combining the Zionist morale [of the Holocaust] and identification with the Jewish people in the Diaspora; Jewish studies have been intensified in the TALI system with the aid of the "People and the World" [Shenhar] Committee and through all kinds of *midrashoth* that flourish in the non-religious public and are integrated into schools, youth movements, and community organizations.

(Dror 2009:15)

As we have shown in this chapter, the tendency to infuse "secular" education with more and more religious Jewish content pre-dated the establishment of the State of Israel in 1948 and has been intensifying ever since. Underlying this tendency is the realization that Jewish religion is the foundation of Jewish nationality and of Jewish national ideology – Zionism. This realization is shared by all political and ideological streams of Jewish Israeli society, including the purportedly secular Jewish renewal movement alluded to by Dror in the citation above (see Chapter 4). The other side of the religionization coin is the decline, with certain ups and downs, of liberal, universalist elements in the "secular" Jewish educational system.

In the state-religious educational system religionization has taken the form of *Charedization*, with gender segregation of primary schools – as a rule from the fourth grade on but in many cases from the very first grade – being the most obvious manifestation of that process. The educational material that is being taught in that system has also become more religious, with gender segregated schools leading the way in emphasizing Jewish studies and de-emphasizing general subjects such as science, mathematics, and social studies, as well as normative values such as democracy, citizenship, and human rights.

Gender segregation, of both students and teachers, has affected the higher education system as well, as universities and colleges, with encouragement from the state, are vying to attract the lucrative *Charedi* business. While *Charedi* attainment of higher education signifies a certain degree of opening to the modern surrounding society, this opening comes with a heavy price tag: legitimization of gender segregation in the institutions of higher education and violation of the liberal values of equality and human dignity, entrenched, supposedly, in Israel's constitutional law. Moreover, the policy of attracting *Charedim* to higher education has so far shown only meager results, while the erosion of liberal values which it entails is quite real.

Civic education has been a particularly contentious arena in the process of religionization of the educational system because it is where the contradiction between Israel's self-definition as a Jewish and as a democratic state comes most clearly to the fore. Should Israeli democracy be substantial (liberal) or procedural; should its citizenship be liberal or ethno-national, formal or active, emphasizing citizens' rights or citizens' duties; should Israeli political culture prioritize universalism or particularism? These questions are at the core of the debate between liberal Zionists such as Kremnitzer and Tamir and religious-nationalists such as Geiger, Sa'ar and Bennett. Whatever the merits of their arguments, secular liberal Zionists are clearly on the retreat politically and on the defensive ideologically, and the state educational system, including its "secular" branch, is being molded in accordance with a religious-nationalist vision.

Notes

1 For an overview of the issue of religion in the Israeli educational systems from a legal perspective see Ha-Cohen 2017.

2 A third educational system, in which the language of instruction is Arabic, was established for Israel's Palestinian citizens.

3 It has been suggested that elementary schools may be introducing gender segregation in order to sift out the students with lower socio-economic status, whose parents (who tend to be Mizrachi "traditionalists") oppose gender segregation (Finkelstein 2014:30; Hermann et al. 2014:205).

4 This anxiety was instigated in large measure by the small group of young intellectuals, the Young Hebrews (commonly known as the "Canaanites"), who sought to establish a direct link between the ancient Hebrews and the Zionist settlers in Palestine, severing the latter's ties to Diaspora Jewry (Shavit 1987; Shikli 2004:33).

5 The State Education Law of 1953 allows 75 percent of the parents in a particular cohort to determine 25 percent of the curriculum taught to that cohort according to their preferences.

6 Available at: www.mako.co.il/home-family-kids/education/Article-c4c3d17b5b6e241 006.htm (in Hebrew; accessed July 7, 2017).

7 For a discussion about the onset of resistance by some secular parents to these processes see Kashti 2017b.

8 A treatise of the Mishnah dealing with ethics.

9 Available at: www.binyanshalem.org.il/7/5/%D7%A0%D7%A9%D7%99%D7%9D_ %D7%A9%D7%9E%D7%97%D7%95%D7%AA (accessed September 29, 2017).

10 Due to the change of government in 1996 no final report was submitted by the Kremnitzer Committee (Kremnitzer 2013:36).

11 For the opposite view of the book see Halleli Pinson's analysis:

> The book, under the guise of adopting a pluralist approach and presenting a variety of views that exist in Israeli society, takes a clear position on the question of the appropriate definition of the State of Israel ... The book makes a distinction between the Zionist approaches – the appropriate approaches ... and the approaches that reject Israel's definition as Jewish or as democratic and are therefore on the margin...

(Pinson 2006:15)

Bashir Bashir has argued that

> Despite its reputation as expressing liberal and progressive tendencies, as a matter of fact the Kremnitzer Report displays conservative tendencies in that it does not seek to promote a profound, structural and transformative change in Israeli policy and Israeli identity which are, *inter alia*, exclusivist, colonialist and tribalis.

(Bashir 2013:281)

12 An exception is the permission granted 18–22-year-olds to study for the matriculation examinations or on a preparatory program in an institution of higher education (CHE 2016:15).

13 Figures here and elsewhere may vary in different sources because of different ways of defining who is "*Chared*" (Regev 2016:23–4).

14 Only the Open University, a correspondence school, admits everyone.

15 Cf. The First Letter of St. Paul to Timothy (2:11–12): "Let the woman learn in silence with all subjection. But I suffer not a woman to teach, nor to usurp authority over the man, but to be in silence."

16 For gender segregation in other spheres of Israel's social life and the argument that gender segregation is a form of sexual harassment as defined in Israeli law, see Triger 2012; 2013.

17 The exclusion of women professors from teaching male students has not been authorized, or even mentioned, by the CHE but is operative in practice (HCJ 6500/17:8, 31–7).

References

Almog, O. (1997) *The Sabra – A Profile*, Tel Aviv: Am Oved (in Hebrew).

Arad, U. and Yaffe, M. (2006) "The Place, Contribution and Role of NGOs in the Area of Education for Judaism as Culture in the General State Educational System and its Community Space," *Panim: Everyone Deserves Jewish Culture* www.panim.org.il/p-120 (in Hebrew; accessed October 25, 2013).

Avnon, D. (2016) "The New Citizenship: Ethnic, National, Majoritarian," *Giluy Da'at*, 10: 3–15.

Azrieli, Y. (1990) *The Knitted Kipot Generation: The Political Revolution of the Young in the NRP*, n.p: Avivim (in Hebrew).

Bashir, B. (2013) "Between Ethno-Nationalism to Decolonization of Israeliness," in Avnon, D. (ed.), *Civic Education in Israel*, Tel Aviv: Am Oved, pp. 276–87 (in Hebrew).

Ben David-Hadar, I. (2016) "Education for All: The Israeli Ultra-Orthodox Schools," *Educational Practice and Theory*, 38: 23–39.

Biton, K. (2014) "Between the Sacred and the Profane: Patterns of Accommodation in the Relations between Religion and State in Israel – Analysis of the Issue of the Core Curriculum," MA thesis, Department of Political Science, Tel Aviv University (in Hebrew).

Boaz, H. (2002) "The Struggle over Women's Suffrage in the Period of the Yishuv," *Teoria U-Vikoret*, 21: 107–31 (in Hebrew).

Brown, B. (2017) *The Haredim: A Guide to Their Beliefs and Sectors*, Tel Aviv: Am Oved (in Hebrew).

CBS (2013) *Israel in Numbers, 2013*, Jerusalem: Central Bureau of Statistics (in Hebrew).

CBS (2016) *Projection of Students in the Educational System for the Years 2017–2021: Methodology and Findings Report*, Jerusalem: Central Bureau of Statistics (in Hebrew).

CHE (2016) *Expanding the Charedi Population's Access to Higher Education in the Next Five Years*, Jerusalem: Council on Higher Education (in Hebrew).

Chemo, N. ((n.d. [2012]) *Issues in Jewish Education among a Group of Policy Makers in the Educational Field – Executive Summary*, Jerusalem: Avi Chai (in Hebrew).

Cohn, M. (2016) "Expanding Access to Higher Education for the Charedi Population Toward the Next Five Years: Position Document for the Public Hearing" (letter addressed to the Council on Higher Education), n.p., copy on file with the authors.

Conforti, I. (2009) "The New Jew in Zionist Thought: Nationalism, Ideology and Historiography," *Israel* 16: 63–96 (in Hebrew).

Darom, N. and Kashti, O. (2013) "How Are the Secular State Schools Making Tshuvah, *Haaretz Weekend Magazine*, December 27, www.haaretz.co.il/magazine/.premium-1.2200680 (in Hebrew; accessed November 7, 2014).

Dattel, L. (2017) "Loss of Control: How the Budget for Jewish Culture Studies has Sprung Up – And Where did the Money Go?," *Haaretz*, June 7.

Dror, Y. (2007) "Teaching the Bible in the Schools of the Labor and Kibbutz Movements, 1921–1953," *Jewish History* 21: 179–97.

Dror, Y. (2009) " 'Nurturing Jewish Consciousness' in the Israeli Educational System: From 'Negation of the Diaspora' in the Period of the Yishuv to 'Jewish Peoplehood' in Our Own Days," in Sabar Ben-Yehoshua, N., Shimoni, G., and Chemo, N. (eds.), *Jewish Peoplehood*, Tel Aviv: Beit Hatfutzot (in Hebrew).

Eliav, B. (ed.) (1988) *The Jewish National Home: From the Balfour Declaration to Independence*, Jerusalem: Keter (in Hebrew).

Faitelson, J. (2011) *Demographic Trends and their Implications for the Educational System in Israel*, Jerusalem: The Institute for Zionist Strategy (in Hebrew).

Finkelstein, A. (2014) *The Religious Public Education in Israel: Status Report, Tendencies and Achievements*, Part 2, Kibbutz Be'erot Yitzhak: Ne'emaney Torah Ve-Avoda (in Hebrew).

Firer, R. (1985) *The Agents of Zionist Education*, Tel Aviv: Hakibbutz Hameuchad/Sifriat Poalim (in Hebrew).

Fischer, S. (2014) "The Crises of Liberal Citizenship: Religion and Education in Israel," in Seligman, A. (ed.), *Religious Education and the Challenge of Pluralism*, Oxford: Oxford University Press, pp. 119–49.

Geiger, I. (2009) *Civics Studies: Education or One-Directional Indoctrination?* Position Paper. Jerusalem: Institute for Zionist Strategy (in Hebrew).

Geiger, I. (2013) "Indicators for Civic Education in a Jewish Nation-State," in Avnon, D. (ed.), *Civic Education in Israel*, Tel Aviv: Am Oved, pp. 85–105 (in Hebrew).

Greenblum, D. (2016) *From the Bravery of the Spirit to the Sanctification of Power: Power and Bravery in Religious Zionism 1948–1967*, Ra'anana: Open University Press (in Hebrew).

Ha-Cohen, A. (2017) "'Teach the Boy in His Own Way!?': Religion, Autonomy, Separatism and Pluralism in the Educational System and Judicial Review of Them," in Gordon, O. (ed.), *Edmond Levy Book*, Tel Aviv: Nevo, pp. 39–52 (in Hebrew).

Herman, S. N. (1970) *Israelis and Jews: The Continuity of an Identity*, New York: Random House.

Hermann, T., Be'eri, G., Heller, E., Cohen, C., Lebel, Y., Mozes, H., and Neuman, K. (2014) *The National-Religious Sector in Israel 2014*, Jerusalem: Israel Democracy Institute (in Hebrew).

HCJ 6500/17 (Ruling of the Israeli High Court of Justice). *Dr. Yofi Tirosh and Others vs. the Council on Higher Education and Others, Request for Order Nisi* (in Hebrew).

Hod, R. (2017) "A Short Story on Privatization and Religionization," *Haaretz*, September 3 (in Hebrew).

Ichilov, O., Salomon, G., and Inbar, D. (2005) "Citizenship Education in Israel – A Jewish-Democratic State," *Israel Affairs*, 11: 303–23.

IDI (2016a) *Statistical Report on Ultra-Orthodox Society in Israel*, Jerusalem: Israel Democracy Institute.

IDI (2016b) *Annual of Charedi Society in Israel*, Jerusalem: Israel Democracy Institute (in Hebrew).

Israel Religious Action Center (1992) *Budgeting the Religious Sector in Israel*, Jerusalem: Israel Movement for Progressive Judaism (in Hebrew).

Kafkafi, E. (1991) *A Country Searching for Its people: The Abolition of the Labor Educational Stream*, Tel Aviv: Hakibbutz Hameuchad (in Hebrew).

Kashti, O. (2017a) "Orthodox Bodies Have Taken Over a Program for Pluralist Teaching of Judaism," *Haaretz*, March 19 (in Hebrew).

Kashti, O. (2017b) "The Secular Parents are Planning to Come Ready to the School Year," *Haaretz*, July 11 (in Hebrew).

Kashti, O. (2017c) "Education Ministry Initiates: A Religious Organization Will Guide Seculars How to 'Bring About Behavioral Change in Children'," *Haaretz*, September 28 (in Hebrew).

Kashti, O. (2017d) "The Ministries for Gender Inequality: The Government is Turning Gender Segregation into a Norm," *Haaretz*, November 17 (in Hebrew).

Kashti, O. (2017e) "Struggling Against Religionization in the Religious Public Too," *Haaretz*, December 8 (in Hebrew).

Kashti, O. (2017f) "Hadata Shmadata: Bennett Says There is no Religionization – The Money, the Books, and the Curriculum He is Proud Of Prove Differently," *Haaretz*, July 7.

Kedar, N. (2009) *Mamlachtiyut: David Ben-Gurion's Civil Thought*, Midreshet Sde-Boker: Ben-Gurion Research Institute (in Hebrew).

Kelman, N. (2010) "Seeding the Field of Jewish Renewal in Israel," *Journal of Jewish Communal Service*, 85: 81–3.

Knesset (2010) *Some Aspects of the Condition of Jewish Studies in the [Secular] State System*, Jerusalem: The Knesset Research and Information Center (in Hebrew).

Knesset (2014) "Data on Academic Educational Institutions for the *Charedi* Public," Jerusalem: The Knesset Research and Information Center, n.p., copy on file with the authors (in Hebrew).

Kolatt, I. (1998) "Religion, Society and State in the Period of the National Home," in Almog, S., Reinharz, J., and Shapira An (eds.), *Zionism and Religion*, Hanover, NH: University Press of New England, pp. 273–301.

Kremnitzer, M. (1996) *To Be Citizens: Civics Education for All Students in Israel*, Jerusalem: State of Israel – Ministry of Education (in Hebrew).

Kremnitzer, M. (2013) "Thirteen Years of the Report 'To Be Citizens'," in Avnon, D. (ed.), *Civic Education in Israel*, Tel Aviv: Am Oved, pp. 33–44 (in Hebrew).

Kremnitzer, M. (2016a) "This is Not the Way to Build Citizen Education, Or: Reality Surpasses All Imagination," *Giluy Da'at* 10: 1–8 (in Hebrew).

Kremnitzer, M. (2016b) "State Education Law and the Civics Book," Israel Democracy Institute, www.idi.org.il/articles/3327 (in Hebrew; accessed April 26, 2017).

Laws of the State of Israel (2000) "State Education Law" (Amendment No. 5), *Laws of the State of Israel*, 1729: 122 (in Hebrew).

Laws of the State of Israel (2008) "State Education Law" (Amendment No. 10), *Laws of the State of Israel*, 2168: 660–1 (in Hebrew).

Liebman, C. S. and Don-Yehiya, E. (1983) *Civil Religion in Israel: Traditional Judaism and Political Culture in the Jewish State*, Berkeley, CA: University of California Press.

Liebman, C. S. and Don-Yehiya, E. (1984) *Religion and Politics in Israel*, Bloomington, IN: Indiana University Press.

Liefschitz, H. (2017) *Civics Matriculation Examinations*, Position Paper No. 33, Kohelet Forum.

Malach, G. (2014) *A "Kosher" Degree: Academic Studies in the Haredi Sector*, Jerusalem: The Institute of Urban and Regional Studies, The Hebrew University of Jerusalem (Floersheimer Studies No. 4/27; in Hebrew).

Malach, G. and Kahaner, L. (2016) "Gender and Sector Separation in Academic Studies for the Charedi Population," Report Submitted to the Council on Higher Education – The Committee for Budgeting and Coordination, n.p., copy on file with the authors (in Hebrew).

Malach, G., Kahaner, L., and Regev, E. (n.d. [2016]) "The Five-Year Plan of the Council on Higher Education – The Committee for Budgeting and Coordination for the Charedi Population for 2012–2016: Evaluation Study and Recommendations," n.p., copy on file with the authors (in Hebrew).

Ministry of Education (2000) *To Be Citizens in Israel: A Jewish and Democratic State*, Jerusalem: State of Israel – Ministry of Education (in Hebrew).

Ministry of Education (2009) "Response to Dr. Isaac Geiger's Position Paper," September 24, n.p., copy on file with the authors (in Hebrew).

Molad (2017) *Propagating: How the Religious Right Took Control of Values Education in the [Secular] State System*, Jerusalem: Molad – The Center for Democratic Renewal (in Hebrew).

Pedahzur, A. and Perliger, A. (2004) "The Structural Paradox of Civic Education in Israel," *Megamnot*, 43: 64–83 (in Hebrew).

Peled, Y. (1992) "Ethnic Democracy and the Legal Construction of Citizenship: Arab Citizens of the Jewish State," *The American Political Science Review*, 86: 432–43.

Pinson, H. (2006) "Between a Jewish and a Democratic State: Contradictions and Tensions in the Civics Curriculum," *Politika*, 14: 9–24 (in Hebrew).

Pinson, H. (n.d. [2013]) *From Jewish and Democratic State to Jewish State Period: Analysis of the New Chapters in the Civics Textbook "To Be Citizens in Israel: A Jewish and Democratic State,"* Jerusalem: Association for Civil Rights in Israel (in Hebrew).

Rabinowitz, A. (2017) "Increase in the Number of Charedi Educational Institutions that Joined the State Charedi System and Teach the Core [Curriculum]," *Haartez*, September 1.

Regev, E. (2016) "The Challenges of Integrating Haredim into Academic Studies," in Weiss, A. (ed.), *State of the Nation Report: Society, Economy and Policy in Israel*, Jerusalem: Taub Center for Social Policy Studies in Israel.

Riger, E. (1940) *Hebrew Education in Palestine, Part One: General Principles and Trends*, Tel Aviv: Dvir (in Hebrew).

Sagi, A. and Schwartz, D. (2017) *From Realism to Messianism: Religious Zionism and the Six-Day War*, Jerusalem: Carmel (in Hebrew).

Sagiv, N. (2011) "Approaches to Bible Teaching in Elementary Schools of the General and Labor Educational Streams from 1910 to the 1960s," MA thesis, Chaim and Joan Konstantiner School of Education, Tel Aviv University (in Hebrew).

Schiff, G. (1977) *Tradition and Politics: The Religious Parties of Israel*, Detroit, MI: Wayne University Press.

Secular Forum (2017a) "Indicator for Examining Textbooks for State Elementary School," *Secular Forum Website* (accessed April 26, 2017).

Secular Forum (2017b) "The New Jewish-Israeli Culture Curriculum: A Position Paper by the Secular Forum," *Secular Forum Website* (accessed April 25, 2017).

Shafir, G. and Peled, Y. (2002) *Being Israeli: The Dynamics of Multiple Citizenship*, Cambridge: Cambridge University Press.

Shapiro, Y. (1984) *An Elite Without Successors: Generations of Political Leaders in Israel*, Tel Aviv: Sifriat Poalim (in Hebrew).

Shapiro, Y. (1996) *Politicians as a Hegemonic Class: The Case of Israel*, Tel Aviv: Sifriat Poalim (in Hebrew).

Shavit, Y. (1987) *The New Hebrew Nation: A Study in Israeli Heresy and Fantasy*, London: Frank Cass.

Sheleg, Y. (2010) *From Old Hebrew to New Jew: The Jewish Renaissance in Israeli Society*, Jerusalem: Israel Democracy Institute (in Hebrew).

Shenhar, A. (1994) *People and the World: Jewish Culture in a Changing World*, Jerusalem: Ministry of Education – The Committee for Examining Judaic Studies in State Education (in Hebrew).

Shenhar, A. (2007) "A Crisis in Judaic Studies – and the Academic World is Silent," *Kivunim Chadashim*, 16: 77–82 (in Hebrew).

Shenhar, A. (2012) "'Between Heritage and Culture of Israel' and 'People and the World'," *Studies in Education*, Haifa: Haifa University, pp. 18–25 (in Hebrew).

Shikli, E. (2004) "TALI Education: The Development and Realization of an Educational Idea under Conditions of a Changing Reality," PhD dissertation, Jerusalem: Jewish Theological Seminary (in Hebrew).

Shir, Z. (2014) *Gender Separation in State-Religious Elementary Schools*, Jerusalem: Bank of Israel – Periodical Papers 2014.06 (in Hebrew).

Silver, E., Pascal, L., Korev, A., and Shapira Rosenberg, E. (2012) *Examining Directions of Work in the State Educational System (Non-Religious) in the Jewish Sector*, Jerusalem: Avi Chai.

Skop, Y. (2015) "Sharp Increase in the Separation between Girls and Boys in the State-Religious Elementary Education," *Haaretz*, August 25.

Steinmetz, M. (2016) "Ministry of Education Data Reveal: Only One in 10 *Charedim* Entitled to *Bagrut*," *Walla News*, August 1, https://news.walla.co.il/item/2984523 (in Hebrew; accessed January 29, 2018).

Swirski, Shlomo (1990) *Education in Israel: Schooling for Inequality*, Tel Aviv: Breirot (Hebrew).

Taylor, C. (2011) "Western Secularity," in Calhoun, C., Juergensmeyer, M., and Van Antwerpen, M. (eds.), *Rethinking Secularism*, Oxford: Oxford University Press, pp. 31–53.

Triger, Z. (2012) "Gender Segregation as Sexual Harassment," *Tel Aviv University Law Review*, 35: 703–46 (in Hebrew).

Triger, Z. (2013) "The Self-Defeating Nature of 'Modesty'-Based Gender Segregation," *Israel Studies*, 18: 19–28.

Zameret, Z. (1997) *Across a Narrow Bridge: Shaping the Education System during the Great Aliya*, Sede Boker: Ben-Gurion University Press (in Hebrew).

Zameret, Z. (2003) *Israel's First Decade: The Development of the Education System*, Tel Aviv: Open University Press (in Hebrew).

Zucker, Norman L. (1973) *The Coming Crisis in Israel: Private Faith and Public Policy*, Cambridge, MA: The MIT Press.

6 The IDF: from religionization to theocratization

In *The Jewish State* Theodor Herzl declared: "We shall keep our priests within the confines of their temples, in the same way as we shall keep our professional army within the confines of their barracks" (Herzl 1934:71, cited in Abramov 1976:63). The Israel Defense Forces is not a professional army but a "people's army," based on mandatory regular and reserve service, and in recent years "our priests" – Jewish Orthodox rabbis – are increasingly finding their way into its barracks.

The issue of the role of Jewish religion and of religious Jews in the IDF has two somewhat contradictory but related aspects: the de facto exemption of *Charedi yeshiva* students from military service altogether, and the growing prominence of Religious Zionists in combat roles and in the military command structure.

Charedim and military service: sharing the burden or division of labor?

A major factor in the institutional growth of the *Charedi* communities in recent years has been the exemption from military service granted to *Charedi yeshiva* students in 1948 in order, initially, to help rebuild the world of *yeshivot* that had been destroyed in the Holocaust (Stadler and Ben-Ari 2003:25, 31; Stadler 2004:71; Brown 2017:296–303; Leon 2017:12). Mandatory military service of three years for men and about two years for women is required by law of all citizens of Israel, with the exception of women who are married, pregnant or mothers. In addition, men, mostly, are required to serve in the military reserves for two or three decades following their regular service. As a matter of policy, citizen-Palestinian men, with the exception of those belonging to the Druze and Circassian minorities, and all Palestinian women, are administratively exempted from service by not being called up (but can volunteer for service if they want). Jewish women can be exempted if they declare that military service violates their religious beliefs, and they have the option of doing an alternative, civilian service; this option is taken mostly by national-religious women (about 30 percent of whom currently do serve in the military, to the chagrin of most national-religious rabbis) (Ettinger 2015; Magal 2016:129–48).

Charedi and some national-religious *yeshiva* students, and students in Druze religious schools, are granted administrative deferments to the end of their studies, as are a very small number of college students each year. Unlike the college students and students in national-religious *yeshivot* (see below), however, the vast majority of *Charedi yeshiva* students in effect do not serve even after they graduate (Hofnung 1991; Y. Cohen 1993; Ilan 2000:113–48; Peres and Ben-Rafael 2006:127–9; Gal 2012; Zicherman and Cahaner 2012:39, 47 and sources cited therein; S. Cohen 2013; Malchi 2013; Y. Levy 2015:104–10; Brown 2017:296–319).

Charedi objection to military service, both at the level of the rabbinical establishment and at the level of the *yeshiva* students themselves, does not stem from pacifism or disregard for the importance of the IDF or of military defense in general. On the contrary, most *Charedim* hold the IDF in high regard and consider it to be a vital institution for the security of the country. Their objection to military service stems primarily from concern that the experience of military service will "corrupt" their young men (there is obviously no question of drafting *Charedi* women), will draw them away from a religious life devoted to Torah study, and in this way will "threaten the boundaries of the community and thus … potentially lead to its very destruction" (Stadler and Ben-Ari 2003:30–3; Stadler 2004:71–2). The argument based on the threat of corruption of the youth is buttressed by another argument – namely, that national defense must have two aspects, both physical and spiritual. While the IDF provides physical defense, the *yeshivot* provide spiritual defense, which is no less, if not more important. The issue, then, is not about sharing the burden of military service but rather a division of labor between earthly soldiering and "other-worldly soldiering" (Stadler and Ben-Ari 2003:24–8; Stadler 2004:75).

Objection to military service among *yeshiva* students themselves is apparently not as solid as among their rabbis. Quite a few, it seems, would actually like to have the escape route from the *yeshiva*, as well as the challenge, the excitement, and the sense of fulfillment that military service could provide, as long as arrangements were made that would allow them to maintain their religious lifestyle in the military. Paradoxically, these young men see, or fantasize, the military as a space of freedom compared to their regimented life in the *yeshiva*. The rabbis who head the *yeshivot*, and the community in general, exert very strong pressures on the young men not to enlist, because this will obviously weaken their hold over their young generation (Stadler and Ben-Ari 2003:32, 35–43; Stadler 2004:74, 79–81, 83–6; Stadler et al. 2008:220).

In the fifty years between 1948 and 1998, 70,000 deferments of military service, most of them de facto exemptions, had been granted, mostly to *Charedi yeshiva* students. In 2003 such deferments were held by 39,200 young *Charedi* men and in 2010 by 63,000. In 2011 the number declined to 54,000 but had risen to about 60,000 at the time of writing. The rate at which deferments have been granted has been accelerating rapidly in recent years: 2.5 percent of the male draft-eligible cohort were granted deferments in 1968, 5.3 percent in 1988, 9.2 percent in 1999, and 13 percent in 2010 (Horovitz 1989:10, 68–9; Hoffman

1989:233; Hofnung 1991:245; Israel Religious Action Center 1992:166; Gonen 2000:4; Ilan 2000:114, 126; State Comptroller 2011; IDI 2012; Y. Levy 2015:104–10).[1]

Since only full-time *yeshiva* students (*shetoratam umnutam* – whose Torah study is their vocation) are eligible for deferments, and since deferments become exemptions once their holders reach the age of forty-one (thirty-five if they have four children or more), most of these students continue to study, or at least be registered in *yeshivot*, and do not enter the labor market for many years, if at all. Thus while the average age of leaving a *Charedi yeshiva* in Israel is forty-two, in the United States, where no special privileges accrue to *yeshiva* students, the average leaving age is twenty-five. It has been calculated that the absence of *Charedi* men from the labor market costs the Israeli economy 9.4 billion shekels (about 2.5 billion US dollars) annually in lost production (Ilan 2000:259–63; Gonen 2000:16; Pundak et al. 2012).

State subsidies for *yeshivot* are based on enrollment, so *yeshivot* have no interest in terminating their students, bona-fide or otherwise. Thus in 1993 the number of full-time adult male *yeshiva* students reported by the Ministry of Religious Affairs was 50,000, in 1997 it was 71,000 and in 2012 114,000. These numbers, the accuracy of which is notoriously doubtful, represent practically the entire cohort of draft-eligible men in the *Charedi* communities. Both the numbers and the phenomenon of entire age cohorts that go on to advanced religious studies in *yeshivot* are without parallel in Jewish history (Berman and Klinov 1997:10n15; S. Cohen 1997a:96; Adva 1998, esp. pp. 21–2; Gonen 2000; Ilan 2000:126; *Hiddush* 2012). Needless to say, this situation could not have been sustained without massive state subsidization: state expenditures for Jewish religious educational institutions in 2013 was 760 million shekels (about 220 million US dollars), or 46 percent of all subsidies granted by the state to cultural institutions (Amsterdamski 2014).

The recent fluctuations in the number of deferment holders result from strenuous efforts on the part of secular civil society and some secular political parties to eliminate the arrangement of *torato umnuto* in order to "equalize the burden" of military service and enable *Charedi* men to enter the labor market in greater numbers (Y. Levy 2015:288–93). (The fact that military service has come to be seen as a burden rather than a privilege in the non-observant, more affluent sector of the society is significant; see below.) These efforts have taken the form primarily of appeals to the High Court of Justice against the legality of this arrangement. After a number of appeals had been turned down, the first breakthrough on this front occurred in 1998 when the Court decided that, given the large number of deferments granted in 1996 (7.4 percent of the draft-eligible cohort in that year), this arrangement could no longer be based on administrative decisions and must be regulated by primary legislation (Brown 2017:309; HCJ 1877/14, §3 of Chief Justice Naor's opinion).

In 2002 a law regulating these deferments, known as the Tal Law, was enacted, nicknamed after Zvi Tal, the Orthodox retired Supreme Court justice who headed the committee that drafted it. The law authorized the Minister of

Defense to continue to issue deferments, but, importantly, provided the *Charedi yeshiva* students with an escape route after four years of deferred service, in the form of a shortened military or civilian service following which they would be exempted from military service and be free of the need to remain in the *yeshiva*. The law was criticized severely both by liberals, for failing to "equalize the burden" of military service, and by the *Charedi* rabbinical establishment, including the *Charedi* political parties, for requiring even a shortened military or civilian service as a condition of receiving the exemption. A great deal of pressure was put on *Charedi yeshiva* students not to take advantage of the provisions of the Tal Law, and as a result the High Court of Justice in 2012 declared it to be unconstitutional for failing to achieve its declared purpose and thus unjustifiably violating the principle of equality and the human dignity of those who do serve in the military (Stadler and Ben-Ari 2003:20; Brown 2017:311–12; HCJ 1877/14, §7 of Chief Justice Naor's opinion).

General elections that were held in 2013 and 2015, resulting in different constellations of power between liberal and *Charedi* political parties, have led to further legislation, the essence of which, camouflaged by flowery rhetoric, has been to legalize the deferments system without any substantive change. One new element in this legislation has been the setting of quotas for *Charedi yeshiva* students to enroll in military or civilian service each year and conditioning the deferments granted to individuals on the fulfillment of those quotas. However, the quotas were set very low and were ignored in practice. As a result, in September 2017 the High Court of Justice declared this new legislation unconstitutional as well and determined that it be voided in a year's time (Greilsammer 2014:141–3; Brown 2017:315–17; HCJ 1877/14). This is where things stand at the time of writing.

Parallel to these political and judicial maneuvers, increasing numbers of young *Charedi* men have been enlisting in the IDF, in spite of the strong community pressures against it. In 2016 2850 *Charedi yeshiva* students, or 25 percent of the *Charedi* draft-eligible cohort, did enlist, primarily in their own special units.[2] As we saw, many young *Charedi* men find the prospect of military service appealing in its own right, and many are tired of the life of poverty and dependency to which they are destined by the prevailing *torato umnuto* arrangement. Prevented from joining the labor force or seeking secular education at least until the age of thirty-five, for fear of being drafted, they are forced to depend on state subsidies and on their wives' earnings for their livelihood. The changed attitude of some of them is reflected in their rate of participation in the civilian labor force, which in 2015 was 45.6 percent for *Charedi* men aged 25–64, up from 38.7 percent in 2009. This compares with 85.3 percent in the general male population, 87 percent among non-*Charedi* Jewish men, and 76.5 percent in the population as a whole (BOI 2012:195, 204; CBS 2015; IDI n.d. [2017]).

Religious Zionists

Unlike the *Charedim*, who "tend to differentiate between two kinds of soldiering which are both important to the security of the country and the people," the earthly and the other-worldly, "for the national-religious, this-worldly service is sanctified in terms of other-worldly considerations" (Stadler and Ben-Ari 2003:40). Thus, as the motivation to serve, especially as a career, has declined with liberalization among many non-observant, middle-class youth, the role of national-religious youngsters in the military has steadily become more pronounced (Hofnung 1991:232–48; Y. Levy 1997:178; 2015; Inbar 1996; S. Cohen 1997b; Shafir and Peled 2002:237–8; Magal 2016; Siboni and Pearl Finkel 2017). Estimates of the ratio of Religious Zionist officers in the combat officer corps vary, but there is no question that it is a significant ratio; that it is disproportionate to their share of the Jewish population (approximately 12 percent [CBS 2011:8]); and that it is increasing at both the junior and senior officer levels. A number of Religious Zionist officers have achieved general ranks, and one has reached the position of Deputy Chief of Staff of the IDF. Clearly, the national-religious sector has replaced the labor settlement sector as provider of quality manpower to the Israeli military (Leibel and Gal 2012:104–5; Sadan 2016:20–1; Yefet 2016:253n123).

According to some observers this process has resulted in growing politicization and decreasing professionalism of the IDF. Others have interpreted the process in exactly the opposite way – an attempted retreat from the neo-liberalism and post-modernism that had plagued the IDF since the Lebanon war of 1982 to the traditional spirit of a resolute and effective war machine (Y. Levy 2007; Drori 2012; Leibel 2012; Loebel and Lubish-Omer 2012; Magal 2016:245). Be that as it may, the prominence of Religious Zionist officers and enlisted men in the infantry brigades has caused concern that under certain circumstances they may obey their rabbis and defy military orders – to dismantle West Bank settlements, for example. This concern stems from the fact that a high proportion of Religious Zionist recruits join the IDF through a network of religious educational institutions with which they continue to maintain contact during their service (and beyond) (Magal 2016:296; Y. Levy 2017–2018:178–83).

The first of this kind of institution to be established – *yeshivot hesder* (arrangement) – were set up in the mid-1960s and their numbers increased rapidly after the wars of 1967 and 1973. Students in these *yeshivot* perform a shortened military service (currently seventeen months), in their own separate units, combined with their religious studies. The original purpose of *yeshivot hesder* was to enable Religious Zionist young men to overcome the sense of inferiority they felt toward two other groups of young men in the society: *Charedim*, who devoted their lives to sacred studies and did not serve in the military, and the non-observant, who performed meaningful military service in defense of their country.

In order to prevent their youngsters from joining one or another of these camps, Zionist rabbis devised these *yeshivot* in which the students can both immerse themselves in religious study and perform meaningful military service. The IDF agreed that they would serve for a shorter period, in their own special units, thus reducing the risk that their military service will induce them to stray from the religious fold. *Yeshivot hesder*, many of which are located in the occupied Palestinian territories, have been hotbeds of radical Jewish nationalism and major recruiting grounds for Gush Emunim. Prime Minister Yitzhak Rabin's assassin, Yigal Amir, was a graduate of one of these *yeshivot* (and was a law student at the national-religious university, Bar-Ilan, when he committed the murder) (S. Cohen 1997a:105–39; Y. Levy 2015:66–82, 94–104, 188; Magal 2016:115–28).

The short military service performed by students of *yeshivot hesder*, and the fact that they serve in their own special units, made promotion, and thus having significant influence on the IDF, more difficult. These *yeshivot* were also criticized for enabling their students to do less than the full service required of other young men (Y. Levy 2015:127; Yefet 2016:252n119). A solution to these problems was devised in the late 1980s in the form of a new institution: preparatory religious schools (*mechinot*), where graduates of state-religious high schools spend a year or two in religious studies combined with orientation for military service, and then serve the full three years in regular military (mostly army) units.

The idea behind the *mechinot* is that intensive religious study would inoculate their students against the secular temptations presented by military life, so they could safely serve in any unit and even pursue a military career, without their religious commitment being weakened (Lebel 2016). In addition, most of the *mechinot* are located in the occupied Palestinian territories, and their political orientation is also ultra-nationalist and anti-liberal. Together, *hesder* and *mechinot* graduates currently account for about 10 percent of the IDF's ground combat forces and, as indicated, a highly disproportionate share of the command structure up to and including the brigade commander level (Y. Levy 2015:125–40, 169–71).

Yagil Levy has made an important distinction between two different processes occurring within the IDF: religionization – "a cultural change that increases the influence of religious culture on the military, or seeks to give religious meaning to military activity," and theocratization – "a shift from cultural influence to the involvement of religious authorities in the running of the military," to the detriment of the latter's professional autonomy (Y. Levy 2015:134, 138, 183, 366; 2017–2018).

Religionization could be the effect of the more significant presence of religious soldiers, and especially of religious officers, in the IDF, and of the general religionization of the society. It has manifested itself in such minor issues as cleaning up the language used by soldiers, ending the practice of stealing military equipment from other military units, and stricter observance of the Sabbath and of *kashrut* (Magal 2016:241–2). Much more significantly, religionization has resulted in coming to view Israel's wars as holy wars. Thus, as mentioned above, during Israel's military operation in Gaza in the summer of 2014 the commanding officer of the Givati infantry brigade, Colonel Ofer Vinter, a graduate of the oldest *mechina*, located in the West Bank settlement of Eli, called on his troops to fight "the terrorists who defame the God of Israel" (Y. Levy 2015:157). This unprecedented call for religious war by a senior IDF commander caused a public uproar, but Vinter has not been reprimanded and has since been promoted.

Theocratization is the effect of the involvement of civilian rabbis – teachers in *yeshivot hesder* and *mechinot*, as well as these teachers' own rabbis – in both the daily affairs and operational decisions of the IDF. It has manifested itself in turning to civilian rabbis in questions of *Halacha*, including questions that have to do with permissible ways of interacting with female soldiers. More importantly, from a political standpoint, theocratization removes the issue of the Jewish settlements in the occupied Palestinian territories from the realm of mundane politics, hence from the purview of the military command and the elected political leadership, and turns their preservation into a divine commandment (Y. Levy 2015:154–75, 183; 2017–2018:178–83).

To counter this argument, critics point to the withdrawal of Jewish settlements from Gaza in 2005, which encountered strong opposition by some, but not all, important Zionist rabbis, and did not trigger massive resistance by religious soldiers against taking part in that operation. That example, however, should do little to allay concerns about the future behavior of these soldiers if the need arises to remove Jewish settlements from parts of the West Bank. In order to remove 8,000 Jewish settlers from Gaza, an easily isolated region of no religious significance to Jews, Prime Minister Ariel Sharon, a military hero idolized by both the settlers and the IDF, had to deploy the entire man and woman power of all of Israel's security forces. Moreover, the Gaza withdrawal was not carried out in agreement with the Palestinians, or in order to facilitate peace with them. It was carried out unilaterally, in order to make Israel's control of Gaza more efficient. In fact, the lack of explicit resistance by religious soldiers resulted from a series of "grey" agreements between the IDF and some civilian rabbis not to deploy their followers in the actual removal of the settlers from their homes (Rubin 2014:58–9; Y. Levy 2015:189–94, 208–19; cf. Magal 2016:274–94). Judging by this example, removing even 100,000 settlers from the West Bank, in order to enable the establishment of a minimally territorially contiguous Palestinian state, would be an impossible task.

A third institution that has played a crucial role in the religionization/theocratization of the IDF is the chief military rabbinate. Unlike military chaplaincies in liberal democratic states, the IDF rabbinate does not cater to the religious needs of religious soldiers only, but is entrusted, rather, with ensuring the character of the IDF as a *Jewish* military organization (Y. Levy 2015:59–60; 2017–2018:187–90; Yefet 2016:254). This role manifested itself initially in safeguarding the *kashrut* of military kitchens and the observance of the Sabbath in military units (in accordance with the commitments made in the Status Quo Letter of 1947; see Chapter 3). In recent years, however, its role has evolved to cover much more significant areas, such as conversion to Judaism of "Law of Return eligible" non-Jewish soldiers (see Chapter 3), who are pressured by the IDF to convert through a fast-track conversion course (ACRI 2017); women's place in the IDF; motivating the soldiers to fight; and, most importantly perhaps, military ethics (Sheleg 2010:67; Yefet 2016:254–5; Y. Levy 2018; see also An. Shapira 2014:153–4).

With the expansion of the role of the military rabbinate and of *yeshivot hesder* and *mechinot*, the position of military rabbi has increasingly come to be filled by erstwhile combat officers (Y. Levy 2015:333; Magal 2016:299–302), many of whom are *chozrim biteshuvah* (see Chapter 4). Concomitantly, the continuing ties of the graduates of *yeshivot hesder* and *mechinot* to the civilian rabbis running those institutions, whose rabbinical authority far exceeds that of the military rabbis, has forced the latter to allow civilian rabbis to play a greater role in the life of the IDF. The resultant "competitive cooperation" (Y. Levy 2015) between these two rabbinical communities has affected all areas entrusted to the IDF rabbinate, or usurped by it.

Since the 1970s, and more prominently since the 1990s, the IDF has pursued a policy of integrating women into all military roles, with the exception of clearly front-line combat. Currently only 8 percent of military roles are closed off to women (Y. Levy 2015:249–52). This policy has brought male and female soldiers into close contact in many cases, violating the religious stricture against such intimacy. A subsidiary issue has been women singers in military ceremonies and social events, because at least by some interpretations of Jewish religious law, men are forbidden to listen to the singing of women, which is considered to be an erotic activity (Hollander 2014). Religious soldiers have complained to their civilian rabbis of being forced into close proximity with women and of the requirement that they attend events where women were singing. Working through the military rabbinate, and in some cases directly *vis-à-vis* senior commanders, the civilian rabbis have been able to bring about adjustments to the military rules that would minimize the potential for such friction.

While the IDF has not succumbed completely (yet?) to the demands of those rabbis in this matter, it has gone a long way toward appeasing them and their soldier constituents (Y. Levy 2018). Thus, in 2017 the Chief Military Rabbi, Brigadier General Eyal Karim, determined that religious officers could not serve in mixed gender combat units, of which at the time of writing there were four battalions. On the other hand, he also determined that religious soldiers should participate in military events that include singing by women, but should concentrate on other things while the women are singing (Harel 2012; Y. Levy 2013; 2015:248–97, 330; An. Shapira 2014:147–8; Magal 2016:320–37; Yefet 2016:225; G. Cohen 2017; Tirosh 2017).[3]

As mentioned above, the legitimacy crisis alluded to by Liebman and Don-Yehiya (1983) and the liberalization of the Israeli economy and society since 1985 (Shafir and Peled 2000; 2002) have reduced the motivation of the veteran Ashkenazi middle class, including its labor settlement sector, to serve in the military, especially as a career. This was the primary reason behind the IDF's interest in recruiting Religious Zionists to its combat units and to careers in the military. Faced with a motivational crisis among its traditional pool of quality manpower, the IDF turned to religion as a source of inspiration both to serve "meaningful service" and to sacrifice one's life if necessary (Y. Levy 2015:52–3, 102; 2017–2018:177, 188, 192).

In the early 2000s the IDF adopted a program named "Mission and Uniqueness" (the title of one of Ben-Gurion's books) to enhance Jewish consciousness among its soldiers. The rationale for the program stated, in part:

The IDF relies on various events, traditions, opinions, symbols and rituals drawn from the treasure of Jewish historical memory in order to consolidate the *national* consciousness of those who serve in it ... The IDF should build the *national* consciousness of its soldiers, on the basis of the values and collective memory of the Jewish people ... in a way that enables them to see themselves as belonging [to Judaism] and to identify with it.

(Cited in Sheleg 2010:65, emphasis added)

The military rabbinate was entrusted with the task of buttressing the soldiers' motivation by raising their "Jewish consciousness." In 2010 the mission of the military rabbinate was redefined to include (in typical military circular language) "developing Jewish consciousness in religious matters [i.e., developing Jewish religious consciousness] among the IDF's commanders and soldiers ... in order to enhance [their] fighting spirit" (Y. Levy 2015:332, citing the State Comptroller's 2012 report; see also 327–36). Accordingly, the Chief Military Rabbi in 2006–2010, Avichai Rontzki (formerly an infantry officer), declared:

Part of my job, perhaps the main part, as Chief Military Rabbi, will be to connect the soldiers to the values of Judaism ... After all, you can't bring the French [Foreign] Legion here. A soldier must understand why he [*sic*] is here [in Israel]. If his only interest in life is to have a good life, why is he here?

(Y. Levy 2015:332)

The fact that Rontzki, his colleagues, and his successors had been combat officers in the past has made their use of religion to buttress the fighting spirit of the troops more credible with the soldiers.

Not only the motivation to fight, but the mode of fighting as well, has been affected by the use of religion to boost the morale of the troops. Prior to entering Gaza in December 2008, Rontzki, by his own account, "read to the soldiers the [Biblical] chapters dealing with Samson's revenge against the Philistines, *a national revenge* ... When they returned from battle the soldiers told me that this discourse had greatly empowered them" (Y. Levy 2015:336, emphasis added).

If the purpose of fighting is national revenge, rather than defeating the enemy's military force, for example, then the distinction between combatants and non-combatants, which is at the core of the law of war, will necessarily be dimmed. Moreover, if in war the IDF is executing a sacred mission, foretold in a divine plan, then the enemy resisting it is committing an "historic crime" and is viewed in its entirety, combatants and non-combatants alike, as a demonic being standing in the way of God's will (Luz 1999:368–9, 374–7; Barzel 2017:142–3; Sagi and Schwartz 2017:112–13; Y. Levy 2017–2018:183–7). Coupled with growing sensitivity among the general Jewish public to military casualties, a consequence of the sacralization of military operations has been that safeguarding Israeli soldiers has come to take precedence over safeguarding the lives of Arab civilians.

The military rabbinate and many civilian rabbis have done a great deal to legitimize this approach, as have secular military thinkers concerned with adapting the laws of war to the reality of the "war on terror" (Kasher and Yadlin 2005; Guiora 2011/2012; Sharvit Baruch 2012; Peled 2012; Y. Levy 2015:336–42; Yefet 2016:254). As a result, during Israel's punitive operation in Gaza from December 2008 to January 2009 between 1,200 and 1,400 Palestinians were killed, about half of them civilians, and only 13 Israeli soldiers, about half of them by friendly fire (Goldstone 2009; Margalit and Walzer, 2009:22). In the 2014 operation in Gaza over 2,100 Palestinians were killed, 1,500 of whom were civilians, and 71 Israeli soldiers (as well as 6 Israeli civilians) (Malinsky 2015; Weil and Azarova 2015).

Summary

As related in Chapter 3, the self-transformation that Religious Zionism had undergone in the 1960s, especially after 1967, included "moving from the back-seat to the drivers' seat" of the State of Israel. A crucial element in this move was "meaningful service" in the IDF, supported by a network of religious-military institutions – *yeshivot hesder* and *mechinot*.[4] With the liberalization of the Israeli economy and society, which began shortly afterwards, the motivation to serve, especially as a career, declined markedly among the IDF's traditional pool of quality manpower – the veteran Ashkenazi elite, especially its labor settlement sector. The IDF therefore turned to the Religious Zionist sector, and to Jewish religion in general, in order to try to overcome this shortage.

The convergence of the IDF's and Religious Zionism's interests resulted in Religious Zionist soldiers and officers, many of them West Bank settlers, coming to play a significant role in the IDF, especially in its infantry units. This, naturally, also enhanced the place of religion and of rabbis, both military and civilian, in the life of the IDF, coming into conflict, *inter alia*, with its efforts to integrate women into most of its units. The "religionization" and then "theocratization" of the IDF (Y. Levy 2015) have together raised the issue of "bifurcated loyalty" (Rubin 2014) – will religious soldiers, at the moment of truth, obey their commanders or their rabbis, should contradictory instructions be issued by these two sources of authority? So far this issue has not come to the fore in a significant practical way, in part at least because the IDF has been very receptive to the rabbis' demands. But the issue continues to loom under the surface. The problem will be exacerbated, of course, should *Charedi* men begin to enlist in significant numbers as well.

Notes

1 Since the size of draft-eligible cohorts is considered a military secret, these figures should be taken as approximations only.
2 Available at: www.mako.co.il/news-military/security-q3_2017/Article-7d456d70e79be51 004.htm (accessed December 22, 2017).

3 As a civilian, before his appointment as Chief Military Rabbi, Karim had objected to women serving in the IDF, permitted the raping of enemy women in war (theoretically), called homosexuals sick, and justified discriminating against Arabs in employment. When his appointment as Chief Military Rabbi was challenged at the High Court of Justice he apologized for expressing these views (G. Cohen 2017).

4 For a literary depiction of the life of religious recruits in the IDF pre-1967 see Be'er 1987.

References

Abramov, Z. S. (1976) *Perpetual Dilemma: Jewish Religion in the Jewish State*, Rutherford, NJ: Fairleigh Dickinson University Press.

ACRI (Association for Civil Rights in Israel) (2017) "Letter to Commanding General, Human Resources Branch, IDF," January 22 n.p., copy on file with the authors (in Hebrew).

Adva (1998) *Government Budgetary Allocations to the Charedi Jewish Sector* (written by Swirski, Sh., Connor, E., and Yechezkel, Y.), Tel Aviv: Adva Center (in Hebrew).

Amsterdamski, S. (2014) "46 Percent of State Support went to *Yeshivot* and *Kolelim*," *Calcalist*, January 19 (in Hebrew).

Barzel, N. (2017) *"Redemption Now": The Beliefs and Activities of the Jewish Settlers in the West Bank and Israeli Society*, Bnei Brak: Hakibbutz Hameuchad (in Hebrew).

Be'er, H. (1987) *The Time of Trimming*, Tel Aviv: Am Oved (in Hebrew).

Berman, E. and Klinov, R. (1997) *Human Capital Investment and Nonparticipation: Evidence from a Sample with Infinite Horizons (or: Jewish Father Stops Going to Work)*, Jerusalem: The Maurice Falk Institute for Economic Research in Israel (Discussion Paper no. 97.05).

BOI (2012) *Bank of Israel Report 2011*, Jerusalem: Bank of Israel.

Brown, B. (2017) *The Haredim: A Guide to Their Beliefs and Sectors*, Tel Aviv: Am Oved (in Hebrew).

CBS (2011) "Selected Data from the Israel Statistical Annual No. 62, 2011," www.cbs.gov.il/reader/newhodaot/hodaa_template.html?hodaa=201111240 (accessed November 7, 2014).

CBS (2015) Press Release. *Labour Force Survey Data, May 2015*, Jerusalem: Central Bureau of Statistics (in Hebrew).

Cohen, G. (2017) "Chief Military Rabbi: A Religious Officer Cannot Serve in a Mixed Unit," *Haaretz*, April 26 (in Hebrew).

Cohen, S. (1997a) *The Scroll or the Sword?: Dilemmas of Religion and Military Service in Israel*, Amsterdam: Harwood Academic Publishers.

Cohen, S. (1997b) "Towards a New Portrait of the (New) Israeli Soldier," *Israel Affairs*, 3: 77–114.

Cohen, S. (2013) *Divine Service?: Judaism and Israel's Armed Forces*, Burlington, VT: Ashgate.

Cohen, Y. (1993) *Giyus Cahalacha: On the Release of Yeshiva Students from the IDF*, Jerusalem: Ne'emaney Torah Vaavoda (in Hebrew).

Drori, Z. (2012) "The Gap between the Kippah and the Beret: How Does the IDF Deal with the Process of Hadata?" in Gal, R. (ed.), *Between the Kippah and the Beret: Religion, Politics and the Military in Israel*, Ben Shemen: Modan, pp. 115–50 (in Hebrew).

Ettinger, Y. (2015) "The Number of Religious Women who Join the IDF Doubled Since 2010," *Haaretz*, May 6 (in Hebrew).

Gal, R. (ed.) (2012) *Between the Kippah and the Beret: Religion, Politics and the Military in Israel*, Ben Shemen: Modan (in Hebrew).

Goldstone, R. (2009) *Human Rights In Palestine And Other Occupied Arab Territories*, Report of the United Nations Fact Finding Mission on the Gaza Conflict, UN Human Rights Council.

Gonen, A. (2000) *From the Yeshiva to the Workplace: The American Experience and Lessons for Israel*, Jerusalem: The Floersheimer Institute for Policy Studies (in Hebrew).

Greilsammer, I. (2014) "Ben-Gurion's Status Quo and Moving the Frontlines Between Hilonim (Secularists) and Datiim (Religious)," in Berlinerblau, J., Fainberg, S., and Nou, A. (eds.), *Secularism on the Edge: Rethinking Church–State Relations in the United States, France, and Israel*, Basingstoke: Palgrave Macmillan, pp. 135–44.

Guiora, A. N. (2011/2012) "Determining a Legitimate Target: The Dilemma of the Decision-Maker," *Texas International Law Journal*, 47: 315–36.

Harel, A. (2012) "Women's Singing in the Military: Boycotting Official Ceremonies will be Forbidden; Exemptions will be Given from Entertainment Events Only," *Haaretz*, January 3 (in Hebrew).

HCJ 1877/14 (Ruling of the Israeli High Court of Justice). *The Movement for Quality Government in Israel vs. The Knesset and Others.*

Herzl, T. (1934 [1896]) *The Jewish State*, n.p., Library of Alexandria.

Hiddush: For Religious Freedom and Equality (2012) "All Time High in Yeshiva Student Numbers: About 114,000," http://hiddush.org/article-2344-0-All_time_high_in_yeshiva_student_numbers_about_114000.aspx (accessed April 10, 2018).

Hoffman, C. (1989) *The Smoke Screen: Israel, Philanthropy and American Jews*, Silver Spring, MD: Eshel Books.

Hofnung, M. (1991) *Israel – Security Needs vs. The Rule of Law*, Jerusalem: Nevo (in Hebrew).

Hollander, A. Y. (2014) "Halachic Multiculturalism in the IDF: Rulings of Official Religious Authorities in Israel Concerning 'Women's Singing'," *Modern Judaisn*, 34: 271–86.

Horovitz, M. (1989) *Rabbi Schach*, Jerusalem: Keter (in Hebrew).

IDI (2012) *Equality of the Burden or the Burden of Equality: Towards the Annulment of the Tal Law and the Implications of Drafting Yeshiva Students to the IDF*, Jerusalem: Israel Democracy Institute (in Hebrew).

IDI (n.d. [2017]) *Charedi Employment Army*, Jerusalem: Israel Democracy Institute (in Hebrew).

Ilan, S. (2000) *Charedim Ltd.*, Jerusalem: Keter (in Hebrew).

Inbar, E. (1996) "Contours of Israel's New Strategic Thinking," *Political Science Quarterly*, 111: 41–64.

Kasher, A. and Yadlin, A. (2005) "Military Ethics of Fighting Terror: An Israeli Perspective," *Journal of Military Ethics*, 4: 3–32.

Leibel, T. (2012) "From 'The People's Army' to 'The Jewish People's Army': IDF Force Building between Professionalization to Militarization," in Gal, R. (ed.), *Between the Kippah and the Beret: Religion, Politics and the Military in Israel*, Ben Shemen: Modan, pp. 205–41 (in Hebrew).

Leibel, T. and Gal, R. (2012) "Between Military-Society Relations and Religion-Military Relations: The Different Faces of *Hadata*," in Gal, R. (ed.), *Between the Kippah and the Beret: Religion, Politics and the Military in Israel*, Ben Shemen: Modan, pp. 83–113 (in Hebrew).

Leon, N. (2017) "Introduction," *Democratic Culture*, 17: 9–18 (in Hebrew).

Levy, Y. (1997) *Trial and Error: Israel's Route from War to De-Escalation*, Albany, NY: SUNY Press.

Levy, Y. (2007) *Israel's Materialist Militarism*, Lanham, MD: Lexington Books.

Levy, Y. (2013) "The Military as a Split Labor Market: The Case of Women and Religious Soldiers in the Israel Defense Forces," *International Journal of Politics, Culture and Society*. (Online), http://link.springer.com/article/10.1007%2Fs10767-013-9146-7#page-1 (accessed October 20, 2013).

Levy, Y. (2015) *The Divine Commander: The Theocratization of the Israeli Military*, Tel Aviv: Am Oved (in Hebrew).

Levy, Y. (2017–2018) "The Theocratization of the Israeli Army and its Drivers," *The Public Sphere*, 13: 169–96 (in Hebrew).

Levy, Y. (2018) "The Chief of Staff of Religionization," *Haaretz Weekend Magazine*, January 19, pp. 46–8 (in Hebrew).

Liebman, C. S. and Don-Yehiya, E. (1983) *Civil Religion in Israel: Traditional Judaism and Political Culture in the Jewish State*, Berkeley, CA: University of California Press.

Loebel, U. and Lubish-Omer, S. (2012) "'To Return to What We Were': Wearers of Knitted Kippah as a Conservative Opposition to a Post-Modern Military," in Gal, R. (ed.), *Between the Kippah and the Beret: Religion, Politics and the Military in Israel*, Ben Shemen: Modan, pp. 151–203 (in Hebrew).

Luz, E. (1999) *Wrestling in River Yabok: Power, Morality, and Jewish Identity*, Jerusalem: Magnes (in Hebrew). Available in English as *Wrestling with an Angel: Power, Morality, and Jewish Identity*, trans. Swirsky, M., New Haven, CT: Yale University Press, 2003.

Magal, Y. (2016) *The Story of the Religious Zionists' Army Integration*, Tel Aviv: Yedioth Ahronoth (in Hebrew).

Malchi, A. (2013) *Charedi Men in Technological Military Service: Integration of Shachar Course Graduates in the Labor Market – Evaluation Study Report*, Jerusalem: Ministry of Industry, Commerce and Labor (in Hebrew).

Malinsky, A. (2015) "Death is in the Eye of the Beholder: A Study of Casualty Count Framing in the 2014 Israel–Gaza Conflict," *Critical Studies on Terrorism*, 8 (3): 491–502.

Margalit, A. and Walzer, M. (2009) "Israel: Civilians and Combatants," *The New York Review of Books*, LVI/8: 21–2.

Peled, Y. (2012) "From Oslo to Gaza: Israel's 'Enlightened Public' and the Remilitarization of the Israeli-Palestinian Conflict," in Stavrianakis, A., Selby, J., and Oikonomou, I. (eds.), *Militarism and International Relations: Political Economy, Security, Theory*, London: Routledge.

Peres, Y. and Ben-Rafael, E. (2006) *Closeness and Conflict: Cleavages in Israeli Society*, Tel Aviv: Am Oved (in Hebrew).

Pundak, C., Peled, M., and Levy, D. (2012) "The Economy Pays 9.4 Billion Shekels Because of Non-Employment of Charedim," *Calcalist*, July 22. www.calcalist.co.il/local/articles/0,7340,L-3577777,00.html (in Hebrew; accessed November 6, 2014).

Rubin, A. (2014) "Bifurcated Loyalty and Religious Actors' Behaviour in Democratic Politics: The Case of Post-1967 Religious Zionism in Israel," *Religion, State and Society*, 42: 46–65.

Sadan, E. (2016) "Who Are You, Religious Zionism? – Questions and Answers from Right and Left," *Sons of David – Eli: People of Faith in the World of Action*, www.bneidavid.org/DocsUpload/010270/Doc_10270.pdf (in Hebrew; accessed May 6, 2016).

Sagi, A. and Schwartz, D. (2017) *From Realism to Messianism: Religious Zionism and the Six-Day War*, Jerusalem: Carmel (in Hebrew).

Shafir, G. and Peled, Y. (2000) *The New Israel: Peace and Economic Liberalization*, Boulder, CO: Westview.

Shafir, G. and Peled, Y. (2002) *Being Israeli: The Dynamics of Multiple Citizenship*, Cambridge: Cambridge University Press.

Shapira, An. (2014) "Israel's 'Religious Secularism'," in Berlinerblau, J., Fainberg, S., and Nou, A. (eds.), *Secularism on the Edge: Rethinking Church–State Relations in the United States, France, and Israel*, Basingstoke: Palgrave Macmillan, pp. 145–55.

Sharvit Baruch, P. (2012) "Legal Dilemmas in Fighting in Asymmetrical Conflicts," *Army and Strategy*, 4 (1): 37–45 (in Hebrew).

Sheleg, Y. (2010) *From Old Hebrew to New Jew: The Jewish Renaissance in Israeli Society*, Jerusalem: Israel Democracy Institute (in Hebrew).

Siboni, G. and Pearl Finkel, G. (2017) "Motivation Crisis in Recruitment to Combat Service," *Overview* 997, Institute for National Security Studies.

Stadler, N. (2004) "Taboos, Dreams and Desires: Haredi Conceptions of Militarism and the Military," *Israeli Sociology*, 6: 69–90 (in Hebrew).

Stadler, N. and Ben Ari, E. (2003) "Other-Worldly Soldiers? Ultra-Orthodox Views of Military Service in Contemporary Israel," *Israel Affairs*, 9: 17–48.

Stadler, N., Lomsky-Feder, E., and Ben-Ari, E. (2008) "Fundamentalism's Encounters with Citizenship: The Haredim in Israel," *Citizenship Studies*, 12: 215–31.

State Comptroller (2011) *Annual Report 62*, Jerusalem: State of Israel – State Comptroller Office (in Hebrew).

State Comptroller (2012) *Annual Report 63*, Jerusalem: State of Israel – State Comptroller Office (in Hebrew).

Tirosh, Y. (2017) "Modesty on Parade," *Haaretz Weekend Magazine*, June 2, p. 8.

Weill, S. and Azarova, V. (2015) "The 2014 Gaza War: Reflections on *Jus ad Bellum, Jus in Bello*, and Accountability," in A. Bellel (ed.), *The War Report: Armed Conflict in 2014*, Oxford: Oxford University Press.

Yefet, K. C. (2016) "Synagogue and State in the Israeli Military: A Story of 'Inappropriate Integration'," *Law and Ethics of Human Rights*, 10 (1): 223–94.

Zicherman, H. and Cahaner, L. (2012) *Modern Ultra-Orthodoxy: The Emergence of a Haredi Middle Class in Israel*, Jerusalem: Israel Democracy Institute (in Hebrew).

7 Nationalism and religion in the visual fine arts field

In 2008 Gideon Ofrat, the prominent Israeli art critic, historian, and trenchant hegemonic gatekeeper, asked: "Is an Artistic Cultural Revolution Taking Place among Those Who Wear Knitted Kippot [i.e. religious Zionists]?" (Ofrat 2008). Puzzled by the substantial increase in the number of religious players within the fine arts field, and suspecting the absurd proposal of challenging the secular hegemony in that field, he stated: "It is doubtful that religious artistic expression could confront [successfully] the multi-layered ideational complexity of art in the 2000s" (Ofrat 2008:175). For

> [w]hen the religious aspect merges with the national aspect [as it does in the works of religious Zionist artists] the result is illustrative didacticism, whose sophistication is extremely poor. Most [religiously] observant artists [who are] very popular among the religious Jewish public, affirm art whose faith-based, ideological content sinks it into a shallow swamp that has nothing to do with the complex form–content synthesis of the 150 years of modern (not to mention post-modern) art ... It seems that I will not be mistaken if I add that these artists have no interest in integrating into this modern/post-modern fabric, believing, naively, in a proud Jewish alternative.
>
> (Ofrat 2008:170)

In an earlier essay, published in 2003, Ofrat, echoing Kant's conception of fine arts (see below), juxtaposed the philosophy of the politically liberal Left with that of the political Right epitomized by Religious Zionism:

> Upholding the alliance between: People-Land-Torah contradicts all the principles of good art as the people [nation] precedes the I, as the Land is the negation of universal expression, and as the Torah affirms the superiority of law and tradition over liberty and creative anarchism. The holy trinity of People-Land-Torah assumes the One – one is our God, one is our Torah, one is our Land, one is our (chosen) People. These are unity and uniformity that mandate centralism of God-father-rabbi-leader. The Left, on the other hand, risks anarchy and licentiousness, but gains the

humanism of rebellion and the authenticity of the doubt and the search. These are the values of good art...

(Cited in Eider 2008:1–2)

Writing from the opposite ideological perspective, in 2010 Yair Sheleg, a religious Zionist journalist and public intellectual, noted that while in major cultural fields such as music, literature, poetry, and film one could observe a "renaissance" in religious creativity, there was no substantial religious presence in the field of plastic arts. Sheleg provided a two-tiered explanation for this absence: First, the prohibition against the depiction of representations of "real-life" expressed by the second of the Biblical ten commandments: "Thou shalt not make unto thee any graven image, or any likeness of anything that is in heaven above, or that is in the earth beneath, or that is in the water under the earth"; and second, constraints stemming from the religious concern for modesty and chastity which is much more pronounced in relation to visual images than it is in relation to text (Sheleg 2010:98–9).

Indeed, for the first nine decades of Zionist settlement (from the 1880s to the 1960s) explicitly religious Jewish artworks were barely visible within the hegemonic core of the fine arts field in Palestine/Israel. Since the 1970s, however, the seemingly secular hegemony in the field is being contested. In analyzing this process – the religionization of the Israeli fine arts field – we will rely on Pierre Bourdieu's key analytic concepts of *field*, *agent*, and *habitus*. A field, according to Bourdieu, is a conflictual space inhabited by agents, which constitutes a complex, layered network of individuals and institutions who share mutual interests while exerting power in the pursuit of advancement and secure positions. Agents both structure the settings of the field and are being structured by them, and the more powerful agents, those who possess greater capital of the kind that is relevant to the field, play a greater role in structuring the field and producing hierarchies within it. Each agent embodies a set of dispositions which are shared by similar others and make up the *habitus* of the agent, which is being projected in the agent's social, economic, and cultural tastes and activities (Bourdieu 1984; 1993; 1995).

After a brief discussion of the problematic engagement of religious Jews with visual arts production, in this chapter we explore the transformative practices and dynamics undergone by the Israeli fine arts field through three major epochs, from the initial stages of its development at the end of the nineteenth century to the present. The first period lasted from the Fifth Zionist Congress in Basel in 1901 to the middle of the 1920s. During that time the art field established the rationale for its own construction, grounding the visual narrative of a homeland for the Jews in the mythical textual memories of Biblical Israel. The second period saw the construction and formation of a visual culture proficient with the fine arts visuality of the Western cultural world. In the third, current period, we are witnessing the integration into the field of a religious layer of artistic creativity. From the middle of the 1920s to the end of the twentieth century the fine arts field reflected Zionism's universalist aspiration to be counted among the secular democratic national liberation movements. In the current stage, however, the pendulum is swinging toward the particularistic, Jewish and religious pole of Jewish Israeli culture.

Kant, aesthetics, Jews

In 1790 Immanuel Kant published his third critique – *The Critique of Judgment* (Kant 1987 [1790]; 2007 [1790]).[1] In the book Kant stressed the exceptional state of fine arts as distinct from any other human productive category. The uniqueness of fine arts stemmed from the juxtaposition of the sensual (taste, beautiful) and the intellectual (aesthetic, judgment). As such, fine arts were removed from the ideas of Nature, Science, and the mechanical\functional\ practical arts and were rooted intrinsically in individual choice which makes for "production through freedom" based on an "act of will" and integrating "reason at the basis of its action" (Kant 2007 [1790]:132, §43). The infinite sensuous and intellectual material sources of production in the artist's domain made possible the unlimited conditions for creative activity freed of remuneration, thus liberated from the shackles of vending human labor under what would later come to be called capitalism. With modernity, the artist, the generator of fine artistic products, became the executor who replaced eminent religious *presentations* with non-religious *representations*: "We look [at art] as something which could only prove purposive (be a success) as play, i.e. an occupation which is agreeable on its own account..." (Kant 2007 [1790]:133, §43).

Yet, the artistic creative process does have its rules:

> ... in all free arts something of a compulsory character is still required, or, as it is called, a *mechanism*, without which the *spirit* [*Geist*], which in art must be *free*, and which alone gives life to the work, would be bodyless [*sic*] and evanescent.
>
> (Kant 2007 [1790]:133–4, §43, emphasis in the original)

However, the rules of artistic creation could not be learned, transcribed technically or scientifically, in regard to the creative artistic process, as the artistic talent is embedded in the

> *Genius* ... [i.e.] the talent (natural endowment) which gives the rule to art. Since talent, as an innate productive faculty of the artist, belongs itself to nature, we may put it this way: *Genius* is the innate mental aptitude (*ingenium*) *through which* nature gives the rule to art.
>
> (Kant 2007 [1790]:136, §46, emphasis in the original)

Visual representations have a binary character: the lesser ones, those that belong to the category of mechanical arts, have a functional purpose, which involves labor conditioned by training and learnt practices. The fine arts, on the other hand, reflect the subject, the artist who possesses additional extraordinary aptitudes over the natural – i.e., genius, the "guardian and guiding spirit bestowed upon a human being at birth" (Kant 2007 [1790]:137, §46). The

> "Spirit" in an aesthetic sense, signifies the animating principle in the mind, [...] but that whereby this principle animates the soul – the material which it employs for that purpose – is that which sets the mental powers into a swing that is purposive, i.e. into a play which is self-maintaining and which strengthens those powers for such activity.
>
> (Kant 2007 [1790]:142, §49)

The artist/genius is an extraordinary human being, possessing capabilities of play between imagination and understanding. Furthermore, as the creative process cannot be traced or transcribed scientifically, "genius ... gives the rule as *nature* ... [and] Nature prescribes the rule through genius not to science but to art, and this only *in so far as it is to be fine art*" (Kant 2007 [1790]:137, §46, emphasis added). Only the Genius, the artist endowed by nature with "talent," could produce fine art works to appear as nature: "... the purposiveness [of the product of fine art] in its form must appear just as free from the constraint of arbitrary rules as if it were a product of mere nature" (Kant 2007 [1790]:135, §45). Moreover, the artist/genius, the pivot of the art field, bears a social function: "Fine art [...] is a mode of representation which is intrinsically purposive, and which, although devoid of an end, has the effect of advancing the culture of the mental powers in the interests of social communication" (Kant 2007 [1790]:135, §44). Thus, the artist functions as the transmitter of universal signifiers.

Packaging the fine art product as a universal signifier involves the activity of judgment in taste and beauty, as "It is only in respect of judgment that the name of fine art is deserved" (Kant 2007 [1790]:148, §50). However, "The judgment of taste ... is not a cognitive judgment, and so not logical, but is aesthetic – which means that it is one whose determining ground cannot be other than subjective" (Kant 2007 [1790]:35, §1). How could the judgment of taste and beauty be socially communicative if it is subjective? For that Kant devised the term "subjective universality": Because the judgment of taste "must involve a claim to validity for everyone, and must do so apart from a universality directed to objects, i.e. there must be coupled with it a claim to subjective universality" (Kant 2007 [1790]:43, §6). "For we may say universally, whether it concerns beauty in nature or in art: *beautiful is what we like in merely judging it* (rather than either in sensation proper or through a concept)" (Kant 1987 [1790]:174, §45, emphasis in the original).

Kant distinguished between "determinative" and "reflective" judgment. While the former denoted "the ability to think the particular as contained under the universal" (Kant 1987 [1790]:18, §IV), "reflective judgment" denoted that judgment is aesthetic: "Hence aesthetic art, as art which is beautiful, is one having for its standard the reflective judgment and not bodily sensation" (Kant 2007 [1790]:135, §44). Aesthetic judgment, the act of cognition folded within the free play of imagination and understanding, necessitates a certain cultivation and dis-interested contemplation which could free one from reliance on just the senses. It is a source of liberation from the natural instincts:

> For the basis of this pleasure is found in the universal, though subjective, condition of reflective judgments, namely, the purposive harmony of an object ... with the mutual relation of the cognitive powers (imagination and understanding) that are required for every empirical cognition.
>
> (Kant 1987 [1790]:31, §VII)

According to one of Kant's translators, Werner Pluhar,

> Kant's "deduction" of judgments of taste ... established the universal sub-jective validity of the feeling of pleasure in these judgments ... [F]or, Kant argued, this feeling cannot be directed to anything but the conditions of (empirical) judgment as such (harmony of imagination and understanding), and these conditions can be presupposed to be the same in everyone.
>
> (Kant 1987 [1790]:lxxxvii)

Although fine arts, as opposed to the practical arts, are "devoid of an end," they form a cardinal layer in the fabric of modern society. The artist, the spiritual mediator between nature and the constructed human world, produces the artistic object, which obtains a communicative value, through educated, skillful judg-ment. Alluding to the liberal theory of a social contract as the basis of society, Kant attributed to fine arts a key role in forging inter-class solidarity:

> The age and the peoples in which the vigorous drive towards a social life *regulated by laws* – that which converts a people into an enduring com-munity – grappled with the huge difficulties presented by the trying problem of bringing freedom (and therefore equality also) into union with constraint (more that of respect and dutiful submission than of fear). And such must have been the age, and such the people, that first discovered the art of reciprocal communication of ideas between the more cultured and cruder sections of the community, and how to bridge the difference between the breadth and refinement of the former and the natural simpli-city and originality of the latter – in this way hitting upon that mean between higher culture and self-sufficing nature, that forms for taste also, as a sense common to all mankind, that true standard which no universal rules can supply.
>
> (Kant 2007 [1790]:183, §60, emphasis in the original)

By "social life regulated by laws" Kant means a civil society, "a stable polity [based on] principles of justice rather than sheer force" (Guyer 2014:457). The crucial role played by fine arts in enabling such a society points to the close con-nection, for Kant, between aesthetics and morality. According to Paul Guyer:

... although in its purest form, the free play of our understanding and imagination that constitutes the experience of natural beauty does not *presuppose* any judgment of moral value, the very fact of the existence of natural beauty appears to confirm that the world is hospitable to our goals, especially our moral goals, while our experiences of natural sublimity and artistic beauty both involve the free play of our cognitive powers *with* morally significant ideas, and thus are distinctively aesthetic yet morally significant. Kant's account of fine art in particular, the traditional focus of aesthetic theory, is that it makes the most important ideas of morality, which are otherwise bare abstractions, palpable to us *through* the free and creative play of the imagination.

(Guyer 2014:430, emphasis in the original; see also 452–8)

Even more than fine arts, what Kant calls the "sublime," a realm of aesthetic judgment to be distinguished from taste and beauty, is intimately tied to morality. Kant describes the sublime as "an object (of nature) the presentation of which determines the mind to think of nature's inability to attain to an exhibition of ideas" (Kant 1987 [1790]:127). The sublime is "primarily a response to nature rather than works of art," a response that is not purely pleasurable but that is "negative," in that, akin to awe, it involves both pleasure and pain: "a moment of pain due to an initial sense of the limits of our imagination followed by pleasure at the recognition that it is our own power of reason that challenges and reveals the limits of our imagination." Unlike beauty, the sublime cannot be experienced through immediate sensible encounter with external objects alone; it must be approached with "certain ideas, ultimately moral ideas." For Kant, the explication of the sublime is part of aesthetics because it gives moral significance to natural phenomena, in that it demonstrates "our moral superiority to nature, the fact that our moral choices are not determined solely by merely natural forces," and in that sense we are free (Guyer 2014:431, 444–6; Kant 1987 [1790]:127).

In his book, *Heidegger and "the jews,"* [*sic*] Jean-François Lyotard discussed the Kantian concept of the sublime, contrasting it to art:

The sublime cannot be produced, nor does it "project" itself, it simply happens. Art is an artifact; it constructs its representation. Art cannot be sublime; it can "make" [i.e., attempt to represent] sublime, and this is not better than beautiful, only more ridiculous. In lieu of a thesis, a pose.

(Lyotard 1990:45)

Moreover, Kant's notion of the sublime

as the combination of pleasure and pain, as the trembling ... of a motion both attractive and repulsive at once, as a sort of spasm, according to a dynamic that both inhibits and excites ... bears witness to the fact that an "excess" has "touched" the mind, more than it is able to handle. That is why

the sublime has no consideration for form, why it is an "unform." For form
is what gives the given, even with respect to imaginative representations.

(Lyotard 1990:32)

To illustrate the sharp distinction, indeed the direct contradiction, between
beauty and the sublime, Kant referred to the Biblical Second Commandment:

Perhaps there is no more sublime passage in the Jewish Law than the commandment: Thou shalt not make unto thee any graven image, or any likeness of anything that is in heaven or on earth, or under the earth, etc. This
commandment can alone explain the enthusiasm which the Jewish people,
in their moral period, felt for their religion when comparing themselves with
others ...

(Kant 2007 [1790]:104, §29)

By rating the Second Commandment as "sublime" and placing it over the sensible, Kant, who defined the terrain and prescribed the rules for the modern understanding of visual fine arts, opened the discourse of Jewish aniconism, the Jews'
absence from this newly defined cultural sphere.

Aniconism refers to the ambiguous "historiographic myth that certain cultures, usually

monotheistic or primitively pure cultures, have no images at all, or no figu-
rative imagery, or no images of the deity." Jewish aniconism implies that
Jews are a People of the Book rather than a People of the Image. Proponents
of Jewish aniconism deny the existence of authentic Jewish traditions in
painting, sculpture, and architecture. They concede that Jews imitate, in production and reception, the foreign art of their host or neighboring cultures.
They claim that Jewish attitudes toward visuality and the visual arts range
from indifference to suspicion and hostility.

(Bland 2000:3, 8)

This has become a major stratum in the discussion of Jewish identity and Jewish
visual art from the nineteenth century until the present time.

By banning mimetic representations of the imaginary, Biblical law, embodied
in the Second Commandment, furnished the imagination with potentially bound-
less freedom. Thus, the constraints on sensuous visual perception endowed
ancient Judaism with an ethical form of morality, as freedom and autonomous
free will could be exercised under the moral law. However, by releasing the Jews
of the burden of visual representation and pulling them closer to the sublime, the
Second Commandment erected a divide in European societies and designated
the Jew as the Other which will not convert, assimilate, or integrate into the
majority. Thus, the Jew became the symbol of the uncanny, unfathomable Other
within Western societies.

Integration vs. nationalization: Hermann Cohen and Martin Buber

By the end of the eighteenth century the prospects of political, social, cultural, and economic integration in Western and Central Europe posed real threats to the traditional Jewish communities, while presenting new possibilities for individual Jewish existence. Jewish philosophers well-versed in Enlightenment philosophy responded to the challenges presented, in an attempt to carve an agreeable and congenial space for the Jewish Other. Their narratives were attempted explorations into the structuring of precise mechanisms which could reconcile the antimony of the universal and the particular.[2] Their prolific discussions addressed the meaning of being Jewish in the particular historical junction of time and space.

Hermann Cohen, a German Jewish neo-Kantian philosopher (1842–1918), was one of the prominent protagonists in the project of seeking accommodation between the modern European universal and the traditional Jewish particular. He strived to exhibit similarities between *Deutschtum* and *Judentum*, between liberal German Protestantism and Judaism, and envisioned the union of "ethical-religious values and modern social norms." In his endeavor an individualistic, depoliticized Jewish religion was to provide the spiritual ethics, while the German Enlightenment, embodied in the German state, provided "its ethical cultural legacy." This messianic vision of a Judaic-Protestant culture imagined an idealized humanistic community based on the idea of "ethical monotheism," which would grow out of the correspondence between Christian Protestantism and ethical writings derived from the Old Testament (Myers 2001:198, 211; Bland 2000:19; Batnitzky 2011:53–9).

Cohen asserted that not Christianity, as Kant had averred, but rather Judaism, as a religion of law, "best represents a religion of reason, because the sources of Judaism, meaning the Jewish textual tradition, express the purest form of monotheism." To establish his claim about the nature of Judaism, Cohen enlisted Pentateuch law, prophetic preachings, and Biblical psalms denoting moral values such as righteousness, justice, and freedom. By removing the heavy weight of Jewish rituals and rabbinical authority, Cohen envisioned the enhancing of Jewish ethical humanistic law, in harmony with philosophical scientific thinking, since "one of the chief goals of philosophy, as a scientific enterprise, was to clarify the central role of the ethical in human thought and behavior" (Myers 2001:203).

What hindered the realization of monotheism, Cohen argued, were the Protestants themselves, and they could "clear away their own obstruction [only] by understanding their reliance on Jews and Judaism. Until they are able to do so, the Jewish people will suffer vicariously for the sins of Protestants" (Batnitzky 2011:54, 58): "[A]s Israel suffers, according to the prophet [Isaiah], for the pagan worshippers, so Israel to this very day suffers vicariously for the faults and wrongs which still hinder the realization of monotheism" (cited in Batnitzky 2011:56). However, "Jewish suffering should not be relieved through a political solution, as Zionists propose," for "Judaism is not a nation within a nation but instead a community that is bound together by laws that only Jews are obliged to follow." Coalescing particularism and universalism, Cohen insisted that "the Jewish religion exists not just for the sake of Jews but also for all of humanity; in its particularity, the observance of Jewish law by Jews preserves pure mono-theism for all peoples." Zionism, therefore, "destroys the world-historical mission of the Jewish people, which is to model pure monotheism for the nations of the world" (Batnitzky 2011:55–8).

Following Kant, Cohen viewed Jewish aniconism as a great virtue, for ani-conism was essentially tied to pure monotheism: "the veracity of the Jewish con-sciousness of God is precisely the reason for the aversion to the plastic arts." For God is "absolutely the archetype for the mind ... for the love of reason, but not an object for mimetic reproduction." Therefore, "[t]he plastic arts [*Plastik*] and painting [*Malerei*] were kept at a safe distance from the pure worship of God." Monotheism reflected chaste aniconism, while polytheism reflected iconism, as presented in Hellenistic culture. The cultural state of aniconism relieved the need for visual representations of the seen, yet facilitated artistic expression through poetry. For "[p]oetry ... the original language of literature, is able to make spir-itual thoughts more inward than can the visual arts." Thus "what the religious consciousness loses in the visual arts [*bildenden Kunst*], it makes up for amply through lyrical poetry ... Monotheism makes no concessions to the visual arts, for thereby the unique God would come to danger" (cited in Bland 2000:17–18). Furthermore,

> Cohen ... invoked the "poetically articulated" notion that Moses "carved human pyramids." Cohen explained that this implicitly superior and com-pensatory "artwork of people" (*Kunstwerk der Menschen*) was achieved "by means of the laws." He concluded that "the laws themselves can therefore not be without all artistic value," especially not without the artistic value associated with the verbal art of "poetry."
>
> (Bland 2000:17)

A contemporary German Jewish philosopher, Martin Buber (1878–1965), held the opposite view from Cohen's on both Zionism and Jewish fine arts. Buber was a key member of the Democratic Fraction within the World Zionist Organization, which advocated "cultural Zionism" in opposition to Herzl's strictly "political Zionism" (Batnitzky 2011:155–60). At the Fifth Zionist Con-gress in Basel, in 1901, Buber addressed the delegates on the subject of Jewish art (Schmidt 2003:8; Presner 2007:71–3). For him, the sublime, aniconistic char-acter of Jewish religion was not a virtue but a drawback, as it impaired the evo-lution of national consciousness among the Jews:

> The excess in soul power that we possessed at all times expressed itself in the exile merely in an indescribably one-sided spiritual activity that blinded the eyes to all the beauty of nature and of life.

We were robbed of that from which every people takes again and again joyous, fresh energy, the ability to behold a beautiful landscape and beautiful people. The blossoming and growth beyond the ghetto was unknown to us and hated by our forefathers as much as the beautiful human body ... The very thing in which the true *essence of a nation* expresses itself to the fullest and purest, the sacred word of the *national soul*, the artistic productivity, was lost to us.

(Buber 1999:48, emphasis added)

"In our days," however, Buber continued, thanks to the emancipation of Western European Jews, "the visual art of our people [has] blossomed in unexpected splendor ... Our tribe, which has for so long produced scholars who hated life, began to create artists" (Buber 1999:55; cf. Presner 2007:77–8).

To demonstrate this newfound Jewish artistic vitality, Buber, together with artist Ephraim Moshe Lilien and author Berthold Feiwel, curated an art exhibition at the Fifth Zionist Congress in 1901, the first European Jewish fine art exhibition ever (Schmidt 2003; Presner 2007:65–105). At the exhibition eleven artists presented 48 works which, by and large, "depicted Jewish themes along one of two trajectories: the authentic, heroic tradition of Jews in antiquity and the contemporary [abject] situation of Jews in exile" (Presner 2007:65). According to Buber, in those artworks "the play of the atmosphere around objects, the integration of individual items into the surrounding environment, the broad concept of space, the strange inward movement ... [were recognizable] elements of Jewish perception and formation" (Buber 1999:55).[3]

Figure 7.1   Ephraim Moshe Lilien. Illustration for *Der Jüdische Mai* (*Jewish May*) in Rosenfeld, Morris, *Lieder des Ghetto*, Berlin: Benjamin Harz Verlag (1902).

An iconic drawing by Lilien, *The Jewish May*, illustrates the spirit of the art-works presented at the Congress (although this particular drawing was created in 1902). Like Buber, Lilien was a "cultural Zionist" and contributed visual designs, photographs, illustrations, prints and fine art works for the movement's publications. "The Jewish May" was one of a number of illustrations he made for a book of poems by the Yiddish socialist Zionist poet, Morris Rosenfeld, *"Lieder des Ghetto"* (Berlin: Benjamin Harz Verlag, 1902).

The illustration was done in the *Jugendstil* style (the German version of Art Nouveau), yet was saturated with symbolic and neo-romantic representations of Zionist visual iconography. On the left side of the visual plane, a stereotyped representation of an old Jew was depicted, bound and immersed in barbed wire, guarded by snakes. In the background thorns and a raven symbolized death and decay. The figure's arms were desperately extended in a frail begging gesture, yet with hope toward the sunrays directed at him over an imaginary non-European landscape, sketching a river flowing from a mountain to the valley in the direction of the stifled figure, all surrounded with lush vegetation, palm trees and flowers.

Art as national education

The task that Jewish art could perform for Zionism, according to Buber, was, first and foremost, national education:

> Jewish art is for us a great educator. It is a teacher for a living perception of nature and people, a teacher for a living feeling of all that is strong and beautiful, a teacher for this perception and feeling that we lacked for so long and that we may now recover through the visual and poetic productions of our artists.
>
> (Buber 1999:51)

In a more practical vein, Buber viewed art as an important tool of Zionist propaganda. At the beginning of his speech at the Fifth Zionist Congress he cited approvingly Max Nordau's article "The Zionism of Western Jews" where Nordau, Herzl's chief lieutenant, characterized "Jewish art as a first class propaganda tool" (Buber's words, not Nordau's). That propaganda, Buber argued, should be aimed primarily at the Jewish "propertied classes," from whom the movement could raise money but who at that stage were largely hostile to Zionism (Buber 1999:47; Nordau 1936 [1901]; Mosse 1993:161–75).

Buber, and Nordau, were not unique among European nationalist thinkers in assigning national significance to fine arts. In the late nineteenth century Polish Positivist thinkers argued that

> ... national interest had to take precedence over artists' desire for personal expression. Works of art and literature had to become weapons in the battle for cultural and therefore national survival. Polish artists and writers had an

obligation to preserve Polish culture at home and to testify to its continual existence abroad. It was their patriotic duty to produce works that in concrete ways benefited their compatriots: that refined people's taste, provided them with a common base of cultural references, and nurtured their patriotism. Most importantly, they had to instill in the Polish people a sense of common destiny and national solidarity that could overcome ingrained class animosities, regional differences and divergent political views.

(Brzyski 2001:167)

Similarly,

... the arts had a long record in France of being used to advance what powerful individuals had construed as the national interest ... [M]onarchs had understood the dynastic advantage to be drawn from a carefully crafted cultural policy, and such lessons had not been lost on their political rivals, from the Jacobins of the 1790s to their republican successors of a century later.

(Hargrove and McWilliam 2005:9–10)

And, in a general way, for the nineteenth-century European bourgeoisie, "art as a projection of beauty stood for the true, the good, and the holy, and so did the national stereotype, which reflected and personalized the character of the nation" (Mosse 1993: 122; see also Etin 1991).

Writing in 1936, Walter Benjamin famously summed up the process of the enlistment of visual fine arts in the service of politics, tying it to technological changes that enabled, for the first time, the mechanical reproduction of works of art:

An analysis of art in the age of mechanical reproduction must do justice to these relationships, for they lead us to an all-important insight: for the first time in world history, mechanical reproduction emancipates the work of art from its parasitical dependence on ritual. To an ever greater degree the work of art reproduced becomes the work of art designed for reproducibility. From a photographic negative, for example, one can make any number of prints; to ask for the "authentic" print makes no sense. But the instant the criterion of authenticity ceases to be applicable to artistic production, the total function of art is reversed. Instead of being based on ritual, it begins to be based on another practice – politics.

(Benjamin 1936)

No less important than the political task that Jewish art could perform for Zionism was what Zionism could do for Jewish art. The rebirth of Jewish creativity could materialize fully only in the Land of Israel:

A national art needs a soil from which it grows and a sky to strive for. We Jews of today have neither. We are the slaves of many different soils, and our thoughts rise to different skies. In the deepest depths of our soul we have no soil and no sky. We have no homeland ... A whole and complete Jewish art, like a whole and complete Jewish culture in general, would be possible only on Jewish soil.

(Buber 1999:50)

Art education was essential in Buber's view as an empowering leverage in the process of the "'formation' and even the 'redemption' of the Jewish people by serving the Zionist project of state formation" (Presner 2007:73). Under the influence of Friedrich Schiller's *Letters upon the Aesthetic Education of Man* (Schiller 2002 [1795]), Buber argued for the centrality of aesthetic education in grasping the best part of human moral nature and happiness, thus potentially enabling the redemption of the Jewish people from the degeneration caused by Exile. For Schiller the goal of "aesthetic education" was "the cultivation of a new, ideal humanity in a new, ideal state." In similar vein, for Buber aesthetic education was critical to the "regeneration of both the individual Jew and the people as a whole, before the Zionist state could be realized" (Presner 2007:82–7). In Presner's summation, "Buber and other early Zionist ideologues of regeneration thus rooted their ideas in Enlightenment notions of progress and improvement: Jews could change, develop, and evolve." Those ideas of progress and improvement were Eurocentric and in no small measure rooted in "the cultural context of [German] modernist conceptions of the racial and aesthetic state" (Presner 2007:75, 78).

Establishment of the Israeli fine arts field

The Zionist movement stirred exuberance and hope among Jewish intellectuals and artists in its formative stages, at the very beginning of the twentieth century. A foreseeable and conceivable transformative shift, from degeneration to regeneration, in an old–new space populated by new Jews, was imagined by many. At the Seventh Zionist Congress in 1905, Professor Boris (Shlomo-Zalman Dov-Baruch) Schatz (1866–1932), the visionary who was to construct the visual cultural field in Palestine, proposed the formation of a Jewish art academy based on a synthesis of the "*alt/neu*," like the title of Herzl's utopian novel, *Altneuland* (Herzl 2000 [1902]). Schatz had met Herzl in Vienna in 1903 and became an ardent Zionist. With Herzl's endorsement his proposal for the construction of the first modern arts and crafts school in the Middle East was approved by the Congress and Jerusalem was designated as the chosen location to house the Academy: "In the desolated land of Israel, in withered Jerusalem, there we will construct a tranquil corner for our Hebrew art" (Schatz 1923). Schatz labored intensively to materialize the proposed project and referred to the endeavor as "*Beit midrash le'omanut*," the new nation's visual cultural institution, which would open its doors in 1906.

Beit midrash is a gendered Jewish institution intended exclusively for men, devoted to the study of the Talmud and rabbinical literature. Adding to "*beit hamidrash"* the words "for Arts" (*le'omanut*) signified a paradox in terms, as the study of visual art had been totally excluded from orthodox religious Judaism. Schatz named his *beit midrash le'omanut "Bezalel"* (literally "in the shadow of God"), a Biblical reference to the chief craftsman of the Tabernacle, Bezalel Ben-Uri, who was appointed by Moses to build the Ark of the Covenant. The Academy of Arts and Crafts, as well as an art museum, were established in 1906 with Schatz as their first Director. With the inauguration, Lilien joined the studio faculty of the Academy (Manor 2005:18–39; Saposnik 2015:1658).

Schatz's animated life journey mirrored the trajectories opened to European Jews upon the historical waves which transpired in the second half of the nineteenth century, up until the First World War – modernization, Enlightenment, emancipation, and *haskala* (Jewish Enlightenment). He was born in 1866 in a small town, Varniai, in present-day Lithuania, to a typical ultra-Orthodox Jewish family. He was the son of a *cheder melamed* (a teacher in a boys' elementary school in the traditional Jewish educational system). At the age of 16, while studying in a *yeshiva* in Vilnius, he enrolled in the Vilnius School of Drawing and took night studio classes, in addition to studying the Russian language. A year later he distanced himself from his Orthodox Jewish family and from the Jewish Orthodox way of life and left the *yeshiva*. He devoted himself to studio arts, first in Vilnius, later on in Warsaw, and finally in the Mecca of the new – Paris, where he arrived in the year of the *Exposition Universelle* in 1899.

In 1888, nine years before the First Zionist Congress, while studying in Warsaw and at the age of 22, Schatz published an article arguing for the importance of visual arts production, particularly fine arts. He named the article: "Work of Art" (*melechet machshevet*) and published it in *Hatzfirah* (The Siren), a popular Hebrew scientific and literary daily edited by the future Zionist leader, Nahum Sokolow, and published in Warsaw (Schatz 1888a; 1888b). Celebrating modernism, *Hatzfirah* catered to the European Jewish intelligentsia, and between the years 1881 and 1890 it circulated beyond Europe as well.

In his article Schatz addressed the neglect of the visual fine arts in Jewish cultural life, arguing for their inclusion on an equal basis with music, poetry, and literature. Unaware of, or ignoring the Kantian interpretation of the Second Commandment, as well as Hermann Cohen's negation of Jewish fine arts production, Schatz evaded the raging debate over Jewish aniconism – the prohibition of visual arts production in Judaism. He embraced enthusiastically the potential embedded in Jewish emancipation and *haskala*, which unlocked social, cultural, and economic new fields for Jews to integrate into. Becoming involved with the field of visual fine arts, in Europe – an exclusive terrain of the Christians – appeared to Schatz and other modernist Jews as the proper activity Jews could engage in, in order to expand their horizons socially, economically, and culturally. For "it is well known that famous paintings elevated and revitalized Christianity among the people throughout the world" (Schatz 1888b:3).

Schatz's article, written in Biblical Hebrew, was three-dimensional: it dealt with art and nature, with exclusion by social discrimination, and with inclusion by unfolding the idea of the new – rebirth. In the first part Schatz echoed Kantian concepts of nature, beauty, ethics and the artist, the genius:

> All that is alive, the human, the animal, the reptile, the birds, will sense the beauty and the pleasure of the seen and the heard [in nature] ... mortals will delight in viewing the gracefulness of paintings ... created by those who already in the womb were called upon to mimic nature.
>
> (Schatz 1888a:2–3)

Exclusion and inclusion in the fine arts field were narrated thus:

> Nature did not give everyone the talent to explore its roots and observe its foundations, to know how wonderful that picture is ... But there are many who exhibit signs of talent for painting in their early childhood, before their minds are developed ... If only good fortune provide them with an opportunity to fulfill their creative potential they climb the ladder of art to become exemplary models ... famous painters whose names are admired and sanctified. But many of them, especially among the children of our people, had bad fortune and their talent went to naught. This talent, and all the talents for the sciences and arts, which the creator endowed them with equally with their brothers, were doomed, lost in the circumstances of time and its hardships ... However, as soon as the spirit of the European enlightenment began to invigorate the children of Israel numerous Hebrew painters began to blossom, some of them gaining world recognition as they stand on the scaffoldings of this precious artistry, while only thirty years ago there was no one who excelled in that art among the Jews of Russia.
>
> (Schatz 1888a:3)

Jewish artistic talent – for painting and sculpture – was evident in the wealth of craft works in synagogues, produced by Jewish artisans. Yet those talents shunned their potential artistic genius, obeying the Second Commandment prohibition and thus maintaining the myth of the Other within Christian society:

> Is it only now that talent was renewed among them [the Jews]? We know today that many of those who appreciate works of fine arts – painting and sculpture – mostly among the Christians, collect the fine craft works they see on Eastern [walls of synagogues] and the engravings on Holy Arks, for in this work is reflected [the Jewish artisans'] extraordinary talent, without them being aware of the treasure hidden in their lap. Thus their talent vanished as they were called "craftsmen" and could not deliver any advantage to themselves or to others.
>
> (Schatz 1888a:3)

According to Schatz, construction of a Jewish visual fine arts field would disentangle the distorted state of the social and spiritual existence of European

Jews. By his assessment, the creation and distribution of paintings and sculptures simulating Biblical and spiritual Jewish icons would strengthen the people's spirit, morals, national sentiments and social refinement. Moreover, the new field would produce new economic opportunities for Jewish artists. Schatz's article, written at the end of the 1880s, was a call for Jewish fine arts artists to seize the changes in historical time and space and integrate into the social, cultural and economic European states. It was not as yet a Zionist call for the structuring of a visual fine arts field in a Jewish nation-state.

In 1889 Schatz was one of the many artists who flocked to Paris. He enrolled in the *Académie Cormon* run by the *Beaux-Arts* professor and artist Fernand Cormon, an acclaimed Parisian who exhibited his paintings in the "Salon de Paris," the official art exhibition of the hegemonic *Académie des Beaux-Arts*.

Paris, at end of the nineteenth century and the beginning of the twentieth, was the vibrant cultural hub where European, and a few American, artists congregated in the new dynamic cultural terrain, at the transformative junction leading to a society of mass production. Schatz, however, chose the conservative path and resisted the avant-garde in perceiving, theorizing, and creating visual fine arts. Exposed to the vast cultural versatility of Paris, Schatz distanced himself from the cultural milieu of the vivacious modernist individualistic avant-garde and chose to master the established hegemonic "romantic" and "realist" visual artistic styles. These were for him the perfect tools for recreating the symbolic visual vision of a nation's glorious past, real or imagined. Between the years 1890 and 1900 he produced artworks depicting mythical Biblical and post-Biblical figures such as Moses, Moses's mother, Jochebed, the heroine Judith, and Matthias the Maccabee.

The sculpture of Matthias the Maccabee – portraying the iconic Jewish historical figure of the Cohen (priest) who led a successful revolt against the Hellenistic kingdom of Syria in the second century BC – was exhibited in Paris in 1895 and inspired Prince Ferdinand Koburgsky, who in 1908 would be crowned as the Tsar of Bulgaria. The prince offered Schatz the position of official court sculptor and invited him to establish an academy of art as well. Over the span of eight years Schatz affiliated himself with the Bulgarian visual arts field while involved in the State School of Art in Sofia, which he helped found in 1896, and in his own creative artwork. His artistic agenda was national, the visualization of the people of Bulgaria and their iconic figures (Kotlyar 2008). However, in 1903 Schatz experienced a divorce crisis and was devastated by the Kishinev pogrom of that year (Penkower 2004; Kotlyar 2008:15). These events sharpened his nationalist sentiments toward the idea of "The Land of Israel for the People of Israel."

While in Bulgaria, motivated by his mentor and friend, the Russian Jewish artist Mark Antokolsky (Glants 2010), and inspired by the paintings of the French "realist" Gustave Courbet, Schatz perceived education in the visual fine arts as a crucial method of refining the masses (cf. Kant 2007 [1790]:183, §60). The State School of Art in Sofia, in which he served as master of sculpture and applied crafts, integrated popular visual culture in the form of weaving, carving,

ceramics, jewelry and imagery, reflecting the ruler's and people's patriotic sentiments (Kotlyar 2008:7). He believed that the introduction to visual fine arts
would diffuse prejudices against the Other who inhabited the same territory.

In a letter he addressed to Ivan Shimshanov, Chairman of the Society for the
Support of Art in Bulgaria, Schatz elaborated his ideas of the future of art in
Bulgaria: "In my view, the first step in the growth of art in any country must be
the gradual education of the artistic sensibility of the masses" (Kotlyar 2008:6).
Furthermore,

> A society which has set such a goal for itself must nurture an [aesthetic]
> taste among the public, create the conditions for a union of all art workers,
> and provide them with all possible moral and material support, so as to
> enable art and the art industry to advance.
>
> (Kotlyar 2008:6)

Viewing visual arts as a vital leverage in Jewish integration, Schatz, like
Antokolsky, believed it would carve trajectories and integrative opportunities for
the betterment of European Jewish life.

A disciple of the Enlightenment, modernism and the "new," and trained in the
conservative "academic fine arts," Schatz distanced himself from the vibrating
European cultural scene provoked by the cultural avant-garde. His career and artistic pursuits reflected the unsettled existence of Jews in late nineteenth-century
Europe. Embracing modernism, the herald of freedom, enabled Schatz and other
Jewish thinkers and cultural creators to retain their Jewish cultural and religious
identity, yet integrate into their societies and contribute their talent to the general
good. However, personal and social traumatic events re-routed Schatz, now relieved
of royal patronage, to take an active and leading part in the Zionist movement.

In 1906 Schatz settled in Palestine and, as mentioned, established the first
Arts and Crafts Jewish Academy there, funded by the Bezalel Society in Berlin
(Schmidt 2003:184). He wanted the school to be located at a point overlooking
the Temple Mount (not yet on the Temple Mount itself, as in his utopian book of
1924; see below), but had to settle for a plot in the rapidly developing western
part of the city (Saposnik 2009:177–8). The speedy implementation of his 1905
proposal reflected Schatz's entrepreneurial, managerial, political, and artistic
skills, as well as the power of his conviction regarding the significance of the
institute for materializing the Zionist vision.

Palestine, however, was not Bulgaria. Schatz faced a major impediment as
the people who populated the land of Palestine were Arabs, not Jews. So he and
his colleagues labored on inventing an imagery to unveil the representation of
the "Real" – "The Land of Israel to the People of Israel." The result was a brew
concocted out of an eclectic, hybridized style, an assemblage of European high
and low art, such as *Art Nouveau* and *Jugendstil*, nineteenth century European
artists' interpretations of mythological Biblical texts, and the folkloristic styles
of the local inhabitants of the Middle East, the Arabs. This amalgam produced a
new "authentic," Orientalist visual language.

The newly invented visual Jewish *lingua franca*, Schatz believed, would become a vital element in several fields that formed essential components in the practical construction of the Zionist project in Palestine: the ideological, educational, cultural, and economic fields. The visualization of despondent Diaspora Jewry contrasted with the resurrected bright Biblical scenery of Palestine would crystallize the optimistic prospect of transforming the Jewish state of existence from de-territorialized "organs without body" to a re-territorialized body complete with organs (Neumann 2011).

This applied not only to Diaspora Jewry but also to the stagnant de-territorialized ultra-Orthodox Jewish community in Jerusalem, who spoke Yiddish and Arabic, and was perceived by Zionists as an unproductive community which managed its sustenance mainly on donations. As a commentator using the pen name "pilgrim" wrote in 1903, he [pilgrim] arrived in Jerusalem after a few years abroad and found that no one spoke to him in Hebrew and no one refused a handout (cited in Saposnik 2009:173). Thus, "normalizing" the Jewish community in Palestine would entail developing a productive economy. For that purpose Schatz founded craft workshops which were to become an integral part of Bezalel.

Toward the end of the First World War, in 1917, the Ottoman rulers of Palestine came to a strategic decision, to exile systematically and brutally the European Jews who resided in Jerusalem and other places in southern Palestine, as they were suspected of potentially being in service as a fifth column to the advancing British forces. Schatz was deported to Damascus and subsequently to Tiberias and Safed in the northern part of Palestine. While in exile there he composed a utopian text named *Jerusalem Rebuilt: A Daydream*, which was published in 1924 (Schatz 1924).

In this book Schatz envisioned Jerusalem as a socially, economically, and culturally modern metropolis. In the eastern part of the city, on the Temple Mount, he imagined a secular temple devoted to Jewish culture. In this new, Third Temple, there would be no animal sacrifices to the monotheistic God. Instead, the Temple would be immersed in Jewish artistic creativity. In addition, and adjacent to the Temple, a whole complex of modern institutions would be built, such as a global center for peace, a university, cottage industries and more. As for the Dome of the Rock (referred to by Schatz as the Omar Mosque):

> In the west side of the city across from Jaffa Gate on the mountain recognized by the lower pool, I could spot the proud dome of Omar mosque – Omar mosque – which previously was erected on Temple Mount and was transferred to the beautiful mountain as a memento token to the Arabs, our good neighbors who guarded and preserved our holy places with great devotion.
>
> (Schatz 1924:9; Zalmona 1985)

Schatz died in 1932 while fundraising on behalf of his academy in the United States. The Bezalel art school had already been closed down by 1929. Coincidentally, or maybe not, that year was "Year Zero" of the Israeli-Palestinian conflict, according to historian Hillel Cohen, because of the wide-ranging Palestinian uprising ("riots" in Israeli parlance) that took place that year (H. Cohen 2015). The school would re-open in 1935 and would become the most prestigious academy of arts and crafts in Israel up until the present.

One of Bezalel's fine arts students in its early period was Reuven Rubin, a 19-year-old aspiring artist from Romania. Reuven, as he is universally known, had secured a modest stipend from Dr. Adolf Stand, a Zionist activist from Austria-Hungary who recommended him to Schatz, and reached the shores of Palestine in 1912. He studied for only one year at Bezalel, however. Faced with the harsh realities of Palestine and disappointed by Bezalel's fine arts program which, at that time, was dedicated to the production of Jewish memorabilia and various sorts of crafts and barely engaged in visual fine arts, he left for Paris in 1913 and enrolled at the *École des Beaux-Arts*. Throughout his life Reuven, "the most prolific and the most successful artist in the Jewish settlement in Palestine in the 1920s" (Manor 2002:75), travelled between Palestine, later on Israel, and the Western cultural centers, mainly Paris and New York. In 1923, while in Palestine and residing in Tel Aviv, the vibrant new bourgeois Jewish town, Reuven painted "Moses and the Burning Bush," styled in late nineteenth-century symbolist and post-impressionist imagery.[4]

The center of the painting projected a representation of a dominating naked male figure barefooted and rising above a heap of shed black rags. The right hand's index finger pointed to the man's body as responding to God's voice: "Here I am," while the left hand repels the seemingly intense fire originating from an unconsumed bush. In front of the figure, gazing at the fire, is a white sheep or goat, and in the background there are prickled pear cactuses and trees, presumably olive trees, the two iconic plants of Palestine. In the back of the figure a nursing black goat and a napping white sheep or goat are portrayed.

Depiction of a naked Moses within a Burning Bush scene is a unique repres- entation found only in Reuven's painting. The representation connoted the birth of the virile masculine "new Jew," endowed with a sacred mission by an unme- diated vocal interaction with the God of the Abrahamic faith. The symbolic imagery created by Reuven reflected Zionist ideology as projected in culture, namely, the Zionist "revolution" as the rebirth of the "new Jew" rooted in Bibli- cal mythology in a specific geographical space, The Land of Israel. In the words of Chaim Nachman Bialik, Israel's national poet, reviewing Reuven's work as a painter:

> It is clear to me that Hebrew art, like Hebrew epic, if it has any hope, must be rooted in the legend of our [ancient] past. It will sprout from this past and will delve deep into it in search of influence … The ways of Hebrew legend of the past are the ways of Hebrew art of the future. There is no other way.
>
> (Cited in Manor 2002:83)

Reuven was among a group of modernist artists in Palestine who extended the Zionist visual cultural field as envisioned by Boris Schatz by importing the modern European visual art styles of the end of the nineteenth and the beginning of the twentieth century. Unlike the romantic and "realistic" styles, which dominated Schatz's Bezalel work, these artists worked in visual styles such as impressionism, post-impressionism, expressionism and post-expressionism, through which they expressed their inner feelings and their vision of Palestine as a "physical space." The interrelated, juxtaposed imagery of modern European artistic styles, Biblical mythology, and "*midrashim* about *Eretz Yisrael*" (Manor 2002:83)[5] projected onto the Palestinian landscape artworks saturated with Orientalist imagery (Manor 2002:129).

An illustrative example is Nahum Guttman's 1927 painting "A Holiday in the Jaffa Orchards." The Hebrew word for orchard is "*pardes*," which is also an acronym referring to types of approaches to Biblical exegesis in rabbinical Judaism or to interpretation of text in Torah study. Guttman appropriated the concept and placed it in the environs of the oldest port city in continuing use in the Western world, Jaffa, known for its brand of oranges exported to Europe. In a projection of naïve art, veiled Moslem women, viewed mostly from the back, were portrayed walking leisurely or lying down in a citrus grove, with a train, the icon of modernity, passing in the background. Juxtaposing the perceived mystery and idleness of the Orient with a dynamic icon of modernity under the heading of a rabbinical concept conveyed in a very subtle way the early Zionist belief that Jewish settlement in Palestine will "save [the Arab community] from its economic straits, raise it up from its social degradation, and extricate it from its bodily and moral degeneration" (Neumann 2011:86).[6]

The Bezalel art academy re-opened its doors in 1935 named "The New Bezalel School for Arts and Crafts" and headed and supported mainly by German Jews fleeing the persecution of Nazi Germany. The "New Bezalel" program and principles tended toward the spirit of the German Arts and Crafts School – the *Bauhaus*, established in Weimar in 1919. The school's creed reflected utopian socialist aesthetics, based on the notion of a classless society and the collapse of the Kantian binary between fine arts and applied arts. Its founder, the architect Walter Gropius, published a manifesto stating the creed of the school:

The ultimate aim of all visual arts is the complete building! To embellish buildings was once the noblest function of the fine arts; they were the indispensable components of great architecture. Today the arts exist in isolation from which they can be rescued only through the conscious, cooperative effort of all craftsmen. Architects, painters and sculptors must recognize anew and learn to grasp the composite character of a building both as an entity and in its separate parts ... The old schools of art were unable to produce this unity, since art cannot be taught. They must be merged once more with the workshop ... Let us then create a new guild of craftsmen without the class distinctions that raise an arrogant barrier between craftsman and artist! Together let us desire, conceive and create the new structure of the future, which will embrace architecture and sculpture and painting in one unity and which will one day rise towards heaven from the hands of a million workers like the crystal symbol of a new faith.

(Forgács 1995:27)

Desolated Germany after the First World War had no place or market for fine arts. Combining Marxist ideas and Kantian aesthetic notions ("since art cannot be taught") in a vision of technological modernist economy inspired the *Bauhaus*. It was, for the school, the right historical moment for carrying out Kant's Enlightenment idea of "refining the masses" by developing a modernist design compatible with early twentieth-century mechanical industry. The painter Mordecai Ardon, who attended the *Bauhaus* for five years (1921–1925), was elected to become Director of the New Bezalel.

From its inception, then, the Israeli visual arts field was tinted with socialist ideas: Schatz's scheme of cottage industry was influenced by the British theorist John Ruskin and the artist William Morris, who set handiwork workshops to be included in a rapidly growing industrialized society (Schatz 1924; Manor 2002: 16). And New Bezalel, as mentioned, was influenced by the *Bauhaus*. These ideas gave cultural expression to the Labor Zionist Movement's "conquest of land and labor" practices (Chapter 2), yet the visual arts field developed in major cities, primarily Jerusalem and Tel Aviv.

While Bezalel functioned as the visual field's pillar in Palestine, additional artists' associations sprung up in those cities. Among them were the notable Young Hebrews (known derisively as "Canaanite") artists who, replacing "*Eretz Yisrael*" with "Canaan," called in their work for a new Hebrew culture feeding on the history and narratives of the Middle Eastern peoples, cutting off the bond with Europe and European Jewish culture (Avnery 2017).

In a discussion which took place in 2002, three major Israeli cultural figures discussed the meaning of the iconic sculpture *Nimrod*, created by the German-born Jewish sculptor Izhak Danziger in 1939. They were Ruth Calderon, a future Member of Knesset and the founder of *Alma-Beit Midrash*, a cultural and intellectual center for the "secular" study of the Bible and the Talmud combined with literature, poetry, philosophy and the arts (see Chapter 4), and two key contemporary gatekeepers of the Israeli art field: Galia Bar Or, the legendary former curator and Director of the Ein Harod Museum, and Gideon Ofrat, the art historian and curator.

The Biblical character Nimrod is described as "a mighty hunter before the Lord," the primordial father of all hunters, and as king of Shenar, an area in southern Mesopotamia. But the root from which his name came is "to rebel," and in Talmudic literature he is depicted as the despised idolater who erected the Tower of Babel challenging the monotheistic God. Nimrod also features in ancient Middle Eastern mythology as a mighty figure with divine powers. Here he is portrayed as an uncircumcised virile hunter-warrior whose bow had become his backbone. Danziger took the hawk on Nimrod's shoulder from Egyptian art, underscoring the link between his sculpture and the ancient pagan world. Nimrod, endowed in the public view with a "Canaanite" aura, became an iconic visual cultural symbol in the ideological pendulum swing between the Zionist modernist yearning for universalist secularity and for pre-modern particularist Jewish religiosity.[7]

Trying to locate the sculpture on this ideological spectrum, Bar Or and Ofrat pointed to archeological research indicating that, visually, Nimrod echoed Nubi-Egyptian rather than Canaanite imagery. Toward the end of the conversation Calderon asked a question: "[Are] Judaism and Hebraism estranged from each other in view of Danziger's work?" – attempting to enlist the fine arts in support of her thesis on the close relations, indeed the inseparability, of local Hebraism and Judaism. Bar Or, who would curate the *Matronita* exhibition in 2012 (see below), evaded the question, but Ofrat responded eagerly, sealing the conversation:

> For me it is a profound paradox, as the essence of Judaism as I understand it is the negation of place. It is non-territorial and the embodiment of longing from within negation, a perpetual Diasporic and nomadic existence ... So Nimrod portrays a localism which is in direct contradiction to Judaism, because of its territoriality.[8]

In our view, however, Calderon diagnosed correctly the Gordian knot tying together Hebraism, or Israeli Zionism, and Jewish religion, perceiving an inherent natural continuum from Hebraism to Jewish religion in the context of a national Jewish being in the world. However, in 2002 her attempt to throw a mantle of Jewish religiosity over the "Canaanite" movement encountered resistance from the hegemonic agents in the art field.

Fine arts and the state

Even before Israel's declaration of independence in 1948 the fine arts field functioned as a paradoxical liminal space: On the one hand the *topos* encompassed the ideology of the regime (Labor Zionism), and on the other the movement encouraged (capitalist) autonomous, universal, creative individual expression. The two thresholds, we believe, constructed the working contract between the politically hegemonic core and the individual creative agents of the field. Thus, while the political regime recruited artists on behalf of the Zionist endeavor, the artists held deep convictions as to their autonomous creative status which meant, at that point in time and space, the merger of the political collective agenda with belief in individual autonomy. That symbiosis disclosed the conditions under which artists could cooperate with the political regime and yet maintain a veneer of creative autonomy. The political hegemony erected social institutions to maintain that symbiosis economically (Katz and Sela 1999):

- The educational system, which employed artists as art teachers (Steinhardt 2014:68–9).
- The Jewish Agency and the *Histadrut*, which purchased artworks, assisting artists financially (Katz and Sela 1999:21, 27).

- *Amanut L'am*, a state agency which has been paying for fine arts from the center of the country to be presented in the periphery (Katz and Sela 1999:7–8, 17).
- Commissioning sculptors to erect memorials commemorating fallen soldiers in the public space (e.g., Gilat 2005).

In 1948 the prominent abstract painter, Yossef Zaritsky, President of the Israel Painters and Sculptors Association, who was chosen by the state to represent Israel in the international art exhibition, The Venice Biennale, formed an artists' group named *New Horizons*, in order to promote abstract painting, the dominant visual narrative of Western modernity at the time. Under the theme, "we have no past, we have no history" (Manor 2009:66n111) the group developed its "lyrical abstract" style as the visual expression of the statist civil religion, focused on the building of a new, modern state.

"Lyrical abstract" corresponded to Abstract Expressionism, the hegemonic Western artistic style originating in the 1950s. "We have no past, we have no history" meant deletion of any visual traces of the past, obliterating Diaspora Jewish references and symbols in the process of the production of fine art. Thus "lyrical abstract" represented the amputation from the fine arts field of mythological Biblical memory, of contemporary Diasporic memory, underlined by the Holocaust, as well as of the tragic predicament of the Palestinian defeat (the *nakba*). It presented a re-territorialized site, a terrain on which the future of Israeli visual culture would be constructed, in line with the visual plan presented in the European and American fine arts field.

Between 1949 and 1952 Zaritsky lived on a kibbutz, Yechiam, during the summer, where he taught painting classes. Yechiam, founded in 1946, is located in the northern part of the country, in Western Galilee. Among the founding members of the kibbutz were Hungarian Holocaust survivors; its neighbors were the Bedouin residents of the village Khirbat Jiddin, which would be destroyed only two years later, in the war of 1948. Characteristically of war, the villagers abandoned their habitat, leaving behind ghost dwellings and ruins, vacant spaces dispersed in the landscape. Zaritsky's painting, *Yechiam*, created in 1952, had no reference to the past, either of the physical space or of the human members of the kibbutz. It consisted, rather, of a colorful abstract composition. Yet the title disclosed not only the location, but also the vision of the young modern state as conveyed by the autonomous artist – a future free of the burden of recent history, Jewish or Palestinian.[9]

The ideological spirit of the young state reverberated in the visual as a "document" in four ways: First, the abstract visual plan corresponded to the visuality of modern paintings produced mainly in New York and Paris; second, the abstract style emptied of identifiable imagery echoed the state's political agenda of the "melting pot," the erasure of any cultural traces of individual and social inter-Jewish ethnic identity and to a large extent Jewish religious identity as well; third, Zionist national sentiments were enhanced over religious sentiments; and fourth, the work represented the hegemony of the modern Jewish state, a product of the re-territorialization of the Jews, while concealing the "real," the tragedy of de-territorialization of the Palestinians.

The latter was illuminated, for example, in the painting of the exiled Gazan painter Ismail Shammout.[10] Unlike Zaritsky, Shamout painted in a "realistic" style. His 1954 painting, *We Will Return*, depicted a "frozen" stream of refugees on the move, a frozen split second where an old man looks sideways and a terrified young child looks up at him as if trying to decipher the old man's gaze. Absent from the composition is the middle generation, the boy's parents. The imagery denotes the totality of de-territorialization, the absence of the present through the generational gaze. Zaritsky's and Shamout's representations connoted the future: the Israeli one unfolded an optimistic future, the Palestinian unfolded disintegration, pessimism, and angst.

"Lyrical abstract" turned out to be Israel's hegemonic display window in the visual fine arts field. Yet, at the same time, socially conscientious artworks, portraying the hardships encountered by Jewish immigrants and the plight of the Palestinians who became Israeli citizens after the 1948 war, were on the periphery of the visual arts' hegemonic core. Such were the works of Yohanan Simon, Naftali Bezem, Ruth Schloss, Gershon Knipsel and Avraham Ofek (Bar Or and Ofrat 2008:14, 21–3). National symbols were also present in the public space, in the form of visual communications and propaganda in what was called "lower art." Completely absent from the field, however, was visual art produced by Orthodox artists relaying their religious culture. Thus, their work was excluded, for example, from the *Hegemony and Plurality* exhibition at the Ein Harod Museum of Art (see below). (Bar Or and Ofrat 2008:14, 23–5).

Art education

Art education in the early stages of schooling was a significant component of the secular Zionist educational system. Already in 1935 every student in the secular Zionist teacher training institutions had to take a painting class, as art teachers were responsible for decorating the schools during national and Jewish holidays. After the establishment of the state, art education occupied an important place in the state educational system, functioning as a political mechanism that provided the conceptual framework for meshing individual aspirations with the collective national agenda (Steinhardt 2014:64–6).

The state-religious educational system, as well as the *Charedi* system, were indifferent to art education and to the fine arts field in general. They saw their goal as the production of a "*Halachic* man" (Safrai 2013:264). For that purpose an Orthodox student in the religious systems had to focus on word and text, and not be distracted by imagery such as representations of human bodies. However, within the state-religious educational leadership there were a few voices which argued for the introduction of visual arts instruction. They relied for their arguments on Rav A. I. Kook's openness to Zionist culture, expressed, e.g., in the quote: "The profane will be sanctified and sanctity will be renewed" (Safrai 2013:266). When the Bezalel academy was opened in 1906 Rav Kook sent a letter to its founders praising the idea of building such an institution, which he viewed as "part and parcel of the redemption materializing in front of our eyes." Kook considered the appreciation of beauty in nature and fine arts as a crucial element of the human spirit.[11] Yet he alerted against the non-Jewish (Christian) perceptions of the visual fine arts and warned that beauty itself must not transgress the bounds of *Halacha* (Ben Shlomo 1989; Safrai 2013:269).

Nonetheless, even the national-religious educators who favored the introduction of art education did not see art as a means of developing their students as well-rounded personalities. They saw art education, rather, as providing students with tools that could help them encounter the "other" surrounding the national-religious enclave (Safrai 2013:266). Thus, for twenty-one years after the establishment of the state the state-religious educational system refrained from introducing art classes in its schools, as debates of this issue continued to brew in the state-religious system and in the national-religious public in general.

Generally speaking, the habitus of the religious Orthodox prohibited partaking in the field of fine arts. However, discussions among the state-religious educational leadership for and against art education disclosed a continuing paradox: on the one hand strict observance of *Halachic* law, and on the other an ardent resolve for total integration with the cultural fields of modern Israel. As summarized by Professor Yonah Frankel, a professor of Jewish thought at the Hebrew University of Jerusalem, the difficulty in accepting fine arts and art education stemmed from the fact that

> teaching the history of fine arts requires dealing with pagan art, dealing with nudity in the framework of the plastic arts and dealing with salient Christian church art. Currently we cannot train [art] teachers for the religious sector in our own institutions, only in non-religious ones, namely universities, and there "*Halacha* will be transgressed."
>
> (Safrai 2013:273)

Alluding to the craftsmanship displayed in the woodwork of many old synagogues, Frankel's proposed solution to these difficulties was to recognize that "*Halacha* has many faces." Then, in 1969, the Young *Mizrachi* Women's House, a women teachers' seminary in Tel Aviv, began to offer introductory fine art courses in its curriculum (Safrai 2013:273).

Religious art making

For more than five decades the Jewish religious presence in the Israeli fine arts field was minimal. In 2008 Israel's six major art museums hosted a multiple-site exhibition to celebrate the country's sixtieth anniversary, named "60 Years of Fine Art in Israel," with the exhibition in each museum dedicated to one decade of the country's history. While the segmentation of the history of Israeli art into decades was quite arbitrary, the exhibition catalogs outlined the narrative of the hegemonic center of the visual arts field. The exhibition representing the first decade, 1948–1958, was named *Hegemony and Plurality* and was shown in the iconic kibbutz, Ein Harod, located in the Jezreel valley, where the art museum is called The Temple of Art (*mishkan le'omanut*).

Like the exhibitions mounted in the other five museums, the Ein Harod exhibition projected imagery, form, contents, and titles which corresponded to practices common in museums in the Western world, and completely ignored art produced by religious artists. It offered a re-reading of Israel's first decade by adding the word "plurality" to "hegemony," but plurality did not encompass Jewish religious art. Rather, the curators, Galia Bar Or and Gideon Ofrat, included in the show "low art" works produced for decorating kibbutzim dining halls on Jewish holidays and displayed them in the museum's secondary spaces.

Figure 7.2 Meir Ben Uri, *Jacob's Ladder* (1957). Dry etching, 94 × 146 cm. Collection of Ben Uri Museum. Reproduced with permission of Ben Uri Museum.

These works consisted of visual presentations of Jewish holidays and were painted on paper or sackcloth in gouache paints, which made them portable and recyclable. Thus the first decade exhibition was characterized by selective inclusion within hegemonic exclusion.

Works of the "secondary" holiday artists, other than their holiday decorations, were presented in the main exhibit spaces as well, with one exception. Meir Ben Uri was an Orthodox religious artist and an architect who in his later years founded a museum for religious fine art on the second floor of his house in a Haifa suburb. Ben Uri's work, the only one created by a religious artist, was included with the holiday paintings in the secondary spaces of the exhibition, but his individual artworks, such as, for example, *Jacob's Ladder*, were not presented in the main spaces of the museum, like the works of the other holiday painters. The reason for that may be found in Ofrat's statement: "The plastic arts are anti-iconic. There is no hidden God beyond forms and materials, only fragments of Godly monuments scattered in the dark, and emptiness" (Ofrat 2000). Indeed, after sixty years of Israeli art, Israeli Jewish religious art was still excluded from the canon.

In 1998 Abraham Levitt, a researcher in the conservative Shalem Institute, offered a revisionist narrative describing the historical dynamics of the Israeli art field. In an article titled "Israeli Art on its Way to a Different Place," published in Shalem's *Azure* Journal (Levitt 1998), Levitt denoted the production of contemporary Israeli art as "degenerate processes," and suggested five stages through which the Israeli fine arts field had gone by that time:

- The first period, from 1906 to the mid-1920s, saw the establishment of the Jewish art community in Palestine led by Boris Schatz, whose vision Levitt described as admiration for the power and vitality of the ancient Jewish people (Levitt 1998:103).
- The next stage began in the second half of the 1920s. Artworks created in this decade, as against the previous one, had non-Jewish themes. Excited by the build-up of the Zionist project around them, artists contemplated the local landscape, its Palestinian inhabitants, and the Jewish "pioneers" in a modern European style, characterized by Levitt as "Orientalist" (Levitt 1998:105–6). Their work was devoid of any relation to the historical mythological place or its Jewish history, real or imagined. For example, the painting *The Train Passing Through Neve Tzedek*, painted by Ziona Tager in 1920 (not mentioned by Levitt), recorded the artist's experience by depicting, in the prevailing contemporary European style, a train rushing through the heart of a neighborhood of the first Zionist city, Tel Aviv.
- The third stage, Levitt argued, transpired in the 1930s, with the influx of German Jews to Palestine. Those refugees fleeing Nazi Germany, "discovered a growing interest in the material aspect of the land without bonding with the Jewish people" (Levitt 1998:106). Their art projected repugnance toward the under-developed place and toward Zionist ideology proclaimed by the "*Ostjuden*" (Eastern European Jewish) leadership. Moreover, their art

Figure 7.3 Ziona Tager, *The Train Passing Through Neve Tzedek* (1920). 46 × 55 cm. Private collection. Reproduced with permission of Avraham Katz Oz.

had no value for the Jewish people. Such is the morbid feelings projected, according to Levitt, by the woodcut *An Alley in Jerusalem* by Jacob Stein-hardt,[12] who expressed in his works "guilt feelings and a pained wish for reconciliation with the Arabs ... [and] grief and rage over the results of Jewish settlement in the Land of Israel" (Levitt 1998:108).

- The deterioration continued, according to Levitt, in the fourth stage, with the establishment of the State of Israel in 1948. In that period artists shunned national and religious sentiments. He emphasized the influence of the "New Horizons" group and the "Canaanites" on the future of the Israeli fine arts field. The two movements, Levitt argued, shared the same ideology: The favorite theme of New Horizons was the sunlight illuminating the Israeli landscape, while the Canaanites' was the Middle Eastern peoples, current and ancient. Furthermore, already in the 1950s and 1960s prominent artistic voices, such as those of Naftali Bezem and Igael Tumarkin, were contesting the core tenets of Zionism. Bezem's work from 1957 titled *In the Courtyard of the Third Temple* (not mentioned in the article), relayed the artist's

Figure 7.4 Naftali Bezem, *In the Courtyard of the Third Temple* (1957). Gouache on cardboard, 70 × 100 cm. Collection of Tel Aviv Museum of Art. Reproduced with permission of Shlomo Bezem and Tel Aviv Museum of Art, photograph by Avraham Hai.

response to the murder of forty-three Israeli Palestinian citizens by the Israeli police in Kafr Qasim in 1956. The painting portrayed three women mourners and a dead baby holding an identity card. Framed by the title *In the Courtyard of the Third Temple*, an allusion to the State of Israel, Bezem criticized the horrendous IDF military action, hence the modern state itself.

Shortly after the war of 1967 the sculptor Igael Tumarkin exhibited a mutilated soldier's figure in a sculpture made of discarded firearms and bronze, named *He Walked in the Fields* (the title of the iconic 1947 novel by Moshe Shamir celebrating the Palestine-born new Jew, the *Sabra*), protesting the militaristic exaltation which followed the results of that war.

Bezem's and Tumarkin's voices would become the *bon ton* of the hegemonic group in the fine arts field in later years.

• The fifth stage, in the 1990s, projected, according to Levitt, the final detachment from national and religious values. Levitt attributed this estrangement from Jewish values to the 1993 Oslo Accords, the blowing winds of peace, economic liberalization, the introduction of civil society, identity politics, and feminism. All of these wove the conditions for the fine arts field to relieve itself of its ideological, national and/or religious burdens. Thus, the 1990s engendered strong sentiments of rootless desire for nomadism and preparations

Figure 7.5 Igael Tumarkin, *He Walked in the Fields* (1967). Bronze, partly painted, 175 × 46 × 48 cm. Collection of Tel Aviv Museum of Art. Reproduced with permission of the artist and Tel Aviv Museum of Art, photograph by Ran Erde.

for departure from the Land of Israel. Levitt attacked artworks and exhibitions influenced by post-modern, post-colonial, identity politics and feminist rhetoric, the language of the global discourse. And he concluded:

> Boris Schatz hoped to establish in the Land of Israel an art community which will erect a "Temple" in the desert for the Jewish people returning to their homeland. However, it lasted only for three, four generations. After the beginning of the great vision and dream Israeli art offers nothing to the Jewish soul, no haven, no rescue … Israeli artists uprooted the land of the forefathers from their heart, even if they are physically present there, in their spirit they abandoned the land and displaced themselves to the desert, through sea or land … [But] the gravest self-contempt rising from the studios of Israeli art may prepare the stage for a counter reaction, for a revolution that will radically change the cultural map of Israel.
>
> (Levitt 1998:118)

Twenty years after Levitt, the non-observant, kibbutz-born writer, novelist, and literary critic Assaf Inbari, also assessed that the cultural field in Israel was distorted since: "We seculars have abandoned Judaism, just like the ultra-Orthodox abandoned the State" (A. Inbari 2017).[13] Echoing Schatz's vision, Inbari argued that:

> We [seculars] should be forging a modern, pluralistic, enlightened halakha. That's what the pioneers tried to do. They knew that Judaism was never static. Judaism always transformed itself and was relevant. They tried to create a modern, nationalist framework. They invented new rituals, they dealt with day-to-day ethics. They had a form of political theology. That's what Judaism is supposed to be. We should be confronting – on Jewish terms! – those rabbis who think that Judaism means excluding women or ignoring the Palestinians on the West Bank.
>
> (A. Inbari 2013)

Inbari yearns for "Hebrew culture," folded in "modern Jewishness," rather than "Israeli culture," which, accordingly, reflects "modern detachment." "Hebraic culture is a Jewish alternative, not an alternative identity to Jewish identity," he argues. "Israeli culture silenced the Hebraic one," since in the 1970s the "art scene projected alienation from Zionism, the land of Israel and a large section of the people of Israel … Realization of the colonial and occupation reality drove the cultural sector of the society into detachment from the Hebraic culture." Furthermore: "Judaism without God is an empty word." Positioning God in the center means reinforcing the religious dimension of the state. Thus:

> Jewish renewal must take the form of renewed encounter with Jewish faith. Just as it needs to open up to the statist dimensions, the aesthetic dimensions, the up-to-date challenges that Rabbinical Judaism is fleeing from, so it must open up to the metaphysical dimension without which Judaism is just folklore.
>
> (A. Inbari 2017)

Orthodox artists: a quest for change within religious Jewish orthodoxy

Levitt's prediction of a coming "revolution" in the Israeli fine arts field is materializing now in evolving narratives among Religious Zionist as well as *Charedi* rabbis, intellectuals, educators, and artists as to the legitimacy of producing fine arts in general, and visual fine arts in particular, within the confines of *Halacha*. Rabbis who head *yeshivot hesder* are crucial participants in the "modernization" discourse regarding visual arts and the *Halacha*, seizing the opportunity to enlist the fine arts as a form of leverage in constructing bridges between the Orthodox and non-observant ways of life, just as *yeshivot hesder* succeeded in reconciling Torah study with meaningful military service (Chapter 6). Rav Yuval Sherlo, who heads a *yeshivat hesder* in Petach Tiqva, relied on Rav A. I. Kook's theologizing in defense of his support for the fine arts. Kook saw spiritual creativity as the place

> for nourishing the powers of the soul, the imagination, sensitivity and other soul tools. All those tools are the amalgamation of knowledge, aspiration, sensitivity and study ... Culture and art are major endeavors as they target the imagination in order to shape the image of man in the present and the preparation for the Lord's command in the future as appears in the prophecy.
>
> (Sherlo 1998; see also 2000)

Leaning on Rav Kook's theology and *Halachic* interpretations aids the religious supporters of visual arts in countering the conservative Religious Zionist rabbis who oppose the production of visual fine arts, using the metaphor of a "slippery slope" to warn against the dire consequences of such activity.

Matronita *and beyond*

In 2012 the Ein Harod Museum of Art hosted an exhibition, *Matronita*, which presented the work of Orthodox feminist artists committed to the world of *Halacha*. The museum director, Dr. Galia Bar Or, observed that

> [f]or many years now, the two essential aspects of the "Matronita" project – art created in Israel in a distinctively feminist context, and art created from within the religious Jewish world – seem to have been absent from the canon of Israeli art.
>
> (Bar Or 2012:202; Matronita 2012)

It was this absence that *Matronita* aimed to correct.

Matronita was the first comprehensive exhibit of religious Israeli women artists. Its two curators were Orthodox Jews – Dvora Liss and David Sperber (Matronita 2012). The exhibition turned out to be a challenging event in the Israeli cultural ontology that year, by introducing, for the first time in the hegemonic core of the art field, feminist art created by Orthodox women who were totally committed to *Halacha*. Concurrently with global feminist art, many of the works exhibited dealt with the humiliating situations and exclusion of women in the *Halachic* regime and legitimized by male authority. However, in the variety of works exhibited there was no insinuation of the collapse of the overbearing walls of *Halacha*, only a beam of light directed at the absurd situations in which women are placed within the existing codex. The works represented a cry against oppressive male mastery. The visual language chosen by the artists was that of the conventional canonic art practices, utilizing a tool box comprised of generic contemporary tools, expressing the specific content of their living space.

Not all the works shown in *Matronita* had specifically feminist content (see Chapter 8). In many of them the feminist statement consisted of the very fact of art being created by Orthodox religious women commenting on public issues in the public sphere. Thus, Andi Arnovitz's 2009 work, *Vest of Prayers*, shown in *Matronita*, was described by the curator, Dvora Liss, as "a Jewish response to the suicide vests worn by terrorists" (Liss 2012:191). The materials Arnovitz assembled to create the vest were rolled worn-out pages of prayer books, strings, and Japanese paper. Many hundreds of scrolls organized in dense layers, sharply contrasted to the screws and nails wrapped in cylinders around the suicide bombers' explosive belts. The artwork referenced religion by the prayer book pages and clearly represented its message of a binary metaphor: Jewish religious humanism and culture versus Moslem barbarism; transcendence versus violence.

The series of oil paintings by Ruth Kestenbaum Ben-Dov, *Prayer Rugs* were created in 2003–2005 (No. 3 was shown in *Matronita*; No. 2, shown below, was not). In her works she presented a juxtaposition of Jewish and Moslem religious ritual articles, such as a *parochet*, the curtain that covers the Torah Ark containing the Torah scrolls in a synagogue, and Moslem prayer rugs, with texts from the two religions' Holy Scriptures. In No. 2 the *parochet* turns into a prayer rug. The Hebrew text around the rug is taken from the prayer *Aleinu Leshabeach*

Figure 7.6 Andi Arnovitz, *Vest of Prayers* (2009). Found prayerbook pages, threads, and Japanese paper. Collection of the artist. Reproduced with permission of the artist.

(It Is Our Duty to Praise) and the word God, which was on the *parochet* in Hebrew, is written in Arabic on the rug, together with a sentence from a Jewish prayer. The sentence, boldly painted on top of the painting in Hebrew, is "And we bend our knees, and bow down."

On the face of it, Kestenbaum Ben-Dov's painting series projects a yearning for Jewish-Moslem peace and coexistence, expressed through presentations of inter-religious metaphorical cross-breeding between Judaism and Islam, tantamount to the collapsing of modernist, nationalist, secular processes of ethnic purification. However, the prayer *Aleinu Leshabeach* begins with the words: "It is our duty to praise the Master of all … who has not made us like the Gentiles … for they worship vanity and emptiness and pray to a god who cannot save," and these phrases appear in Kestenbaum Ben-Dov's work. So while the painting is supposed to project a yearning for peace and coexistence, the text on its margins conveys a message of Jewish superiority.

Debbie Kampel, a resident of the West Bank settlement of Alon Shvut born in South Africa, paints in the so-called realistic style. She responded to a question about her work, *Reality Check*:

> In South Africa the policy was clearly of oppression. It is true that in Israel severe violations do occur, and the IDF sometimes behaves immorally, but

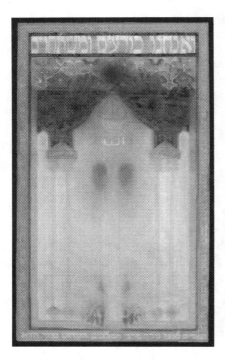

Figure 7.7 Ruth Kestenbaum Ben-Dov, *Prayer Rug No. 2* (2003). 125 × 80 cm. Collection of the artist. Reproduced with permission of the artist.

this is not the policy. The terrorist acts produced it. Still, I have a hard time with the checks the Arabs have to go through.[14]

On another occasion she stated: "my painting shows an aspect of daily coexistence between soldier and civilian, young and old. My paintings bear witness to the human moments. There are no stereotypes – just people, human beings, interacting, acknowledging and embracing their common humanity."[15]

Kampel's gaze, as an Orthodox Jewish Israeli citizen residing in the occupied Palestinian territories, made her idealize a particular instance of the physical human contact between the occupying Israeli citizen-soldier and the occupied non-citizen Palestinian men and women in the spaces of Judea and Samaria. Her work of art turned into a lopsided documentation of the colonial matrix of citizens and non-citizens, which is the signified of the artwork, while its textual signifier, ironically, is *Reality Check*.

As against Kampel's *Reality Check*, Herman Peled's *Violinist at Beit Iba Checkpoint*,[16] lifted from a very short videograph of a Palestinian man playing the violin in front of an Israeli army officer in a space controlled by the military, is a work of multiple signifiers. The visually inscribed traces on a surface densely filled with historically displaced memories. The image brought an interval of reflection to most Israelis, an almost sublime moment, when the

Figure 7.8 Debbie Kampel, *Reality Check* (2003). 100 × 110 cm. Collection of the artist. Reproduced with permission of the artist.

fold was fractured, and could not refold (Ehrenberg 2016). The Jewish victims of persecution and discrimination crossed a threshold, the Borgesian map was torn apart to reveal the surface of the iron wall, that of a victim becoming victimizer; an unacceptable, forbidden, mental state, which echoed of ultimate immorality and vice.

The image sabotaged symbolic structures planted in the collective Israeli cultural memory, those structures that constructed the new Jew, the Zionist, the Nietzschean *Übermensch*, the one who underwent a metaphorical transformation from the last Jew, the Diasporic, the weak, the nomadic, the wanderer, void of patriotic and national and territorial feelings. It was a terrifying moment of realization that the semiotic displacement of the figure of the fiddler visualized and symbolized, in the contemporary historical junction, the landscapes of the new victims of political repression. These landscapes are not exclusive anymore. The Palestinians are now the inhabitants of these semiotic territories.

Documenting the Palestinian fiddler at the checkpoint made it clear that there are no empty territories in the Promised Land. And yes, victim can become victimizer. In this way the connection between the symbolic and the subjective was shortened, marking the collapse of the imaginary Jewish-Zionist liberal morality. This interpretation is based on a binary conception, on the basis of which Kampel's circumventing language, based on hybridity, cannot be constructed.

Figure 7.9 Horit Herman Peled, *Violinist at Beit Iba Checkpoint* (2004). Still from a videograph. Collection of the artist. Reproduced with permission of the artist.

Porat Salomon is a major player in the art field through his art and also through the Orthodox art academy he founded in Jerusalem – *Pardes*. The setting of his visual work, *Shabbat*, which portrays a young settler family seated at a seeming, but peculiar, Sabbath dinner. At the time he produced this work the artist was a resident of Bat Ayin, a Jewish settlement in the West Bank considered to be one of the more extreme ideologically nationalist settlements. Being a student of the late Rav Menachem Forman, Salomon views the religious paradigm as the only viable one for dialogue between Israelis and Palestinians.[17] For him, the issue of sovereignty over the Temple Mount is the core of the dispute between Israelis and Palestinians:

> I'd like to bring together architects, intellectuals and religious people of all persuasions to plan anew the Holy Basin area, where the main shrines of the three religions are located in Jerusalem, as a wound at the heart of the world; to create a space where people come to experience not what is but what is missing, where they come to yearn … People won't come to monuments of power or to phalluses reaching the sky, but to create the ultimate wilderness everywhere, including the Western Wall.[18]

"To conquer the center" was the sub-title of an article by *Haaretz* art critic Shaul Setter, reviewing the exhibition *Tzena U-Re'ena* ("Come Out and See,"

Figure 7.10 Porat Salomon, *Shabbat* (2009). Photograph, 70 × 50 cm. Collection of the artist. Reproduced with permission of the artist.

the title of a famous book of *midrashim* in Yiddish written for Jewish women in 1616) exhibited at Ben-Gurion University, followed by an academic conference in April 2017 (Setter 2017). Setter argued that while in dialogue with the Western discourse of contemporary high art, the artists who participated in the exhibition projected a monolithic perspective contextualized in gender and Jewish religious identity connoted by the insinuated symbolic meaning of a "trinity": "Femininity, Israeliness, and Religion," a code to be deciphered as an exclusive Jewish territory emptied of all the others, namely Arab Israeli women citizens. The University's announcement indicated the theme of the exhibition: the religious identity of the participants – *Charedi*, national-religious, formerly religious, *chozrim biteshuvah*, and settlers, as projected within their communities and visualized by different media and styles of artwork.

One of the works: *Tzuk Eithan* [solid rock], *Me?* ("The Gaza War of 2014") created by a *chozeret biteshuvah* artist, Sigal Maor, communicated the circumstances and consequences of the 2014 Gaza war, triggered by the kidnap and murder of three *yeshiva* students in the West Bank by Palestinian Arabs. The video artwork depicted a woman embroidering repeatedly the portraits of the three slain Israeli youth on a khaki Israeli combat shirt branded with IDF in Hebrew letters, while the artist expressed her thoughts and feelings via voiceover, reaffirming the reasoning, urge and legitimacy of the war waged on Gaza in 2014.

Figure 7.11 Sigal Maor, *Tzuk Eithan* [solid rock], *Me?* (2014). Embroidered IDF shirt. Collection of the artist. Reproduced with permission of the artist.

Maor is not a settler; she resides in the southern part of central Israel, in Ashdod. Yet the art critic linked the diversity of religious identities folded among the participant artists with the politics of the right: "what the exhibition obscures [is] that Israeli religious female artists are right-wing artists," whose works, according to Setter, projected sentiments of patriotism, unity, and acceptance of the loss of soldiers' lives. Setter pointed to the increasing practices of religionization *vis-à-vis* the art field, as expressed in the exhibition:

> [T]hese female artists mostly come from the ascending group in the population, increasingly demanding a hold in state institutions. Following education, the IDF and the Supreme Court, the cultural field is the objective. The national-religious segment of the society demands greater presence in the cultural fields.[19]

One of the leading national-religious artists working today is Avner Bar Hama, who graduated from *Merkaz Ha-Rav yeshiva* and is a prolific artist, curator, educator and an active agent in the process of religionization in the art field.[20] In 2017 Bar Hama was appointed Head of the Department of Arts in the Ministry of Culture and Sports. Prior to that he had been a member of the Israeli Council for Culture and Art – an advisory body to the Minister of Culture and Sports.

In May 2015 the right-wing Likud politician, Miri Regev, was made Minister of Culture and Sports. She immediately proceeded to threaten to withdraw funds from cultural activities that she deemed to be in opposition to government policy. A case in point was the Elmina Theater in Tel Aviv-Jaffa run by the acclaimed Israeli Palestinian actor and director Norman Issa and his Jewish partner, the playwright Gidona Raz. Since Issa refused to perform in the occupied Palestinian territories (OPT), the Minister threatened to cut off his theater's funds. The threat triggered protests against the Minister in public and in social media channels by agents active within the cultural field.[21]

In response to the protest Bar Hama published an article titled "This is Kicking Time," criticizing the protestors and calling on right-wing religious artists to cease producing "nice, polite" visual works and to start to create critical, angry, and infuriating art, contesting the hegemony of the non-observant in the art field. Furthermore, in this article Bar Hama condemned the alleged conviction of the hegemonic artists that their task was to defend the minority and the oppressed:

> They focus on "our cousins" [the Palestinians] – the murderers. When freedom of expression indiscriminately plays into their hands this could harm the nation which resides in Zion [the Jews]. It is about time that our male and female artists will reflect in their artistic work the other side and will not let the alleged "humanistic" arena control the Israeli art scene that until today speaks in unanimously one voice for the Palestinians and never for our right on this land.
>
> (Bar Hama 2015)

Assuming an essentially modernist position, Bar Hama stated that: "Fine art is not folklore and not craft ... It is cultural structuring ... striving for spiritual expression that touches the depth of human soul" (Bar Hama 2015). Bar Hama draws his deep convictions about what Jewish fine arts ought to be from a blend of vague Kantian concepts packaged dialectically in Rabbi A. I. Kook's references to fine arts: "The undertaking of fine arts [literature, painting, sculpture] is perpetually to disclose all the spiritual concepts immersed in the depth of the human soul ... [This] is the duty of artwork" (Bar Hama 1999).

David Sperber is a constitutive figure in the structuring of the religious visual fine arts discourse. An art historian, curator, professor, and art critic who, like Bar Hama, is a graduate of *Merkaz Ha-Rav* and *yeshivat hesder Har Etzion*, located in the West Bank. Sperber co-curated the *Matronita* exhibition in 2012, as well as other major Jewish art exhibitions. Both Sperber and Bar Hama ground the fine arts field in individual artistic expression confined within the bounds of *Halacha*. Yet while Bar Hama recourses to right-wing nationalist rhetoric, Sperber recourses to the rhetoric of multiculturalism, projecting a liberal standpoint. Both of them protest the exclusion of Orthodox religious artists from participation in the hegemonic center of the visual arts field. However, while Bar Hama blames the exclusion on the politically liberal convictions of the hegemonic agents in the fine arts field, Sperber blames it on the binary "nature" of modernism. Employing identity politics and feminist narratives Sperber blames modernist practices for the exclusion of Orthodox religious artists in the name of the "secular discourse, that adopted modern conventions by which art is conceived as a field that has nothing to do with religion" (Sperber 2010:23).

In 2013 Sperber, voicing aesthetic judgment, the perfect modernist tool of the discourse, targeted Bar Hama's artistic work for criticism, tagging it as right-wing, nationalistic, "embarrassing Photoshop" artwork. Sperber asserted that "the foundation of creation ... in the art field ... is judgments of taste and value ... which turn a creation from mere visual culture to a work of art ... What is required here are skills, sensitivities, subtleties" which presumably are lacking in Bar Hama's work (Sperber 2013). This statement clearly contradicts, however, the binary-denying post-modern discourse that Sperber relied on in criticizing as modernist the exclusion of Orthodox religious works of art from the mainstream of the Israeli art field.

At the end of 2017 Bar Hama published an article with the title "Bennett, Do Not Ignore the Plastic Arts." It was an open letter to the Minister of Education Naftali Bennett, calling upon the religious public "to stop being afraid and enter the influential plastic arts arena" which is currently "ruled by those who kick and defy Judaism" (Bar Hama 2017). Like most religious actors in the fine arts field, Bar Hama criticized the non-observant hegemonic agents in the field for systematically excluding the creative products of religious artists. Furthermore, he claimed that those hegemonic agents refuse to endow the Israeli art world with the treasures of the "Jewish bookcase" that Jewish religion has to offer. He called upon religious artists to put up a resistant stand against the existing artistic apparatus and against the indifferent religious and rabbinical establishment ... The duty of fine arts today is also to mend society and point out its maladies. And yet, in this period, when the status of the artist is integral and influential in society, we are absent.

(Bar Hama 2017)

Moreover, while artists who sympathize with the Palestinians are rewarded by the hegemonic institutions of the fine arts field, funded by the state, artists who project humanistic values while expressing agony and suffering over Palestinian terror attacks are being ignored (Bar Hama 2017).

The veracity of Bar Hama's claim can be illustrated by comparing the reception of his digital work, *Hasam Gvulech Shalom*, to the oil painting by the Druze female artist, Fatma Shanan Dery, *Razan 2012*. Both works depict a typical, iconic Israeli landscape, long perceived as the conceptual base of "classic" Israeli fine arts, and in both works cultural symbols are depicted in the foreground, embedded in a painterly photographic scene. In Shanan Dery's painting it is an image of a woman standing in a field staring downward at a rug, while in Bar Hama's digital painting, it is a three-dimensional image of a Greater Land of Israel map. The map is inscribed with the verse "the land flowing with milk and honey" modified by exchanging "gold" for the original "flowing." The title of the work is a verse from Psalms, "The one who initiates peace will be content,"

Figure 7.12 Avner Bar Hama, *Hasam Gvulech Shalom* (2005). Digital work, dibond print, 110 × 170 cm. Collection of the artist. Reproduced with permission of the artist.

meaning "peacemaking is a precondition for prosperity." In this work Bar Hama played on the political sensitivities of the liberal hegemonic group in the art field who view peace as conditioned on the two-state solution to the Israeli-Palestinian conflict. The interplay between the visual and the text in Bar Hama's work produces a counter statement – peace and prosperity are in reach, conditioned on maintaining Jewish control over Greater Israel (cf. Chapter 3).

The oil painting created by Fatma Shanan Dery, a young but already established Druze woman artist active in the Israeli fine arts field, was presented in her solo exhibition at the prestigious Tel Aviv Museum of Art in 2017, whereas Bar Hama's work has never been presented in a major museum in Israel (Sperber 2013). The rug in the foreground of the painting connotes a reference to the home in most cultures, and certainly in Druze culture. The displacement of the rug in a typical, distinctive, iconic Israeli background (the field being a reference to the Zionist pioneering ethos of the "conquest of land") alongside the figure of a non-Jewish woman, depicted as a Western female figure standing in the field, project metaphorically the spirit of the liberal Jewish state, which grants the non-Jewish citizen, the "other," integrative equal opportunities.

Contrary to Shanan Dery's artwork, Bar Hama's work does not comply with the narrative of the liberal Israeli fine arts field. While Shanan Dery's work "speaks" the right language of the contemporary *bon ton*, that of feminism and identity politics, Bar Hama's challenges the discourse with a provocative counter

Figure 7.13 Fatma Shanan Dery, *Razan 2012* (2012). 80 × 100 cm. Private collection. Reproduced with permission.

narrative, an embarrassing political abomination in the eyes of most key players in the Israeli fine arts field as currently constituted, unworthy of being called an artwork (Sperber 2013). The juxtaposition of the two works presents a paradoxical situation: while Bar Hama holds key institutional positions in the visual art field, his work is rejected by the aesthetic gatekeepers of the field, whereas Shanan Dery's works are rewarded by them.

Charedim in the visual arts field

The visual arts were introduced to *Charedi* communities initially by artists who made *teshuvah* in the 1970s (Chapter 4). Thus, Yitzhak (Ika) Israeli was a well-known painter who grew up in a Labor Zionist family and in the 1960s was a pillar of the bohemian scene in Tel Aviv. The bohemian scene then was made up of artists, writers, and theatre people, as well as senior IDF officers – an extraordinary association between cultural agents and those of the soldierly world, reflecting the *zeitgeist* of the emerging Jewish Israeli cultural field.

In June 1967, two weeks after the end of the war, Israeli and his (non-military) friends sent a letter to *Davar*, the *Histadrut*'s daily, asking the government and the IDF for respectful and dignified rule over the Palestinians in the occupied territories, in order to avoid anti-Israel propaganda abroad (Israeli 1967). Israeli began his personal process of *teshuvah* at the end of the 1960s when, like other members of the bohemian circles, most famously the comedian, actor and film director, Uri Zohar, he was frustrated with the contradiction between Labor Zionist ideals and the reality of war and military occupation. At the same time he also realized the shallow emptiness of his own bohemian existence (cf. Wexler n.d.). He joined a Lithuanian (anti-Chassidic) *Charedi* community in Jerusalem where the Second Commandment was strictly enforced as one of the means of preserving the segregation of the community from the wider Israeli society.

However, while Israeli, by now a rabbi and a major proselytizer in the *teshuvah* movement, gradually withdrew from his old lifestyle, his visual artistic desire did not abate. Together with a former Israeli film star, Mordechai "Popik" Arnon, he founded "To'Ar" (Tora and Art association). In 2003 the association founded the Shelter Art Gallery in the *Charedi* quarter of Mekor Chaim in West Jerusalem as a gallery for Jewish art, created by religious artists from all walks of life and levels of talent, and showcasing modern Jewish art and Judaica.

In 2017 Noa Lea Cohen became Director of The Shelter Art Gallery. The place then became a vibrant location for *Charedi* cultural gatherings, as well as for other culture lovers, artists, gallery goers, and curious non-observant visitors. According to its Director, the gallery provides a space to quench the growing thirst within the Orthodox community for individual cultural expression. Cohen herself identifies religiously as *Chardalit* (feminine inflection of the combination of *Charedi* and Mafdal, Hebrew for the NRP), usually a nickname for Religious Zionists who become more observant, *Charedi* style. However, in Cohen's case the direction was reversed: she was a *Charedit* who embraced religious Zionism, a move which facilitated connection to the general culture. The eventful program of the gallery, situated at the heart of a *Charedi* neighborhood in Jerusalem, denotes an additional juncture in the network of fields undergoing religionization.

Chana Goldberg, an established artist in the religious art scene and an active member of the gallery, perceived the gallery to be an agent of change beyond the *Charedi* community, as she addressed the difficulty of religious women art students:

> In the classical religious world, there is no room for self-expression; it is something that would even be considered offensive. I taught at a girls' yeshiva high school of the arts, a place that was fairly "light" religiously, and where students were encouraged to speak up. Once I asked each student to come up with a single sentence. Every one of them offered a quotation. Some quoted from Maimonides, some from Van Gogh. Not a single one offered a sentence of her own. The Jewish sages never say anything without citing a source. It is a culture of quotation.
>
> (Arad 2017)

In 2014 Bezalel opened an academic fine arts department dedicated exclusively to teaching *Charedi* women, the first class of which graduated in 2017.[22] Thus, by the beginning of the twenty-first century a growing community of Orthodox artists and art teachers, mainly women, has been formed, as well as a conversation about the meaning of integrating into the hegemonic art discourse, while reflecting on the religious Jewish content in their works. In the words of Porat Salomon:

> [Our] dream is not to create a separatist, alternative art world, but on the contrary – to create an art community that will enter the art world, that will succeed in generating [a] conversation within the art world. Today the trend in the art world is [one] of cultural identities: Chinese and African art, for example. And I think that religious art is also a kind of tribe with its own conversation. In order to conduct its conversation accurately, it needs some kind of internal happening.
>
> (Rief 2013)

Summary: Nimrod's circumcision

Whether due to the Second Commandment prohibition on representing living creatures, or because of their particular living conditions in the Diaspora, or both, for most of their history Jews had refrained from producing visual fine arts. Toward the end of the nineteenth century, following the Enlightenment and their emancipation in Western Europe, Jews began to enter the fine arts field. Zionism encouraged this trend enthusiastically, viewing the fine arts as an essential component of any national culture. This led to the establishment by Boris Schatz of the Bezalel Academy of Arts and Crafts in Jerusalem as early as 1906.

Since its inception in 1906 the hegemonic core group in the fine arts field in Palestine/Israel played a crucial integral role in the processes of state- and nation-building, reflecting in their artworks the prevailing civil religion. The war of 1967 marked a turning point in this respect, as the territories occupied in that war, particularly those in the West Bank, ignited the messianic vision of the Greater Land of Israel for the People of Israel among large sectors of the Jewish Israeli public. The 1973 Yom Kippur war enhanced this messianic vision for many, especially Religious Zionists, but brought disillusionment for others, including most agents active in the fine arts field, who came to be increasingly critical of the state and even of Zionism.

As the Zionist journey back to the homeland expanded in time and space, the interlaced presence of the natives, the non-Jewish inhabitants of Palestine, as occupied subjects, burdened the conscience of liberal Jewish citizens. In the 1990s, as the Oslo Accords failed and non-citizen Palestinians became a prolonged presence, the visual arts field adopted conceptual tools to analyze and reflect upon the results of the erosion of the democratic facet of the Israeli state's social contract. The binary narrative of a Jewish democratic state could not

Figure 7.14 Shai Azulai, *Nimrod's Circumcision 2* (2008). 42 × 50 cm. Collection of the artist. Reproduced with permission of the artist.

contain the reality of the "new Jew" as military occupier. Adopting post-modernist, post-colonial, feminist, and in-between hybrid theories evading these binary principles accommodated the visual fine arts field to the new reality, enriching it in the process.

The non-binary narratives allowed for the incorporation of Jewish and non-Jewish "others" in the hegemonic core of the field – first Palestinian citizens and then, more grudgingly perhaps, Orthodox Jews. This inclusion in the midst of exclusion functioned as a mirrored image which facilitated and prolonged the illusion of the harmony between the two constitutive principles of the state – Jewish and democratic. However, as the political conflict with the Palestinians and economic liberalization progressed, the liberal aspects (in all but the economic sense) of the civil religion weakened, creating a void which is now being filled by the Orthodox religious agenda. Until recently the void in the visual arts field was filled primarily by liberal Orthodox agents represented by David Sperber and religious feminist artists. Lately, however, ultra-nationalists like Avner Bar Hama have been making strides into the field, encouraged by the political powers-that-be.

As stated by the Religious Zionist artist Porat Salomon: for us art "continues an ancient conversation that has been going on in the *beit midrash* for thousands of years and now we would like to carry it on into the arts" (cited in Rott 2013:50). The *Charedi chozer biteshuvah* artist, Shai Azulai, has articulated this transformation most powerfully in his painting, *Nimrod's Circumcision*, shown in an exhibition called "We Shall Bring a Prophet" (in Hebrew a play on words: *navi navi*). In his painting Danziger's iconic "Canaanite" Nimrod sculpture is surrounded by a group of *Charedim* and is being circumcised (metaphorically castrated).[23]

Notes

1 For reasons of textual clarity we are using two different translations of Kant's Critique of Judgment, also known as Critique of the Power of Judgment (Kant 2000 [1790]).
2 A project still ongoing among Western Jews, according to David Myers (2001:214).
3 Not all of the artists exhibiting at the Congress were supporters of Zionism or of Buber's understanding of it. For example, Hermann Struck, an Orthodox Jew and well-known etcher, was among the founders and for some time the President of the *Mizrachi* movement, the Democratic Fraction's rival within the World Zionist Organization (Schmidt 2003:95–7).
4 Available at: www.imj.org.il/collections/269416 (accessed January 25, 2018).
5 Midrashim (sing. Midrash) are texts by ancient Jewish sages (250 BC–AD 625) meant to interpret Biblical passages.
6 Available at: http://www.museumsinisrael.gov.il/he/items/Pages/ItemCard.aspx?IdItem=ICMS-NGU-7948 (accessed February 1, 2018).
7 Available at: https://artsandculture.google.com/asset/nimrod/OQGFM_ok8fkVzg?hl=en (accessed December 23, 2017).
8 Available at: http://tarbut.cet.ac.il/ShowItem.aspx?ItemID=24cc4181-e22e-4870-a7e2-3b4285abd262&lang=HEB (accessed December 19, 2017).
9 Available at: www.tamuseum.org.il/he/collection-work/8305 (accessed February 1, 2018).

10 Available at: https://i.pinimg.com/originals/d5/09/79/d50979d888baa004f2ad6571e76
    f92b9.jpg (accessed February 5, 2018).
11 Rav Kook reportedly considered Rembrandt to be one of the righteous persons to
    whom the hidden light (a Kabbalistic concept) was revealed in his generation (Safrai
    2013:271).
12 Available at: http://museum.imj.org.il/artcenter/includes/itemH.asp?id=395669.
13 Available at: www.thetower.org/article/assaf-inbari-is-looking-for-a-home/.
14 Available at: www.maarav.org.il/archive/classes/PUItemd896.html?lang=HEB&id=329
    (accessed December 15, 2017).
15 Available at: https://www.embracingourdifferences.org/gallery/2009-gallery/reality-
    check/646/?back=gallery (accessed December 13, 2017).
16 Available at: www.horit.com/violin.htm (accessed February 10, 2018).
17 Available at: www.inn.co.il/News/News.aspx/338141 (accessed January 15, 218).
18 Available at: www.haaretz.com/.premium-settler-artist-lives-by-light-of-utopia-1.5402279
    (accessed January 15, 2018).
19 Available at: www.haaretz.co.il/gallery/art/.premium-1.4068982 (accessed February
    2, 2018).
20 Available at: www.maarav.org.il/archive/classes/PUPrint455c.html?id=1151&lang=
    HEB (accessed January 5, 2018).
21 Available at: www.jpost.com/Israel-News/Culture/Arab-Israeli-actor-Norman-Issa-
    refuses-to-cross-the-Green-Line-405545 / www.ynet.co.il/articles/0,7340,L-4666590,00.
    html (accessed December 13, 2018).
22 Available at: www.haaretz.com/israel-news/culture/leisure/.premium-1.781695 (in
    Hebrew; accessed February 4, 2018).
23 Available at: www.bac.org.il/specials/project/shsh-ahry-hahgym/article/nbvaha-shmg
    shymha-at-aatzmha-mha-hakshr-byn-tzvk-aytn-lnbvaha (in Hebrew; accessed January7,
    2018).

References

Arad, R. (2017) "Inside Israel's Only *Glatt Kosher* Art Gallery," *Haaretz*, May 31.
Avnery, U. (2017) "We Swear to You, Homeland, on the Day of Your Bitter Humiliation:
    Great and United You Will Rise from the Ashes," *Haaretz*, December 29.
Bar Hama, A. (1999) "Time to Unveil Contemporary Jewish Art," *Bisde Chemed*, 4,
    www.daat.ac.il/he-il/kitveyet/bisde_hemed/bar-hama-hasifat.htm?printview=true   (in
    Hebrew; accessed January 16, 2018).
Bar Hama, A. (2015) "This is Kicking Time," *Musaf-Shabat – For Torah, Contempla-
    tion, Literature and Art*, July 13, https://musaf-shabbat.com/2015/07/13/ (in Hebrew;
    accessed January 16, 2018).
Bar Hama, A. (2017) "Bennett, Do Not Ignore the Plastic Arts," *Musaf-Shabat – For Torah,
    Contemplation, Literature and Art*, November 6, https://musaf-shabbat.com/2017/11/06
    (in Hebrew; accessed January 16, 2018.
Bar-Or, G. (2012) "Foreword," in *Matronita: Jewish Feminist Art*, Ein Harod: Ein Harod
    Museum of Art, pp. 7–9 (in Hebrew).
Bar Or, G. and Ofrat, G. (2008) *The First Decade: Hegemony and Plurality*, Ein Harod:
    Ein Harod Museum of Art (in Hebrew).
Batnitzky, L. (2011) *How Judaism Became a Religion: An Introduction to Modern Jewish
    Thought*, Princeton, NJ: Princeton University Press.
Ben Shlomo, J. (1989) *The Song of Life: Chapters of Rav Kook's Teaching*, Tel Aviv:
    Ministry of Defense.

Benjamin, W. (1936) *The Work of Art in the Age of Mechanical Reproduction*, www. marxists.org/reference/subject/philosophy/works/ge/benjamin.htm (accessed February 1, 2018).

Bland, K. P. (2000) *The Artless Jew: Medieval and Modern Affirmations and Denials Of The Visual*, Princeton, NJ: Princeton University Press.

Bourdieu, P. (1984) *Distinction: A Social Critique of the Judgment of Taste*, trans. Nice, R., Cambridge, MA: Harvard University Press.

Bourdieu, P. (1993) *The Field of Cultural Production: Essays on Art and Literature*, New York: Columbia University Press.

Bourdieu, P. (1995) *The Rules of Art: Genesis and Structure of the Literary Field*, trans. Emanuel, S., Stanford, CA: Stanford University Press.

Brzyski, A. (2001) "Between the Nation and the World: Nationalism and Modernism in *Fin de Siécle* Poland," *Centropa* 1: 165–79.

Buber, M. (1999) "Address on Jewish Art," in Schmidt. G. G. (ed.), *The First Buber: Youthful Zionist Writings of Martin Buber*, Syracuse, NY: Syracuse University Press, pp. 46–68.

Cohen, H. (2015) *Year Zero of the Arab-Israeli Conflict 1929*, trans. Watzman, H., Waltham, MA: Brandeis University Press.

Ehrenberg, J. (2016) "Introduction," in Ehrenberg, J. and Peled, Y. (eds.), *Israel and Palestine: Alternative Perspectives on Statehood*, Lanham, MD: Rowman & Littlefield, pp. vii-x.

Eider, D. (2008) "The Gatekeepers – On the 'Exclusion': The Politicization of the Aesthetic in the Art Discourse in Israel," *The Protocols*, 10: 1–31, http://bezalel. secured.co.il/zope/home/he/1220527665 (in Hebrew; accessed November 3, 2017).

Etin, R. A. (1991) *Nationalism in the Visual Arts*, Washngton, DC: National Gallery of Art.

Forgács, E. (1995) *The Bauhaus Idea and Bauhaus Politics*, trans. John Bátki, Budapest: Central European University Press.

Gilat, Y. (2005) "Artists Rewriting the Mythos: The Alexander Zeid Memorial and Works that Came in Its Wake," *Israel*, 8: 119–43.

Glants, M. (2010) *Where Is My Home? The Art and Life of the Russian-Jewish Sculptor Mark Antokolsky, 1843–1902*, Lanham, MD: Lexington Books.

Guyer, P. (2014) *A History of Modern Aesthetics, Volume 1: The Eighteenth Century*, Cambridge: Cambridge University Press.

Hargrove, J. and McWilliam, N. (2005) "Introduction," in Hargrove, J. and McWilliam, N. (eds.), *Nationalism and French Visual Culture, 1870–1914*, Washington, DC: National Gallery of Art, pp. 9–15.

Herzl, T. (2000 [1902]) *Old New Land*, trans. Levensohn, L., Princeton, NJ: Marcus Wiener Publishers.

Inbari, A. (2013) "Assaf Inbari is Looking for a Home," *The Tower Magazine*, 6 www. thetower.org/article/assaf-inbari-is-looking-for-a-home/ (accessed February 5, 2018).

Inbari, A. (2017) "Hebrew Culture Cannot Be a Culture of Atheists," *Haaretz*, October 23.

Israeli, I. (1967) "With Clean Hands," *Davar*, June 25 (in Hebrew).

Kant, I. (1987 [1790]) *Critique of Judgment*, trans. Pluhar, W. S., Indianapolis, IN: Hackett Publishing Company.

Kant, I. (2000 [1790]) *Critique of the Power of Judgment*, trans. Guyer, P. and Matthews, E., Cambridge: Cambridge University Press.

Kant, I. (2007 [1790]) *Critique of Judgment*, trans. Meredith, J. C., Oxford: Oxford University Press.

Katz, E. with Sela, H. (1999) *The Beracha Report: Cultural Policy in Israel*, Jerusalem: The Van Leer Jerusalem Institute (in Hebrew).

Kotlyar, E. (2008) "The Making of National Art: Boris Schatz in Bulgaria," *Ars Judaica*, 4: 43–60.

Levitt, A, (1998) "Israeli Art on its Way to a Different Place," *Azure*, 6: 102–29.

Liss, D. (2012) "Tzena Ure'ena," in *Matronita: Jewish Feminist Art*, Ein Harod: Ein Harod Museum of Art, pp. 198–201.

Lyotard, J. F. (1990) *Heidegger and "the Jews,"* trans. Michel, A. and Roberts, M. S., Minneapolis, MN: University of Minnesota Press.

Manor, D. (2002) "The Dancing Jew and other Characters: Art in the Jewish Settlement in Palestine During the 1920s," *Journal of Modern Jewish Studies*, 1: 73–89.

Manor, D. (2005) *Art in Zion: The Genesis of Modern National Art in Jewish Palestine*, London and New York: Routledge Curzon.

Manor, D. (2009) "Joseph Zaritski and Rafi Lavie: Artists as Leaders," *Israel*, 15: 33–66.

Matronita (2012) *Matronita: Feminist Jewish Art*, Ein Harod: Ein Harod Museum of Art (in Hebrew).

Mosse, G. L. (1993) *Confronting the Nation: Jewish and Western Nationalism*, Hanover, NH: University Press of New England.

Myers, D. N. (2001) "Hermann Cohen and the Quest for Protestant Judaism," *Leo Beck Institute Yearbook*, XLVI: 195–214.

Neumann, B. (2011) *Land and Desire in Early Zionism*, trans. Watzman, H., Waltham, MA: Brandeis University Press.

Nordau, M. (1936 [1901]) "The Zionism of Western Jews," in Nordau, M., *Max Nordau to His People: Political Writings, First Book*, Tel Aviv: Hozaah Medinit, pp. 123–33 (in Hebrew).

Ofrat, G. (2000) "The Philosophical Error and the Religious Chance," *Studio*, 115: 40–51.

Ofrat, G. (2008) "Is an Artistic Cultural Revolution Taking Place among Those Who Wear Knitted *Kippot?*" *Kivunim Chadashim*, 17: 164–76 (in Hebrew).

Penkower, M. N. (2004) "The Kishinev Pogrom of 1903: A Turning Point in Jewish History," *Modern Judaism*, 24: 187–225.

Presner, T. S. (2007) *Muscular Judaism: The Jewish Body and the Politics of Regeneration*, Abingdon: Routledge.

Rief, Racheli. (2013) "Art Has an Opportunity to Revive Judaism," *Shabat: Makor Rishin Supplement for Torah, Thought, Culture and Art*, February 15, http://musafshabbat.com/ (in Hebrew; accessed November 7, 2014).

Rott, N. (2013) "Different Interpretations of Art," *Etrog*, 26: 46–51 (in Hebrew).

Safrai, A. (2013) "Art Education in the State-Religious Educational System," in Gross, Z. and Dror, Y. (eds.), *Religious Education in Israel and the Diaspora*, Tel Aviv: Tel Aviv University, pp. 264–86 (in Hebrew).

Saposnik, A. B. (2009) "Secularized Zionist Sanctity in Creating the World of the New Jew," *Israel*, 16: 165–94 (in Hebrew).

Saposnik, A. B. (2015) "Wailing Walls and Iron Walls: The Western Wall as Sacred Symbol in Zionist National Iconography," *American Historical Review*, 120: 1653–81.

Schatz, B. (1888a) "Art Work," Part 1, *Hatzfirah*, 216: 2–3.

Schatz, B. (1888b) "Art Work," Part 2, *Hatzfirah*, 217: 3–4.

Schatz, B. (1923) "Our Way," *Gideon Ofrat's Warehouse*, https://gideonofrat.word-press.com/2011/01/16/%D7%94%D7%97%D7%96%D7%95%D7%9F-%D7%A9%D7%9C-%D7%91%D7%A6%D7%9C%D7%90%D7%9C-1929-1906/ (accessed February 1, 2018).

Schatz, B. (1924) *Jerusalem Rebuilt: A Daydream*, Jerusalem: n.p.

Schiller, F. J. C. von (2002 [1795]) *Letters upon the Aesthetic Education of Man*, Black-mask (Online), www.blackmask.com (accessed November 6, 2017).

Schmidt, G. G. (2003) *The Art and Artists of the Fifth Zionist Congress, 1901*, Syracuse, NY: Syracuse University Press.

Setter, S. (2017) "High as the Grass: Art in Be'er Sheva Has Something to Learn from Football," *Haaretz*, May 7, www.haaretz.co.il/gallery/art/.premium-1.4068982 (in Hebrew; accessed December 29, 2017).

Sheleg Y. (2010) *From Old Hebrew to New Jew: The Jewish Renaissance in Israeli Society*, Jerusalem: Israel Democracy Institute (in Hebrew).

Sherlo, Y. (1998) "Reflections on the Issue of Culture and Art," *Zevulun Book*, Jerusalem: Ministry of Education, pp. 407–21 (in Hebrew).

Sherlo, Y. (2002) "Image of the Religious Artist," *Tlalei Orot*, 10, www.daat.ac.il/daat/kitveyet/taleley/dmuto-2.htm (accessed February 6, 2018).

Sperber, D. (2010) "Judaism and the Art Discourses in Israel," *Akdamot*, 24: 13–23 (in Hebrew).

Sperber, D. (2013) "The False Branding of Avner Bar Hama," *Erev Rav*, www.erev-rav.com/archives/25828 (in Hebrew; accessed February 2, 2018).

Steinhardt, M. (2014) "The Training of Art Teachers: An Historical View," *Mofet Journal*, 54: 62–7 (in Hebrew).

Wexler, E. (n.d.) "Dahn Ben-Amotz, the Zionist Ethos and a Spiritual Crisis," n.p., copy on file with the authors (in Hebrew).

Zalmona, Y. (1985) *Boris Schatz*, Jerusalem: Keter (in Hebrew).

8 Orthodox feminism

Religious nationalism joins state, territory and culture primarily by focusing on family, gender and sexuality: by defending the traditional family, as the key generative site of social reproduction and moral socialisation, against economic and cultural forces that weaken its authority or socialising power; by upholding traditional gendered divisions of labour within and outside the family; and by promoting a restrictive regulation of sexuality, seeking to contain sexuality within the family.

(Roger Friedland, cited in Brubaker 2012:13)

The masters of all slaves rely, for maintaining obedience, on fear; either fear of themselves or religious fears. The masters of women wanted more than simple obedience, and they turned the whole force of education to effect their purposes. All women are brought up from the very earliest years in the belief that their ideal of character is the very opposite to that of men; not self will, and government by self control, but submission and yielding to the control of others.

(John Stuart Mill, *The Subjection of Women*, (1999 [1869]))

In 1982 Professor Yeshayahu Leibowitz, the famous Israeli irreverent academic, Orthodox religious thinker and public intellectual, wrote:

the topic called "the woman in Judaism" is a vital issue for Judaism today, more so than all the political problems of the people and its state. Avoiding serious treatment of this matter endangers the very continued existence of religious Jewry in our world.

(Cited in Ross 2007:19)

According to legal scholar Frances Raday, in Israel "women are the ultimate victims of the deference to religious over egalitarian values." As she elaborated:

The incorporation of religious patriarchy [in Israel] takes effect on two levels. First, it excludes women from participation in policy-making or holding office in the public activities delegated to the institutions of the religious communities [such as rabbinical courts, municipal religious councils, synagogues, etc.]. Second, it subjects women to patriarchal norms in those spheres of social life regulated by these institutions, and particularly the domestic sphere.

(Raday 1996:226–7)

Or, as phrased by Orthodox feminist historian Margalit Shilo, "in Orthodox institutions women are discriminated twofold: they are absent, and their interests are viewed through male perspectives" (Shilo 2006:82). The reason, according to Dan Chyutin, is that "the Bible, as a text written by and for men, situates women as the quintessential Other, and thus acts as the condition for an institutional marginalization of womanhood that covers all spheres of Jewish religious life" (Chyutin 2016:39; Kehat 2008:24–30; P. Lahav 2013; H. Lahav 2016:19–20).[1] Moreover,

[t]he presence of the Arab-Israeli conflict and the Jewish-Israeli fear of the "demographic threat" posed by Arabs became a determining element for women's existence in Israel, as motherhood was established as a path to civil status for women, marking them "bearers of the collective." In the context of the Jewish national collective this carries not only the actual biological reproductive function of women, but also the determination of the boundaries of national identity ... [due to] the matrilineal attribute of Judaism, namely the rule that designates the mother as the "transmitter" of Jewish identity, and hence of the membership in the Jewish people.

(Halperin-Kaddari and Yadgar 2010:911)

As discussed above, this reality was manifested in the exclusion of marriage and divorce from the purview of the Women's Equal Rights Law in 1951 and the exclusion of religious institutions from its amendment in 2000 (see Chapter 3). Moreover, although Israel signed the UN Convention on the Elimination of All Forms of Discrimination against Women (CEDAW) in 1980 and ratified it in 1991, it entered, on religious grounds, reservations pertaining to two of the Convention's articles: Article 7(b), on equality in Political and Public Life, and Article 16, on equality in Marriage and Family. The reasons for the reservations, respectively, were the religious prohibition on the appointment of women as judges in religious courts, and personal status laws of the various religious communities in the country. In 1997 the UN committee monitoring CEDAW suggested that in order to comply fully with the Convention Israel "should complete the secularization of the relevant legislation, place it under the jurisdiction of the civil courts, and withdraw its reservations to the Convention" (Halperin-Kaddari 2000:345–6; Raday 1996:226).

In this chapter we analyze the response of *Orthodox*, primarily national-religious, feminists to women's exclusion and marginalization by this religious patriarchy, a response which in Albert Hirschman's terms can be characterized as "voice," rather than "exit," because of these women's "loyalty" to the

Halacha. This response accords well with Hirschman's suggestion that in organizations where entry is by birth and the price of exit is high voice will be the strategy of choice of disaffected members (Hirschman 1970:97–8; Ross 2007). In Shilo's words, Orthodox feminists

> would like to continue to maintain uncompromising loyalty to the overall framework (family, congregation, community), while at the same time making exhaustive efforts to modify that framework and invest it with new, egalitarian content (though the term "egalitarian" is part of the rhetoric of the Orthodox feminists, its exact meaning has so far not been clarified).
>
> (Shilo 2006:82)[2]

In terms of the general theories of the relations between religion and women's rights, in the first and second waves of feminism in the early twentieth century and in the 1960s and 1970s, respectively, "religion has systematically been connected to women's oppression," seen as the basic grounds of inequality between women and men (Bracke 2008:52). Thus, "[a]s the secular and rebellious daughters of the Enlightenment, feminists were raised on rational argumentation and detached self-irony. The feminist belief system is accordingly civic, not theistic, and is viscerally opposed to authoritarianism and orthodoxy" (Braidotti 2008:3). However, the post-secular turn in feminism, as in many other fields, has enabled religious women sympathetic to feminism, both Jewish and others, to develop a reconcilable discourse which claimed to settle the inevitable paradox of the combination of religion and feminism. Theorists of hybridization constructed a narrative which weaved together the discourses of religion and feminism and was supposed to evade the binary paradox (Sperber 2012 and sources cited there).

Israeli Orthodox religious feminists who, generally speaking, fall into the "conformist" category – feminists whose religion takes priority over their feminism (Kehat 2008:19; Yanay-Ventura 2014:3; H. Lahav 2015:362–4) – have been making their voices publicly heard, with some success, in five different ways or issue areas:[3]

1   The appointment of Leah Shakdiel as the first female member of a municipal religious council in her town of Yerucham in 1987.
2   The efforts of Women of the Wall since 1988 to pray aloud as a group, with a Torah scroll and wrapped in prayer shawls, at the Western (Wailing) Wall.
3   The authorization of women to act as advocates in rabbinical courts (*toanot rabaniyot*) since 1991.
4   The establishment of the religious-feminist organization, *Kolech* (Your Voice) in 1998.
5   The production of religious-feminist art, exhibited in a major museum for the first time in 2012.

According to historian Anita Shapira, the phenomenon of Orthodox women struggling "for equal rights in religious observance within their own society" stems from their empowerment as their families' main breadwinners, in the case of *Charedim*, and as enhancing their families' standard of living, in the case of the national-religious, by working outside the home (An. Shapira 2014:148–9). As they see it, in conducting these struggles Orthodox religious feminists have not been defying the *Halacha* but have offered legitimate interpretations of it that support their demands. As described by one commentator, theirs has been a "divide and rule" strategy – marshaling the views of certain respectable rabbis against the positions of the conservative Israeli rabbinical establishment (Uzan 2016:144–7).

At the core of this strategy is the claim that in reality *Halacha* consists of two layers: an immutable core layer of divine origin, and an historical, or "public policy" layer constructed by humans in accordance with changing historical circumstances and therefore amenable to change (Shamir et al. 1997:336–40, 345; Ross 2007; Berner 2012). In her study of Shi'i piety in Lebanon, Lara Deeb has coined the term "authentication" to describe "a process within a religious tradition, grounded in textual study and historical inquiry, as well as in a notion of rationality, and driven by a desire to establish a 'true' meaning of faith, taking distance from tradition" (cited in Bracke 2008:59). This, we believe, is a very apt description of what Orthodox Jewish feminists in Israel are engaged in.

Leah Shakdiel

In 1987 Leah Shakdiel was elected by the municipal council of her town, Yerucham, to serve on the local religious council, a body that supervises the supply of religious services in the locality. The Chief Rabbinate of Israel opposed her appointment and the Minister of Religious Affairs refused to appoint her to that position, primarily on two grounds: (1) modesty requires that men and women not married to each other do not share the same space and if Shakdiel became a member of the religious council men who adhere to *Halacha* would not be able to serve there; and (2) women are prohibited from holding positions of authority over men. Shakdiel appealed to the High Court of Justice, which made the Minister of Religious Affairs instate her in the position. The decision was written by Justice Menachem Elon, an Orthodox religious Jew. He concluded that since membership in a religious council, an administrative and not a religious body, does not require *Halachic* knowledge, the exclusion of women on ground (1) was unwarranted. Second, Elon determined that important rabbinical opinions hold that if a woman is elected by the public to a position of authority, there is no prohibition against her filling that position (Y. Cohen 1991; T. Cohen 2006; Irshai and Zion-Waldoks 2013:298–301).

Even so, by 2012 only 6 percent of the members of local religious councils were women, and not even one had served as chair of a religious council (Knesset 2012:13; Irshai and Zion-Waldoks 2013:312). Following the municipal elections of 2013, by 2016 only one third of local religious councils, which are appointed jointly by the local authority (45 percent), the local rabbinate (10 percent) and the Minister of Religious Affairs (45 percent), have been formed.[4]

Women of the Wall

Women of the Wall (WoW) are a group of American and Israeli Jewish women that was formed following the first international conference of Jewish feminists held in Jerusalem in 1988 (Jobani and Perez 2017:40). Their wish is to pray aloud as a women's group in the women's section of the Western Wall in Jerusalem while wrapped in traditional prayer shawls (albeit different from the ones used by men) and holding a Torah scroll.[5] They summarize their demands as the three T's: Tfila (prayer), Torah, Tallit (prayer shawl).[6]

While the women in the group belong to all streams of Judaism, they conduct themselves in accordance with the strictures of Orthodox Judaism, as understood by their Orthodox members. These practices, when performed by women, have not been universally opposed by *Halachic* authorities through the ages, but they are fiercely opposed by the Orthodox rabbinical establishment in Israel, including, most importantly, the rabbi in charge of the Western Wall. The main argument of the opponents is that the rituals practiced by WoW contradict "the local custom" at the Wall, as established since Israel occupied East Jerusalem in 1967.[7] This is an argument that carries a lot of weight in *Halachic* reasoning but that clearly belongs to the historical layer of *Halacha*. An additional, related, argument has been that WoW's prayers offend the religious sensibilities of other worshippers at the Wall and have disturbed the peace in that some of those other worshippers have physically attacked WoW members when they attempted to pray there (Raday 2008; P. Lahav 2015; Shakdiel 2002; Reiter 2016; Uzan 2016; Jobani and Perez 2017:20, 29, 34–5, 39).[8]

The broader purpose of WoW, at least of its Israeli members, is to fight religious patriarchy in Israel. They aim to bring about a change in the overall status of women in Israeli society by changing their religious status, beginning with the prohibition on women in relation to the three T's: "Women of the Wall work for a redefinition of their identity as religious women. They work against Jewish patriarchy in accordance with a feminist strategy that demands equality within Orthodox religion, not through exit from it" (Raday 2008:402; 2013:296; Reiter 2016:84; Jobani and Perez 2017:24–7). And they focus their work at the very site that is considered to be most sacred for Judaism, both religiously and nationally – the Western Wall – where their activities get the most publicity.[9]

Israeli Jews are about equally divided on whether WoW should be allowed to pray aloud at the Wall. Among the national-religious 66 percent oppose that while 13 percent favor it, and among *Charedim* the figures are 81 and 13 percent, respectively (Pew 2016:199). WoW's struggle has gone through a number of court rulings, including three rulings by the High Court of Justice, and a number of governmental committees trying to satisfy both WoW, who enjoy wide support among American Jews (Reiter 2016:89), and the Orthodox establishment, which possesses a great deal of political leverage in Israel. Overall, the courts have recognized in principle WoW's right to pray at the Wall according to their wishes, but deferred to the "local custom" and to considerations of public order in denying them that right in practice.[10] At the time of writing no arrangement satisfactory to both sides has been found and WoW continue to pray at the Wall at the beginning of every month (according to the Jewish calendar) and continue to be harassed by some of the other worshippers and by the police (Irshai and Zion-Waldoks 2013:301–7; P. Lahav 2015; Reiter 2016; Jobani and Perez 2017:44–52).

Women advocates in rabbinical courts

Rabbinical courts, staffed by men only, have exclusive jurisdiction over marriage and divorce of Jews and parallel jurisdiction with civil family courts over related matters such as financial settlements, alimony, child custody and support, etc. Litigants in rabbinical courts can be represented by lawyers, male or female, but they can also be represented by special "rabbinical advocates" (*toanim rabaniyim*) who are knowledgeable in *Halacha* and are authorized to appear in these courts only. Until 1991 only *yeshiva* graduates, i.e., only men, could become rabbinical advocates. In 1991 the regulations were changed so that graduates of any educational institution recognized for this purpose by the Great (i.e., highest) Rabbinical Court could serve as rabbinical advocates. This opened the way for women to fill this role and the first institution training them for that purpose was opened in Jerusalem (Shamir et al. 1997; Irshai and Zion-Waldoks 2013:307–9). In the words of Margalit Shilo:

> The initiators of the concept of female rabbinical advocates had a twofold agenda: (i) to reinforce the voice of women, who felt that they were being silenced and discriminated against in the rabbinical courts, and (ii) to support them in *halachic* negotiations and heighten their awareness of their rights according to *Halacha*.
>
> (Shilo 2006:84)

Rabbinical advocates have to pass qualifying examinations conducted by the Chief Rabbinate, which initially made every effort to prevent women from passing the examinations. The institute training women to be rabbinical advocates appealed to the High Court of Justice and following the Court's intervention women began to be qualified as rabbinical advocates (Shamir et al. 1997:327–30; Irshai and Zion-Waldoks 2013:308).

Unlike Leah Shakdiel, WoW, and *Kolech*, the women who work as rabbinical advocates are careful not to describe themselves as feminists, a term that carries a negative connotation among their potential Orthodox clientele (Shamir et al. 1997:340–6; Irshai and Zion-Waldoks 2013:311n210). Still, their entry into the field of rabbinical courts is an important breakthrough for Orthodox women in that they have been officially recognized as *Halachic* experts, albeit of the lowest kind. Their presence in these courts has also enhanced the chances of Orthodox women, who may be reluctant to reveal their domestic problems to a man, to receive a fair hearing (Shamir et al. 1997:331–3).

Kolech

Kolech is the main Orthodox feminist organization in Israel, numbering a few hundred members and committed to "adherence to Halacha and gender equality" (Shilo 2006:86). It was established in 1998 by Hannah Kehat, following the establishment of a similar organization, Jewish Orthodox Feminist Alliance (JOFA), in the United States a year earlier. *Kolech* is involved in such activities as women's Torah studies, the issue of *agunot* and divorce-refused women, and educational reforms in girls' schools. It holds well-attended annual conferences dealing with issues relating to the status of women in Judaism as well as other issues, considered from an Orthodox feminist perspective (Shilo 2006; Israel-Cohen 2012:30–2).

The term "*kolech*" invokes a dual association. On the one hand, the Talmudic saying, "A woman's voice is a genital," used to prohibit the singing of women in front of men, but on the other, the verse from the Song of Songs, "Let me hear your voice, for your voice is sweet," which, according to Hannah Kehat, *Kolech*'s founder, "may be interpreted … as the unique promise of the Almighty, throughout human history, to listen to the female voice" (Israel-Cohen 2012:30; Berman 1980; Halperin-Kaddari and Yadgar 2010:915).

Religious-feminist art

A bold attempt to provide a platform for Orthodox female voices through the medium of fine arts was undertaken in *Matronita*, the first comprehensive exhibit of religious feminist artists' work (Matronita 2012; Chapter 7). According to art historian David Sperber, the religious feminist

> creative space is intimately connected to the general art world, but still relates explicitly to the religious space, and especially to the world of *Halacha*, which is generally foreign to the majority society and to the Israeli art discourse. It is, then, a marginal and minority art that comes from a cultural world which is aware of its otherness, and seeks to create critical art that touches in its foundation a unique world stemming from a *Halachic-religious* discourse.
>
> (Sperber 2012:49)

Like the other manifestations of Orthodox feminism discussed in this chapter, the works in *Matronita* represented a (more or less explicit) cry against oppressive male mastery, without, however, challenging the boundaries of *Halacha* itself.

A representative example was a work by Chana Goldberg titled *Shulchan Aruch* (literally, a set table), which is the key legal codex of the *Halacha*, compiled in the sixteenth century. Goldberg's work consisted of Xerox pages of text and images from an Orthodox children's book, socializing children to their respective gendered roles. The *Shulchan Aruch* became the signifier of the work,

Figure 8.1 Chana Goldberg, *Shulchan Aruch* (2003). Photocopies of illustrations from books for children, and framed terylene tablecloth, 20 × 30 × 40 cm. Ein Harod Museum of Art. Reproduced with permission of the artist and Ein Harod Museum of Art.

while the text and the visuals constructed the signified – a gendered binary space where a man and boys were sitting around the table studying from sacred books while a woman and girls were sweeping the floor around them. The functional object – the table – was transformed into a place which gathered the hegemonic male members of the family in a learning field, with ideas hovering over them, while the females supplied the logistical base for the males' intellectual activity (Sperber 2012:64–6; Chapter 7).

"A Story with a Woman and a Robe: Immersion of Converting Women" (not shown in *Matronita*) is a straightforward video art installation created by the artist/filmmaker Nurit Jacobs-Yinon[11] (Raz and Jacobs-Yinon 2013). The performed work is narrated in three parts: the first depicts a staged double immersion (*tvilah)* in the *mikveh* (ritual bath) by a non-Jewish woman seeking conversion to Judaism while being watched by three male *dayanim* (rabbinical court judges). The second part communicates the immersed woman's thoughts, written by Rivka Lubitch, an Orthodox *toenet rabanit* (Raz and Jacobs-Yinon 2013:13); and the third reveals the attitudes of three rabbis, versed in *Halachic* law, regarding the value of modesty in the context of the scene of ritual immersion – three men staring at a robed woman dipping twice in the water.

The *Halacha* regulates all bodily practices. Liquids are a constant presence in ritual practices and water becomes the major symbolic transmitter of cleanliness, as well as of purity and individual and social transformation. *Mikveh* immersion is a crucial *Halachic* bodily ritual exercised by Jewish men and women performing religious acts. In the Jewish Orthodox regime, which in Israel enjoys a monopoly over conversion to Judaism (*giyur*), immersion is considered to be "the main act of the conversion process for women and men alike." The ritual symbolizes and finalizes the acceptance of Judaism by the convert after a lengthy period of Jewish religious studies (Rav Chaim Druckman, interviewed in the video; see also Charbit 2014:163).

Jacobs-Yinon's video work begins with three faceless men entering the ritual space while passing a glass door shadowed by a blurred image of a woman. Their faces absent from the first opening shot, the male figures are identifiable as observant Jews by the *tzitizit* (specially knotted ritual fringes) hanging on the sides of their black slacks. In the next episode the Balanit (female *mikveh* attendant) knocks on the door saying (you can come in) "please," with a reflection of a shadowy hand sketched on the glass door. The Balanit hugs the woman and escorts her to the steps leading down to the water. Gazed at by the men through a back shot viewpoint leading to a front viewpoint, the staircase bar blocking the vision of the men, the woman descends the staircase toward the water. Then she immerses herself twice in the water. Between the two immersions she recites a prayer (in Hebrew with an American accent) while clutching her shoulders. There is no eye contact between the witnessing men and the robed woman while she enters. However, between the two immersions and her exit from the water she glances for a split second at the men. After exiting the water she is hugged and congratulated by the Balanit with the blessing "*Mazal Tov*." The first part of the video ends with the wet, robed woman slipping away into the room she entered from at the beginning while pressing her hand from inside the room on the glass door, connoting a plea for help.

The second part of the video, titled "The Female Convert's *Midrash*" (homiletic exegesis of the Torah), relates a story in which a gentile woman asks to be converted to Judaism and is instructed by three rabbis to immerse herself in water in front of their eyes. She refuses to do so on grounds of modesty, asking that her immersion be supervised by a woman. Initially the rabbis refuse, but then they concede, appoint a woman to supervise women's immersions, and praise the convert woman for her righteousness. The final words of Lubitch's *midrash* end with "the rabbis had only to learn from Abraham our forefather and Sarah our foremother ... For Abraham would convert the men and Sarah would convert the women" (Raz and Jacobs-Yinon 2013:13; see also Tichochinsky 2008).

The third part of the work consists of three monologue interviews with prominent Religious Zionist rabbis, projected simultaneously on three monitors and titled "The *Beit Din*" (rabbinical conversion court). The three rabbis discuss the modesty/immodesty issue in the context of the long tradition of non-Jewish women's immersion as a crucial element in their conversion process. Whereas in Judaism modesty is required of women only, and is a hallmark of the patriarchal nature of the religion, men are prohibited from gazing at a woman's immodesty

– in essence any exposed part of her body, other than her face and hands (Raday 2013:290–2). Two of the rabbis, considered to be liberal to a certain degree, relate to the ritual as problematic (Rav David Stav) and embarrassing (Rav Dr. Benny Lau) in terms of the latter prohibition, and both of them generally support a change. The third, more conservative rabbi, Rav Druckman, does not see any modesty issue in men viewing a woman clad in a robe immersing herself in water and coming wet out of it. All three, however, are wary of the possibility of a "slippery slope" within the tradition in case the witnessing of the immersion, a function of the rabbinical court, were to be done by women, who are not qualified to appear as witnesses in that court.

The gendered, seductive title of the work, "A Story with a Woman and a Robe," insinuates an imaginative visual of a sensual, veiled, naked woman's body in a private space. However, the sub-title, "Immersion of Converting Women," constructs a transitory liminal space inside an ancient Jewish ritual, where the sensuous and the formal are fused into a traditional intact archetype. The artwork contested an inflexible performative traditional practice led and controlled only by men. In the video work inflicting blindness on the designated men made their testimony of the immersion inconsequential and subsequently stripped the ritual of legitimacy, from the *Halachic* point of view. However, legitimacy was reinstated with the three rabbis' commentary on the issue of modesty in the mechanics of women's immersion in the *mikveh* ritual.

Jacobs-Yinon espoused the critical feminist signifiers, "the body as a site" and "the male gaze" (Jay 1999:170–1), and designated the female body as the place for interrogating the concepts "modesty/immodesty," where a binary analysis had to be undertaken. In "A Story with a Woman and a Robe" the woman seeking Jewish conversion was doubly gazed: by the "blind"/fragmented bodies of the austere *dayanim* and by the spectators. However, by interviewing only rabbis in the third part of her work, rather than women who had undergone that ceremony, for example, the artist's mild, respectful contestation of the practice did not really challenge the boundaries of the *Halachic* world.

Exhibited in galleries and disseminated virally, the video artwork/installation was widely discussed and interpreted within the Israeli milieu of culture studies and art history. Modernist and post-modernist analyses referenced liberal feminist narratives of the "male gaze." The work interlaced with *Kolech* and became an additional node in the new web of Jewish Orthodox women struggling for "equal opportunities for women in the public arena, including the advancement of women's rights in religious and *Halachic* spheres,"[12] without, however, breaking out of that sphere.

Equality between women and men, and modesty, contextualized within a particularistic religious framework, were the foundational bricks in Jacobs-Yinon's activist art work. The hybridization of feminism and religion enabled her to appropriate universal values to be interpolated within the boundaries of a religious space. This formed an artistic discourse corresponding to Deleuze and Guattari's notion of "lines of flight," which connote the overcoming of existing boundaries without really transgressing them (Deleuze and Guattari 1983). As we saw, Hannah Goldberg's work also did not offer any agency of liberation or emancipation. The limited scope of both artists' challenge to the prevailing religious norms becomes obvious when contrasted, for example, with the work of the African-American artist, Betye Saar. In her work, *The Liberation of Aunt Jemima*, the stereotyped representational image of "Aunt Jemima," the serving domestic help, is transformed into an active, defiant agent by the placing of a rifle in her hand, alongside the broom.[13]

Summary

Feminist stirrings among Orthodox Jewish women, which began with the liberalization of Israeli society in the mid-1980s, have been an aspect of the general effort on the part of the Orthodox, primarily the Religious Zionists, to integrate into the mainstream of the society. Given the monopoly which rabbinical courts have over marriage and divorce of Jews, the inferior status of women in the *Halacha* and in all Orthodox institutions has been an issue between the Orthodox and non-observant Jews in Israel. To ameliorate this problem Orthodox feminists have sought to enhance the status of women within the prevailing understanding of *Halacha* without, however, transgressing the boundaries of *Halacha* itself.

The introduction of female advocates in rabbinical courts illustrates both the value of these efforts and their limitations. Women's prospects of having their day in a rabbinical court have improved by the availability of these female advocates, but no serious effort has been made to include women as *judges* in these courts, which continue to rule on the basis of *Halacha*, a blatantly patriarchal body of law. Whatever constraints have been placed on the ability of rabbinical courts to discriminate against women have been placed by the state and especially by the civil court system (Hirschl 2010:143–7), not by women working from within the Orthodox world.

Similarly, the work of feminist Orthodox artists to expose religious norms and practices which are discriminatory, exclusionary, and humiliating toward women have remained at the level of exposition, without offering any real alternative. Breaking into the mainstream of the Israeli art field, in exhibitions such as *Matronita*, these artists convey to the general public the notion that the Zionist Orthodox world is not a closed caste, immune to internal criticism. This gives credence to the notion that there is pluralist variety in that world, akin to the pluralism of the society at large, and that processes of change are taking place in that world, hence it should not be viewed as threatening to the non-observant. This message is enhanced by the, still very limited, engagement of *Charedim* with the fine arts field, in institutions such as the Shelter Art Gallery (Chapter 7).

Notes

1 For a generalization of these arguments see Stopler 2008.
2 For a critique of this kind of response see P. Lahav 2015:55.

3 We are not going to discuss the many and varied activities undertaken by Orthodox religious feminists within the confines of the religious institutions themselves, such as synagogues, religious educational institutions, religious courts, etc. A major issue dealt with by Orthodox feminists within the field of religious institutions is that of *agunot* (deserted wives whose husbands disappeared without being officially dead or divorced) and of women whose estranged husband refuses to grant them a divorce (*get*) (Halperin-Kaddari and Yadgar 2010:910). We are also not going to discuss the vast Jewish feminist theological literature. For more comprehensive treatments see Ross 2007; Kehat 2008; Israel-Cohen 2012; Irshai and Zion-Waldoks 2013; Yanay-Ventura 2014; Zion-Waldoks 2015; see also Shafir and Peled 2002:95–109).

4 Available at: www.shatil.org.il/node/85958 (accessed August 30, 2017).

5 The Western Wall Plaza is organized as an Orthodox synagogue, with a partition between the men's and women's sections and Torah scrolls available in the men's section only, which occupies two-thirds of the space. The first attempt to install such a partition between the men's and women's areas, in September 1928, led directly to the Palestinian uprising of 1929 (Shakdiel 2002:136, 145–6). For the significance of the Wall in Zionist and Israeli culture see, e.g., Saposnik 2009:180–8; 2015.

6 Revealingly, only in English do these three Hebrew words begin with the same letter, T. For the influence of American Orthodox feminism on its Israeli counterpart see, especially, Uzan 2016; Shamir et al. 1997:322.

7 Interestingly, WoW, made up of very liberal women, do not address the question of how the Wall came into Israel's possession in 1967 in the first place. For a failed attempt to connect WoW's struggle with the Israeli-Palestinian conflict right at the beginning see Shakdiel 2002:140–1.

8 Using the analytical framework of ethnocracy (Yiftachel 2006), Shakdiel identifies a national, as well as religious, element in the opposition to WoW (cf. Raday 2008:409).

9 Not all Orthodox Jews approve of the cult of the Wall. In July 1967, barely a month after Israel's occupation of East Jerusalem, Yeshayahu Leibowitz, for example, called it "diskotel" – a combination of a discotheque and the *Kotel* (Wall) – and described the enthusiastic pilgrimage to it by Israeli Jews during the holiday of *Shavuot* (Pentecost) as a sacrilege unprecedented since the placing of an "abomination" in the Temple by the Hellenistic king Antiochus IV Epiphanes in the second century BC (Leibowitz 1967).

10 Through no fault of their own, WoW's struggle has become entangled with the struggle of the non-Orthodox streams of Judaism for recognition at the Wall and in Israel in general (Shakdiel 2002:133; Irshai and Zion-Waldoks 2013:313–14n215; Jobani and Perez 2017:49–52). The latter struggle lies beyond the scope of this book.

11 Available at: https://vimeo.com/193788929 (accessed January 12, 2018).

12 Available at: www.kolech.org.il/en/ (accessed January 12, 2018).

13 Available at: www.mondriaanfonds.nl/en/fff-3/ (accessed February 9, 2018).

References

Berman, S. J. (1980) "Kol 'Isha," in Landman, L. (ed.), *Rabbi Joseph H. Lookstein Memorial Volume*, New York: Ktav Publishing House, pp. 45–66.

Berner, T. (2012) "Religious Feminism: Beginnings and Directions," in *Matronita: Feminist Jewish Art*, Ein Harod: Ein Harod Art Museum, pp. 180–97 (in Hebrew).

Bracke, S. (2008) "Conjugating the Modern/Religious, Conceptualizing Female Religious Agency: Contours of a 'Post-secular' Conjuncture," *Theory, Culture & Society* 25: 51–67.

Braidotti, R. (2008) "In Spite of the Times: The Postsecular Turn in Feminism," *Theory, Culture & Society* 25: 1–24.

Brubaker, R. (2012) "Religion and Nationalism: Four Approaches," *Nations and Nationalism*, 18: 2–20.

Charbit, D. (2014) "Israel's Self-Restrained Secularism from the 1947 Status Quo Letter to the Present," in Berlinerblau, J., Fainberg, S., and Nou, A. (eds.), *Secularism on the Edge: Rethinking Church–State Relations in the United States, France, and Israel*, Basingstoke: Palgrave Macmillan, pp. 157–71.

Chyutin, D. (2016) "'The King's Daughter is All Glorious Within': Female Modesty in Judaic-Themed Israeli Cinema," *Journal of Jewish Identities*, 9: 39–58.

Cohen, T. (2006) "Feminine Religious Leadership: Modern Orthodoxy in Israel as a Case Study," *Democratic Culture*, 10: 251–96 (in Hebrew).

Cohen, Y. (1991) *Women in Public Leadership: The Dispute over Women's Membership in Religious Councils*, Jerusalem: Ne'emaney Torah Va'avoda (in Hebrew).

Deleuze, G. and Guattari, F. (1983) *Anti-Oedipus: Capitalism and Schizophrenia*, Minneapolis, MN: University of Minnesota Press.

Halperin-Kaddari, R. (2000) "Women, Religion and Multiculturalism in Israel," *UCLA Journal of International Law and Foreign Affairs*, 5: 339–66.

Halperin-Kaddari, R. and Yadgar, Y. (2010) "Between Universal Feminism and Particular Nationalism: Politics, Religion and Gender (In)Equality in Israel," *Third World Quarterly*, 31: 905–20.

Hirschl, R. (2010) *Constitutional Theocracy*, Cambridge, MA: Harvard University Press.

Hirschman, A. O. (1970) *Exit, Voice, and Loyalty: Responses to Decline in Firms, Organizations, and States*, Cambridge, MA: Harvard University Press.

Irshai, R. and Zion-Waldoks, T. (2013) "Modern-Orthodox Feminism in Israel – Between Nomos and Narrative," *Mishpat Umimshal*, 15: 233–327 (in Hebrew).

Israel-Cohen, Y. (2012) *Between Feminism and Orthodox Judaism: Resistance, Identity and Religious Change in Israel*, Leiden: Brill.

Jay, M. (1999) "Returning the Gaze: The American Response to the French Critique of Ocularcentrism," in Weiss, G. and Fern Haber H. (eds.), *Perspectives on Embodiment: The Intersections of Nature and Culture*, London: Routledge.

Jobani, Y. and Perez, N. (2017) *Women of the Wall: Navigating Religion in Sacred Sites*, New York: Oxford University Press.

Kehat, H. (2008) *Feminism and Judaism: From Collision to Regeneration*, Tel Aviv: Ministry of Defense Publishing House, "Broadcast University" Library (in Hebrew).

Knesset (2012) *Religious Councils*, Jerusalem: The Knesset – Research and Information Center (in Hebrew).

Lahav, H. (2015) "Post-Secular Jewish Feminist Theology?" *Journal of Modern Jewish Studies*, 14: 355–72.

Lahav, H. (2016) "What do Secular-believer Women in Israel Believe in?" *Journal of Contemporary Religion*, 31: 17–34.

Lahav, P. (2013) "Israel's Rosit the Riveter: Between Secular Law and Jewish Law," *Boston University Law Review*, 93: 1063–83.

Lahav, P. (2015) "The Women of the Wall: A Metaphor for National and Religious Identity," *Israel Studies Review*, 30: 50–70.

Leibowitz, Y. (1967) "The Diskotel," *Haaretz*, July 21 (in Hebrew).

Mill, J. S. (1999 [1869]) *The Subjection of Women*, College Station, PA: Penn State Electronic Classics, pp. 18–19.

Pew (2016) *Israel's Religiously Divided Society*, Washington, DC: Pew Research Center.

Raday, F. (1996) "Religion, Multiculturalism and Equality: The Israeli Case," *Israel Yearbook on Human Rights*, 25: 193–241.

Raday, F. (2008) "A Demand for Equality in the Definition of Religious Identity: The Case of Women of the Wall – A Saga at the Supreme Court," *Ha-Mishpat*, 13: 401–25 (in Hebrew).

Raday, F. (2013) "Modesty Disrobed – Gendered Modesty Rules under the Monotheistic Religions," in Failinger, M. A., Schiltz E. R., and Stabile S. J. (eds.), *Feminism, Law, and Religion*, Farnham: Ashgate, pp. 283–306.

Raz, S. and Jacobs-Yinon, N. (eds.) (2013) *A Story with a Woman and a Robe: Immersion of Converting Women*, Tel Aviv: The Zaritsky Artists' House (in Hebrew).

Reiter, Y. (2016) "Feminists in the Temple of Orthodoxy: The Struggle of the Women of the Wall to Change the Status Quo," *Shofar: An Interdisciplinary Journal of Jewish Studies*, 34: 79–107.

Ross, T. (2007) *Expanding the Palace of Torah: Orthodoxy and Feminism*, Tel Aviv: Am Oved (in Hebrew).

Saposnik, A. B. (2009) "Secularized Zionist Sanctity in Creating the World of the New Jew," *Israel*, 16: 165–94 (in Hebrew).

Saposnik, A. B. (2015) "Wailing Walls and Iron Walls: The Western Wall as Sacred Symbol in Zionist National Iconography," *American Historical Review*, 120: 1653–81.

Shafir, G. and Peled, Y. (2002) *Being Israeli: The Dynamics of Multiple Citizenship*, Cambridge: Cambridge University Press.

Shakdiel, L. (2002) "Women of the Wall: Radical Feminism as an Opportunity for a New Discourse in Israel," *Journal of Israeli History*, 21: 126–63.

Shamir, R., Shitrai, M., and Elias, N. (1997) "Religion, Feminism, and Professionalism: The Case and Cause of Women Rabbinical Advocates," *Megamot*, 38: 313–48 (in Hebrew).

Shapira, An. (2014) "Israel's 'Religious Secularism'," in Berlinerblau, J., Fainberg, S., and Nou, A. (eds.), *Secularism on the Edge: Rethinking Church–State Relations in the United States, France, and Israel*, Basingstoke: Palgrave Macmillan, pp. 145–55.

Shilo, M. (2006) "A Religious Orthodox Women's Revolution: The Case of Kolech (1998–2005)," *Israel Studies Forum*, 21: 81–95.

Sperber, D. (2012) "Jewish-Feminist Art in the Religious Space," *Migdar*, 1: 43–78 (in Hebrew).

Stopler, G. (2008) "'A Rank Usurpation of Power' – The Role of Patriarchal Religion and Culture in the Subordination of Women," *Duke Journal of Gender Law & Policy*, 15: 365–97.

Tichochinsky, M. (2008) "'And the Woman Immerses the Woman': Immersion of a Woman for Conversion in front of a *Beit Din*," *Akdamot*, 21: 65–82.

Uzan, E. (2016) "From Social Norm to Legal Claim: How American Orthodox Feminism Changed Orthodoxy in Israel," *Modern Judaism*, 36: 144–62.

Yanay-Ventura, G. (2014) "Orthodox Feminist Identities in Israel – A New Look on Feminism and a New Look on Orthodoxy," *Migdar*, 3: 1–24 (in Hebrew).

Yiftachel, O. (2016) *Ethnocracy: Land and Identity Politics in Israel/Palestine*, Philadelphia, PA: University of Pennsylvania Press.

Zion-Waldoks, T. (2015) "Politics of Devoted Resistance: Agency, Feminism, and Religion among Orthodox Agunah Activists in Israel," *Gender & Society*, 29: 73–97.

9   Film, TV, media

Film

Until the turn of the millennium Israeli cinema did not engage in a serious positive way with Jewish religious themes or with the various Jewish religious communities that exist in Israeli society. Prior to that, primarily two cinematic genres had addressed Orthodox Jewish reality, both by way of ridiculing it: The *Kuni Lemel* series, and similar films, which mocked the Ashkenazi ultra-Orthodox as a Diasporic avatar that needed to be gotten rid of, and the so-called *Bourekas* films, which presented religiously traditional Mizrachim as good-natured buffoons (Gebel 2006:23; Recanati 2010:31–40; Friedman and Hakak 2015:51–2; Peleg 2016:15). Obviously, both kinds of films were made by non-observant Israelis.

The reason for this attitude, as explained by Yael Friedman and Yohai Hakak, was that

> [w]orking in the service of the national project and Zionist ideology, Israeli cinema in the first few decades of the state's existence spoke predominantly of and for the hegemonic center of Israeli society, which was secular, Ashkenazi, and male. By and large reflecting the Eurocentric imaginary of Zionism, with its intrinsic ambivalence toward both traditional (Diasporic) Judaism and the Middle East, Israeli cinema looked to the West for its sources of inspiration. Western notions of universalism and humanism shaped much of the themes, images, and narratives of this cinema.
>
> (Friedman and Hakak 2015:51)

In this way, argues Isaac Recanati,

> [t]he religious Jew was "symbolically eliminated" from the Zionist land-scape, and the emerging Israeli stage was left open for the main actor: the pioneer, the secular Sabra. The negation of the Diasporic Jew in cinema and his presentation as a stranger and the "other" as against the "new Jew" born in Israel was done parallel to the adoption of a pseudo-Biblical Jewish iden-tity, leaping over the entire period of exile.
>
> (Recanati 2010:44; see also 49–50)

The 1999 film *Kadosh* (Saint), by the non-observant director Amos Gitai, was the first major Israeli film "to portray religious characters as real, living, breathing people and not caricatures" (Peleg 2016:35). The plot tells of two *Charedi* sisters' love problems: one is happily married but must be divorced from her husband because they cannot have children together, and the other is in love with a *Charedi* man who served in the IDF and is therefore ostracized by their community (see Chapter 6). Prevented from marrying the man she loves, she is forced to marry another man, presented as a narrow-minded and violent religious zealot. The film is harshly critical of *Charedi* society, representing "Charedi women as pitiful victims of abuse and Charedi men as cruel, violent, and ignorant chauvinists" (Dardashti 2015:87). At least in the view of one religious critic, "although its investigation into the details of *Charedi* life is relatively accurate ... [it is] like a short incursion by *National Geographic* into the primitive world of the religious in their backwardness" (Recanati 2010:116). Another, non-observant, critic argued that *Kadosh* evinced "a sense of real threat to secular Israel from growing internal religious forces" (Peleg 2016:40; see also Daniels 2008; Chyutin 2016:49–52).

The major breakthrough in the presentation of the religious sphere in Israeli films (and television) occurred as a result of the establishment of a Religious Zionist film and television school, *Ma'aleh*, in 1989, followed by film and media programs that were established in many high schools belonging to the state-religious educational system (Kimmel 2002; Recanati 2010). *Ma'aleh* was a conscious product of Religious Zionists who felt marginalized by the mass media and by the hegemonic culture in general and decided, beginning in the early 1980s, to enter and occupy leadership positions in all spheres of Israel's social life, including the media.

Thus Yisrael Harel, a leader of Gush Emunim and editor of its major organ, *Nekuda*, asked, rhetorically, in 1984 "why don't we [Religious Zionists] have creative people?" Uri Ohrbach, a prominent religious Zionist media and cultural figure, called upon young Religious Zionists to prefer service in the IDF's weekly magazine, *Ba-Machane*, and in the military radio station – common training grounds for future careers in the mass media – over service in elite combat units. Many other commentators and educators called upon the Religious Zionist public to "enter the media of mass communications." At least some of the founders of *Ma'aleh*, and its political and financial backers, saw it as a school for training mouthpieces for the dominant ideology of the West Bank settlers in the wider Israeli public (Recanati 2010:52, 57, 73, 81–2; Jacobson 2004).

The Religious Zionists' urge to find their voice in the media was intensified following the assassination in 1995 of Prime Minister Rabin by Yigal Amir, a Religious Zionist law student, when the Religious Zionist public felt it was unjustly accused by the hostile secular media of responsibility for the assassination (Recanati 2010:72; Gebel 2006:5–6). In the words of one *Ma'aleh* graduate, Avishai Azulai:

> With the help of *Ma'aleh* religious people will enter the decision making circles in [the] television [industry], will no longer be afraid to express

themselves, and will achieve the final goal: conquest of the media ... *What happened in the IDF, where our people have become senior commanders, will happen in the media as well.*

(Cited in Recanati 2010:81, emphasis added; cf. Gebel 2006:19)

Between 1992 and 2008 about 175 students graduated from *Ma'aleh*. These graduates had produced thirty-eight short feature films and thirty-four documentaries as senior projects. The overall themes of the films, as summarized by Recanati, point to the individualization of the consciousness of the third generation of Religious Zionists in Israel (thirty-somethings in the first decade of the millennium) – a move from collective ideological concerns to engagement with personal and family issues.

The main conflict presented in the films is that between the desire for personal autonomy and freedom, and the Orthodox institutions and traditions that stifle that desire. A major focus is women's efforts to redefine gender roles in the family and the community and the frustration of these efforts by powerful conservative forces. The *Halacha* and its Religious Zionist interpreters are questioned in the course of these quests, but, generally speaking, the borders of *Halacha* are not transgressed. Politically, Israel's rule of the occupied Palestinian territories is taken as a matter of fact given in the background, neither questioned nor ideologically affirmed in the films; Palestinians and non-observant Israelis are conspicuous in their absence. (It should be noted that the scripts of these films require prior approval by the school.) (Recanati 2010:232, 234–7, 242; Jacobson 2004:38–40).

A number of *Ma'aleh* graduates, although fewer than the school's founders had hoped for, have found work in the film and television industries as writers, directors and producers. More importantly, perhaps, senior figures in the organization itself have gone on to fill key executive roles in the media industry.

Mordechai Shklar, a graduate of *Merkaz Ha-Rav yeshiva* (see Chapter 3) who ran *Ma'aleh*'s parent organization, Ma'aleh – the Center for Religious Zionism – at the time of its establishment, went on to become Chairman (1999–2002) and then Director General (2002–2006) of the Second Television Authority that regulates the commercial channels and cable television, as well as commercial radio stations. He then proceeded to become Director General of the Israel Broadcasting Authority (2006–2011) which controlled public television and radio and was closed down in 2017. In these roles he aggressively promoted religious personnel and religious programming in the media outlets for which he was responsible (Recanati 2010:56, 292). In 2014 he established a religious cable television channel, Channel 20, which he currently heads. Another *Merkaz Ha-Rav* graduate, Udi Leon, was Director General of *Ma'aleh* (1996–1997), established the Gesher Multicultural Film Fund (GMFF), which supports films produced by minority groups in Israel, including the Jewish religious groups, and is currently manager of priority and diversity programming at Keshet, Israel's primary commercial television channel (Recanati 2010:67, 126, 147).

Parallel to the development of *Ma'aleh* in the 1990s, both non-observant and religious filmmakers began to incorporate religious themes in their work.[1] In 2000 a US-born Religious Zionist director and screenwriter, Joseph Cedar, released *Time of Favor*, the first Israeli film created by a religious director and the first to deal seriously and positively (at least by some interpretations) with issues of religiosity in Israeli society. The plot of the film takes place in a *hesder yeshiva* in the West Bank (see Chapter 6) and revolves around a conspiracy to blow up the Moslem shrines on the Temple Mount in order to replace them with the Third Jewish Temple. The hero is a Religious Zionist "new Jew" – a handsome, upstanding, highly esteemed, ideologically motivated religious company commander in the IDF, contrasted with the main non-observant hero, presented as materialistic and weak (Peleg 2016:94–8; Recanati 2010:116–22). However, the film was not received with universal acclaim by the Religious Zionist public, nor was Cedar's next film, *Campfire*, which depicted sexual abuse and its cover up in a small Religious Zionist community preparing to settle in the West Bank. Cedar, it should be noted, is the only major national-religious filmmaker whose films, at least the earlier ones, deal with broad social and political issues rather than exclusively with personal and family concerns (Recanati 2010:122–4, 127–8, 144; Chyutin 2016:47–9).

Charedi *films*

In the same year as *Time of Favor*, Yehuda Grovais launched *Jewish Revenge*, a *Charedi* film series consisting of five action B-movies designed for male consumption on DVD. By 2008 Grovais had produced over 80(!) such films, aimed at a very specific population: marginal *yeshiva* students (known in *Charedi* parlance as *shabab*) who are not really fit for this type of education but who continue to enroll in a *yeshiva* in order to avoid military service (see Chapter 6) (Be'er 1987:89; Vinig 2011: 44; Friedman and Hakak 2015:51). In Grovais's own words:

> Our Yeshiva boys that "go bad" … go to see Van Damme and Steven Seagal. They don't go to see European cinema.… My goal is to provide an alternative to Van Damme that is appropriate for our public … an alternative for leisure activities.
>
> (Cited in Friedman and Hakak 2015:53)

Other *Charedi* producers had been producing this type of film as well, without receiving rabbinical authorization for them (Friedman and Hakak 2015:55). In 2010, however, a number of important *Charedi* rabbis prohibited the use of home computers for the purpose of entertainment, an edict which dealt a severe blow to the DVD film industry. Another problem that afflicted the industry was unauthorized copying and downloading of the films, which undermined its economic viability. As a result, at the time of writing the only *Charedi* film industry that actually exists is the one made by and for women (see below) (Vinig 2011:19, 45–6; Aharoni 2017:59–60).

The plots of the *Jewish Revenge* series depict a non-observant intelligence agent whose daring mission in Israel's defense is about to be frustrated. The mission is rescued at the last moment by the *Charedi* hero, whose intellectual prowess turns out to be superior to, but not a substitute for, the physical prowess of the non-observant one. The *Charedi* hero also instructs his non-observant counterpart about the true nature of Jewish heroism and Jewish revenge and in this way brings about his spiritual transformation to the point, in some of the films, of embracing Jewish religion. "Non-Jewish men appear in the films as one-dimensional characters and are depicted stereotypically as untrustworthy, sometimes evil, and sometimes inadequate or stupid." The message directed at the films' *Charedi* audience at one and the same time legitimizes and humanizes secular Zionism and appeals to the audience's desire for a more physically active life and for taking part in Israel's defense, contrary to the positions held by the community's rabbis (see Chapter 6). Overall, according to Friedman and Hakak, the films express the *Charedim*'s desire to "integrate but not assimilate" into mainstream Israeli society (Friedman and Hakak 2015:59, 65, 69–70; Aharoni 2017:61; cf. Stadler and Ben-Ari 2003; Stadler 2004).

A completely different kind of *Charedi* film, meant for distribution in the society at large, is *Ushpizin* (Guests), produced in 2004 by the *Charedi* (and previously Religious Zionist and non-observant) screenwriter and actor Shuli Rand, who wrote the script and starred in the film, and the non-observant director, Gidi Dar. *Ushpizin* was the first film to be shown in Israel in which religious actors played religious characters out of identification with them and a wish to project their beliefs and values onto the broader society. (Rand received permission from his Breslav Chassidic rabbi to produce the film.) (Recanati 2010:124–7; Vinig 2011:29–30; Peleg 2016:40–4).

Its plot depicts a penniless and childless Breslav Chasidic couple, *ba'alei teshuvah*, on the eve of the holiday of *Sukkot* (Festival of Tabernacles), which they are not able to properly prepare for because of their poverty. After praying to God with great devotion the husband is shown an allegedly abandoned *sukkah* that he can take a hold of and the couple receives, by pure chance, a gift of 1,000 US dollars from a local charity. All they need now for a proper celebration of the holiday are guests (*ushpizin*) in their *sukkah*, at which point two escaped convicts, one of them a friend from the husband's own criminal past, appear on their doorstep. The two guests, the only non-observant characters shown in the film, create mayhem in the couple's household and in the neighborhood, and the husband's restrained reaction to that is rewarded, nine months later, by the birth of a male child.

While to an outside observer the *Charedi* couple may seem naïve, even primitive, and full of superstition, the film was received with great enthusiasm by the Israeli audience and by the critics. According to Recanati,[2] who summarized the views of a number of religious critics, the film "touched on great theological questions," yet "a blessed, unmediated, intimacy exists in the film throughout its length between the human characters and the hidden God" (Recanati 2010:125). However, the film was not considered by *Charedi* filmmakers and audiences to be a *Charedi* film, primarily because it violated the proscription against showing men and women together, even though in this case the two were married to each other (Vinig 2011:29–30; Friedman and Hakak 2015:54).

Ushpizin was also seen as presenting the *Charedi* world to a non-observant audience in a way that the non-observant audience could accept. According to Yaron Peleg, a non-observant literary scholar, "even the most hardened of secular hearts cannot but rejoice with the destitute couple, whose goodness and honesty are rewarded so handsomely and in such a timely manner" (Peleg 2016:42). Unlike the *Jewish Revenge* series, *Ushpizin*

> ... does not have an integrative agenda and makes no claim other than to ask viewers to recognize the community as different but legitimate. In the name of contemporary multiculturalism, the film's religious community wishes to be seen as equal to other communities in postmodern, post-Zionist Israel.
>
> (Peleg 2016:43)

A particularly successful genre of *Charedi* films are films made by women for the consumption of exclusively female audiences in public screenings. (As opposed to the male-directed films mentioned above which were distributed on DVD to be watched on home computers.) Unlike the male-produced films, since the women's films are to be shown in public they require prior authorization from the rabbis, who impose strict conditions of modesty and gender segregation on the content and production process of the film, as well as censoring their themes and the messages they convey so as not to transgress the established religious norms. The rabbis also prohibit the distribution of these films on DVD (Vinig 2011; Friedman and Hakak 2015:50; Aharoni 2017:62–3).

Two important considerations lay behind the rabbis' reluctant decision to permit film (and theater) production by and for *Charedi* women in the first place. One was the need to fill women's and girls' free time, since they are not obligated to engage in religious studies like the men are. The other was the economic potential of this industry, as women are by and large the main income earners in *Charedi* families and the film industry, despite the lack of state and foundation subsidies, is a source of income for the women engaged in it (Vinig 2011).

With very few exceptions, like *Ushpizin*, *Charedi* films, unlike the ones produced by Religious Zionist filmmakers, have not been funded by either the state or private foundations (Vinig 2011:69, 112, 155–6; Friedman and Hakak 2015:52–4). The reason is that the prevailing cinematic discourse in Israel,

> [r]ooted in European art cinemas, and typical of the world film festival circuit ... is a cinematic discourse that perpetuates a dichotomy between art and popular cinema, privileging the auteur over genre, the image over dialogue and action, and the small, personal narrative over spectacle and grand narrative.
>
> (Friedman and Hakak 2015:53–4)

In Yehuda Grovais's words:

> If I was willing to give the [film] funds what they want to see on the screen, I too could have been embraced by the establishment of Israeli cinema, like filmmakers from other "minority groups." But they [the film funds] say they are looking for art, truth, exposure, when they actually mean images that would reinforce their stereotypical notions of Charedi life.... Charedi cinema is not cinema about Charedim but for Charedim.... I seek primarily to provide an alternative source of home-grown entertainment. Ideally, these films will reinforce Charedi values while allowing the escapist pleasure of Hollywoodic fantasies.
>
> (Cited in Friedman and Hakak 2015:54)

However, the decline of the DVD film industry had made Grovais turn to making the kind of films that the funds would approve of and indeed in 2006 one of his films, *Where Will My Help Come From*, was given a grant by the Gesher Fund.[3]

Grovais's characterization of his DVD films holds true for the *Charedi* women's films as well. The plots of their movies usually revolve around the adoption or kidnapping of children, in many cases in the context of the Holocaust, with a sub-plot that focuses on familial dynamics, usually mother–daughter relations and issues surrounding education, modesty and the efforts to arrange a marriage for the daughter. (Arranged marriage is the only kind of marriage in *Charedi* society.) In the absence of a male figure in the films, the mother is presented as the strong, wise and stable head of the family who is the guardian of traditional religious values and norms. Thus Attara, the mother figure in the film *Sgurim* (Closed), directed by Dikla Gol, says to her daughter:

> We do not encourage craziness. We do not encourage diverging from the rules. The Sabbath comes in exactly when the Sabbath comes in, not a minute earlier or later. It doesn't matter if a person prayed for too long or did not finish cooking on time. The Sabbath comes in exactly when the Sabbath comes in.
>
> (Vinig 2011:120, 130–9)

The daughter, a teenage student in a *Charedi* girls' high school (commonly referred to as a *seminar*), is the one who very gingerly attempts to express some independence of mind in the form of doubts and misgivings about the oppressive *Charedi* lifestyle, although never about the tenets of Jewish religion or the major rules of behavior of the particular *Charedi* sect depicted in the film.[4] At the end the mother, naturally, prevails and the established order is maintained.

Divine providence plays a major role in these films, emphasizing humans' inability to exercise control over their fate. Passions, especially romantic passions, are absent from the films, and evil is presented, if at all, in very moderate forms. When love appears it is invariably in the form of friendship between two female characters. Non-Jews and non-observant Jews are always depicted in a negative, unchanging light whereas *Charedi* Jews, even if they go astray, eventually mend their ways and come back to the fold (Vinig 2011:94–107, 114).

Initially most of the women engaged in producing *Charedi* films as writers, directors and actors lacked proper training in this field and tried to learn by doing. The only exception were *ba'alot teshuvah* who had worked in the industry before their conversion. In order to try and professionalize the field, a number of institutions began to offer courses in the different aspects of filmmaking (Vinig 2011:72, 85–90). In 2010 the Gesher Fund, which promotes multicultural film, set up a training project for *Charedi* women filmmakers. (Separate, of course, from the project set up for *Charedi* men in 2006). In 2014 *Ma'aleh* opened a special branch for *Charedi* women. Its message to potential students stated, in part:

> If you have a burning need to create art which makes a significant statement, feminine and Jewish, you are invited here, to an educational experience, professional training and creation that will fill your entire substantial, emotional and artistic world. The *Charedi* branch was opened with the encouragement and blessing of rabbis and educational women and sees in you the vessel that contains real, essential Jewish content![5]

According to Marylin Vinig, a *Charedi* filmmaker who has written the only published study of *Charedi* women's films to date, "when considering facts, *Charedi* [film] creation will be found wanting, but when considering intentions, then *Charedi* film creation is the exciting Israeli phenomenon of the two-thousands" (Vinig 2011:112). The facts are the low professional quality of the films, the banality of their story lines, and the restrictive cultural and financial conditions under which the industry must work. What is exciting is the opening, albeit very limited, of *Charedi* society to this novel field of cultural expression as a way of beginning to come to terms with the surrounding modern society (Vinig 2011:54–6), and, especially, the leading role played by women in this process.

Television

Until 1992 Israel had only one, public, television channel. Religious programming and religious staff – nine men out of about one thousand professional employees – working on that channel were confined to a specific department – Jewish Heritage – which was poorly funded and produced low-quality programs of very limited interest to the general public. In 1992 the television market was opened up with the introduction of two commercial channels. In that decade religious themes began to appear in documentary and drama programs as well (Recanati 2010:48, 50, 131).

Since the 2000s there has been a "religious transformation, even revolution … [in] Israeli television … with respect to the representation of Jewish religious themes" and the presence of religious reporters, commentators and anchor people on the various TV channels (Peleg 2016:19). While in the 1990s religious issues were discussed primarily as current affairs, in the 2000s such issues were treated primarily in original dramatic programs and religiously oriented talk shows. This transformation was due in no small part to the work of people like Mordechai Shklar and Udi Leon, but also to the efforts of the private US-based Avi Chai Foundation, which

> has been active since the 1990s in supporting various educational and cultural initiatives in Israel designed to bridge the gap between the secular and the religious, as the foundation puts it, and to introduce Jewish traditional themes into Israeli popular culture primarily through the arts.
>
> (Peleg 2016:19)

> Through its investment of tens of millions of dollars toward Israeli art and media that engage with Jewish themes, the Avi Chai Foundation has financed pop culture content in music, television, film, journalism, and other platforms. By way of such endeavors, Avi Chai – *by far the biggest player in the realm of Israeli media* – and other organizations with similar goals attempt to encourage Israelis to explore their Jewishness, thereby shifting Israeli identities and notions of religiosity.
>
> (Dardashti 2015:79; emphasis added)

"AC [Avi Chai] identified television as one of the most valuable tools for capturing 'the heart,' and sought to utilize it to humanize religious Israelis for the largely secular Israeli viewing audience" (Dardashti 2015:87).

Although by 2008 no full-length feature film had been produced by a *Ma'aleh* graduate, two of its graduates, Hava Dibon and Eliezer Shapira, produced a popular television series, *Srugim* (Knitted; a nickname for religious Zionists because of the knitted skull cap worn by the men), that ran between 2008 and 2012 (Recanati 2010:249–50; Burg n.d. [2013]; Peleg 2016:109–11).

At that time *Srugim* was the only major television show with Jewish content not supported by Avi Chai, because its characters were all religious and did not interact with non-observant Israeli Jews. The show focused on a group of young, single religious Zionist men and women, a community referred to in religious Zionist slang as a "swamp." It was modeled on *Friends* and *Sex and the City* and "the romantic worries of the characters ... stem[med] from their agency as self-aware modern members of an otherwise antiquated religion" (Peleg 2016:109; Hermann et al. 2014:33n36). The effect of the show was to humanize and de-politicize Religious Zionism for the benefit of the non-observant audience (Burg 2006:23), an approach shared by most *Ma'aleh*-produced films and television shows and by most screen-arts products stemming from the national-religious sector as a whole.

This approach of Religious Zionism to the screen arts, which allegedly fails to combine art and faith and endow the combination with theological meaning, has been criticized from within that sector:

[Religious Zionism] flocked to the screen arts without recognizing that the placing of human beings at the center, with their pleasures and satisfactions, including the ones that are considered base, and the power of the director to shape the screen as he wishes and make his choices in a supposedly completely free manner, are central to them. Without them [the screen arts] have no existence. [Religious Zionism] took upon itself to create interest in accordance with modern-Western conventions and adapted itself to the modern, or post-modern, pace, conception of conflict and dramatic construction, without trying to offer a formal alternative ... Thus it sought to tell its own stories, to present pseudo-independent content, but with the accepted Western language and form.

(Cited in Recanati 2010:294)

From our perspective in this book, however, this approach is precisely the correct one for a social sector that seeks to establish cultural hegemony over its society from an initial position of relative weakness (cf. Chapter 7).

Looking at the place of religion and the religious in the general television industry, two studies conducted by the Second Broadcasting Authority, which regulates the commercial television channels, in 2003 and 2004–2005, examined the exposure levels of different social groups in prime-time programs on the two commercial television channels (Laor et al. 2004; 2006). The studies showed an under-representation of both the national-religious and *Charedi* sectors, with a slight increase in the later study in the presentation of national-religious figures, from 6 to 7 percent. The most significant increase in the presentation of national-religious figures was in reality and game shows, from 7 percent in 2003 to 19 percent in 2004–2005, which may be an indication of the mainstreaming of this sector (Laor et al. 2006:2, 16–25; see also Recanati 2010:141–2).

A limited study of Channel 1 (the now defunct public channel) news, conducted between April and June 2005, found that the national-religious sector, comprising about 12 percent of the population, received 16 percent of the coverage, more than the Mizrachim, comprising 29 percent of the population, who received only 15 percent of the coverage, and more than Israel's Palestinian citizens, comprising 19 percent of the population, who received only 4 percent of the coverage (Bar-Lev 2007:29).

Qualitatively, the Second Broadcasting Authority studies developed an index for measuring the way the different groups were presented, positively or negatively, based on previous work by Gadi Wolfsfeld (1997). The index is made up of three variables: "status" – a figure's biography, behavior and role in the item; "back-door entry" – the extent to which the group is characterized by deviant behavior; and the extent to which the figures belonging to each group are presented anonymously or with their proper names (Laor et al. 2006:4, 32–52). Based on this index, in the secularizing 1990s religious issues were covered negatively in over 50 percent of the cases (they were covered positively in 27 percent and the rest did not display any clear value orientation), whereas in the 2000s they were presented positively in over 50 percent of the cases and negatively in only 17 percent (see also Y. Cohen 2005; 2012; Recanati 2010:142–3; Evans 2011).

Other indications of the growing interest, and role, of Religious Zionists in the media of mass communications are the establishment in 2003 of a religious Jewish paid cable television channel, Azure, that, however, went out of business because of low subscription numbers and resultant financial difficulties in 2006. It was replaced in 2014 by cable Channel 20 established by Mordechai Shklar (previously the Legacy Channel) (Recanati 2010:135–8). In 2008 a *Charedi* cable television channel, *Hidabroot* (Conversation), was established to be watched by *Charedim* on home computers, since they are not supposed to watch television or own television sets. *Hidabroot* was established by a *teshuvah-*promoting organization with the same name and its declared purpose is to reconcile religious and non-observant Israeli Jews through conversation. Its broadcasts deal primarily with religious issues and with other issues that are of concern to the *Charedi* community (Vinig 2011:25–6).[6]

An innovative study based on analysis of television reviews published in two leading newspapers, *Haaretz* and *Yediot Aharonot*, in 1985 (as a benchmark year) and in 1990–2014, revealed that, according to the qualitative index mentioned above, in 1985 and throughout the 1990s negative coverage of religious issues on Israeli television channels clearly exceeded positive coverage, whereas since the turn of the millennium, and especially since 2009, the trend has been reversed. Similarly, in the 1990s most religious personalities and themes appeared in current affairs and talk shows focusing on religion-related controversies – *Charedi* military service, controversial statements made by various rabbis, the secular-religious "culture war," etc. – where the religious were presented as inciting the controversy and were asked to defend their positions. In the 2000s, on the other hand, religious figures and themes began to appear in Israeli dramatic series, where they are no longer treated as a threatening "other" but are rather presented as a legitimate component of normative Israeli society (A. Schwartz 2015).

Summary

Like the other social fields surveyed in this book, the screen arts and media of mass communications have undergone a profound transformation in terms of both the participation and portrayal of Orthodox Jews, both Religious Zionists and *Charedim*. Until the 1990s Orthodox agents were largely absent from this field, and Orthodox Jews were portrayed mostly negatively in it, if at all. This began to change in the 1990s with the establishment of the Religious Zionist film school, *Ma'aleh*, and the introduction of commercial television stations. The great leap forward, however, occurred in the 2000s, following the breakdown of the Oslo peace process and the outbreak of the second *intifada*. As the general Jewish public became more receptive to national-religious messages, and as growing numbers of film and television artists "returned" to Jewish religion, Orthodox agents have become much more visible in this field, and religion and the religious have come to be portrayed in it in mostly positive terms.

Critics from within the Orthodox world have complained that Orthodox film and television creators have not developed their own cinematic language but have used, rather, the prevailing language of these media to convey their own specific content. In our view this was the right strategy since these Orthodox agents active in the screen arts field did not aim to create their own artistic niche, but have sought to integrate into the actually existing field and, if possible, achieve a dominant position within it. So far they have not achieved dominance within that field but they have certainly established a very prominent presence in it.

Notes

1 The distinction between religious and non-observant in this context is somewhat problematic, because many film makers who deal with religious issues have shifted from one category to the other.
2 Recanati is a Religious Zionist and a former Director General of *Ma'aleh*.
3 Available at: www.gesherfilmfund.org.il/Info.aspx?PageID=69 (accessed July 4, 2017).
4 *Sgurim* was considered too daring a film because the daughter, Batya, had too many non-conformist thoughts. It was therefore banned in many *Charedi* girls' high schools and was thus a commercial failure (Vinig 2011:66, 110–11).
5 Available at: www.maale.co.il/he/program/orthodox, in Hebrew (accessed June 1, 2017).
6 Available at: www.hidabroot.org/ad_manager/gotourl/989 (accessed July 5, 2017).

References

Aharoni, M. (2017) "'Other' *Charedi* Identities: Representation of the Modern *Charedi* and of the Manual Worker in Communal *Charedi* Films in Israel," *Democratic Culture*, 17: 53–86 (in Hebrew).
Bar-Lev, J. (2007) "Representation of Minorities in Public Broadcasting," MA thesis, Department of Communications, Ben-Gurion University (in Hebrew).
Be'er, H. (1987) *The Time of Trimming*, Tel Aviv: Am Oved (in Hebrew).
Burg, H. (n.d. [2013]) "Torah and Creation: Television Works of Religious Creators as an Expression of the Tension between Religion and Modernity in Religious Zionism," n.p., copy on file with the authors (in Hebrew).
Chyutin, D. (2016) "'The King's Daughter is All Glorious Within': Female Modesty in Judaic-Themed Israeli Cinema," *Journal of Jewish Identities*, 9: 39–58.
Cohen, Y. (2005) "Religion News in Israel," *Journal of Media and Religion*, 4: 179–98.
Cohen, Y. (2012) *God, Jews and the Media: Religion and Israel's Media*, London: Routledge.
Daniels, J. S. (2008) "Scripting the Jewish Body: The Sexualized Female Jewish Body in Amos Gitai's *Kadosh*," in Abrams, N. (ed.), *Jews and Sex*, Nottingham: Five Leaves.
Dardashti, G. (2015) "Televised Agendas: How Global Funders Make Israeli TV More 'Jewish'," *Jewish Film & New Media: An International Journal*, 3: 77–103.
Evans, M. (2011) "Exacerbating Social Cleavages: The Media's Role in Israel's Religious-Secular Conflict," *Middle East Journal*, 65 (2): 235–51.
Friedman, Y. and Hakak, Y. (2015) "Jewish Revenge: Haredi Action in the Zionist Sphere," *Jewish Film & New Media: An International Journal*, 3: 48–76.
Gebel, A. (2006) *The National-Religious Public and the Media: A Love-Hate Relationship*, Tel Aviv: Tel Aviv University, Chaim Herzog Institute for Communications, Society and Politics (in Hebrew).

Hermann, T., Be'eri, G., Heller, E., Cohen, C., Lebel, Y., Mozes, H., and Neuman, K. (2014) *The National-Religious Sector in Israel 2014*, Jerusalem: Israel Democracy Institute (in Hebrew).

Jacobson, D. C. (2004) "The Ma'aleh School: Catalyst for the Entrance of Religious Zionists into the World of Media Production," *Israel Studies*, 9: 31–60.

Kimmel, M. (2002) "Religious Youth Make Movies – Educational Aspects," *Water from His Buckets: Annual of the Religious Teachers' College*, 13: 283–300 (in Hebrew).

Laor, N., Elephant Lefler, N., and Inbar-Lankri, Ch. (2004) *The Present and the Absent in Prime Time: Cultural Diversity in the Broadcasting of Commercial Television Channels in Israel*, Research Report, Second Authority for Television and Radio (in Hebrew).

Laor, N., Elephant Lefler, N., and Inbar-Lankri, Ch. (2006) *The Present and the Absent in Prime Time: Cultural Diversity in the Broadcasting of Commercial Television Channels in Israel*, Follow-up Report, Second Authority for Television and Radio (in Hebrew).

Peleg, Y. (2016) *Directed by God: Jewishness in Contemporary Israeli Film and Television*, Austin, TX: University of Texas Press.

Recanati, I. S. (2010) "Religious Zionism and the Screen Arts: 'Ma'aleh' School, Its Students and their Films as a Test Case," PhD dissertation, Department of Contemporary Jewry, Bar-Ilan University (in Hebrew).

Schwartz, A. (2015) "Representation of the Religious Population and Religious Issues in Newspaper Coverage of Television Programs," a paper presented at the *Religionization of the Public Sphere* conference, Department of Political Science, Tel Aviv University.

Stadler, N. (2004) "Taboos, Dreams and Desires: Haredi Conceptions of Militarism and the Military," *Israeli Sociology*, 6: 69–90.

Stadler, N. and Ben-Ari, E. (2003) "Other-Worldly Soldiers? Ultra-Orthodox Views of Military Service in Contemporary Israel," *Israel Affairs*, 9: 17–48.

Vinig, M. (2011) *Orthodox Cinema*, Tel Aviv: Resling Publishing (in Hebrew).

Wolfsfeld, Gadi. (1997) *Media and Political Conflict: News from the Middle East*, Cambridge: Cambridge University Press.

10 Conclusion

> Israel is standing today in a fateful junction in front of the strategic move of the
> new Religious Zionism. As against a well-organized Religious Zionist establish-
> ment, permeated with a feeling of historic deprivation, motivated by overbearing
> revolutionary zeal, and suspicious of the legal authorities of the state, stand the
> powers of the Zionism that had founded the state in a position of weakness, while
> the Zionist idea that had motivated the establishment of the state is today in a
> state of crisis.
>
> (Ben-Sasson 2015:6)

The religionization of Jewish Israeli society since 1967, we have argued in this
book, is manifested primarily in two ways: the growing prominence of Religious
Zionists in various social institutions and fields – the military, fine arts, the
media of mass communications – and the evolution of religious Zionism toward
becoming the culturally hegemonic worldview among Israeli Jews. As a would-
be hegemonic worldview, religious Zionism encompasses a range of levels of
religious observance and nationalist fervor, from close to ultra-Orthodoxy on
one end up to modern Orthodoxy and "Judaism as culture" on the other, and
from messianic ultra-nationalism to a very liberal version of Zionism.

As we have shown in Chapter 3, the religious Zionist periphery of Religious
Zionism is at least as large as the core group itself. The most dynamic element
within Religious Zionism, however, and the one that has contributed in the most
significant way to the evolution of religious Zionism toward cultural hegemony,
is its messianic-activist nucleus, comprised of followers of the two Rav Kooks,
father and son, and epitomized by Gush Emunim.

Taking advantage of the weakness of Labor Zionism alluded to in the citation
above and in Chapter 2, that group was able to set the agenda for Israel's relation
to the territories it captured in 1967 and to their Palestinian residents. As a result,
by 2011 the number of Jewish settlers in the West Bank, including East
Jerusalem and the areas annexed to it by Israel in 1967, was over 700,000 – more
than 20 percent of the total population of the West Bank – making the two-state
solution to the Israeli occupation, favored by the international community and by
many in Israel itself, no longer feasible (Ghanim 2012:98; 2016; Herman Peled

and Peled 2011; Ehrenberg and Peled 2016; Peled and Herman Peled 2016). It is not purely symbolic that a peripheral member of that messianic-activist group, Yigal Amir, assassinated the Prime Minister who might have implemented the two-state solution, Yitzhak Rabin.

Cultural hegemony in the Gramscian sense is held by a social group, not by an abstract worldview. In our case too, while religious Zionism is becoming a hegemonic worldview, actual hegemony in the cultural-political sense is reverting to Religious Zionism. Like all hegemonic groups, in order to build and maintain its historic bloc Religious Zionism must find ways to accommodate the interests of other, more or less closely related, social groups. Thus, the historic bloc forged by Gush Emunim, as described in Chapter 3, has been expanded to include some *Charedim*, traditionalists, and non-observant Jews committed to "Jewish renewal."

As *Charedim* gradually integrate into the surrounding society, by entering the military, academia, the media, the fine arts field, and the labor market in growing numbers (IDI 2017a), they in effect, if not in word, begin to adhere to religious Zionism. By the same token, the Jewish Home party, current incarnation of the National Religious Party led by Naftali Bennett, son of American *ba'alei teshuvah*, appeals to a certain traditionalist and non-observant constituency, and its number-two leader, Ayelet Shaked, currently the Justice Minister, is a non-observant woman (Ben-Sasson 2015).[1] In order to attract traditionalist and non-observant Jews, Religious Zionism does not need to moderate the nationalist aspect of religious Zionism, but rather its religious aspect. As for *Charedim*, if they want to integrate into the Zionist mainstream without giving up their traditional way of life, religious Zionism is their only option.

Supported by its historic bloc and following a well thought-out long-term strategy, Religious Zionism has been making inroads into several key fields of Israel's social life – education, the media, fine arts, the military – in order, as they put it, to "move from the backseat to the driver's seat" of the State of Israel (Ben-Sasson 2015). The IDF, the institution most trusted by the Jewish Israeli public (IDI 2017b:120) and of obvious importance for the security of the country as well as its continued occupation of the Palestinian territories, was first to be "captured" through the religious-military institutions of *yeshivot hesder, mechinot*, and the military rabbinate, aided by the declining motivation of non-observant middle-class youth to perform "meaningful service" or choose the military as a career. The most immediately visible effect of this development is growing pressure to institute gender segregation in the military, to the point of exempting women from mandatory military service altogether.

In the educational field, not satisfied with having their own autonomous system, Religious Zionists, who have controlled the Ministry of Education for much of the past forty years, have used this position of power to infuse religious and ultra-nationalist content into the "secular" educational system, beginning at the kindergarten level. In the higher education field, efforts to recruit *Charedim*, especially *Charedi* men, have resulted in the proliferation of gender segregated classrooms, buildings, even campuses, in gross violation of the principles of gender equality and human dignity. Gender segregation, as early as the first grade, is being instituted in the state-religious school system as well, as this system is becoming more extreme in its religious observance.

Religious Zionists, followed by *Charedim*, have also established a presence in the arts field, both within the visual fine arts and the screen arts. The latter – film and television – of obvious value for shaping public opinion, have been entered into first through the establishment of educational institutions providing professional training, and the support of powerful foreign foundations such as the Avi Chai Foundation. In the field of visual fine arts the hegemonic gate-keepers have resisted the incursion of Orthodox artists longer than in any other field, using aesthetic judgment as a vehicle of exclusion. Orthodox artistic entre-preneurs, mostly Religious Zionists but increasingly *Charedim* as well, have been using post-modern, multicultural, and feminist discourses, as well as polit-ical positions of power, in order to overcome these obstacles, with impressive results. Their first major breakthrough occurred in 2012 with the *Matronita* Orthodox feminist exhibition at the Art Museum of kibbutz Ein Harod, an icon of Labor Zionist ideology and settlement strategy (see the celebrated dystopian novel by Amos Kenan, *The Road to Ein Harod* [Kenan 2001]).

It would be a mistake, however, to believe that the religionization of Israeli society had begun from point zero. As we have shown, a deeply rooted religious element was embedded in Zionism and the State of Israel from the very beginning. Zionism's relations with Judaism has been entangled in a paradox – Zionism needed to "rebel" against the traditional, "religious," Jewish way of life, yet its object – the Jewish "nation" – was constituted by the very religion it "rebelled" against. And that religion is public and practical, not private and limited to belief as in most Western nation-states. In other words, Zionism has had to contend with a dual imperative – it needed to privatize religion in order to break up the traditional Jewish community so it could be nationalized, and mobilized in the service of nationalism and the nation-state. At the same time Zionism also needed to maintain the public, collective char-acter of Judaism, in order to claim that Jews were a nation.

Political implications

In Israel, as in many other countries, religiosity is very strongly correlated with right-wing nationalist political positions. This correlation affects particularly three significant issue areas – the Israeli-Palestinian conflict, where religiosity correlates with intransigent political positions; attitudes toward democracy, including the rights of non-Jewish citizens and residents of the country; and gender relations (Luz 1999; 2003; Hellinger 2008; Halperin-Kaddari and Yadgar 2010; International Crisis Group 2013, especially pp. 33–9; Don-Yehiya 2014; Bagno-Moldavski 2015; Barzel 2017).[2]

In 1994 Charles Liebman posed the question:

> Why has Israeli Judaism been transformed in the direction of particularism and ethnocentrism and not in the direction of morality, universality and

political liberalism? In other words, why [is] … Israeli Judaism less and not more compatible with the conditions that are vital for the existence of a stable democracy?

(Liebman 1994:136)

His answer was that, especially since 1967, political authority in the national-religious camp has crystallized in the rabbinical establishment which, by and large, tends to be particularistic and xenophobic, and has shifted away from more liberal religious intellectuals and politicians. Indeed, the transformation of the National Religious Party from a very moderate party on the questions of Israel's relations with the Arabs to an ultra-nationalist party corresponded with the growing political weight of the rabbis, particularly Rav Z. Y. Kook, within it. What enabled the rabbis to achieve this position of authority, according to Liebman, was the alliance they forged with right-wing secular politicians who needed their endorsement for legitimating their territorial-political ambitions in the territories occupied in 1967 (Liebman 1994:140, 143; see also Luz 1999, especially 362–92; Sagi 2011:140–2; International Crisis Group 2013:5–6; Hermann et al. 2014:38–9, 109–13; Ben-Sasson 2015).

As can be seen in Table 10.1, a quarter of the Jewish public in Israel, but almost 90 percent of *Charedim* and two-thirds of the national-religious would prefer observing the *Halacha* over respect for democratic principles, should there be a conflict between the two. Accordingly, 86 percent of *Charedim* and almost 70 percent of the national-religious, as against almost 30 percent of all Jews, favor making the *Halacha* state law for Jews in Israel (Pew 2016; Hermann et al. 2014:74–97; cf. Ben-Nun Bloom et al. 2011). As for the rights of the Palestinian citizens and residents, there the national-religious hold more extreme right-wing

Table 10.1 Political attitudes of Israeli Jews by level of religiosity, 2014–2015 (percent)

	Religious Zionists	*Charedim*	*General Jewish*
Democracy compatible with Jewish State	79	58	76
Prefer *Halacha* over democracy	65	89	24
Halacha should be state law for Jews	69	86	29
Arabs should be expelled or transferred	71	59	48
Jews should have more rights (do not agree)	61	40	70
Anyone who refuses to declare Israel the nation-state of the Jewish people should lose the right to vote	62	64	44
Settlements help security	68	50	42
Settlements hurt security	13	13	30
Only Jews should vote in a referendum on peace	50	–	33
All Israeli citizens should vote in a referendum on peace	16	–	25
Vital decisions in the area of national security should be made by a Jewish majority	92	94	72

Sources: Hermann et al. 2014; 2016; 2017; Pew 2016.

views on some issues than the *Charedim*: whereas over 70 percent of national-religious respondents agree that "Arabs should be expelled or transferred from Israel," less than 60 percent of *Charedim* do so, as against nearly half of the general Jewish public (Pew 2016:6, 17, 196).[3] On the other hand, only 40 percent of *Charedim* as against 61 percent of the national-religious and 70 percent of the general Jewish public *do not agree* that Jewish citizens should have more rights than non-Jewish ones (Hermann et al. 2016:156–7). Similarly, over 60 percent of *Charedim* and of the national-religious, as against 44 percent of the general Jewish population believe that "anyone who refuses to declare that Israel is the nation state of the Jewish people" should lose the right to vote (Hermann et al. 2017:8).

On the question of whether or not Jewish settlements in the occupied Palestinian territories (OPT) enhance Israel's security, a clear majority among the national-religious believe that they do, as against one half of the *Charedim* and less than half of the general Jewish public (Pew 2016:182; cf. Hermann et al. 2017). If a referendum were to be held about the future of the OPT and peace with the Palestinians, one half of the national-religious sector, broadly defined, as against one third of the general Jewish public prefer that only Jews participate in that referendum. Sixteen percent of the former and one quarter of the latter prefer that all Israeli citizens take part in it. In general, over 90 percent of both the national-religious and *Charedim* feel that vital decisions in the area of national security should be made by a Jewish majority, as against 72 percent who feel that way in the general Jewish public (Hermann et al. 2014:139–40, 249; 2016:161–2).

These attitudes of the religious Zionist public are rooted in a profound belief in the moral superiority of Jews and the sanctity of their mission to establish their sovereignty over the entire Land of Israel, for the sake of *global human* redemption. According to Rav Eliezer Waldman, head of a Hebron *yeshiva*, Israel's wars are holy wars because they are a constitutive element in "the struggle for world peace and for the redemption of humanity in its entirety. Peace will come to the world only after the nations of the world recognize the People of Israel's exclusive ownership of the Land of Israel" (cited in Luz 1999:372). Therefore, according to Rav Levinger of Gush Emunim, the Palestinians

> [s]hould be partners in the process of the redemption of the People of Israel, not fight it. On the contrary, they bring disaster on themselves by their current behavior, not physically, but spiritually … It must be explained to them that here there is going to be redemption of the People of Israel and of the entire world, and therefore they have to change their attitude towards the whole [Zionist] enterprise, and be for the People of Israel, help and support us in settling [the Land of Israel], not interfere with us.
>
> (Cited in Luz 1999:372)

In the words of Ehud Luz, a scholar of Jewish national-religious thought:

> A way of thinking which attributes sanctity to political reality itself and gives a-priori religious-moral approbation to everything that is being done

for that reality, leads necessarily to the swallowing-up of politics by religion – or of religion by politics. This is a conception that refuses to recognize not only the limitations of reality but also the moral limitations of politics. The great historical justice of redemption overshadows the little injustices that take place in everyday life. This conception sees the main danger not in the moral corruption that awaits us as a result of the unmitigated use of force, but in the weakness of faith that is manifest in the willingness to concede and to compromise under the pressure of the hostile nations of the world.

(Luz 1999:380, 388–9)

Regarding the status of women, according to the 2009 Guttman Center survey, two-thirds of *Charedim*, nearly twice as many as among the next group – the national-religious – agreed that "it is best if the man works to support the family and the woman stays home and takes care of the children." This is ironic, of course, because in the *Charedi* sector it is usually the wife who supports the family while the husband studies in the *yeshiva*, or pretends to. Only among the *Charedim*, according to that survey, is a majority (60 percent) satisfied with the current status of women in Israel, while all other Jewish religious groups believe it should be modified. Interestingly, where the *Charedim* and the national-religious come together is on the statement "a woman can fulfill herself even without children," with which both groups disagree at very high rates – 78 and 73 percent, respectively, a rate of disagreement twice as high as among self-defined secular Jews. This meeting of the *Charedi* and national-religious minds indicates that for the national-religious public demographic considerations trump their concern about the status of women in the society (Guttman Center 2012:57).

Causes

As presented in the Introduction, de-secularization of the public sphere is a well-known and widely commented upon phenomenon in much of the world. Students of this phenomenon have explained the resurgence of public religion largely in terms of the failure of secular ideologies (nationalism, liberalism, socialism) to provide normative and emotive foundations for collective action, and the failure of scientific approaches (rationalism, positivism, methodological individualism) to provide a meaningful understanding of reality. More specifically, rapid technological change, neo-liberal economics, and the decline of the welfare state have all been counted among the factors contributing to heightened alienation and the need for religion to counter it.

In addition to these general causes, the religionization of Jewish Israeli society, we argue, has resulted from the convergence of a number of factors specific to Israel. The legitimacy crisis caused by the 1967 and 1973 wars put into question both the justice of Zionism and Israel's ability to guarantee the security of its Jewish citizens. These anxieties were intensified by the breakup of the Oslo peace process and the outbreak of the second *intifada* in 2000. The failure of the

Oslo peace process also signified the end of the two-state solution to the Israeli-Palestinian conflict, hence to the possibility of maintaining a Jewish demographic majority in Israel. Coupled with this, the halting and uneven, but still real, integration of Israel's Palestinian citizen into the mainstream of society intensified the siege mentality of many Israeli Jews and their need to erect higher cultural (as well as physical) walls around themselves in order to preserve their identity.

Naturally, the legitimacy crisis affected particularly hard the then hegemonic Labor Zionist Movement. The military success of 1967 was followed by political paralysis and inaction and the traumatic war of 1973 sealed the fate of the Labor party as Israel's dominant party and of Labor Zionism as the culturally hegemonic worldview. To complete its downfall Labor led the way in liberalizing the economy, thus depriving itself of the economic mainstay of its hegemony – the *Histadrut*. Meanwhile Religious Zionism was reinvigorated by the messianic-activist young guard of the NRP which formed itself into Gush Emunim and began to aggressively settle in the occupied Palestinian territories, with or without a wink from the Labor government and, after 1977, with the explicit blessing of the Likud governments. In the context of a legitimacy crisis, neo-liberalism, the erosion of welfare services, a national conflict with no end in sight, and the decline of Labor hegemony, all in a society that was never really secular,[4] Religious Zionism was ideally placed to make its religious-nationalist ideology the hegemonic worldview of the society. It was aided in this endeavor by a broad historic bloc stretching from many *Charedim* wishing to integrate into the surrounding society to the supposedly non-religious movement for Jewish renewal.

Toward a constitutional theocracy?

Ran Hirschl, who coined the term "constitutional theocracy," identified four features that characterize that kind of regime:

1   adherence to some or all core elements of modern constitutionalism, including the formal distinction between political authority and religious authority and the existence of some form of active judicial review;
2   the presence of a single religion or religious denomination that is formally endorsed by the state, akin to a "state religion";
3   the constitutional enshrining of [that] ... religion as *a* or *the* main source of legislation and judicial interpretation of laws – essentially, laws may not infringe on injunctions of the state-endorsed religion;
4   a nexus of religious bodies and tribunals that ... are ... granted official jurisdictional status on either a regional or a substantive basis and operate in lieu of, or in uneasy tandem with, a civil court system. Most important, their jurisdictional autonomy notwithstanding, some key aspects of religious tribunals' jurisprudence are subject to constitutional review by higher courts, often state created and staffed (Hirschl 2010:3, emphasis in the original).

Does Israel qualify as a constitutional theocracy, then? In our view, while several important features of constitutional theocracy certainly do exist in Israel, at the moment it would be incorrect to classify it under that category, although it may be on its way there:

1   Especially since the "constitutional revolution" of 1992–1995, that inau-gurated judicial review of primary legislation by the High Court of Justice, Israel's constitutional law has incorporated many elements of modern constitutionalism (Hirschl 2010:142; Shafir and Peled 2002:260–77). However, the two 1992 statutes that constituted that "revolution" – Basic Law: Human Dignity and Freedom and Basic Law: Freedom of Occupation – stated that their purpose was to embed in basic legislation Israel's values as a *Jewish* and democratic state. Still, Israel's semi-written constitution does recognize the distinction between political and religious authority, although that distinction, as we have argued in this book, is being eroded.

2   Israel defines itself, constitutionally, as a Jewish state, and a political party that seeks to challenge that definition cannot participate in Knesset elections (Peled 1992). As mentioned above, almost half of the Jewish public in Israel believes that people who do not accept that definition should be disenfranchised. While Israel accords other recognized religious communities a degree of autonomy in running their own affairs (as well as exclusive jurisdiction in matters of marriage and divorce of their con-stituents), the state's definition as a Jewish state clearly places these other religious communities in an inferior position *vis-à-vis* the Jewish majority. To illustrate, government budgetary allocations for religious services of the non-Jewish religious communities, which constitute about 20 percent of the population, are currently about 10 percent of the total budget for religious services.

3   The Foundations of Law Act – 1980 states that legal lacunae should be filled by the courts according to "the principles of freedom, justice, honesty and peace of Jewish heritage" (Hirschl 2010:141; B. Porat 2016:5). A bill currently working its way through the Knesset would add "the principles of Jewish law" to those principles, in order to enhance the weight of Jewish law in Israel's legal system. Still, at the present time it cannot be said that in Israel "laws may not infringe on injunctions of the state endorsed religion," for there are laws, especially in the case law created by the High Court of Justice, that infringe on injunctions of Jewish religion in areas such as conversion to Judaism, women's rights, HLBTQ rights, observance of the Sabbath, etc. (Hirschl 2010:143–7).

4   "A nexus of [state created] religious institutions and tribunals;" the Chief Rabbinate (with branches going all the way down to the neighborhood level), rabbinical courts, and religious councils, does exist in Israel and plays a prominent statutory role in key areas of social life, primarily mar-riage and divorce, *kashrut*, burial services, and the observance of Sabbath

laws. However, constitutionally, these institutions are subject to "the general principles of administrative and constitutional law" such as "gender equality, reasonableness, proportionality, natural justice, and procedural fairness." In 1995 the Supreme Court determined that "all religious tribunals, including the Great Rabbinical Court, are statutory bodies established by law and funded by the state; [therefore] *in principle*, all aspects of their judgments are ... subject to review by the Supreme Court" (Hirschl 2010:142–3, emphasis added).

Israel is not a theocracy, then, constitutional or otherwise, but broad and profound processes of transformation are shaping its dominant culture and institutions in a religious Zionist form. We cannot predict, of course, what the future will bring, so we conclude with the powerful words of Hebrew University scholar of German literature Christoff Schmidt:

> In a continuing political emergency it seems that the national-religious platform, far beyond its numerical strength in the Knesset, is picking up steam and successfully undermining the legitimacy of secular culture. This culture, in a desperate search for new sources of legitimacy, which could replace the classical utopias of civil equality and the brotherhood of peoples, also tends to accommodate itself to the demand to be "Jewish" ... A concern is taking shape that ... Israeli secular culture is preparing itself for the exit of the Jew from his Enlightenment, for which he himself is to blame.
>
> (Schmidt 2018)

Notes

1 The NRP had only two women Members of Knesset in its history and no woman in a leadership position. The *Charedi* political parties have never had a woman MK.
2 For attitudes toward the Arabs in religious-Zionist thought see D. Schwartz 2011; 2015.
3 The Pew survey did not distinguish, in asking this question, between Israel's Palestinian citizens and the non-citizen Palestinian residents of the OPT, an omission that reduces the value of this finding. However, a study conducted by the (late) Tel Aviv University political science professor Asher Arian in 2002, at the height of the second *intifada*, may provide some clues as to the distribution of opinion regarding these two Palestinian population groups. Among the general Jewish public Arian found that 46 percent favored the "transfer" of the Palestinian residents of the OPT, whereas "only" 31 percent favored the "transfer" of Israel's Palestinian citizens. Among supporters of the Mizrachi *Charedi* political party, Shas, 60 percent supported the "transfer" of the non-citizen Palestinians. These figures are very similar to the Pew findings, so we may cautiously conclude that by the transfer of "Arabs" Pew's respondents understood the non-citizen Palestinian residents of the OPT, rather than Israel's Palestinian citizens (Arian 2002:29; Peled 2006).
4 We realize the problematic nature of this statement in view of the post-secular turn in the social sciences and humanities that challenges the secularization thesis, but our argument does not require a resolution of this point.

References

Arian, A. (2002) *Israeli Public Opinion on National Security 2002*, Tel Aviv: Tel Aviv University – Jaffee Center for Strategic Studies (Memorandum No. 61) (in Hebrew).

Bagno-Moldavski, O. (2015) "The Effect of Religiosity on Political Attitudes in Israel," *Politics and Religion*, 8: 514–43.

Barzel, N. (2017) *"Redemption Now": The Beliefs and Activities of the Jewish Settlers in the West Bank and Israeli Society*, Tel Aviv: Hakibbutz Hameuchad (in Hebrew).

Ben-Nun Bloom, P., Zemach M., and Arian A. (2011) "The Religious Experience as Affecting Ambivalence: The Case of Democratic Performance Evaluation in Israel," *Democratization*, 18: 25–51.

Ben-Sasson, H. (2015) "With Uplifted Eyes: The New Agenda of the National-Religious Leadership," Molad: The Center for Democratic Renewal, www.molad.org/articles/% D7%91%D7%A2%D7%99%D7%A0%D7%99%D7%99%D7%9D- %D7%A8%D7%9E%D7%95%D7%AA (in Hebrew; accessed September 30, 2017).

Don-Yehiya, E. (2014) "Messianism and Politics: The Ideological Transformation of Religious Zionism," *Israel Studies*, 19: 239–63.

Ehrenberg, J. and Peled, Y. (eds.) (2016) *Israel and Palestine: Alternative Perspectives on Statehood*, Lanham, MD: Rowman & Littlefield.

Ghanim, H. (2012) "Not Exactly Apartheid: The Dynamics between Settler Colonialism and Military Occupation," *The Public Sphere* 6: 95–112 (in Hebrew).

Ghanim, H. (2016) "Not Exactly Apartheid: The Dynamics between Settler Colonialism and Military Occupation," in Ehrenberg, J. and Peled, Y. (eds.), *Israel and Palestine: Alternative Perspectives on Statehood*, Lanham, MD: Rowman & Littlefield, pp. 97–114.

Guttman Center (2012) *A Portrait of Israeli Jews: Beliefs, Observance, and Values of Israeli Jews, 2009*, Jerusalem: Israel Democracy Institute and Avi Chai–Israel.

Halperin-Kaddari, R. and Yadgar, Y. (2010) "Between Universal Feminism and Particular Nationalism: Politics, Religion and Gender (In)Equality in Israel," *Third World Quarterly*, 31: 905–20.

Hellinger, M. (2008) "Political Theology in the Thought of 'Merkaz HaRav' Yeshiva and its Profound Influence on Israeli Politics and Society since 1967," *Totalitarian Movements and Political Religions*, 9: 533–50.

Herman Peled, H. and Peled, Y. (2011) "Post-Post Zionism: Confronting the Death of the Two-State Solution," *New Left Review*, 67: 97–118.

Hermann, T., Be'eri, G., Heller, E., Cohen, C., Lebel, Y., Mozes, H., and Neuman, K. (2014) *The National-Religious Sector in Israel 2014*, Jerusalem: Israel Democracy Institute (in Hebrew).

Hermann, T., Heller, E., Cohen, C., Bublil, D., and Omar, F. (2016) *The Israeli Democracy Index – 2016*, Jerusalem: Israel Democracy Institute (in Hebrew).

Hermann, T., Heller, E., Lazar-Shoef, T., and Omar, F. (2017) *The Israeli Democracy Index – Summary*, Jerusalem: Israel Democracy Institute.

Hirschl, R. (2010) *Constitutional Theocracy*, Cambridge, MA: Harvard University Press.

IDI (2017a) *Charedi Society Annual – 2017*, Jerusalem: Israel Democracy Institute (in Hebrew).

IDI (2017b) *Democracy Index – 2017*, Jerusalem: Israel Democracy Institute (in Hebrew).

International Crisis Group (2013) *Leap of Faith: Israel's National Religious and the Israeli-Palestinian Conflict; Middle East Report No. 47*, Brussels: International Crisis Group.

Kenan, A. (2001 [1984]) *The Road to Ein Harod*, trans. Hutzpit, M., London: Saqi Books.

Liebman, C. S. (1994) "Religion and Democracy in Israel," *Zmanim: A Historical Quarterly*, 50/51: 132–44.

Luz, E. (1999) Wrestling in River Yabok: Power, Morality, and Jewish Identity, Jerusalem: Magnes (in Hebrew). Available in English as:

Luz, E. (2003) *Wrestling with an Angel: Power, Morality, and Jewish Identity*, trans. Swirsky, M., New Haven, CT: Yale University Press.

Peled, Y. (1992) "Ethnic Democracy and the Legal Construction of Citizenship: Arab Citizens of the Jewish State," *The American Political Science Review*, 86: 432–43.

Peled, Y. (2006) "No 'Arab Jews' There – Shas and the Palestinians," *Palestinian Review of Society and History*, 1: 112–36 (in Arabic).

Peled, Y. and Herman Peled H. (2016) "The Way Forward in the Middle East," in Ehrenberg, J. and Peled, Y. (eds.) *Israel and Palestine: Alternative Perspectives on Statehood*, Lanham, MD: Rowman & Littlefield, pp. 187–99.

Pew (2016) *Israel's Religiously Divided Society*, Washington, DC: Pew Research Center.

Porat, B. (2016) *A Proposal to Amend the Foundations of Law Act, with an Analysis and Critique*, Jerusalem: Israel Democracy Institute (in Hebrew).

Sagi, A. (2011) "Requiem to Religious Zionism – Testimony," in Sagi, A. and Stern, Y. Z., *Barefooted Homeland: Israeli Reflections*, Tel Aviv: Am Oved, pp. 137–44.

Schmidt, C. (2018) "Sketch for My Image as a Stowaway of Jewish-German History," *Haaretz Serafim*, January 5; www.haaretz.co.il/misc/article-print-page/1.5598599 (in Hebrew; accessed April 27, 2018).

Schwartz, D. (2011) "Conquest of the Land of Israel and the Attitude towards its Inhabitants: Viewpoints in Religious Zionist Thought," *Cathedra: For the History of Eretz Israel and Its Yishuv*, 141: 75–104 (in Hebrew).

Schwartz, D. (2015) "Passivity and Negation: The Image of the Arab in Religious-Zionist Thought (1902–1949)," *Democratic Culture*, 16: 277–315 (in Hebrew).

Shafir, G. and Peled, Y. (2002) *Being Israeli: The Dynamics of Multiple Citizenship*, Cambridge: Cambridge University Press.

Appendix

July 9, 2014

Commander's Battle Sheet[1]

Operation "Solid Rock"

Dear Commanders and Fighters,

A great right has befallen us, to command and to serve in the Givati brigade at this time. **History has chosen us to be at the spearhead** of combat against the "Gazan" terrorist enemy which defames, defiles and insults the God of Israel. We have geared up and prepared ourselves for this time and we take upon ourselves this task with a sense of mission and complete humility, while ready to endanger and give our lives in order to protect our families, our people and our homeland.

We will work **together** with power and resolve, initiative and ingenuity and strive for contact with the enemy. We will do everything to accomplish our task in order to eliminate the enemy and remove the threat from the people of Israel. With us **"there is no coming back without accomplishing the task."**

We will work and do everything in order to **bring our boys back safely**, using all the means at our disposal and with all necessary force.

I trust each and every one of you to operate with this spirit, the spirit of Israeli warriors who lead the troops, **"the spirit named Givati."** I turn my eyes to the sky and call together with you, **"Hear O Israel, Adonai is our God – Adonai alone."** God of Israel, please give us success, because we are about to fight for your People of Israel against an enemy that defiles your name. In the name of the fighters of Israel, and especially the fighters and commanders of this brigade, make true for us what is written in the Bible, "For God your Lord is marching with you to fight for you with your enemies to save you" and we will say Amen.

Ofer Vinter, Col.
Commander, Givati brigade

Source: *Haaretz,* July 11, 2014

Note

1 Translated from the Hebrew (see Figure) by Yoav Peled. All emphases in the original.

בס"ד

י"א בתמוז התשע"ד

9 ביולי 2014

דף מפקד לקרב

מבצע "צוק איתן"

מפקדים ולוחמים יקרים,

זכות גדולה נפלה בחלקנו לפקד ולשרת בחטיבת גבעתי בעת הזו. **ההיסטוריה בחרה בנו להיות בחוד החנית** של הלחימה באויב הטרוריסטי יהועזתי" אשר מחרף מנאץ ומגדף, אלוקי מערכות ישראל. נערכנו והתכוננו לעת הזו ואנו מקבלים על עצמנו את המשימה מתוך שליחות וענווה גמורה ומתוך שאנו מוכנים להסתכן ולמסור את נפשנו על מנת להגן על משפחותינו, על עמנו ועל מולדתנו.

נפעל יחד בנחישות ובעוצמה, יוזמה ותחבולה ונחתור למגע עם האויב. נעשה הכל בכדי **לעמוד במשימה** על מנת להכרית אויב ולהסיר את האיום מעם ישראל. אצלנו, "לא חוזרים בלי לבצע".

נפעל ונעשה הכל בכדי **להחזיר את בחורינו בשלום**. תוך שימוש בכל האמצעים העומדים לרשותנו ובכל העוצמה שתידרש.

אני סומך עליכם, על כל אחד ואחד מכם כי תפעלו ברוח זו, רוח של לוחמים ישראלים ההולכים חלוץ לפני המחנה. **"הרוח שתמה הוא גבעתי"**. אני נושא עיני לשמים. וקורא עמכם, **"שמע ישראל ה' אלוקינו ה' אחד"**. ה' אלקי ישראל היה נא מצליח דרכינו, אשר אנו הולכים ועומדים להלחם למען עמך ישראל כנגד אויב המנאץ שמך. בשם לוחמי צה"ל ובפרט לוחמי החטיבה והמפקדים. עשה ויתקיים בנו מקרא שכתוב. "כי ה' אלוהיכם ההולך עמכם להילחם לכם עם אויבכם להושיע אתכם" ונאמר אמן.

"יחד ורק יחד ננצח".

עופר וינטר, אל"מ

מפקד חטיבת גבעתי

Glossary

Agudat Yisrael Ultra-Orthodox Jewish religious political party established in 1912

Aliyah Wave of Jewish settlement in Palestine [literally: pilgrimage]

Ba'alei teshuva People who "returned" to Jewish religion

Beit Midrash House of Jewish religious study

Bnei Akiva The main Religious Zionist youth movement

CBS Central Bureau of Statistics

Charedim (also ***Haredim***) Non-Zionist Ultra-Orthodox Jews

CHE Council on Higher Education

Chozrim biteshuvah People who "returned" to Jewish religion

Cohen Priest

DMC Democratic Movement for Change

Gachelet Ultra-Orthodox group working toward a "Torah state"

Galut Exile

GE Gush Emunim

Halacha (also ***halakha***) Jewish religious law

Haskala Jewish Enlightenment

HCJ High Court of Justice

Histadrut Jewish labor organization in Palestine/Israel established in 1920

IDF Israel Defense Forces

IDI Israel Democracy Institute

Kashrut Jewish dietary law

LZM Labor Zionist Movement

Mechinot Preparatory religious schools

Midrash A text by ancient Jewish sages (250 BC–AD 625) meant to interpret Biblical passages

Mizrachim Israeli Jews hailing from the Moslem world

Mizrachi The Religious Zionist (or national-religious) movement

MK Member of Knesset

NRP National Religious Party, the political arm of *Mizrachi* in Israel since 1956

OPT Occupied Palestinian territories

Sabra A "new Jew" born in Palestine/Israel

SES   Socio-Economic Status

Shas   Mizrachi ultra-Orthodox political party established in 1984

Teshuvah   "Return" to Jewish religion

UNSCOP   United Nations Special Committee on Palestine (1947)

WoW   Women of the Wall

WZO   World Zionist Organization

Yeshiva   School for advanced Jewish religious studies

Yeshivot hesder   Special *yeshivot* [plural of *yeshiva*] where Religious Zionist recruits can study while serving in the IDF

Yishuv   Pre-statehood Jewish community in Palestine

Index

Page numbers in **bold** denote tables, those in *italics* denote figures.

academic fine arts 153, 180
Achdut Ha-Avoda 36, 60
aesthetic education 149
Agudat YIsrael 2, 4, 11, 12, 42, 58, 100–1;
   Ashkenazi independent educational
   systems of 103
agunot, issue of 193, 198n3
al-Aksa intifada 45
aliyah (settlement wave) 2, 32; First
   Aliyah (1882–1903) 32; Second Aliyah
   (1904–1914) 32–3, 70
Alma-Beit Midrash 157
Alterman, Nathan 21, 37
Altneuland (novel) 149
Amanut L'am 159
American Jews 13, 88, 94, 191
American Judaism 12–13
Amir, Yigal 93, 128, 202, 215
aniconism, idea of 143, 145, 150
anti-Israel propaganda 179
anti-religious coercion 100–1
Antokolsky, Mark 152, 153
Arab–Israel war 188; Six Day War (1967)
   2, 16, 63–5, 82, 165, 220; Yom Kippur
   war (1973) 16, 82, 106, 181, 220
Arab Revolt of 1936–1939 37
Arab state system 56
Aranne, Zalman 105–6; Jewish
   consciousness program 105–6
Ardon, Mordecai 157
Arnovitz, Andi 169, *169*
art and media, in Israel 209
art education 18, 149, 160–1
Arts and Crafts Jewish Academy, Palestine
   (*Bezalel*) 153
Asad, Talal 1, 5–8, 23n2
Ashkenazim 20, 22, 86

Aviad, Janet 82, 84, 87–8
Avi Chai Foundation 72, 91, 93, 209, 216
Avnon, Dan 113
Azulai, Shai *181*, 182
Azure (journal) 163
Azure (paid cable television channel) 211

Ba'alei Teshuvah 81, 83, 85, 87–9, 88, 94,
   205, 215
Bar Hama, Avner 175–9, *177*, 182
Bar-Ilan (national-religious university) 14,
   62, 93, 108, 128
Bar Or, Galia 157–8, 162, 168
Bartov, Hanoch 67
Bar-Yehuda, YIsrael 60–1
Beit Din (rabbinical conversion court) 195
Beit midrash 92, 149–50, 182
Ben-Gurion, David 37, 41, 56, 58, 105;
   mamlachtiyut, doctrine of 109
Benjamin, Walter 148
Bennett, Naftali 18, 72, 109, 112, 116,
   176, 215
Ben Uri, Meir *162*, 163
Ben-Yehudah, Eliezer 2
Bernstein, Zalman 72
Bezalel (Israel's leading art school) 4, 150,
   154–7, 160, 180
Bezalel Society, in Berlin 153
Bezem, Naftali 160, 164, 165, *165*
Biblical Land of Israel 64
Binyan Shalem 109; idea of Jewish family
   values 109
Bnei Akiva youth movement 62–3, 71
Bourdieu, Pierre 138
Bourekas films 201
British Peel Commission (1936) 58
Brubaker, Rogers 6

Buber, Martin 144–7, 149
Burg, Joseph 68

Camp David 46
Campfire (film) 204
Cavanaugh, William 5–6
Cedar, Joseph 204
Channel 20 (Legacy Channel) 203, 211
Charedi rabbis 126, 167, 204
Charedi communities: art education 160;
    deferments of military service 124; films
    and cinemas 204–8; in higher education
    113–15; integration of 215; and military
    service 123–6; political parties 126;
    quotas for 126; rabbinical establishment
    126; threat of corruption 124; in visual
    arts field 179–80
Charedi girls' schools 103
Charedi independent educational sector
    103
Chevrat Ha-Oovdim 33
Chozrim Biteshuvah 18, 82, 87, 130, 174
Christianity 6–7, 144, 150
Christian Protestantism 144
citizenship, ethno-national conception of
    112
civic education, in Israel 109–13, 116
civil court system 197, 220
civil religion, of Israel 16, 22, 31–2, 81,
    82, 94, 159, 181–2; decline of 17; value
    system of 17
civil society organization 72
Cohen, Erik 86
Cohen, Hermann 144–7, 150, 155
Cohen, Noa Lea 179
Cohen, Steven 12
consciousness, individualization of 203
constitutional law, of Israel 116, 221–2
constitutional revolution of 1992–1995
    221
constitutional theocracy, features of 220–2
constructive socialism 33
consumer society, rise of 107
Cormon, Fernand 152
corporatist economy 32, 38–40, 48
Council on Higher Education (CHE) 114;
    first five-year plan (2011–2016) 115
counter-nationalism 12
cult of religion 105
cultural hegemony, theory of 21–2, 31, 34
cultural Zionism 145, 147

Dar, Gidi 205
Davie, Grace 19, 22

Deeb, Lara 190
Degel ha-torah (political party)103
democracy, concept of 110–11
Democratic Movement for Change (DMC)
    42
de-secularization of the public sphere,
    causes of 219–20
Diaspora Jews 172; in cinema 201; cultural
    and social values of 104; educational
    attitude toward 105; historical
    connection to the Land of Israel 104;
    middle-class 38; religious practices of
    104; visualization of despondent 154;
    Zionism as rebellion against 104
division of labor 123–6
Dror, Yuval 115, 116
Druckman, Chaim 71, 196
Druze culture 178

East Jerusalem 65, 82, 191, 214
economic liberalization, in Israel 40–6,
    107, 130, 165, 182
Egypt–Israel peace agreement 70
Ein Harod Museum of Art 160, 168, 194
Ein-Vered circle 70
Eisenstadt, S.N. 34
Elon Moreh settlement 68
Emergency Economic Stabilization Plan
    43
Enlightenment 19, 83, 144, 149–51, 153,
    157, 180, 189, 222
entire age cohorts, phenomenon of 125
equality, principle of 115, 126
Eretz Yisrael 9, 10, 82, 84, 156–7
ethical monotheism, idea of 144
ethno-national identity 86
European bourgeoisie 148
European enlightenment 151
European Jews 12, 146, 150–2, 154
Exposition Universelle 150

family law, jurisdiction over 59–60
Feiwel, Berthold 146
feminist belief system 189
Fifth Zionist Congress (1901), Basel 138,
    145–7
films, in Israel 201–8; *Charedi* films
    204–8; Diasporic Jew in 201; DVD
    films 207; Gesher Multicultural Film
    Fund (GMFF) 203, 207; *Ma'aleh*-
    produced 209
fine arts 60 Years of Fine Art in Israel 161;
    academic 153, 180; aesthetic judgment
    140; Buber's view of 144–7; Cohen's

view of 144–7; concept of 137; education of 160–1; establishment of 149–60; exclusion and inclusion in 151; exhibition of ideas in 142; five stages through for 163–7; integration *versus* nationalization of 144–7; in Jewish cultural life 150; Kant's view of 139–43; *Matronita* exhibition (2012) 168–79; in Middle East 149; as national education 147–9; neglect of 150; oil paintings 169; Orthodox artists 167–79; for painting and sculpture 151; *versus* practical arts 141; reflective judgment 140; religionization of 138; and religious art making 161–7; and rules of artistic creation 139; in service of politics 148; and the state 158–60; sublime 142; taste and beauty of 140; as universal signifier 140; visual representations 139, 143, 150

First Zionist Congress (1897) 4, 150

Fischer, Shlomo 62–3, 85

food insecurity 113

Foundations of Law Act (1980) 221

Frankel, Yonah 161

French Revolution 7

Friedman, Yael 201, 205

Frumkin, Gad 100; Frumkin Commission 100

Gachelet 62, 63

galut: concept of 11, 13, 57; *galut* society 57

Gaza 70; Gaza war (2014) 174; Israel's control of 129; military operation in 128; withdrawal of Jewish settlements from 129

Geiger, Isaac 111–12, 116

gender equality, principles of 115, 196, 216

gender segregation: in elementary schools 102, 216; in military 215; in state-religious school system 102–3, 216

General Zionists 36, 58, 100

German Enlightenment 144

German Jews: influx to Palestine 163; persecution of 156

Gesher Multicultural Film Fund (GMFF) 203, 207–8

Givati infantry brigade 1, 18, 128

global village 107

Golan Heights 65, 67

Goldberg, Chana 180, 193, *194*, 197

Gol, Dikla 207

Gramsci, Antonio 21; cultural hegemony, theory of 21–2, 31

Greater Land of Israel 11, 65, 108, 177, 181

Great Recession 41

Gropius, Walter 156

Grovais, Yehuda 204, 207

Gush Emunim 21, 66–71, 202, 218, 220; foundation of 66; leadership of 68; settlement process 67; terrorist activities against Palestinians 67; Zionist settlement project 70

Guyer, Paul 141

Haaretz 1, 173, 211

hadata (religionization of Israeli society) 1, 17, 81; origins of 2

Hagana militia 37

Hakak, Yohai 201, 205

Ha-Kibbutz Ha-Meuchad kibbutz movement 21

Halacha (Jewish religious law) 2, 7, 13, 61, 130, 168, 189–90, 194, 203, 217

Hammer, Zevulun 68, 106, 107

Ha-Poel Ha-Mizrachi 10, 56, 57, 71

Ha-Poel Ha-Tzair 36

Harel, YIsrael 202

Hasam Gvulech Shalom (2005) 177, *177*

haskala (Jewish Enlightenment) 150

Hatzfirah 150

healthcare system 44; household expenditure on **45**; social expenditure on **44**

health tax 44

Hebrew labor 36, 39

Hebrew language 2–3

"Heritage and Culture of Israel" program 108, 112

Herzl, Theodor 2, 4, 7, 123, 145, 147, 149

hesder yeshiva 62–3, 92–3, 204

He Walked in the Fields (1967) 165, *166*

Hidabroot (television channel) 211

High Court of Justice (HCJ) 44, 125–6, 190–1, 221; *see also* Rabbinical Courts

higher education: *Charedim* in 113–15, 215; gender segregation in 116; institutions of 115, 116

Hirschl, Ran 220

Hirschman, Albert 188–9

Histadrut 33–4, 43, 57, 158, 220; cooperative economy of 33; *Hagana* militia 37; institutional structure of 38; institutions and policies of 35–6; investments 39; mode of operation of

Histadrut continued
  38; monopoly of 37; as settlement
  aristocracy 35
Holocaust 8, 105, 115, 123, 159, 207;
  survivors of 39
holy wars 218
human dignity 221; gender equality and
  216; infringement of 115; principle of
  115, 126; values of equality and 116

Immersion of Converting Women 194, 196
income distribution, inequality of 45
individual–state relations 111
Institute for Zionist Education 92
inter-religious marriage 59
intifada 20, 22; *al-Aksa intifada* 45; first
  107; second 94, 211, 219
intra-party generational conflict 67
Israel Defense Forces (IDF): *Charedim*
  and military service 123–6; gender
  segregation in 215; Givati infantry
  brigade 18, 128; involvement of
  religious authorities in 128, 129;
  Judaism of "Law of Return eligible"
  non-Jewish soldiers 129; Kfir brigade
  18; law of war 131; military operation in
  Gaza 1, 128; military rabbi, position of
  129–30; "Mission and Uniqueness"
  program 130; national-religious officers
  in 18; as people's army 123; quality
  manpower in 127; religionization of
  128, 132; religious soldiers 129;
  Religious Zionists in 126–32; role of
  Jewish religion and of religious Jews in
  123; sacralization of military operations
  131; sacred mission 131; Tal Law 125;
  theocratization of 128, 129, 132; victory
  in Arab–Israeli wars 82; women singers
  in military ceremonies and social events
  130; women's place in 129–30; *yeshivot
  hesder* (arrangement) 127
Israel Democracy Institute (IDI) 19, 53,
  113
Israeli Art on its Way to a Different Place
  (1998) 163
Israeli cinema *see* films, in Israel
Israeli economy, liberalization of 40–6
Israeli educational system: *Charedi*
  independent educational sector 103;
  Charedim in higher education 113–15;
  civic education 109–13; Council on
  Higher Education (CHE) 114–15; decline
  of Jewish studies 107; educational
  program adopted under Sa'ar 108; gender

segregation, in elementary schools 102,
  216; in immigrants' camps 100;
  independent school systems 101; Jewish
  education *see* Jewish education; Labor
  educational system 101; number of
  students in the elementary secular state
  system 103; principles guiding 100;
  religious education 101–3; school
  systems, nationalization of 101; state-
  Charedi system 103; State Education
  Law 101, 104, 107; state-religious school
  system 102; Students' Rights Law 115;
  two state systems of 101; unified
  education 100–1
Israeli identity: components of 69;
  definition as a Jewish state 221
Israeli Institute of Applied Social Research
  87
Israeli Judaism 12–13; cultural-ethnic
  significance of 14; emergence of 13; as
  national-state religion 13
Israeli nationalism 68, 108
Israeli–Palestinian conflict 107, 216; two-
  state solution to 20, 214, 220; Year Zero
  of 154–5
Israeli society: liberalization of 15;
  religionization of 108
Israeli welfare state 45
Israeli women 168; Arab Israeli women
  174; status of 59

Jabotinsky, Vladimir 37, 56
Jacob's Ladder (1957) *162*, 163
Jerusalem 4, 64–5, 83, 88, 149, 154, 157,
  173, 179–80, 192
Jewish aniconism 143, 145, 150
Jewish art academy 149
Jewish artworks 138
Jewish calendar 105, 192
Jewish consciousness 105, 131; Aranne's
  program on 105–6; of God 145
"Jewish cultural renewal" movement 81
"Jewish culture" organizations 109
Jewish democracy 69
Jewish education: American Conservative
  rabbis and educators 106; attitude
  toward the Diaspora 105; categories of
  105; decline of Jewish studies in Israel
  107; history of 104; Integrative Stream
  107; in Labor educational system 105;
  in secular state system 104–9; for
  shaping the "new Jew" 105; Shenhar
  Committee 90, 107; students in Jewish
  school systems **55, 56**, 103; TALI

initiative 106; during *yishuv* period 104; and Zionist school systems in Palestine 104
Jewish family values, idea of 109
Jewish heritage 14, 89, 105, 208, 221
Jewish Home party 18, 72, 109, 215
Jewish identity 11, 72, 81, 85, 89–91, 94, 106, 107, 109, 143, 167, 188; crisis of 107; preservation of 17
"Jewish inoculation" program 105
Jewish-Israeli collective, unity of 107
Jewish Israeli culture 16, 19, 139, 179
Jewish-Israeli society 81
Jewish law, principles of 60, 143, 145, 221
Jewish May, The (drawing) *146*, 147
Jewish-Moslem peace and coexistence 170
Jewish National Fund (JNF) 33
Jewish nationalism 62, 116, 128
Jewish Orthodox Feminist Alliance (JOFA) 193
Jewish–Palestinian conflict 37
Jewish public, in Israel 19, 217–18, 221; education and 100
Jewish religion 144; aniconistic character of 145
Jewish religious groups 203, 219
Jewish religious holidays 2
Jewish religious law *see Halacha* (Jewish religious law)
Jewish renewal movement 18, 89–93, 116, 215
Jewish Revenge (*Charedi* film series) 204–6
Jewish school systems, students in **55, 56**; *Charedi* systems 56, 103; elementary system 56, 103; national-religious system 56
Jewish secularism 17, 90
Jewish sovereignty, over Land of Israel 8, 63, 65, 66
Jewish Theological Seminary 106
Jewish tradition, knowledge of 8, 14, 23, 105, 106, 143
Jews, Israeli: definition of 60–2; demographic majority of 220; mission to establish their sovereignty 218; moral superiority of 218; national consciousness among 145; political attitudes by level of religiosity **217**; re-territorialization of 160; and Women of the Wall (WoW) 191
job creation 39
joint secular-religious school system 18
Judaic-Protestant culture 144

Judaism 61, 73, 195; in America 12; as culture 214; in Israel 12–13; and Israeli identity 69; of "Law of Return eligible" non-Jewish soldiers 129; as religion of law 144; religious conversion 61; visual representation of 143
"Judaization" of Israeli society 64
Juergensmeyer, Mark 8

Kadosh (film) 202
Kampel, Debbie 170, *171*, 172
Kant, Immanuel 139–43; account of fine art 142; *Critique of Judgment, The* 139; on judgments of taste 141; refining the masses, idea of 157; on social life regulated by laws 141; on sublime fine arts 142
Karim, Eyal 130
kashrut (Jewish dietary law) 14–15, 56–8, 128–9, 221
Kehat, Hannah 193
Kenan, Amos 216
Kestenbaum Ben-Dov, Ruth 169, 170, *170*
Kfir brigade 18
kibbutz movement 18, 21, 57, 71, 84
Knesset 18, 61; Members of Knesset (MKs) 18; no-confidence vote 101; principles of Jewish law 221
Koburgsky, Ferdinand 152
Kolatt, Israel 58
Kolech (Orthodox feminist organization) 192, 193, 196
Kook, Abraham Isaac Ha-Cohen 3, 9–10, 12, 101, 160–1, 168
Kook, Zvi Yehuda 63–6, 70–1
Kremnitzer, Mordechai 110; Kremnitzer Committee 110–11
Kuni Lemel series 201
Kupat Cholim (Sick Fund) 33, 44

labor market 33, 39, 41, 46, 113, 115, 125, 215
"labor settlement" strategy 33
Labor Zionist Movement (LZM) 2, 4, 21, 46, 56, 62, 71, 220; agricultural model based on manual labor 70; alliance with WZO 35, 38; authority without sovereignty 34; civic virtue of 34; colonial strategy 34–5; "conquest of land and labor" practices 157; corporatist economy and 38–40; decline of 38; educational system and 101; "ethico-political" ideational structure 34; formation of 31–8; *Histadrut*

Labor Zionist Movement (LZM) *continued*
(Association) 33; state-building project
38; weakness of 214
Lahav, Hagar 15
Law of Population Registry of 1965 60
Law of Return of 1950 60–1; definition of
a Jew in 61; "grandfather clause" of 61;
Law of Return Eligibles 61
learning communities 18, 92
legitimacy crisis, among Israeli Jews 16,
94, 130, 219–20
Leibowitz, Yeshayahu 187
Leon, Udi 203
Levine, Daniel J. 3
Levinger, Moshe 69
Levitt, Abraham 163, 165
Levy, Yagil 128
Liebman, Charles 12, 17, 216
Lilien, Ephraim Moshe 146, *146*; *Jewish
May, The* (drawing) *146*, 147
lingua franca 2, 154
Liss, Dvora 168, 169
Lithuanian (non-Chassidic) *Charedi*
educational system 103
Lustick, Ian 48
Luz, Ehud 218

Ma'aleh (Religious Zionist film school)
203, 209, 211; development of 204
mamlachtiyut, doctrine of 109
mamzerim 59
mamzerut 59
Maor, Sigal *174*
Mapai (Land of Israel Workers' Party) 4,
36, 39; control of education system 100;
historic partnership with *Mizrachi*
movement 56–8; Status Quo Letter 58–62
Mapam (United Workers' Party) 101
mass communications 202, 211, 214
Matronita exhibition (2012) 18, 158,
168–79, 193, 194, 216
mechinot 128–30, 132
Mendelssohn, Moses 6–7
Merkaz Ha-Rav yeshiva 63, 66, 175, 176,
203
Migdal, Joel 38
militant nationalism 102
Ministry of Defense 125–6
Ministry of Education 101, 106, 107, 111;
"Essential Concepts for the Teacher"
policy directive 112; Religious Zionists
in 215
Misgav, Uri 1
"Mission and Uniqueness" program 130

Mizrachi (Religious Zionist movement) 4,
36, 62, 71, 95, 101; historic partnership
with *Mapai* movement 56–8
Mizrachi *Charedi* political party (Shas) 12
monotheism, realization of 144–5
Morris, William 157
Mosenson, Ben-Zion 104
Movement for Greater Israel, The 70
Murphy, Emma 40

national capital 37, 39
national citizenship, rights of 34
National Geographic 202
national identity 60, 86, 91, 106, 112, 188
nationalism, idea of 6–8
Nationality Law of 1952 60
national-religious educational system 73,
103
national-religious officers 18
National Religious Party (NRP) 21, 63, 71,
215, 217
nation-state, creation of 34
Nazi Germany 156, 163
New Bezalel School for Arts and Crafts
156
New Horizons 159, 164
Nietzschean *Übermensch* 172
Nimrod's circumcision 180–2
Nimrod sculpture 157–8
non-governmental organizations (NGOs)
72
non-Jewish citizens, rights of 216
non-religious civil marriage 59

occupied Palestinian territories (OPT) 23,
42, 63, 66, 70, 73, 128–9, 171, 175, 203,
218, 220
Ofrat, Gideon 137, 157–8, 162
Old Testament 57, 104, 144
Operation "Solid Rock" 225–6
Oppenheimer, Franz 33
Organization for Economic Co-operation
and Development (OECD) 46
Orthodox Judaism 150; portrayal of 211;
religious feminists 189–90; strictures of
191
Oslo peace process 46, 110; failure of 20,
94, 211, 219; Oslo Accords (1993) 94,
165, 181
"*Ostjuden*" (Eastern European Jewish)
leadership 163

Palestine: *aliyah* (settlement) 2, 32; Arts
and Crafts Jewish Academy 153;

Biblical scenery of 154; conflict with Israel 107, 216; conflict with Jews 37; influx of German Jews to 163; Israel's rule of 203; Jewish colonization in 32; labor movement 4; "labor settlement" strategy 33; occupied Palestinian territories (OPT) 23, 42, 63, 66, 70, 73, 128–9, 171, 175, 203, 218, 220; organized workers' movement in 35; Ottoman rulers of 154; share of Jewish students in 56; Zionist school systems in 104; Zionist settlement in 16, 154
Palestinian uprising of 1929 155, 198n5
parochet 169–70
parochial courts 59
Peleg, Yaron 1, 206
pioneering, notion of 109
plantation colonies *(moshavot)* 32
Pluhar, Werner 141
political Zionism 65, 145
polytheism, idea of 16, 145
pop culture 209
Porat, Chanan 68, 69
poverty rates 113
Prayer Rug No. 2 artwork (2003) *170*

Raanan, Tsvi 84
Rabbinical Courts: *Beit Din* 195; Chief Rabbinate 192; jurisdiction of 59, 192; qualifying examinations 192; women advocates in 192
Rabin, Yitzhak 46, 67, 70, 93, 110, 128, 202, 215
Raday, Frances 187
Rand, Shuli 205
Razan 2012 painting (2012) 177, *178*
Reality Check painting (2003) 170, *171*
redemption of the People of Israel, process of 68, 218
religion: politicization of 107; in public sphere 19; and secularism 5–6
religionization, of Israeli society 1, 16–20, 115, 214, 216; legitimacy crisis and 219–20; reasons for 20, 219–20
religiosity of Israeli Jews: by observance of religious tradition **55**; political implications of 216–19; by self-definition **54**
religious: art making 161–7; conversion 59, 61; convictions 59; patriarchy 187–8, 191
religious education 101–3; principles of 101; state-religious school system 102
religious-feminist art 193–7

religious laws 2, 7, 59, 130
religious life, of American Jews 13
religious soldiers 128–30, 132
religious war 1; call for 128
Religious Zionism 2, 34, 46, 48–9, 56, 137, 167, 181, 203, 211; during 1967–1973 63–6; approach to screen arts 209–10; categories of 54–5; *Charedi* system 56; cultural hegemony 70; on definition of Jews 60–2; demography of 53–6; family law, jurisdiction over 59–60; Gush Emunim 66–71; *Ha-Poel Ha-Mizrachi* 71; hegemony over Jewish Israeli society 70; historic partnership 56–8; middle-class lifestyle and 71; and military service 126–32; on return of the repressed 62–3; socio-economic orientation of 71–2; repressed, return of 62–3
Riger, Eliezer 104
Road to Ein Harod, The (book) 216
Rontzki, Avichai 131
Rosenfeld, Morris 147
Rosenzweig, Franz 3
Rubenstein, Amnon 110
Rubin, Reuven 155
Ruppin, Arthur 33
Ruskin, John 157

Sa'ar, Gideon 108–9, 112
Sabar, Naama 91
Sabbath 4, 15, 56–7, 71, 105, 108, 128–9, 173, 207, 221
Sagi, Avi 108–9
Salomon, Porat 173, *173*, 180, 182
Sandler, Shmuel 66
Schatz, Boris 149–50; scheme of cottage industry 157; Work of Art 150
Schiller, Friedrich 149
Schmidt, Christoff 222
Scholem, Gershom 3
school systems, nationalization of 101
Second Broadcasting Authority 210
Second Commandment 143, 150–1, 179, 180
"secular" education 116, 215
Secular Forum 108
secularism, in Israel 17; concept of 13–15; defined 15
secular nationalism 2–3, 8, 13
self-conscious "developmental states" 38
Seventh Zionist Congress (1905) 149
sexual morality 102
Sgurim (film) 207, 212n4

Shabbat photograph (2009) 173
Shakdiel, Leah 189, 190, 192
Shaked, Ayelet 215
Shammout, Ismail 160
Shanan Dery, Fatma 177–9, *178*
Shapira, Anita 4, 189
Shapira, Moshe Chaim 68
Sharabi, Asaf 89
Sharon, Ariel 22, 45, 129
Shas (political party) 85–8, 95
Shenhar, Aliza 107
Shenhar Committee 90, 107;
    recommendations to enhance Jewish
    studies 107
Shilo, Margalit 188–9, 192
Shimshanov, Ivan 153
Shklar, Mordechai 203, 209, 211
Shulchan Aruch painting (2003) 193, *194*
Siach Lochamim (book) 69, 82–3, 88–9
Sinai 10, 67, 82, 90; Israel's withdrawal
    from 70
social differentiation, process of 20
social discrimination 150
social historic bloc, concept of 21, 22, 32
socialist Zionism, decline of 17, 84, 147
social life 15, 31, 63, 114, 188, 202, 221;
    regulated by laws 141; Religious Zionist
    hegemony in 17, 215
Sokolow, Nahum 150
Sperber, David 168, 176, 182, 193
spiritual ethics 144
Srugim (television series) 209
standard of living 41, 190
state-*Charedi* educational system 103
State Education Law 101, 104, 107;
    amendment of 111; enactment of 109
State Health Insurance Law 44
state-made middle class 39
state-religious educational system 116; art
    education 160–1
state-religious school system 62, 101, 102,
    106; educational activity of 103; gender
    of students and that of the teachers in
    102–3; gender segregation in 102–3,
    216; non-segregated schools 103;
    students' councils 103
State School of Art, Sofia 152
state-secular educational system 56
Status Quo Letter 58

TALI educational system 94, 106–7, 115
Tal Law 125–6
Talmi, Moshe 105
Tamir, Yael 107, 116

taste and beauty, in fine arts 140, 142
teacher training institutions 160
Techiya 70
Tel Aviv 157; Museum of Art 178; Stock
    Exchange 46
television channel, in Israel 208–11; Azure
    channel 211; back-door entry 210;
    Channel 20 (Legacy Channel) 211;
    Hidabroot channel 211; index for
    measuring presentation of different
    groups 210; national-religious sector 210;
    paid cable television channel 211;
    regulation of 210; on religious issues
    210; Second Broadcasting Authority 210
Temple Mount 4, 67, 153, 154, 173, 204
teshuvah movement 81–5, 179;
    establishment of *yeshivot* 88;
    institutionalization of 87–9; *Shas and
    Mizrachi* teshuvah 85–7
Third Jewish Temple 154, 204
Tikvah Fund 72
Time of Favor (film) 204
To be Citizens in Israel 111–12
Torah Ark 169
Torah state, concept of 62–3, 65
Train Passing Through Neve Tzedek, The
    Painting (1920) 163–4
Triger, Zvi 59
Tumarkin, Igael 164–5, *166*
two-state solution, to Israeli occupation of
    OPT 20, 73, 178, 214, 215, 220
Tzuk Eithan Me? artwork (2014) *174*

unified education system 100–1
United Nations (UN) 46; Convention on
    the Elimination of All Forms of
    Discrimination against Women
    (CEDAW) 188; United Nations Special
    Committee on Palestine (UNSCOP) 58
Ushpizin (film) 205–6

Venice Biennale, The 159
Vest of Prayers artwork (2009) 169
vicarious religion 22
Vinig, Marylin 208
Vinter, Ofer 1, 128
visual art 145–6, 150, 152–3, 157, 160–1,
    168, 176, 179, 181; *Charedim* in
    179–80; Jewish 143; production of 138

Waldman, Eliezer 218
Warburg, Otto 33
welfare state 43–5; decline of 20, 219
West Bank 69, 82; Alon Shvut settlement

170; Eli settlement 128; Jewish settlers
  in 214; occupation of 64
Western European Jews 146
Where Will My Help Come From (film)
  207
Wolfsfeld, Gadi 210
woman in Judaism 187
women advocates, in rabbinical courts 192
Women of the Wall (WoW) 94, 189,
  191–2; Israeli Jews on 191; purpose of
  191; right to pray at the Wall 191–2
Women's Equal Rights Law (1951) 59,
  188
World Economic Forum 46
World War I 154, 157
World War II 2
World Zionist Organization (WZO) 31, 35,
  56; cultural Zionism 145; Democratic
  Fraction 145; London Conference
  (1920) 35; WZO–LZM alliance 35

Yadin, Yigael 42
yeshiva network 58, 62–3, 83, 88, 113,
  124–5, 150
yeshivot hesder 129–30, 132, 167, 215;
  purpose of 127
yishuv (pre-statehood Jewish community)
  2, 4, 33, 58, 100; criteria for

membership in 38; economic
  development 37; Holocaust 105; pillars
  of economy of 33; political culture of
  34; *Vaad Leumi* (National Council) of
  37
yishuv kehilati (community settlement)
  70–1
Yom Kippur war (1973) 16, 84, 106, 181,
  220

Zaritsky, Yossef 159–60
Zehut (Identity) 72
Zionism 3–4, 145; colonial struggle to
  inherit the land 69; cultural Zionism
  145, 147; demographic aim of 61;
  ideological foundation of 104; Labor
  Zionist Movement (LZM) *see* Labor
  Zionist Movement (LZM); orthodox
  reactions to 8–12; political Zionism 145;
  as revolution against traditional Jewish
  life 2
Zionist educational system 104, 160;
  Institute for Zionist Education 92;
  schools in Palestine 104
Zionist settlement project 2, 16, 22, 149,
  154
Zionist visual iconography 147
Zohar, Uri 179

Printed in the United States
by Baker & Taylor Publisher Services